The Sharon

The Sharon Kowalski Case

Lesbian and Gay Rights on Trial

CASEY CHARLES

University Press of Kansas

© 2003 by the University Press of Kansas
All rights reserved

Published by the University Press of Kansas (Lawrence, Kansas 66049), which was organized by the Kansas Board of Regents and is operated and funded by Emporia State University, Fort Hays State University, Kansas State University, Pittsburg State University, the University of Kansas, and Wichita State University

Library of Congress Cataloging-in-Publication Data

Charles, Casey, 1951–
The Sharon Kowalski case : lesbian and gay rights on trial / Casey Charles.
p. cm.
Includes bibliographical references and index.
ISBN 0-7006-1233-5 (cloth : alk. paper)
1. Kowalski, Sharon—Trials, litigation, etc. 2. Guardian and ward—Minnesota. 3. Unmarried couples—Legal status, laws, etc.—Minnesota. I. Title.
KF228K63 C48 2003
346.7301'6—dc21   2002154122

British Library Cataloguing in Publication Data is available.

Printed in the United States of America

10 9 8 7 6 5 4 3 2 1

The paper used in this publication meets the minimum requirements of the American National Standard for Permanence of Paper for Printed Library Materials z39.48-1984.

To David Wilson

Others say, Law is our Fate
Others say, Law is our State
Others say, others say
Law is no more
Law has gone away.

And always the loud angry crowd
Very angry and very loud
Law is We,
And always the soft idiot softly Me

If we, dear, know we know no more
Than they about the Law,
If I no more than you
Know what we should and should not do
Except that all agree
Gladly or miserably
That the Law is
And that all know this,
If therefore thinking it absurd
To identify Law with some other word,
Unlike so many men
I cannot say Law is again
No more than they can we suppress
The universal wish to guess
Or slip out of our own position
Into an unconcerned condition.
Although I can at least confine
Your vanity and mine
To stating timidly
A timid similarity,
We shall boast anyway:
Like love I say.

Like love we don't know where or why
Like love we can't compel or fly
Like love we often weep
Like love we seldom keep.

–From W. H. Auden, "Law Like Love" (1940)

Contents

Acknowledgments *xi*

Introduction: Making Justice *1*

1. Injury *16*

2. Counsel *26*

3. Guardians *35*

4. Injunction *58*

5. Hearing *76*

6. Continued Hearing *95*

7. Appeal *114*

8. Publicity *139*

9. Petition *155*

10. New Trial *183*

11. Judgments *230*

12. Remedy *252*

Conclusion: Remaking Justice *264*

Notes *269*

Bibliography *285*

Index *293*

Acknowledgments

I have many to thank for a book that has taken a long time to research and write. I start with Tim Hunt, Professor of English at Washington State University, who in 1993 encouraged my development of a course in law, literature, and politics that led to my discovery of the *Kowalski* case and its compelling narrative.

During the academic year 1996–97, I was a visiting scholar at the Center for Feminist Research at the University of Southern California, studying the case. I thank the staff of the center, Sheila Briggs, and Walter Williams, for support of my project. In California, I was able to use the helpful One Institute and Archives and make copies of archival documents at the office of Deborah Chasnoff in San Francisco. I thank Karen Thompson and Deborah Chasnoff for making those records available to me.

In 1997, I received a Faculty Development Grant from the University of Montana specifically to travel to Minnesota to conduct interviews. My thanks go to the doctors, journalists, judges, lawyers, and witnesses who took the time to share with me their thoughts about the case, especially Mark Kasel and Mark Stodghill. I am also indebted to the Quatrefoil Library in St. Paul for giving me access to its valuable lesbian and gay periodical archives.

Upon my return to the University of Montana in Missoula, I received specialized support from Dr. Jan Wilms, former Director of the Institute for Medicine and the Humanities (IMH), who explained and evaluated medical records for the book. Sue Sampson, research librarian at the Mansfield Library at the University of Montana, has provided invaluable support from the outset of the project, and the Practical Ethics Center at the university gave me a forum to present my research on the case. Other people at the university who have encouraged and supported my project include Bari Burke, Tom Huff, G. G. Weix, Gerry and Terry Brenner, Kevin Goodan, and Ruth Vanita.

In Missoula, I also had the moving opportunity to interview Jason Burrell, a gay man living with a traumatic brain injury. Not only my thanks go out to him, Sharon Kowalski, and all other lesbians and gay men living with handicaps, but also my deep admiration for their courage and stamina. By the same token, writing this book has increased my admiration for those gay, lesbian, bisexual, and transgendered (GLBT) individuals living with HIV/AIDS who continue to honor the importance of their sexual orientation.

Finally, my greatest gratitude extends to those who have taken the time to read and critique drafts of the book in ways that have proved invaluable. My excellent readers have included Annie Dawid, Mona Bachmann, David Wilson, Dee McNamer, Susie and Kittredge Collins (my sister and brother-in-law), Sally Charles (my mother), and Martha Sutro. I thank David A. J. Richards for his support of the inclusion of my autohistory in the manuscript. Finally, the book's most important reader, besides my partner, David Wilson, has been my editor, Michael Briggs, who has championed the book from his first reading of it. My thanks to him and all who helped make this book.

The Sharon Kowalski Case

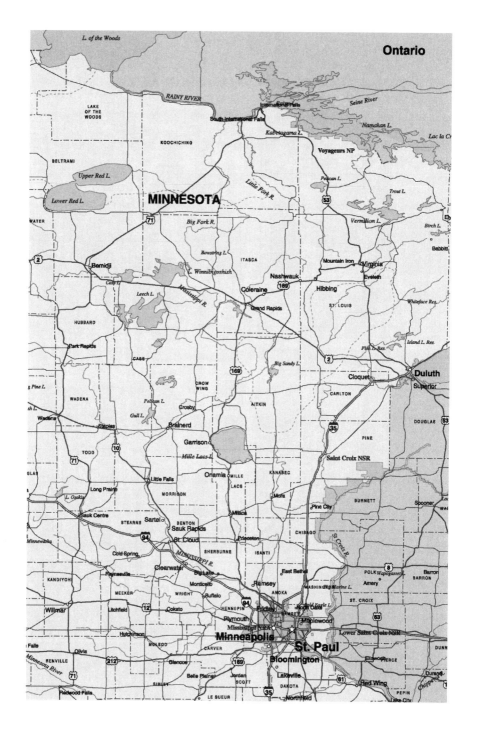

Making Justice

If you don't like the news, go out and make some of your own.
Stephan Ponic, KSAN radio

November 13, 1983, began like any other Sunday in the lives of a quiet couple from Briggs Lake outside St. Cloud, Minnesota — Sharon Kowalski and Karen Thompson, two women who had been living together for the past four years. Later that day, Sharon's car was struck by a drunk driver while she was returning her sister's children to the Iron Range; the impact of the collision would be far greater than anyone could have imagined. The ensuing legal struggle over guardianship of the disabled Sharon is the subject of this documentary — a story of love, law, family, injury, and trial. Part sourcebook, part case study, this history weaves together various versions of this narrative as a way of showing how a private legal dispute between Karen Thompson and Sharon's parents over custody became imbricated in a larger national struggle for lesbian and gay rights.

A retelling of *In re Guardianship of Sharon Kowalski, Ward,* necessarily involves an encounter between law and politics. When, as early as 1984, Karen Thompson started to publicize her story to raise money to pay attorney's fees, her efforts outside the courtroom began to play a major role in the case, demonstrating how law functions as a historically and socially conditioned process, one that is influenced by contexts as seemingly far removed from the public sphere as the bedroom, as the private predilection of romantic lovers. Thompson went out and made justice of her own in a way that has significant implications for our understanding of critical legal studies, theories of legal mobilization, and sexual orientation law. Although *The Sharon Kowalski Case* is primarily a history, a review of these analytical contexts will explain how a guardianship case became a legal landmark in the annals of the lesbian and gay rights movement.[1]

Critical Legal Studies

From the outset, the events surrounding the *Kowalski* case threw into question the concept of justice as a transcendent ideal of fairness, equity, and reason — a blindfolded Athena on a dais holding balanced scales and issuing pronouncements of truth.[2] The law during the tenure of this litigation emerges instead as a contested adjudication that takes place in a network of social forces and pragmatic politics.[3] The threads of Sharon's case are various; they wind themselves into the blindfold of justice — the findings of fact and conclusions of law — in a way that also exposes the ideology behind the notion of a sanctuary of truth within the chambers of stately courthouses. The scientific expertise of medicine, the moral truth of religion, the sensational character sketches of the media, the skilled rhetoric of the public speech — these are some of the discursive voices that intermingle in the affidavits, depositions, trial transcripts, and decisions that make up *In re Guardianship of Sharon Kowalski* from 1983 until 1993, creating a drama of competing archival voices: psychiatrists who testified that Thompson's coming out was devastating, doctors who testified that Sharon had become a helpless child subject to sexual abuse, journalists who wrote of the "silent ordeal" of Sharon's parents besieged by the gay agenda, the cameras of *West 57th Street*, which scanned the bleak winter landscape of the Iron Range. What follows is an account that tries to capture both the narrative flavor of these provocations and the arbitrary judgments that inhabit the accepted objectivity of journalism, medicine, and the law.[4]

This retelling of the *Kowalski* case is also a *true story* in all the conflicting meanings of that phrase — a history with fictions embedded in its facts. Having first come to my attention while I was teaching law and literature, the case unfolds in ways that illustrate the narrative structure of legal history and its connections to literary forms, topics that have also been the focus of recent critical legal inquiry.[5] The Kowalski story contains all the ingredients of a compelling drama, replete with conflicts between worlds urban and rural, gay and straight, male and female, medical and legal; characters driven by religious and political principles, false climaxes, and an ending happy but uncertain. Underlying these components are the particulars of this narrative and their inevitable interface with the generalizations of law, custom, and morality that establishes the weave of this chronology.

The voices of this archive necessarily contain within them the genre of personal testimony, the ethos and pathos of biography, which emerges from interviews, affidavits, direct examinations, and life stories. This history draws not only on the documents in the case — legal depositions, medical records, published newspaper articles — but also on interviews I conducted and letters I read. One major source is Karen Thompson and Julie Andrzejewski's *Why Can't Sharon Kowalski Come Home?* published in 1988 by Spinsters/Aunt Lute. Karen's story is a moving, first-person account of the early stages of the case (1983–87), a heartfelt confessional about a woman coming out and fighting for the right to see her lover. I use it to document the petitioner's actions and reactions, and to supplement the legal and media documents that give a less controlled picture of Thompson's struggle. But *Why Can't* does not supply a fuller archival view, nor does it present the serious complications that Karen's own personality brought to the case. It is one of many sources in this study — legal, medical, media, and political records, as well as interviews with lawyers, judges, journalists, and witnesses.

I would like to add that this history is also more objective than any other account of the case, but I am mindful that the rhetorical nature of any representation makes it impossible to divorce the act of telling the Kowalski story from the presentation of my own making of justice. I know there is no *whole* story that is not also a *side* of the story, just as there is no statement of facts that is not also a *statement* — a qualitative assertion about the events related that is embedded in the selection of archival voices, as well as the type of language used to describe, edit, and arrange them. Writing this book has led me to ask a very fundamental question about my own standpoint: What does it mean for a lawyer turned professor, a gay man who is HIV positive, to write about a case that embodies the concerns of lesbians and the disabled at the turn of the millennium? Even in an era when notions of gender as a natural and unique experience have come under serious question by feminists, how can a man presume to understand the ordeal of Karen Thompson and Sharon Kowalski?[6] How can a California lawyer presume to understand the concerns of the culture of the Iron Range, an asymptomatic carrier of the AIDS virus understand a person with a traumatic brain injury? The exploration of these questions results in the most controversial archival voice in this account — an autoethnography, or what I call an autohistory.[7] Woven into the fabric of the chronology of legal struggle is the story of my own struggle to tell it, the shifting of my own subject position from a teacher who happens to be gay to a gay teacher who becomes an activist inspired by his research to go out and make some justice of his own.

From one perspective, these personal entries, which are appended to the end of each chapter and in the conclusion, do not seem to fit; they are exercises in Foucault's notion of discontinuity, rupture, threshold, and transformation.[8] They do not belong to a traditional legal history but follow the important precedent of scholars, like Patricia Williams, who have led the way in examining the role of subject position in legal analysis. They mark an inquiry into the

limits of my own selfhood as both object and subject and thus come to frame
and situate my own standpoint in relation to the standpoints of others. From
another perspective, however, this autohistory is directly relevant to the precedent and legacy of the *Kowalski* case. These personal entries exemplify how
this story of a same-sex partnership in middle America has influenced gays and
lesbians throughout the country, motivating AIDS activists and other disabled
people of all sexual orientations to work on public and private, local and state
levels to secure the civil rights of same-sex lovers.

Legal Mobilization Theory

The ongoing feud between Karen Thompson and Sharon Kowalski's Iron
Range family unfolded within a context of a burgeoning lesbian and gay rights
movement, culturally, educationally, and politically.[9] The techniques of law
and narrative, archival interweaving, and autoethnography are held together
in this account by the relevance of Sharon's case to current concerns about the
place of the queer in our social fabric. The lesbian and gay civil rights movement is the larger historical framework of the text, but the local issues the case
raises about these concerns complicate and particularize the ongoing national
conversation about those rights among straight and gay people everywhere.

Taking place in the heartland of America, the *Kowalski* case does more than
pit the progressive south of Minneapolis against the socially conservative north
of the Iron Range; it also disunites Sharon's old friends, the discreet and con-
tentedly closeted lesbians of the north, from the feminist and outspoken lesbians of the south whose friendship Sharon cultivated in St. Cloud. As a result,
this conflict figures the larger debate over the closet and the right of privacy
that is invoked as its legal acknowledgment, raising questions about how gays
and lesbians want to live their lives and how heterosexuals want to recognize
them.[10] As Eve Sedgwick has detailed, "The epistemology of the closet is not
a dated subject or a superseded regime of knowing" that lost its value after the
Stonewall Riots in New York in 1969 symbolically marked the beginning of
gay liberation. "The reign of the telling secret," as she describes it, is integral
to this drama of gay uncovering—both to the story of Karen Thompson's
decision to write to the Kowalskis coming out as Sharon's lover and to the story
of the Kowalski family's refusal to believe it.[11]

The closet produces a culture built on discretion, secrecy, and fear by those
both in it and outside it; as a result, it maintains a vitality that defies the injunc-
tions of liberationists and thrives on the mandates of privacy and personal
autonomy. The overused term "homophobia" covers an uneasiness on both

sides of the door that separates gay and straight; it points to fears about both hetero and homo desire that have insinuated themselves into current scripts of self and society. The Kowalski story portrays the open secrecies of the closet not only in a rural culture that passive-aggressively ignores same-sex love, refusing to speak its name while insisting that it does not care as long as "they" don't "flaunt it," but also in an assimilationist lesbian culture that resents those advocates who "advertise" and condemn their discreet "way of life." As Larry Gross points out in his book *Contested Closets,* a standard statement made by both lesbian and gay advocates and their detractors is "that *sexuality is a private matter.* Each side means something different: *Let us live our lives in peace,* and *Get back in the closet.*"[12]

The right of privacy has acted as a double-edged sword in relation to lesbian and gay culture. It has functioned legally both as a protection from government intrusion into private acts between consenting adults as argued in *Bowers v Hardwick* (478 US 186 [1986]), the unsuccessful challenge of Georgia's sodomy law, and as a bar against disclosure of facts that society wants silenced, as in the Minnesota courts' condemnation of Karen Thompson's outing of Sharon Kowalski. Yet the insistence on privacy in both cases is dangerous because it endorses secrecy and legitimates a closet, implying that same-sex love is not acceptable. The history of the *Kowalski* case elucidates the pitfalls of relying on privacy; it teaches us that until acceptance comes legally and socially, publicly and privately — until *we get out of the closet* — we will not live our lives in peace. As Karen Thompson became a more public figure, her stump speech produced the same message: we are vulnerable when invisible, and we pay a price for silence.

In many senses, coming out of the closet is the most important political and legal step that a lesbian or gay man can take. Though the possible consequences vary depending on the recipient of the disclosure — family, spouse, employer, police, military officer, scoutmaster, media — the announcement of one's sexual orientation is an act that emphasizes how law, by the account of legal mobilization theorists, is "a contested terrain of relational power among its citizens."[13] Emphasizing the way courts are forums for social struggles, Frances Zeman's view of law as a desire translated into formal demand captures the initial motivation of Thompson's decision in 1984 to come out and petition for guardianship — her desire to continue to live with her disabled lover. When the courts later barred Thompson from visiting her partner, Karen's recourse to political mobilization in aid of her lawsuit illustrated the interrelation of legal and social power.

The year 1984 was a time of mixed blessings for the burgeoning civil rights movement for lesbians and gay men. Post-Stonewall coalitions in universities,

liberal churches, and feminist organizations had already made inroads in criminal law (twenty states repealed sodomy laws in the seventies), immigration law
(homosexuality was no longer grounds for denying entry into the country), and
school law (lesbian and gay campus groups were protected by the First Amendment) but suffered defeats in the arena of marriage rights in Minnesota, Washington, and Kentucky.[14] In the wake of these efforts, lesbian and gay forces had
formed the Lambda Legal Defense and Education Fund (1972), the National
Gay and Lesbian Task Force (NGLTF; 1973), and the Human Rights Campaign
(HRC; 1980), national organizations that would play a major part in future legal
struggles, including the Kowalski matter. By the eighties the American Civil
Liberties Union (ACLU) had begun to champion lesbian and gay rights, though
Nan Hunter did not start the Gay and Lesbian Project until 1986.[15] These promising advances in social acceptance, however, met with challenges from antigay
evangelical forces, beginning in earnest when Anita Bryant's Save Our Children Network overturned an antidiscrimination law in Dade County, Florida,
in the late seventies. St. Paul and other cities followed the lead of Bryant, a former Miss America, and in 1980 Karen Thompson and the American public
elected Ronald Reagan, ushering in a new era of conservatism. In spite of such
setbacks, lesbian and gay rights had for the first time become a plank in the platform of the Democratic Party in 1980, and by the next presidential campaign
the socially conservative Senator Walter Mondale of Minnesota was talking
about human rights at an HRC fund-raiser in Manhattan.[16]

Even though the struggle for domestic partnership protection had, after the
failed marriage litigation of the seventies, become a dead issue among national
organizations, Sharon Kowalski's domestic rights case, which pitted a socially
conservative father against a lesbian partner, was able to galvanize the lesbian
and gay community when it began to receive national attention in 1987. The
Minnesota litigation brought to the foreground the worst nightmare of lesbian
and gay partners — a legal ban on their freedom to associate. When Karen
Thompson, by judicial fiat, was prevented from having contact with her partner, queer men and women across the country — even in urban ghettos —
identified with her situation and feared the consequences of intervention by
families they had hoped to escape by earlier migrations.

The intervention in freedom to associate was also becoming a greater reality with the advent of the AIDS pandemic, which began to devastate and mobi-
lize the gay community at almost the same time as Sharon Kowalski's struggle.[17]
Thompson's petition for guardianship raised issues of visitation, probate, custody, and medical decision making between same-sex couples that paralleled
those of AIDS while displacing the setting of these questions from urban
enclaves to the "wholesome" Midwest, where two lesbians confronted homo-

phobic forces on the Iron Range. The *Kowalski* case raised similar issues as AIDS litigation without having to confront social stigmas attached to the supposed promiscuity of gay men. Thompson's cause célèbre, which culminated politically on August 8, 1988, in demonstrations all over the country, occurred at nearly the same time that the AIDS Coalition to Unleash Power (Act Up) was expanding nationally into Kansas City, Seattle, and Portland.

There were differences, of course, between these causes, and one of them was gender. Although Karen Thompson did become a grand marshal at the New York City Gay Pride Parade in 1987, she also received support from the women's community, both at home in St. Cloud and nationally with the National Organization for Women (NOW) and among participants in the Michigan Women's Music Festival. The National Committee to Free Sharon Kowalski, with local chapters, was formed in major metropolitan areas with the help of lesbians like singer–songwriter Judy Fjell and feminist groups on campuses and in professional organizations across the country, where Sharon's partner gave talks on the lecture circuit.

As a result of mobilization efforts by Thompson and her supporters, by the time Karen's lawyers filed their last appeal in 1991, amicus briefs came from at least thirteen different groups, including the Metropolitan Community Church, Parents and Friends of Lesbians and Gays (PFLAG), and the Minnesota Alliance for Progressive Action. Persuasive and eloquent briefs by the ACLU, Lambda, and NOW undoubtedly contributed to Judge Jack Davies's 1992 decision to overturn the lower court, award Thompson guardianship, and call Sharon, Karen, and Karen's new partner, Patty, "a family of affinity," but the power to prevail on Thompson's petition most likely came from "a multiplicity of force relations" that probably are not attributable to single groups or individuals.[18] Thompson's grassroots struggle was aided by events as unrelated as Donald Kowalski's largely economic decision to give up control of his daughter, the passage of domestic partnership legislation in Minneapolis, and a fast-growing lesbian and gay media *(Washington Blade, Gay Community News [GCN], Equal Time, [Twin Cities] GAZE)* that brought the case to the attention of national media, including the *New York Times* and television's *West 57th Street*. These social and cultural forces played a role in pointing the legal compass toward an awareness of what legal theorist David Richards calls the "moral slavery" of lesbians and gays in our society.[19]

That slavery is not overcome by legal victories alone. In spite of Sharon Kowalski's successful reunification with her partner in 1992, her opportunities for medical recovery had been seriously undermined by the law's delay. In the early nineties, the couple still faced legal bills and a formidable bureaucracy with regard to disability rights, though the promise of a GLBT-friendly White

House gave activists like Thompson hope. Yet in spite of a Hawaii judiciary calling for same-sex marriage (*Baehr v Lewin*, 852 P2d 44 [Hawaii Supreme Court 1993]), some increased attention to AIDS research, and President Bill Clinton's friendly stance, the nineties unfolded in a way that would defy theories of historical progression in the area of gay civil rights. Media representations did become increasingly prevalent in television *(Ellen)* and film *(Philadelphia)*, but Sharon Kowalski's story failed to reach the silver screen in spite of attempts. Promised mitigation of the ban on lesbians and gays in the military met with a backlash that increased discharges under a flawed "don't-ask-don't-tell" policy. Advances in same-sex partnership in Vermont, Hawaii, and California were counteracted by the passage of Defense of Marriage Acts (DOMAs) by thirty-five states and the federal government. The advent of expensive drugs to treat AIDS stemmed the tide of gay funerals, but there is still no cure, no vaccine, and thousands are still dying annually. The unconstitutionality of laws seeking to prevent government protection of gays and lesbians in cities like Aspen, Colorado (*Romer v Evans*, 517 US 620 [1996]), has not obviated the need for Oregon activists to once again organize and only narrowly defeat a law that would ban discussion of homosexuality in schools.

At the turn of the millennium, Karen Thompson's optimism about her living situation reflects a broader sentiment among activists that in spite of the appointment of an antigay attorney general in the conservative Bush administration, the climate in the United States has changed. "[P]eople get it. People understand. They don't question that it's love. . . . We go in and out of Coburns, our grocery store in town, and we are just like other people," Thompson recently told interviewers.[20] Since then lesbian plaintiffs in a domestic partnership case in Montana have been burned out of their home (February 8, 2002), and though James Dale finds himself able to move to Vermont to enter into a civil union, the Supreme Court has told him his immorality prevents him from participating in the Boy Scouts of America. As *Lesbian/Gay Law Notes* and other publications have chronicled, legal, political, and social barometers in the struggle for GLBT rights continue to fluctuate in ways that make complacency dangerous.[21]

Sexual Orientation Law

In 1983, no law schools in the country offered courses in sexual orientation; in 1995, a quarter of our law schools did, a percentage that no doubt has grown in a field that is replete with hornbooks, journals, law review articles, experts, and courses in many schools.[22] The *Kowalski* guardianship case took place during a period when social theories of homosexuality were shifting from notions of sin and sickness to conceptions of neutral difference, social construction, and genetics.[23] Besides justifying their existence, sodomites were challenging their arrest, ensigns were litigating their discharge from the military, gay and lesbian organizations were demanding the right to meet at Texas A&M University, GLBT nonprofits were demanding the right to tax-exempt status, and lesbian mothers were going to court to keep their children.[24] Sexual orientation law by the 1980s was dividing into discrete areas of study: criminal (sodomy statutes, arrests, hate crimes); employment (military bans, security clearances, private discharge); school (faculty and student rights to organize); immigration (homosexuality as a bar to immigration, and as grounds for asylum); tax and insurance law (domestic partnership rights); and AIDS (disability and discrimination).

Family law had developed its own set of lesbian and gay precedents, covering categories such as same-sex marriage, domestic partnership dissolutions (*Marvin v Marvin* palimony), custody, visitation, adoption, and surrogate parenting. While the three published Court of Appeals decisions that represent the judicial legacy of *In re Guardianship of Sharon Kowalski* have little legal precedent outside the state of Minnesota and the narrow, rarely litigated family law area of guardianship, Judge Davies's final determination granting Thompson's petition in 1991 has become a touchstone for legal reformers in areas of custody law, same-sex marriage litigation, and domestic partnership legislation.[25] What makes the case central to sexual orientation law is precisely the way its influence has radiated beyond its narrow focus as traditional legal precedent.

When Thompson filed her petition in 1984, the legal inroads made in immigration, school, and public employment law were not matched by any progression in domestic relations. As late as 1973, courts were still maintaining their historical position of erasure by silence in the area of custody law; as a result, in divorce cases lesbian mothers and gay fathers were regularly being barred from custody and sometimes even visitation because of "immoral" and "unnatural" behavior.[26] Yet Rhonda Rivera, in her study of sexual orientation cases in the seventies and eighties, documents custody as the "largest single type of lesbian and gay case between 1970 and 1979," which she finds remarkable because out of the forty cases found, twenty-five represented some form of victory in terms of allowed joint custody or visitation for the lesbian or gay appellant, who was most often out of the closet. In the 1978 to 1980 cases, however, homosexuality was a "deciding factor" in the loss of custody, and geography was a better indicator of outcome than how recently the case was determined.[27]

Rivera's research provides a context for the Minnesota litigation over "custody" of the incapacitated Sharon Kowalski, who experts found to be functioning at the level of a six-year-old and therefore in need of a guardian. While guardianship statutes list a number of factors (commitment, preference of the ward, and awareness of social and medical needs) as determinants in the choice of a guardian when a person is found incapacitated, the decision falls within the "best interest" rubric that is also applicable in custody and visitation cases in dissolutions. Sharon's case is thus closely aligned with legal reasoning in child custody cases, even though the analogy is fraught with pitfalls because traumatic brain injury (TBI) patients, in spite of intelligence test results, are not equivalent to children. Notwithstanding this distinction, Karen Thompson's petition for guardianship arose in a legal climate where, in many jurisdictions, a lower court finding that a parent's homosexuality conflicts with the best interests of the child was well within a court's discretion and therefore rarely found to be appealable.[28]

Minnesota's guardian statute, like many, created a rebuttable presumption in favor of a relative of the ward, but Minnesota's other laws did not, as in other states, create a presumption that homosexuals were not in any child's best interest.[29] In Thompson's case, her inability to claim "spousal rights" left her unable to assert the guardian presumption; moreover, the rhetoric of family privilege provided a convenient way for the courts to promote normative heterosexuality without having to prove the "unfitness" of the petitioner's lesbianism, at least until Thompson came under attack for "outing" her partner. Eventually, Thompson's active lesbianism allowed the courts to question her fitness as a guardian of the incapacitated Sharon, who was considered a child even if Karen had been her lesbian partner. The appeals court even gave credence to accusations of sexual abuse by the petitioner, following the historical but statistically invalid association of homosexuality with molestation.[30]

Although Nan Hunter and others have argued that the "best interests" standard continues to permit "a narrow-minded or unsophisticated judge to indulge prejudices about unorthodox behavior," the status of custody litigation post-*Kowalski* has shown some signs of improvement, especially in coastal and more progressive jurisdictions.[31] While several states have created and still maintain presumptions against custody for gay and lesbian parents, and three states explicitly prohibit adoption, other cases have shown that many courts will not deny custody or visitation unless evidence of sexual orientation is combined with other evidence of what is best for the child.[32] While most states still give priority to relatives and spouses, a few states have adopted the Uniform Health-Care (UHC) Decisions Act of 1993, which gives priority to "long-term relationship" with a spousal-equivalent commitment in matters of visitation, medical decisions, and guardianship.[33] The UHC represents an important legislative step taken after the *Kowalski* case.

Provisions of the Uniform Probate Code also defer to valid contracts, like medical powers of attorney, that designate caregivers in case of incapacity. From the outset, Karen Thompson championed the use of powers of attorney and wills as a method by which same-sex couples can protect themselves from heterosexist laws. This important advice has become even more prevalent with the advent of artificial insemination, surrogate mothering, second-parent adoption, and polyparenting. David Chambers, however, has pointed out that such planning not only instantiates an inequality between gays and straights but also, as a practical matter, is unlikely to be undertaken by couples reluctant to face their mortality.[34] As Ruthann Robson has also pointed out, these contracts are sometimes subject to challenges of fraud and undue influence by disgruntled family members.[35] Although not foolproof and definitely the province of the privileged, estate planning is becoming increasingly accessible through the use of books by Nolo Press of Berkeley and other gay and lesbian agencies.[36]

Karen Thompson claimed that she would not have lost Sharon if they had executed the right documents almost as often as she stated that she would not have to retire $300,000 in legal bills if she were Sharon's spouse. The same-sex marriage debate, with its promoters and detractors within the queer community, is well beyond the scope of this book, but the *Kowalski* case must assume its rightful place in the continuing struggle for the provision of the benefits and burdens of the marriage contract for those who are legally unable to marry.[37] The Kowalski litigation took place in a state where, a decade earlier, Minneapolis activist Jack Baker had filed suit with his partner for the state's refusal to give him a marriage license (*Baker v Nelson*, 191 NW2d 185 [Minnesota Supreme Court 1971]).[38] Baker's equal protection arguments were summarily dismissed as inapplicable to a naturally heterosexual institution, and his early efforts created some dubious precedent that led East Coast gay and lesbian advocates to deprioritize marriage cases for more than a decade. Thompson's cause suffered from this low priority. Her outside support came first from the Minnesota Civil Liberties Union (MCLU), which was more interested in the disabled's right to choose an attorney than in Thompson's argument for a de facto marriage. By the time of her appeal in 1991, however, the popularity of Thompson's cause had led Lambda Legal Defense to cite Sharon's predicament as an illustration of the unfairness of exclusive marriage laws and to write briefs on her behalf.

While Thompson was not technically making a legal claim to marriage in her petitions, her lawyers were arguing that her four-year relationship with Sharon was sufficiently committed to be treated as part of the spousal presumption for purposes of determining Sharon's best interests. In the 1980s, however, Karen's lawyers could find few precedents in favor of same-sex domestic rights, outside of the freedom to associate cases in the schools and a

few dissolutions that were treated as *Marvin* partnerships for purposes of property division. In fact, precedent in domestic cases pointed in the opposite direction: homosexuality was cause for separation rather than an approximation of
heterosexuality. Thompson's eventual victory in her petition for guardianship
in 1991 represented a promising change in domestic relations law, one that coincided with another case that was defying the predictions of many gay and lesbian advocacy groups. In 1993, the Hawaii Supreme Court in *Baehr v Lewin*
ruled that the denial of marriage licenses to same-sex partners was unconstitutional sex discrimination. *Baehr* set the stage for renewed litigation in domestic
relations laws for gays and lesbians in the 1990s, a struggle that regularly
detailed the panoply of marital rights gays and lesbians were barred from
enjoying: benefits such as joint tax returns, marital trusts, estate tax deductions,
survivor's benefits, health insurance, and wrongful death claims, as well as
rights to visitation, custody, adoption, and guardianship presumptions.[39] In regard to the latter benefit, the Kowalski case served as a ready reminder of the
seriousness of this lack of equal protection.

In the years since *Kowalski*, the same-sex marriage movement has faced a
set of mixed legal results that reflect the political struggle between influences
of right-wing, primarily sectarian forces and an increasingly uncloseted gay
and lesbian civil rights movement.[40] The *Baehr* litigation led not only to the
rapid passage of a state constitutional amendment in Hawaii fixing the
definition of marriage to opposite-sex couples (1998) but also arguably to the
passage of the myriad DOMAs, including that of Minnesota in 1997. For lesbian and gay scholars who fear assimilation, couplism, and an endorsement of
an institution with a long antifeminist history, however, marriage is not an
honor they dream of, even if most scholars realize that the present denial of
the economic and domestic rights that attach to the troubled institution to gays
and lesbians is clearly discriminatory.[41] In 1999, the Vermont Supreme Court
agreed, holding in *Baker v State* (74 A2d 864 [Vermont Supreme Court 1999])
that its state's marriage clause violated the "common benefits" clause of Vermont's constitution.

The legislative upshot of the Hawaii and Vermont litigation indicates how
the domestic partnership movement is inextricably linked to the struggle for
same-sex marriage, in spite of ideological differences over a symbolic rite. In
2000, the Vermont legislature, in response to the *Baker* ruling, enacted a civil
union bill that gives same-sex domestic partners all the rights of marriage that
the state can confer. The Hawaii legislature in 1997 passed a "reciprocal
beneficiaries" bill that provides some of the benefits of marriage to same-sex
couples. Most recently, the State of California has passed sweeping domestic
partnership legislation that explicitly gives domestic partners parity in matters

of guardianship.[42] Internationally, domestic partnership legislation has also had successes, most famously in Denmark but also in Canada, the Netherlands, South Africa, and most recently Mexico (2001).

The domestic partnership movement, both local and global, public and private, has its own history — one that demonstrates how incremental advances in lesbian and gay recognition are indicative of the unpredictability of power and the consequences of coming out. The movement was well under way at the time of the *Kowalski* litigation, and if Sharon and Karen had lived in a municipality with such a law and been registered as domestic partners at the time of the accident, they might have benefited from visitation rights and might even have enjoyed a rebuttable presumption in favor of Karen's guardianship. The fact that they did not, however, gave the domestic partnership movement more impetus, not only with Minneapolis's passage of a new law in 1991, but also with other laws all over the country. The movement for protection of unmarried couples had actually begun in the 1970s when municipal public registration laws often accompanied antidiscrimination provisions. Some of the laws provided insurance benefits to partners of public employers; others were less substantive, allowing public registration only.[43] Locales like New York (1982), Berkeley (1985), and West Hollywood (1985) were passing such laws at the time of Thompson's litigation. The Minneapolis City Council cited *Kowalski* when it passed a domestic partner ordinance in 1991, directly evidencing the influence of the guardianship case on legislation in Minnesota's largest city, even though that suit was not filed in Hennepin County, where Minneapolis is located, and many of the legal arguments in the case actually reflect a reaction to the social progressiveness of Minnesota's largest metropolitan area.

By 1999, over one hundred cities and counties were providing some benefits to domestic partners, ranging from Seattle to Ithaca.[44] Universities such as Alaska, North Dakota, California, and Washington had joined private eastern schools and many private corporations, including Ford and General Motors, in providing same-sex domestic partners the opportunity to buy into insurance plans.[45] The piecemeal domestic partnership movement has had its detractors. Many advocates argue that same-sex marriage would obviate the need for incremental steps; others say that the fight for such benefits ignores the poor, the single queer, or multiple family units. Polygamy and polyparenting are also part of gay and lesbian culture, and one commentator suggests there is no reason why two women and a man should not be able to register as domestic partners.[46] Thompson's family of affinity currently faces this very issue with its makeup of three women; in fact, Patty Bresser has voiced concerns about what should happen if Karen were to die, since Bresser has no legal ties to Sharon Kowalski.

The legal legacy of the *Kowalski* case in areas of custody, estate planning, and same-sex partnership legislation is as pervasive as it is collateral. Even though under principles of stare decisis the case holds little power, as narrative and political precedent its citations are innumerable. Sharon's separation from her lover for three and a half years illustrated — as much as any example in recent legal history — the need to treat lesbians and gay men fairly. Yet the legislative history of the State of Minnesota, where Karen Thompson resides, sends a crucial message to lesbians and gays who would like to think of themselves as post-gay, assimilated citizens. The very year that Thompson finally moved Sharon into her home, 1993, the Minnesota legislature enacted a law prohibiting quotas based on sexual orientation and barring any advocacy of homosexuality in public schools.[47] In 1997, the state passed its DOMA with a companion law prohibiting recognition of same-sex marriages from other states.

Although sexual orientation law has grown exponentially since Karen Thompson first filed her petition in 1984, recent scholars remind us that it is still "difficult to identify any other group of American citizens who are currently less protected under the United States Constitution than are gays and lesbians."[48] At the turn of the millennium, as William Eskridge has detailed, in most places in the country, the uncloseted lesbian cannot serve in the military, cannot legally marry, commits a crime in eighteen states when she has oral sex, is subject to hate crimes that go uninvestigated, is subject to confiscation of her biological children, and has no recourse in many states if she is fired for being an open lesbian.[49] If her partner is injured, she may also be prevented from visiting her in the hospital, making medical decisions for her, or becoming her guardian. Would the *Kowalski* case end differently today? If two closeted lesbians went through the same legal ordeal, in many jurisdictions there would be no assurance of a different outcome.

The late Tom Stoddard, director of the Lambda Legal Defense Fund, called the Kowalski struggle the most important and compelling legal case concerning lesbian and gay rights in his lifetime. Thompson's legal battle became a rallying cry for a movement reeling from the disability and death associated with the AIDS pandemic, her separation and legal mistreatment dramatizing the deepest fear of same-sex partners. Thompson spoke for an aging lesbian and gay male community; she spoke for rural gays and lesbians everywhere afraid to come out, afraid to face the disparagement and derogatory stereotypes that they lived with externally and internally. She spoke for those who had left homophobic homes while still loving their families, left homophobic towns while still loving the land, left homophobic friends while still wishing for connection. The *Kowalski* case put a face on lesbian and gay discrimination.

It also gave the struggle a narrative structure. The trial of Sharon Kowalski is in this history divided into the chronology of litigation from injury to remedy, with increments of pretrial discovery, injunctive relief, publicity, hearing, decision, and appeal becoming the chapters that mark the stages in the protracted process of going to court and seeking relief. The trial serves as both a structural framework and a metaphor for the state of lesbians and gay men in our society. In the new millennium, citizens of all sexual orientations are finding themselves under oath on the stand "In re the Matter of Same-Sex Love"; each of us is being examined and asked to tell the truth. This book relates the story of how that truth got told in the case of two women from St. Cloud, Minnesota, and how that testimony became law.

Injury

"Who will I say I am?" the visitor asked herself, reading the instructions posted under the intercom. A large locked door stood before her, separating the intensive care unit of St. Cloud Hospital from the rest of the building. Under the push-button intercom system to the left of the entrance, a set of regulations, posted by the hospital for the protection of its severely ill or injured patients, stated that only "family members" were allowed to visit patients in this unit.

At home half an hour earlier, the visitor, Karen Thompson, had received a call from her partner's father, Donald Kowalski, in Nashwauk on the Iron Range.[1] He told her that Sharon and her niece and nephew had been in a car crash about an hour and a half earlier near Onamia. Melissa, Sharon's niece, had been taken to Onamia Hospital; Michael, her nephew, to the University of Minnesota Hospital in Minneapolis; and Sharon to St. Cloud Hospital, twenty minutes from the home in Briggs Lake that the two women shared. Don said he and his wife, Della, would go to Minneapolis directly to check on the boy; Karen assured him that she would go immediately to St. Cloud Hospital. Throwing some of Sharon's clothes into a gym bag, she ran through the rain to her car and completed the twenty-minute drive to St. Cloud in fifteen.

Trying to ignore the import of the regulations she had just finished reading, Thompson finally mustered enough courage to push the speaker button to ask if Sharon Kowalski was there and what her condition was. "What is your relationship?" a disembodied voice demanded over the intercom. Karen replied that she was a close friend who lived with Sharon. "I'm sorry," the speaker replied. "We can't give out information to anyone except immediate family members." Karen tried to explain, stating that she had come in place of Sharon's parents, but the voice was adamant. Unsuccessful, Thompson walked in frustration from the intercom to the waiting room. The woman she had loved for almost four years was probably less than a hundred feet away from her, but because she was not a family member, she was prevented from knowing whether Sharon was living or dying. If they were married, Karen would have been by her side at that very moment; instead, hospital regulations prevented her from caring for the person she was committed to in sickness and in health — at this, the most crucial time in Sharon's life.

Sitting down to wait for someone to emerge from behind the white door,

Karen began to recall a conversation of just a week earlier about the subject she never dared discuss. Sharon had finally used the word "gay" to describe their four-year relationship, asking Karen, "When are you going to acknowledge your sexuality?" The two of them had just been to their first "lesbian" event, a concert by Meg Christian and Cris Williamson in the Twin Cities, but Karen was uncomfortable, feeling labeled and conspicuous. When three or four of her students that she coached came up to greet her during the concert, she was mortified, wishing she could fall between the cracks in the floor. She was not ready to acknowledge her love for Sharon publicly; as far as she was concerned, they were just two human beings who happened to fall in love regardless of gender. "Lesbian" was the last word Karen wanted to apply to their romance (*Why Can't,* 22).

In 1976, more than seven years earlier, Karen Thompson had barely noticed the twenty-one-year-old transfer student from a junior college in the northern Minnesota Iron Range who had enrolled in two of her classes, one called "Competitive Sports for Women" and the other in basketball officiating, at St. Cloud State University, where Karen was an instructor in the Department of Health, Physical Education, Recreation, and Sports Science. Thompson had moved from Ohio, where she had grown up, attended Muskingum College to earn a health and physical education degree, and flirted with joining the Marine Corps, deciding not to accept her commission after a long summer of training. She had taught physical education at Shady Side High School and then for four years at a junior high in Canton. After moving from Ohio to Minnesota to finish her master's degree at St. Cloud, Karen had decided to stay, first as an instructor, later as an assistant professor.

When the quiet student with big glasses who sat in the back row took another class with Professor Thompson the next semester, the thirty-year-old instructor with the brown hair, an oval face, and a lots-of-teeth smile had to relearn her name. Coach Thompson did not remember Sharon Kowalski as particularly outstanding until a year later, when she came to her office asking if Karen needed help with the women's track team. Always in need of a hand, Thompson made the five-foot, eight-inch, 145-pound athlete an unpaid assistant, and for the next four months the two women spent a few hours each day working together during practice. Sharon, a basketball and track star in high school, was enthusiastic, diligent, and regular in attendance on all trips to meets in and out of state. The women's friendship grew as they worked with the team and talked for hours after practice. Eventually Karen opened up enough to tell Sharon about her evangelism program, her church attendance, her Bible study, her two choirs. They began to study the Bible together, in hopes that Sharon would receive Christ into her heart.

At the end of the 1978–79 academic year, Karen received a leave of absence to return to Ohio State University and complete her course work for her doctorate. When Sharon found out that her friend was leaving, she openly expressed her fears that they would become estranged. Karen was, after all, a professor, a doctoral candidate, Sharon just a student nine years younger earning a double bachelor's degree in health and physical education. In response to her friend's concern, Karen gave Sharon a Bible, encouraged her continued growth in her faith, and assured her that their friendship would not wane because of their separation for nine months.

But less than four weeks after the move, Sharon called her friend in Columbus and asked if she could stop by on a motorcycle trip she was taking. Within a week, the two were taking walks together in Ohio, identifying the flora and fauna, going for long rides on Sharon's Honda. Karen came back to St. Cloud that Thanksgiving to visit. After pinning down Sharon during a playful wrestling match, Karen abruptly stood up and withdrew, stating that she didn't want to hurt their friendship. She was beginning to have physical feelings for Sharon that she could not control or understand. But Sharon persisted. She wanted to know what Karen was feeling. Not until the next day, after a sleepless night, was Karen able to articulate her fears about how close she felt to Sharon, who assured her that she had felt the same way for a long time.

In December, Karen flew back to St. Cloud for another visit, carrying a ring. She had decided that she loved Sharon and wanted a committed relationship in the eyes of God. To her surprise, after pulling over during a drive in the country, Sharon almost simultaneously took a ring from her pocket. With serendipitous timing, the exchange of rings and commitment led to a night of passionate love that began that December evening in 1979 (*Why Can't*, 134).

"Are you okay?" a voice asked the distracted Karen. She looked up into the eyes of a priest in the waiting room and immediately began explaining her predicament. He promised to look into the status of Sharon in the intensive care unit (ICU) and report back as soon as possible. Hours had passed since the accident, and she still had no information about Sharon's condition. After the priest disappeared behind the white door, Thompson began pacing, waiting, remembering, thinking about their shared history. Their fourth anniversary was only a month away.

When Karen returned to St. Cloud in June 1980, she and Sharon moved into an apartment for a year, Sharon attempting to make ends meet as a CETA employee teaching visitors about edible plants at the Sherburne Wildlife Refuge while looking for a coaching job, Karen waiting to get back to teaching in September. They knew they loved each other, but they never talked about their sexual orientation, never used the word "lesbian," never discussed the implications of two women loving one another. Karen knew that her church condemned homosexuality, but she did not think of herself as a homosexual. She had fallen in love with an individual, Sharon, and even though her partner was for the first time a woman, Karen felt that gender was irrelevant. In 1981, they moved in with Karen's recently divorced sister, Linda, and jointly decided they had best not discuss their relationship with her. They had fallen into the habit of hiding. Karen rationalized her fear by convincing herself that her love for Sharon was nobody's business but her own. The notion of the closet had no meaning for her; she didn't conceive of herself as being in one and thus felt no pressure to come out. The hiding, though difficult, was automatic, unquestioned, almost unconscious.

Sharon finally secured a teaching position at Big Lake High School in August 1981, and eventually the couple decided to move out of St. Cloud to nearby Briggs Lake, where Karen bought a house in a parklike setting that allowed them to cross-country ski in the winter and canoe and fish in the summer. Although Karen was the legal owner, they thought of the house as theirs together, and Sharon paid what she could toward the mortgage each month. But in June 1983, Sharon lost her job at Big Lake because of budget cuts and was forced to look for work again, while continuing her life as a woman who loved to party, play poker, and drink beer with friends in between quiet times spent with her lover. Both were relieved when St. Cloud State offered Sharon a position as golf coach for the spring semester of the next year, 1984.

Once in a while, Sharon took Karen to her parents' and friends' houses in the Iron Range, in northern Minnesota. Spending an occasional weekend at the Kowalskis' home outside of Nashwauk, Karen became acquainted with Sharon's parents, Don and Della, and her sister and brother, Debbie and Mark. "Save Monday night for me," Sharon had whispered to Karen that rainy Sunday afternoon, buckling her niece and nephew, Debbie's children, into the car, in preparation for the 180-mile drive from Briggs Lake north to Nashwauk (*Why Can't*, 3). They had been happy to baby-sit the kids that weekend, while Debbie and her husband worked on their unraveling marriage. Sharon planned on reaching Debbie's before the rain turned to ice; she would spend the night up on the Range.

On November 13, 1983, a twenty-seven-year-old woman was admitted to the emergency room at St. Cloud Hospital suffering from injuries sustained in a vehicle accident a few hours earlier. She was diagnosed with a severe closed head injury with multiple neurological deficits. A CAT scan demonstrated a right temporal contusion, multiple areas consistent with cerebral hemorrhages, and fixed posture on the right side. The impact of the collision on her brain stem resulted in damage to her cortex, and she was in a coma, unconscious, at the time of admission. She also suffered from multiple orthopedic injuries, including a left proximal femoral fracture (a broken left leg) and fractured kneecaps. She had multiple abrasions and lacerations. Her prognosis was guarded. Her leg was put in traction, and she was sent to the ICU for constant surveillance. The longer she remained alive, the better her chances of survival became, but not until the edema receded could the extent of the damage to the brain cells be assessed. If the patient did survive, recovery would be long-term and incomplete.

Hospital admission records reported that the patient, Sharon Kowalski, was single, born in Grand Rapids, Minnesota, on August 8, 1956. She grew up in the Nashwauk area and had a twenty-six-year-old sister in Hibbing and a twenty-four-year-old brother in St. Peter. Her parents lived in Nashwauk. Her father was retired from Hanna Mining but did some self-employed work at this time in landscaping. Her mother was a homemaker. The patient had completed a high school education, gone to college in Bemidji, Hibbing Community College, and St. Cloud State, where she graduated as a physical education instructor. She was laid off in the spring of 1983 from a job coaching in high school. She was generally interested in physical activity. Prior to the accident, she lived in the home of Karen Thompson in St. Cloud.

Donald Kowalski listened in quiet disbelief as the policeman told him over the phone that his older daughter, a veteran motorcyclist who had driven all over the country, had been involved in a head-on automobile collision an hour earlier near Lake Onamia. He instantly thought of his daughter Debbie's kids, who had been riding back to the Range with Sharon that drizzly November Sunday. Were they OK? The officer could tell him nothing except that the accident was serious and that the three passengers were for some reason sent to three different medical facilities. In a state of shock, Don told Della and then called Debbie. He decided they had better take care of the kids first, quickly preparing for the long drive south, first to Onamia to drop off their daughter to check on Missy, then on to the Twin Cities to check on Michael. He would call Sharon's roommate before leaving to see if she would check on Sharon in St. Cloud. It would be a hell of a drive in the sleet turning to snow — one the Kowalskis, used to their quiet life on the Range, were not pleased about making even under auspicious circumstances.

Since Minnesota became a state in 1858, a north–south division has characterized its economic, political, and social life. The urbanization of the Twin Cities area —

St. Paul and Minneapolis and the surrounding suburbs and towns, including to some degree St. Cloud (about one hundred miles northwest) — has further deepened the split between the politically progressive Minnesota of Walter Mondale and Hubert Humphrey in the south and the rural, working-class mining towns of the north. One of the most renowned sections of Minnesota's northern Arrowhead region, commonly called the Iron Range, is composed of three mountain areas — the Vermilion, Mesabi, and Cayuna. The Range is famous for iron mines, Judy Garland, and Bob Dylan, for towns such as Hibbing, Chisholm, Nashwauk, and Virginia. Since its first permanent European settlement in the 1800s, no part of the state has experienced a greater economic, social, and landscape upheaval than this region, caught in a series of boom and bust cycles, the result of the consumption and exhaustion of natural resources: first animals (fur), then vegetation (white pine forests), then minerals (iron ore). By the end of the twentieth century, the early white settlers — Finns, Slovenes, Italians, Croatians, Swedes, and Poles — had accumulated and spent capital through trapping, sawing, and laying claim to a material world that was now, like its inhabitants, exhausted by the frenzy of free-market activities. For the last 150 years, entrepreneurs had depleted all the resources of the Range, leaving a series of open-pit mines, second-growth forests, and towns with high unemployment rates that were increasingly dependent on service and tourist industries. A report written by a journalist in 1986 about the economic slowdown on the Range offered a striking contrast: from 1981 to 1984, people moved out of the three Iron Range counties — St. Louis, Lake, and Itasca — at four times the rate that Minnesotans in general moved out of the state.[2]

The so-called Range mentality, a fierce independence combined with a distrust of urbanization and its progressive social values, grew out of a history of hard work in hard conditions under hard bosses. The Arrowhead was first visited by the explorers Pierre Esprit Radisson and Médard Chouart de Groseilliers between 1655 and 1660, and except for occasional visits by Jesuits and Franciscans, the Dakota Sioux (later displaced by the Chippewa, or Ojibwa) mainly encountered men interested in fur trading — primarily beavers — seeking to meet the demands of lavish courtiers. By the 1840s, the American Fur Company collapsed from an economy in depression and an overexploitation of the animal population.[3]

At first searching for gold and copper, the next wave of white settlers initially overlooked the towering pines that covered the region, but by the 1870s forests of lumberjacks, from Maine, New York, Canada, Germany, and Ireland, grew up over northern Minnesota. The Arrowhead, which the lumber companies had taken from the hunting-gathering Ojibwa in 1855, was denuded of its forests by the turn of the twentieth century.[4] In 1891, mining operations on the clear-cut Mesabi Range began. The first iron ore was shipped in 1892, and five years later twenty mines were producing three million tons of ore per year. The open-pit method made access to the rich ore relatively easy with steam or electric shovels.

The Iron Range was made up of boomtowns, populated with peoples from over forty nations: lonesome lumberjacks, seasonal immigrants who returned to Europe after six months, gamblers, prostitutes, engineers, hustlers of all sorts — these were the initial inhabitants of Hibbing, Chisholm, Virginia, Eveleth, and Nashwauk. Most of the population was male, most of the businesses were saloons, many of the deaths were suicides.[5] The pioneer period of the Range left a legacy of enterprise, exploitation, and struggle. The earliest town sites consisted of acreage cleared of all vegetation, with mud streets and plank sidewalks. In 1901, one observer described Nashwauk as a hole cut in the forest — the brush burned away — with the stumps extracted only on the main street.[6] Small forest and brush fires surrounded the clearing with smoke and flames; scores of hustling pioneers within the "magic fire circle" were busy as "beavers," erecting stores and dwellings. City governments eventually organized against U.S. Steel and other companies, extracting royalties from them and building elaborate schools and athletic programs. In the 1930 and 1940s, collective bargaining agreements made the iron ore miners among the highest-paid blue-collar workers in the country. Gambling and prostitution were targeted by the Finnish Temperance Union and eventually banned. Women continued to be scarce until well into the twentieth century.

After iron production soared during World War II, with women working in the mines for the first time, emphasis shifted to extracting and processing low-grade taconite ore. New plants were opened in Nashwauk, Keewatin, and Hibbing, when the last boom period began in the 1970s. By 1982, however, the national economic recession and a declining demand for domestic iron ore brought unemployment, plant shutdowns, layoffs, and serious pollution problems. An average of thirty-four people a day were leaving the Range, while others remained trapped by their mortgages or stubbornly held on to the harsh landscape with the tenacity that has marked the identity of Minnesota's "Rangers."

Donald Kowalski took early retirement from Hanna Mining Company, where he had risen to a position of foreman in the taconite mines in the 1960s and 1970s. He had saved enough money to buy some land outside of Nashwauk, where he and his wife, Della, raised three children, Sharon, Debbie, and Mark. He also raised some cattle and operated a bulldozer to supplement his pension, wanting to give each of his children a piece of the property on which to raise their families. His firstborn, however, was not exactly at home on the Range, though she grew up there with considerable popularity and a good education. Sharon, born on August 8, 1956, was an exceptional athlete in high school, holding records in the discus and excelling on the basketball team. The stocky young woman with big glasses, a big smile, and a penchant for big fishing hats loved the outdoors — fishing, hiking, spin casting, canoeing, cross-country skiing — and even worked in the mines for a while. She bought a motorcycle and loved to travel with her friends. Like her mentor Karen Tomberlin, a physical education teacher from Coleraine, Sharon was destined to be a coach, but a freewheeling one. She had the Range in her, loved and hated it, but knew she had to go south to fulfill her potential. Don and Della Kowalski were not ones to interfere with their kids' dreams. They were loving and accepting of most of their daughter's successes and wanderings.

On Sunday, November 13, 1983, Greg Yeager and Wayne Marks woke up in Greg's cabin near Leech Lake, west of the Range in the Chippewa National Forest. The old friends had gone deer hunting that morning but were unsuccessful. They came back around ten-thirty and packed up their belongings. In separate cars they drove to the Blue Heron on Leech Lake and ate, Greg having a rum and Coke with his breakfast around eleven-thirty. When finished, they said good-bye, and Yeager headed south on Highway 169 toward the Twin Cities, listening to the beginning of the Vikings–Green Bay football game. In Garrison he stopped to watch the rest of the game on TV at the Blue Goose, a renowned watering hole in this neck of the woods on the shores of Mille Lacs. The Goose was a big, one-room bar and restaurant with varnished knotty pine walls and pictures of trophy walleye and old settlers. The waitresses wore black skirts, white blouses, and pencils that stuck out of hair buns. The thirty-three-year-old Yeager sat down at the horseshoe bar in front of the television and ordered himself a shot of Bacardi and a Coke. He spent the next three hours watching the Vikings and making his way through six to ten drinks. After the game, Greg asked for another Bacardi and Coke to go, but the bartender refused, telling the patron he would have to drink it there. After being served, Yeager walked out of the Blue Goose with his drink in hand while the bartender turned to change the channel.

Somehow on that Sunday afternoon (it was about three o'clock then), Greg, who by his own admission was pretty drunk at that point, managed to get through Onamia, a little town at the southern end of Lake Mille Lacs, swerving and finishing off his rum. He had an extra bottle in his car. There was not much in it, but he sucked it dry. The police soon received reports of an obviously intoxicated driver who was flattening mailboxes. About four and a half miles south of Onamia, two witnesses in a pickup watched Yeager's truck careening wildly down the road.

On that same cold, drizzly Sunday, Sharon Kowalski was driving north on Highway 169 from St. Cloud to return her niece and nephew to her sister, Debbie Kowalski DiIorio, in Nashwauk. Michael, seven, was in the front, and Melissa, the five-year-old, was in back. As they were approaching Onamia, Sharon was tailing a semi. At the same time, Yeager was driving south, occasionally drifting into the other lane. He managed to swerve out of the way of the oncoming truck but then, in correcting himself, collided head-on with Sharon's two-door Toyota Corolla, injuring Melissa fatally, Sharon severely, and Michael critically. Though both vehicles were totaled, the Corolla had buckled more completely under the impact, the bent hood cracking the windshield. The Minnesota Highway Patrol arrived at the scene of the accident around 3:40, within five minutes of the crash. One witness saw Yeager throw a rum bottle out of his pickup after it landed in a ditch. Greg was taken to a hospital with minor injuries and later pled guilty to Minnesota Penal Code Section 609.21(1) — criminal vehicular operation resulting in death. The drivers and passengers were taken by two ambulances to the hospital in Onamia. Melissa died later. Yeager's blood alcohol level was .22 two hours after the accident.

Two hours after Karen Thompson had arrived at St. Cloud Hospital, the priest emerged from the ICU with a doctor who told her that Sharon had suffered a severe head injury and was in a coma. "I don't know whether she will live through the night," the doctor told a shocked Thompson. "But the longer she does live, the greater her chances of survival will become. The longer she stays in a coma, however, the more severe her head injuries probably will be and more negative the prognosis. It's a waiting game. If she does live we're looking at a long, long time for recovery. Even if she lives, she has been drastically changed and may never be as you knew her before." Karen was sick to her stomach. She could hardly breathe or swallow. The doctor allowed her to visit Sharon for five minutes. Nothing she had heard prepared her for the sight of Sharon lying in traction, her swollen eyes closed, blood seeping through the pores of the skin on her chin and the left side of her face from the impact.

"Why would a lawyer want to become an English teacher?" interviewers repeatedly asked me as I searched for a job after receiving a doctorate at the State University of New York at Buffalo in 1991. My ingenuous reply that I liked reading literature more than depositions was not the answer that academics wanted, I soon learned. It was not about proclivities, one professor finally informed me, not about what you wanted or liked to do; it was about law and literature, a growing field that interviewers expected me to incorporate in my work. In graduate school, I had already made the transition from a student of psychoanalysis and Renaissance literature to a student of queer studies, incorporating homoerotic readings of Shakespeare into my dissertation. During my stay in Buffalo, I had faced some serious hurdles: I had come out professionally, learned that I was HIV positive only months before entering the job market, and helped to start a chapter of Act Up in western New York. These were not announcements I made at job interviews; they were kept as quiet as my status as an inactive member of the California bar.

By 1992, I had developed a course called "Individual Rights in the United States: Law, Literature, and Politics." The course was about the Fourteenth Amendment, about civil rights, about the way literature influenced law, law influenced literature, and both influenced American history. The *Dred Scott* decision, Harriet Beecher Stowe's *Uncle Tom's Cabin*, Charles Chesnutt's *House behind the Cedars*, Toni Morrison's *Beloved*, and John Harlan's dissent in *Plessy v Ferguson* represented the race element of the course. The Communist cases of the 1920s through 1940s, in which citizens were prosecuted for advocating overthrow of the government by force, were studied in conjunction with E. L. Doctorow's *Book of Daniel*, and a segment on women's rights juxtaposed sexual harassment law with Marge Piercy's *Small Changes*.

The final segment of the course, I thought, should deal with the future of civil rights in the United States. What about sexual orientation? Tony Kushner's *Angels in America*? *Bowers v Hardwick*, the Supreme Court case upholding Georgia's sodomy law? Oregon's antigay initiative, Proposition 9—the very law I had marched against in Eugene, the very law that promised to designate me as a gay man, to write my role through a set of moral fictions with or without my consent? "Why does a *gay* lawyer want to be an English teacher?" was a question the job interviewers had not asked, for reasons that pointed directly to the centrality of gay and lesbian concerns to myself and my professions as lawyer and teacher. I started looking at law review articles on sexual orientation, coming across an article entitled "Can Two Real Men Eat Quiche Together? Storytelling, Gender-Role Stereotypes, and Legal Protection for Lesbians and Gay Men" by Marc Fajer. In the middle of his exhaustive study appeared a discussion of *In re Guardianship of Sharon Kowalski* (Minn App 1986), a case that caught my attention because it dramatized discrimination against lesbians and gay men. It read, in fact, like a book.

Counsel

Lesbians are even more invisible than gay men. This is hardly surprising, given the relative invisibility of women's issues and viewpoints throughout our culture. Many women as they grow up are unaware of the existence of women who loved women or even of the word "lesbian." One lesbian emigree, interviewed in the late 1970s, noted, "Your history books do not mention famous lesbians — that some were even queens, like Queen Christina of Sweden, that some were fighters in your revolution, like Deborah Samson. Your children's fairy tales are full of Prince Charmings and their women. . . . Even in your obituaries it is not written that 'Gertrude Stein was survived by her lover of forty years, the woman Alice B. Toklas.' Your commercial advertising tells women to buy perfumes, clothes, makeups, stockings, hair dyes — all to attract *him*. Your novels do not mention it. Even your literary classics do not mention it."

Marc A. Fajer, *Can Two Real Men Eat Quiche Together?*

Donald and Della Kowalski arrived at St. Cloud Hospital at two o'clock in the morning. When Karen Thompson greeted them, she could tell they were exhausted. They had learned of Melissa's death when they dropped their daughter Debbie off at Onamia and decided not to continue on to Minneapolis, where their grandson Michael's condition, they discovered, was improving. Instead, they drove to St. Cloud, where Karen and Della and Don spent the rest of the night at the hospital, taking turns visiting Sharon. Sometime in the middle of that first night, Karen brought up the possibility of obtaining a second medical opinion. The back of her Blue Cross insurance card said such consultations were mandatory in cases of major surgery, and since Sharon was facing a life-or-death situation, Karen asked Don and Della if they would consider another consultation. Don said he was not interested; he thought the doctor knew what he was doing and that they should follow his instructions.

The waiting game continued over the next few days as Sharon's medical condition was monitored. On November 22, surgery was performed on Sharon's leg fracture, and shortly thereafter she was moved from the ICU to a rehabilitation floor. Her skin had cleared, but she was still unresponsive. Karen spent almost all her free time at the hospital — talking to Sharon, reading the

Bible out loud to her, playing music for her, massaging her finger and wrists—willing to try anything to bring her out of her coma. She felt extremely nervous about spending as much time at the hospital as she did, primarily because no one knew the extent of her relation to Sharon. She had talked to others who were visiting loved ones, comparing notes and frustrations, but found herself alienated during those first days. No one knew how close she was to the woman whom she had loved for the past four years, why she was spending inordinate amounts of time at the bedside of her "friend" and "roommate" over whose treatment she had little control.

In the initial period after the accident, the Kowalskis spent as much time at the hospital as they could, but they also had to arrange for their granddaughter's burial and attend to their grandson in Minneapolis. In December, they visited St. Cloud every other week for a few days, often staying with Karen in Briggs Lake, the three of them playing cards and eating dinner together. When Don in passing asked Karen in December how much Sharon owed in rent, Karen felt flummoxed. She was not prepared to tell Don about their relationship. She accepted two months' rent from Don, telling him she would put the money toward Sharon's half ownership of the house. One day in December Karen discovered that the Kowalskis had packed up and left the house without leaving a note. Later that day in Sharon's hospital room, Don asked Karen if she would talk to him in the hall. Her heart sank as they walked down the fluorescent-lit linoleum.

Don and Della had been wondering for a while why Karen was spending so much time at the hospital, why she was monopolizing the visiting hours when they were there, why she was almost shouting into Sharon's ear as she put her face right next to hers, demanding that she wake up. They liked Karen but could not understand what, from their perspective, was intrusive, overbearing behavior in front of their unconscious child. What right had Karen Thompson to sit in their comatose daughter's room and read the Bible to her? Why couldn't she leave poor Sharon alone, let her rest in peace? By December it finally dawned on them that Karen might think of herself as more than Sharon's friend, though they never articulated their suspicions in terms of categories of sexual orientation. They saw Karen as a roommate who was inexplicably intruding into a private family tragedy, a friend who needed to be told to back off.

When Don finally talked to Karen, he tried to put his concerns in the most discreet terms possible. He told her that nobody could love Sharon as much as her family, and that he and Della could take care of Sharon's needs. In his low-key manner, he informed Karen that he did not think it was right for friends to visit as often as Karen was, and that unless she curtailed her presence, he would have to put limits on her hours. "But Sharon might want me here," Karen responded quietly, realizing that if she were Sharon's spouse, which in her mind she virtually *was,* he would never be saying this to her, questioning her involvement. "Don, don't make me tell you more than you want to know," she instinctively stated, afraid of losing contact with the woman she loved (*Why Can't,* 17–18). Don explained that they were planning to take Sharon up to Hibbing as soon as the doctor said she could be moved, planning to bring Sharon home to the Range where they could take care of her.

Undaunted, Karen continued to visit Sharon whenever possible, working with her as the doctors suggested, making sure on one occasion that her lungs were aspirated and preventing a disaster, other times coaxing Sharon to raise her finger, though the doctors remained skeptical of Karen's report of progress, suggesting that sometimes a loved one sees what she wants to see. But within three months of the accident, nurses were corroborating Karen's reports of Sharon's movements in her right hand. Karen spent long hours at Sharon's bedside, trying to make her more alert and responsive, bringing in Ping-Pong and tennis balls for Sharon to hold, putting a pencil in her hand, watching her grow more and more alert each day. At the same time, Thompson continued to be tormented by the troubles she was having with the estranged Kowalskis, fearing that her visitation rights would be suspended or Sharon would be moved. This anxiety led her to the hospital psychologist.

"Should they be confronted, and if so, how?" Thompson asked Charles Chmielewski, a counselor at St. Cloud Hospital. She had just explained to him that she and Sharon were in a long-term relationship, that Sharon was in a coma, that neither of Sharon's parents knew about their daughter's sexual orientation, that they were becoming suspicious of Karen's constant visitation in the hospital, that she herself had told no one about her sexuality, and finally that she loved Sharon and wanted to take care of her (*Why Can't,* 21ff.). Chmielewski saw Thompson professionally a total of ten times between February 14, 1984, and March 26, 1984. He characterized his contact as crisis-intervention therapy, related in large part to Karen's difficulties in knowing what to do in the face of the dilemma that arose as a result of her conflict with Sharon's parents. Chmielewski was impressed with Thompson's concern for Sharon's needs, as well as the level of her commitment. The two of them discussed possible resolutions of the matter, the psychologist positing as one approach sending a letter to the Kowalskis informing them of the women's lesbian relationship. At the next session Karen presented a long letter, which she was considering sending to the parents, a proposal endorsed by the psychologist.

Karen's letter acknowledged Don and Della's parental love but insisted that she, too, loved Sharon. "My love is for an adult, a beautiful, sensitive person who has become my whole world. For over four years we have gotten up to each other, eaten together, played together, shared vacations, and gone to bed to each other every night," Karen announced, revealing her sexual relation without using the word "lesbian." She continued by firmly declaring her stake: "Whether you understand our love is not the issue. Sharon's health and happiness is. We want and need each other. I just cannot believe that you would deliberately hurt your daughter or go against her wishes." Already "unfairly punished" by a drunk driver, Sharon should not be punished further "by taking her away from our home where *she* wanted to be," Thompson continued, insisting that Sharon had chosen to live with her, not with her parents. "I am the single most important person in Sharon's life," Karen declared. "I want to take care of her. I have the right to take care of her. This is what she would have wanted."

At the end of her long missive, Thompson tried to temper some of her emotional fervor. She agreed that "Sharon loves you and needs you too" but reminded Don that "she has not chosen to live her life with you just as you have not chosen at this point in time to live with her. Don, if anything had ever happened to Della, would you have assumed her parents should make all the decisions and take her home to live with them? Well, for Sharon and I the situation is similar to a marriage. We have exchanged rings. I have a right to be involved in any decisions concerning Sharon." Signing her letter "Love in Christ," Karen stated that she would "be happy to sit down and talk" at any time.

Karen Thompson's powerful statement met with anger from the Kowalskis. They had just suffered the loss of their granddaughter, their firstborn was lying in a hospital 180 miles away in a vegetative state that might last forever, and their grandson Michael was still in the hospital. Already suspicious of Thompson's intrusive visitations, Don and Della now realized she was becoming a problem. Their daughter, they knew, was not a homosexual. How could anyone accuse their girl of such behavior when she was too disabled to even speak, when she was lying there in a coma unable to defend herself? What right did Thompson have to intrude on their lives, trying to prevent them from bringing their daughter home to the Range, claiming that she was more important to Sharon than her own flesh and blood? It was plainly outrageous.

Don had already talked to a lawyer about suing the drunk driver for what he had done to their lives, but after reading Thompson's letter he decided to call the former state legislator and well-known local trial attorney, Jack Fena, to make sure that Thompson had no legal leg to stand on. Fena was a name everyone on the Range knew well; he had been a tax judge, had sat in the Minnesota legislature, and knew the court system in his state as well as anybody. He and Don had agreed that Jack would handle the civil action against the drunk driver and the Blue Goose on behalf of their daughter on a contingency fee. The Kowalskis paid nothing to Fena, but the lawyer was entitled to one-third of any settlement and a higher percentage if the case went to trial. Fena was equally incensed when he heard of Thompson's letter, assuring Don and Della that there was no state in the country that recognized the legal rights of homosexuals.

Meanwhile, Debbie Kowalski's reaction to Karen's letter to her bereft parents was swift and decisive. Her sister was *not* a lesbian. Who could possibly believe such a thing? What was this woman doing to her family? She immediately called Karen on behalf of their parents and stated, "You are a sick, crazy person who has made up this whole story. There is no way Sharon is a lesbian. You have written a bunch of trash. My parents never want to set eyes on you again!" Debbie was irate and protective—not about to listen to Karen's attempts to explain over the phone (*Why Can't*, 26ff.).

At some half-conscious level, Karen Thompson probably knew from the time the hospital intercom prevented her access to Sharon that she was bound to face some legal problems if she was to honor her lifelong commitment to Sharon. When she listened to Debbie on the phone, she realized that she would have to consult an attorney, but she had to find one who wasn't blatantly opposed to lesbian and gay relationships. Karen herself was not even convinced she was a lesbian, though she was beginning to understand that her love for Sharon fell under that heading, the label she had avoided for four years but now was having to acknowledge even as she spent nights worrying about the health—the life and death—of her lover.

She finally visited Julie Andrzejewski, a St. Cloud State professor who was known as a feminist and an activist, a lesbian who was involved in a gender equity lawsuit on campus that Karen herself had declined to participate in a few years earlier. Although Karen did not consider herself a feminist and felt threatened by Andrzejewski, she was desperate. After mustering enough courage to knock on her colleague's door, Karen sobbed through her story, soon learning that Julie herself was a lesbian and fully supportive of Karen's situation. Julie would become one of Thompson's greatest allies in the years ahead. When Andrzejewski asked Karen if she was receiving any counseling about these issues, Karen replied that her first priority was legal protection, but "it's scary to think of coming out as being gay when I'm not even sure I am gay. I don't know what I am. I just know I love Sharon. Whatever that makes me, I guess that's what I am. I hate labels and stereotypes. Why do I have to label myself anything?" Karen realized that she had been struggling with these issues for months. At this point she was weary of trying to reconcile her love for Sharon with her love for Christ and her desire to avoid the label "gay," which she knew was, in the eyes of her church, an illness from which one needed to be cured (*Why Can't*, 27).

A few days later, Julie gave Karen the name of an attorney, Peter Donohue, and a religious counselor, Peg Chemberlin of the United Ministries of
Higher Education, a feminist who referred to God as "she." Thompson wasted
no time in contacting Donohue, who agreed to talk to her the next day.
Although sympathetic, he informed her that she basically had no legal rights.
There was no state in the union that recognized by statute a relationship outside of wedlock, nor any that allowed the privileges of a marriage license to
same-sex couples. Even if she could establish the requisites for a common-law
marriage — the sharing of property, a long-term relationship, joint bank
accounts — there was no legal precedent for recognizing that status among
same-sex couples for purposes of any rights other than palimony. More to the
point, however, Sharon remained the final arbiter of her own legal destiny, not
her partner or her parents, Karen discovered, unless she were judged incompetent. Incapacity or incompetency was a legal term, one that signified an individual was mentally unable to make rational choices as determined by a court
in reliance usually on expert medical testimony. From what she had told him,
the lawyer surmised that at this point in time Sharon might be "incompetent"
for purposes of establishing the need for a "guardianship," another complicated legal term.

Guardianship is considered by some legal experts to be the most invasive
form of deprivation of individual rights in society, greater than incarceration.[1]
If a court determines that an individual, the proposed ward, does not have the
ability to care for herself or her property or the ability to make rational decisions,
that individual is declared legally incompetent. Through a statutory process, the
courts then have the power to name a guardian to make decisions for the ward.
Those decisions can be limited to just property or personal decisions, or the
guardianship can be unlimited, giving the guardian the right to make all decisions for the ward, decisions about where to live, whom to see, what medical
attention to seek, and so on. In Minnesota, Karen learned, the statute required
the court to consider "the best interests of the ward" in deciding who was to be
guardian. The statute then listed a number of factors that were relevant in determining that best interest, including but not limited to "the reasonable preference
of the ward" if the ward had the capacity to have a preference.

Questions of whether or not the ward was capable of having a preference
and, if so, how that preference would be determined loomed large in this case,
given Sharon's present difficulty in communicating. Karen was certain that
Sharon would want her as guardian, but she was also fully aware of Don's insistence that Sharon's illness was a family matter. How could Sharon's preference
be proved? Karen learned that there were levels of incapacity, that some wards
could reliably express their preference; others could not; others could but were

judged unreliable in their choice by a court. By statute, the court was also required to take other factors into account in appointing a guardian. The "interest and commitment of the proposed guardian . . . in promoting the welfare of the ward" was a factor, as was the guardian's ability to "maintain a current understanding of the ward's physical and mental status and needs" (Minnesota Statutes Section 525.551). These needs, which the guardian was supposed to understand and be committed to promoting, included food, clothing, and medical care; social, emotional, religious, and recreational requirements; and training and rehabilitation. Karen felt more comfortable on these grounds; she had spent hours with Sharon trying to get her to regain movement and alertness.

The guardianship statute explicitly stated that "kinship is not a conclusive factor in determining the best interests of the ward . . . but should be considered to the extent that it is relevant to the other factors." Her lawyer, however, told her that this language codified or made into statutory law a presumption that existed in previous case law. The Minnesota legislature was saying that courts were allowed to take "kinship" into account in determining guardianship but could not base their decisions solely on that factor. Did kinship include marriage? Was it applicable to same-sex domestic partnership? Would Sharon's family automatically be granted guardianship because of their blood ties? These were the questions the client faced. After talking to Donohue, Karen figured out that she would have no legal rights unless she sought to become Sharon's guardian, an uncertain judicial process that would take away her lover's own freedom and also make their relationship a matter of public record. But if she did not act, Sharon's parents could easily become her guardians and, if they wished, severely limit Karen's right to be with the woman she loved.

The Kowalskis had also consulted their attorney about the financial and emotional hardship they now faced. The question of Sharon's permanent residence arose, for if she legally was a resident of the Kowalskis' home in Nashwauk, there was a chance of collecting a greater amount of injury insurance. Don and Della might be able to use the family auto insurance to increase Sharon's coverage and provide her with a greater amount of money in legal settlement for what would undoubtedly be a long haul of very expensive medical care. The Kowalskis agreed to approach Thompson to see if she was willing to attest that Sharon's permanent address was Nashwauk in order to help her financially. One evening Don swallowed his pride and stopped Karen while she was wheeling Sharon through the corridors of the hospital. He explained the predicament and the proposed solution, but Thompson would have none of it. "Sharon hasn't lived at home for over six years," Karen stated matter-of-factly. "There's no way that the insurance company would accept that as her address."

Don responded in kind, stating bluntly that if Karen really loved Sharon, she would do what she could to help her get as much money as possible. Della, at the end of her rope, stated that they would eventually "get even" with Karen for what she was doing to their family. This contentious encounter was the first of a series of confrontations between Thompson and the Kowalskis, many of which took place in front of Sharon. Don and Della were just plain angry — this so-called friend of Sharon's was adding insults to their injuries, deepening their family tragedy by asserting some perverse attachment to their defenseless daughter. Karen, on the other hand, felt frightened but protective, anxious but zealous in her determination to maintain her attachment to Sharon. Lines of hatred had been drawn around love.

"So who do you think should be the guardian in this case?" I asked my class after introducing the facts of the *Kowalski* case to them as part of the law, literature, and politics course. Silence ensued after the posed question, but I was learning how valuable a teaching tool that vacuum could be. I had been apprehensive about even introducing the sexual orientation issue into this guarded classroom, not being, I thought, the kind of teacher who came out to his classes, preferring to use that forum not as a place of personal confession but as a marketplace of ideas. Professor Charles wanted, for pedagogical purposes, I reasoned, to remain anonymous, objective — a third person, though the issues in the *Kowalski* case were rapidly closing the gap of professional distance.

"It depends," one older woman in the front row finally ventured. "I don't think sexual orientation has anything to do with it. It depends on who can take care of Sharon the best."

"And what she wants," a long-haired young man in the back added. "And if the court thinks gays are immoral, then it won't think being with the woman is in her best interest, so being gay may have something to do with it."

"But I'm saying it shouldn't," the woman replied.

"Would you want to give up your twenty-eight-year-old daughter to a woman who claimed to be her lover of four years?" I asked, reminding the class that in the secret poll I had taken, about a third of them thought homosexuality was wrong. Behind the question lurked the larger issue of how well we know and how much we can trust our partners or our parents — the people we often overestimate under the rhetoric of love.

"Yeah, but if you were married, would you want to give up your wife?" the same student in the back asked. "I don't get it. Let them do what they want. It's their life."

"You might not say that if Sharon was your sister," the young woman next to him suggested. "The thing is that the guardian should be the best qualified, and all this sex stuff is not supposed to be the final word, but it always gets in the way of the law."

"But if homosexuality is immoral or gay marriage not legal, how can you expect a court to make somebody who is gay a guardian?" another student asked.

The discussion continued for a few minutes longer. Many in the class were not talking, unwilling to divulge their views but showing their involvement on their grimacing faces, in the ferocious doodling of their pens. The case not only was blurring the lines between morality, law, and sexual politics; it also was causing students to face or avoid their prejudices about the order of things, their own assumptions about what family was and why it was sacred, about the policing of affinity through categorization. Many were struggling with the tyranny of their silence, their angry refusal to speak out about the unmentionable vice that in this case had become a virtue.

Guardians

She was small and active and sallow; her yellow hair was faded, and looked dry; her blue silk blouses and modest lace collars and high black shoes and sailor hats were as literal and uncharming as a schoolroom desk; but her eyes determined her appearance, revealed her as a personage and a force, indicated her faith in the goodness and purpose of everything. They were blue, and they were never still; they expressed amusement, pity, enthusiasm. If she had been seen in sleep, with the wrinkles beside her eyes stilled and creased lids hiding the radiant irises, she would have lost her potency.

She was born in a hill-smothered Wisconsin village where her father was a prosy minister; she labored through a sanctimonious college; she taught for two years in an iron-range town and when she came to Gopher Prairie, its trees and the shining spaciousness of the wheat made her certain she was in paradise.

Sinclair Lewis, *Main Street: The Story of Carol Kennicott*

On March 2, 1984, in the Probate Division of the District Court of the State of Minnesota, County of Sherburne, Peter S. Donohue filed a petition for appointment of guardian on behalf of Karen D. Thompson, who sought guardianship of both the small estimated estate of Sharon Kowalski ($3,000) and the person of Sharon, who, the pleading stated, "lacks sufficient understanding or capacity to make or to communicate responsible decisions."[1] This boilerplate document eventually caused the filing of a counterpetition on behalf of Donald Kowalski by Kevin Spellacy, a Twin Cities lawyer associated with Jack Fena. A hearing was set for March 23.

Thompson now faced the repercussions of her relationship becoming public, since all filed legal documents were open to inspection by anyone. She feared losing her job, feared being outed to her parents in Ohio by a prying reporter, feared losing Sharon if her petition failed. She had met with Peg Chemberlin, and the two of them had eventually worked through the reconciliation of Karen's Christianity and her homosexuality (*Why Can't*, 27–28). Chemberlin told her that there was nothing in the Bible that condemned love, including the loving relationship between Sharon and Karen, and Thompson concluded she could be both gay and Christian. Chemberlin's support also provided her with the confidence to file for guardianship. Her next step was to come out to her sister Linda, who already had an inkling of Karen's same-sex relations after noticing when the two women were living with her that Sharon's unslept-in bed was always piled with clothes and baseball gloves. After Karen came out to her sister, Linda pledged her support but recommended that their mother, on dialysis for kidney failure, should not be told.

Thompson was still motivated to avoid a hearing. She wrote another letter to the Kowalskis, this one four handwritten pages. "For Sharon's sake," she began, "I am making one last appeal to you to look at things through Sharon's eyes instead of your own, to consider what Sharon would want instead of what you want." Karen told Don and Della she felt compelled to take "legal action" primarily because they would not "make any attempt at communication," because "you've always been more concerned with your own feelings and emotions," and "Sharon's health and future happiness shouldn't be at the mercy of your whims." Thompson's combination of earnestness and judgment permeated the entire letter. Her legitimate concern about protecting "Sharon's rights" and health was coupled with her frustrations about the current arrangement. "I have been forced to practically sneak in and out of Sharon's room," she wrote, "living in constant fear of an open confrontation, and living in anxiety that you will pack her up and take her away." She detailed her insecurities about their pronouncements that they never wanted to see her again and asked why they planned to take "the person I love most in the world" to "an inferior facility in Hibbing just for the convenience of having her closer to *your* home (not *her* home)." The question of the location of Sharon's "home" would become the central concern of the coming litigation. "It isn't my great desire to bring everything out in the open for all to see," Karen put forth at the end of her exhaustive letter, "but I will do whatever is necessary to protect Sharon's physical as well as psychological well-being." She was still "more than willing to sit down and try to talk through things," even though circumstances had forced her to go to court.[2]

Thompson's tactics again backfired. Upon receipt of this missive and the petition for guardianship, the Kowalskis became more convinced that the person they were dealing with was seriously unbalanced. First she had accused their comatose and uncommunicative daughter of being a lesbian — an accusation they had no basis for considering true from their experience. Now Thompson was claiming that she was the best person to take care of their daughter and accusing them of being selfish, childish, and unpredictable. If anyone was unpredictable, from their perspective, it was this woman who was trying to take their child from them, the woman who was costing them a fortune in legal fees, the woman who was unwilling to help Sharon come home.

In their view, Thompson's "last appeal" merely confirmed the importance of their opposition to her petition.

Karen had also sought other means of resolving their differences besides epistolary appeals. She approached a woman in the hospital named Angie Workman, a mother of another hospitalized, brain-injured woman, whom Karen had seen on a number of occasions talking to Don and Della. Over coffee, Karen detailed the difficulties she was having with the Kowalskis, her desire to take Sharon home to Briggs Lake, and her hope that Angie might "reason" with Don and Della. Workman warned Karen of the tremendous responsibility and work involved in home care for someone as disabled as Sharon, but Karen told her that she wanted to give it a chance. During one of their talks in the hospital lounge, Karen related her fear that if she had to sue for Sharon in court, "someone will try to turn the guardianship case into a gay rights battle" (*Why Can't*, 36). Angie agreed to talk to the Kowalskis.

Workman, according to the Kowalskis' attorney, had another version of this conversation to which she was willing to testify. Kevin Spellacy was prepared to produce "live testimony" from Angie Workman that Karen Thompson had told her as early as February 1984 that if she was not successful with her efforts to obtain custody of Sharon Kowalski, she intended to make a "gay rights" issue out of the matter and "take it nationwide." Spellacy's written declaration under oath — his affidavit — was hearsay (i.e., a statement made by someone other than the testifying witness that is offered to prove the truth of the matter stated), but Workman's version of this conversation had emerged as the first piece of evidence in the effort to portray Karen as a publicity seeker.[3]

The Honorable Bruce R. Douglas — heavyset, florid, white-haired — was the first judge to encounter *In re Guardianship of Sharon Kowalski*. For him, the case was not about sexual orientation when he first got it, though in retrospect he realized that everybody involved was suffering from serious denial, including the petitioner. If the case had come up in the nineties, Douglas speculated in a 1997 interview, or even if the lawyers had presented the case as one of same-sex partnership at the outset, the result might well have been different. Courts generally fail when the cultural compass is unclear, the judge speculated, and in 1984 in Sherburne County, Minnesota, the compass was spinning on issues of the rights of homosexuals. If Thompson's lawyers, Beth Ristvedt and Peter Donohue, had hit the sexual preference issue hard enough, Douglas later suggested, they might have created a de facto spousal presumption in the case; that is, they might have established that Thompson, who was coming on quite strongly anyway, was equivalent to a spouse, and since in most of these cases the spouse is the likely candidate for caregiver, she might have been appointed.

Douglas, though he did not follow the case after it left his jurisdiction in 1987, remembered the tragedy of the injury of a woman as athletic as Kowalski and, almost as troubling, the tragedy of the interested parties' complete failure to cooperate. A "liberal" university professor versus a foreman in a Range iron mine — these parties, the judge recalled, were light-years apart in their cultural perspective. Add to that mix the rather strident personalities of the petitioner and Kowalskis' attorney, Jack Fena, and the result was protracted litigation.

During the first scheduled hearing on March 23, 1984, Douglas brought the attorneys for both sides into his chambers for a private discussion of the case; the clients were left out in the courtroom, waiting for a hearing that never took place. Judge Douglas understood the irrationality that often surrounded domestic relations, and like most judges with dockets filled with dissolutions, child custody disputes, and arguments over property settlements (should the golden retriever be split in half?), he made every effort to settle cases before bringing out the clerk, court reporter, and bailiff to hold a hearing. He made no final ruling that first day, but he heard enough to realize that, unfortunately, some action by the court was going to be necessary. He set up separate but equal visitation times, agreed to order one counseling session between Thompson and the Kowalskis, made Sharon temporarily a ward of the court, reset the hearing on guardianship for April 24, and appointed Tom Hayes as attorney for Sharon.

In 1984, Tom Hayes was a probate public defender for Sherburne and Wright Counties, both in the same judicial district in the St. Cloud area. The pay was niggardly. From the get-go, after being assigned the case by Douglas, reading the pleadings, and familiarizing himself with the file, Hayes realized there were large differences between the parties, and his preliminary assessment was that the fight was over money — the money to be gained from the personal injury lawsuit. In his humorous, colloquial parlance, he characterized the parties as being in a "pissing match." The attorney for the Kowalskis, Kevin Spellacy, was part of one of the biggest plaintiff p.i. (personal injury) firms in the state, and they had a vested interest in keeping Sharon in the family. The parents told Hayes a story of initially being impressed with Karen Thompson's graciousness after the accident (the hospitality at her home, the meals, the attention to Sharon); followed by an experience of a level of intrusiveness that left them no room to breathe; then disbelief and shock in reaction to the unwarranted disclosure of their daughter's supposed sexual orientation, the very daughter who had gone to proms and brought boys home on dates. Finally, the Kowalskis articulated a fear of sexual abuse by Thompson.

Also obvious to Hayes was the radical schism between the parties over Sharon's prognosis. On the one hand, the Kowalskis were old-fashioned Rangers, a breed apart even by Minnesota standards, brought up on a medicine of the 1950s and 1960s that saw brain-stem injuries from a very pessimistic point of view. The Kowalskis grieved the total incapacity of their daughter early on, and though they tried desperately to come to terms with her permanent disability, Hayes recognized that this hardworking family would struggle forever with the incapacity, homosexuality, and long-term rehabilitation needs of their daughter. For them, black was black and white was white. On the other hand, Hayes also had to work with Karen Thompson, who, "God love her," was not about to accept fate; unlike the majority of spouses who when faced with such an injury get "the hell out of Dodge," she was convinced Sharon could get better. When Hayes visited his client at that "sweat-box" nursing home in Sartell outside of St. Cloud in May 1984, Karen was there working with her, getting Sharon to squeeze a ball, to respond to questions, to move her limbs — providing the kind of stimulation all the experts agree nowadays that brain-stem-injured people need. Karen was determined to do more from the outset of the case. Such divergent attitudes between the parties, Hayes quickly assessed, were bound to produce an absence of meaningful communication between the two sides. He was in the middle.

In retrospect, the Judge Hayes of 1997, fourteen years later, readily admitted that homosexual relations were not even recognized by the courts in 1984, but he now believed the judiciary was beginning to accept some same-sex partnerships as plausibly committed and capable of the kind of "long-term investment" that the finder of fact would take into account in determining who was the best person to serve as a guardian. Even assuming a common-law presumption in favor of spouses over the family for guardianship, he questioned whether Sharon and Karen's four-year relationship was sufficiently solid for any court to recognize it as tantamount to a marriage. The rings they exchanged meant nothing really, and the question of their monogamy, he recalled, was itself an unanswered one. Ironically, Judge Hayes believed that if Thompson were a man, she never would have gotten guardianship; the judge would have dismissed their relationship as inconsequential beside the everlasting ties of the family. Think about it, he posited, would you want your mom and dad or somebody you had been living with for four years to take care of you if you were disabled for the rest of your life? Of course, he conjectured, had Karen been a boyfriend, what turned out to be World War III would have probably been reduced to a battle. And of course none of this meant that Thompson was not the person most fit to be guardian — she was incredibly dedicated and persevering.

There was homophobia all over the case, Hayes admitted; everyone harbored it, even himself — it was inescapable. But attorneys and judges could not force people to change their ideas — they must empathize with the heartrending situations they found in court battles, knowing nonetheless that it was impossible from their outside position to stand in Don Kowalski's or Thompson's moccasins. Unfortunately, the adversarial system in domestic relations functioned very poorly because it exacerbated emotions that made rational decision making impossible. Judges just hoped they could act in the best interest of the parties, though what they came up with was often a poor approximation of justice. In this case, Hayes admitted, justice may have been impossible.

When the next hearing took place on April 25, Thompson and the Kowalskis were again relegated to the waiting game, sitting outside the courtroom while the lawyers and judge conferred privately in his chambers. Hayes, Spellacy, Ristvedt (Donohue's associate), and Judge Douglas reached a temporary settlement of the dispute, a compromise by which the parties agreed between themselves about their rights and obligations, thus eliminating the necessity of a formal judicial hearing and resolution of the controversy. Thompson reluctantly accepted the settlement; the Kowalskis, more amenable to accepting their lawyers' advice, agreed willingly. The order appointing general guardian of the person and estate of April 25, reflecting the terms of the agreement, appointed Donald Kowalski "guardian of the person and estate of Sharon Kowalski with all the powers enumerated in M.S. [Minnesota Statutes] 525.56 Subds. (3) and (4)" subject to a set of specific conditions. Sharon Kowalski "was not to be moved from the St. Cloud Hospital" unless the Kowalskis, Thompson, and treating physicians agreed on the proposed relocation. Thompson was also given equal access to visitation, medical records, and consultation with physicians. The court recommended that "both parties continue to work on improving communication." Finally, as part of the findings of fact, the court record acknowledged, "Karen Thompson and Donald and Della each have a significant relation to the Ward," and each was a "suitable and qualified person to discharge the trust [of guardian]." But joint guardianship was infeasible, and Karen Thompson agreed to Donald Kowalski's appointment "in order to avoid a contested hearing."[4]

The imperfections of compromise riddled this document, bringing each of the parties only part of what they wanted. Thompson had petitioned for guardianship and now was reluctantly agreeing to give it up to Donald Kowalski upon the advice of her attorney Beth Ristvedt, who told her that a full hearing could well lead to a more unfavorable result. Jack Fena was able to tell his clients that Donald had been made guardian of the estate and person of his daughter, that they had not only staved off Thompson's attempt to take their daughter away but also achieved the first step toward complete control of their daughter.

But there must have been some misunderstanding about the outcome of the hearing, for the Kowalskis were not completely aware of the restrictions on

Don's powers as guardian. The day after the settlement, Don and Della found Karen in the physical therapy room with their daughter, helping the therapist exercise Sharon (*Why Can't*, 41ff.). Don immediately asked why Thompson was there. "What do you mean?" Karen asked. "This is my visitation time." Don announced that he was guardian now and wanted Thompson to leave. While the parties continued their argument, the therapist interrupted to ask them to please step outside. Reaching the door, Karen told the Kowalskis that her visitation rights had not changed under the agreement. "I think you had better contact your attorney to find out what the facts really are," Karen told them as she walked away.

The Kowalskis later found out from their attorney that they were still faced with some restrictions on their guardianship powers and that Thompson was not out of the picture. They were reaching their wits' end, having to drive two and a half hours from Nashwauk to St. Cloud to attend expensive hearings they could not afford, having to face Thompson when they were trying to spend time with their daughter. Both Don's and Della's nerves were shattered — they did not know how much longer they could sustain this disruption in their lives. Little did they realize that the court troubles had just begun.

In fact, the parties were back in the hallowed halls of justice come June. Sharon's auto insurance, which had been paying for her stay at the hospital's rehabilitation ward, had expired, and she was now receiving financial assistance from the State of Minnesota. According to the state, the patient's progress, which Karen believed was slow but remarkable, was not sufficient to warrant her continued stay in the hospital. Even though she was now sitting up in a wheelchair for three or four hours a day, increasing her periods of alertness, smiling for the first time, identifying flowers and spelling their names on an alphabet board, and occasionally eating Jell-O and soft foods, the doctors, who were often skeptical of Karen's reports of progress, had determined that Sharon would have to be transferred to a nursing home. The Kowalskis wanted her to come home to Leisure Hills in Hibbing; Thompson wanted her to stay in the St. Cloud area at Country Manor Nursing Home in nearby Sartell. A hearing on the matter was set for June 24, and Thompson, in collaboration with her attorney, sought affidavits from the staff at St. Cloud Hospital, sworn statements that would attest to the need for Sharon to have Karen nearby for her rehabilitation.

In this period of adjustment, both the Kowalskis and Thompson were having to come to terms with the discomfort, distaste, and disfavor that our culture harbors toward disability. Sharon's loved ones suddenly had to reconcile themselves to the tasks of changing diapers, wiping drool from her chin, treating bedsores, listening to inarticulate sounds from a woman who was once not only healthy but in fact a noted basketball player, hiker, canoer, and biker.

Counselors would later testify that some of the best of us walk away from facing the dissolution of our fantasies about those we care about; some of the best of us pay inordinate sums to put our elders and disabled kin into facilities that prevent us from having to see them on a daily basis. The incapacity to take care of the disabled was often the handicap of those in good health, and rehabilitation specialists had learned not to blame those who walk away from their loved ones. Don, Della, and Karen were confronting the limits of their own capacities to live with a Sharon who had drastically changed both physically and mentally. They faced the same test of love as partners, parents, and friends of AIDS victims and other disabled peoples all over the world who variously avoided, lived with, institutionalized, cried over, dedicated themselves to, or ran away from the fragility of themselves and their loved ones.

Beth Ristvedt came to the June hearing with some substantial testimonials to the dedication and importance of Karen for Sharon's continued well-being. After the initial interview, Peter Donohue had turned the case over to his associate, who on this occasion was armed with four affidavits from employees at the hospital and the favorable testimony of one of the treating physicians, Keith Larson. Occupational and physical therapists and two nurses testified in writing that they had "observed Karen's positive reinforcement and encouragement of Sharon's efforts during her therapy sessions" and that "it could be very detrimental to Sharon's continued progress to be deprived of Karen's continued involvement."[5]

The hearing on June 26 was again held behind the closed doors of Judge Douglas's chambers while the Kowalskis and Thompson waited impatiently in the halls of the courthouse. During the conference, Tom Hayes asked the court to hear from Dr. Keith Larson, one of the treating physicians in the case, who wanted to testify outside of the presence of the Kowalskis or Thompson. The court agreed to allow Dr. Larson to testify in camera (in chambers) so he could speak freely without concern that his comments might affect his ongoing relationship with the caregivers. Judge Douglas admonished the attorneys for both sides to use discretion in communicating the doctor's testimony to their clients, even though it would later become a matter of public record.

Larson, a medical neurologist who had earned his degree in 1975, began treating Sharon in April, in the absence of Dr. Brix, the neurosurgeon who originally treated the patient in November. In May, when the physicians thought Sharon had "plateaued," a staff meeting was scheduled to discuss her possible transfer to a less full-time rehabilitation facility, and on June 1 a consensus was reached that Sharon should move to a nursing home. Larson told Douglas and the lawyers that he had come as a friend of the court "to deliver an observation that I have agonized over, and thought a great deal about." He understood that the court was being asked "for an intensely Solomonly decision," but he felt compelled, after much soul-searching, to give his opinion "that Sharon's friend, Karen, can get out of Sharon [more] physical actions, attempts at vocalization, and longer periods of alertness and attention than can really any of our professional therapists." Dr. Larson did not want to "speculate upon" the reasons for Karen's effectiveness as "a therapist for this patient," but he did want to give his medical opinion that "contact" between Sharon and Karen should "be enhanced or at least not removed entirely." When Tom Hayes then asked if Larson thought the Kowalskis were not able to work as well with their daughter as Karen Thompson was, the doctor answered that it was "fair to say that the parents have certainly tried to elicit somewhat similar responses from Sharon, especially Sharon's mother," but for whatever reason, whether the Kowalskis' "less total contact," or their "emotional makeup," Sharon's parents had not achieved the success that Thompson had in rehabilitating the patient.[6]

The Kowalskis' attorneys were not prepared with expert opinion to counteract Dr. Larson's testimony about Karen Thompson's therapeutic effect. To promote their proposal that Sharon move to Leisure Hills in Hibbing, they primarily argued that the distance between the Kowalskis and their daughter — a two-hour drive in good weather — created a hardship only remediable by Sharon's transfer to this facility in the Range, twenty minutes from their home. As a result, three days after the hearing, Judge Douglas ordered Sharon to Country Manor Nursing Home in Sartell, outside of St. Cloud. Thompson had won the first skirmish. On July 2, 1984, Sharon was moved over the protests of an angry Don, who refused to sign the discharge from the hospital. Social workers in charge of the move had to wait for a court order before putting Sharon, with Karen holding her hand, on to a special transit service bus to Country Manor, an un-air-conditioned facility with wheelchair-accessible grounds that featured a duck pond outside Sharon's window.

Karen remembered the first few months at Country Manor as a time of major progress in Sharon's recovery. On her first day pass, Sharon went back to the house at Briggs Lake and took a nap beside Karen on the waterbed. Later, on weekend passes, Karen videotaped the progress. Sharon even began to vocalize for the first time, according to Karen, saying "I'm cold" and "turn me," to the astonishment of all the medicos around, who thought the ward would never speak again. She was actually able to accomplish some limited writing with a pencil, as observed by the nurses, and learned to drink some liquids with a straw without aspirating them into her lungs. She even accomplished a standing pivot transfer, that is, she was able to stand on her feet with the help of one person and move from chair to bed.

During this tense period, another troubling incident transpired when the

Kowalskis encountered Thompson and her friends returning Sharon from an outing on the very day they had traveled from Nashwauk to visit their daughter. As Thompson recalled the incident, Don and Della "suddenly rushed" in and demanded that Karen "get out" (*Why Can't*, 52–53). They wanted to know why Karen had taken Sharon out on a pass the very day they drove down to see her. According to Karen, Della then assaulted her, grabbing Karen's arms and shoving her against the wall. Leaving Sharon's room, Karen quickly fled down the hallway with her friends, nervous and upset. Some time later, the Kowalskis emerged from Sharon's room with their attorney, Jack Fena, who apologized for the earlier confrontation. Karen told Fena that she had already contacted her lawyer about it. Upon entering the room, Karen discovered that the ring on Sharon's finger was gone.

On August 16, the Kowalskis sought a new remedy in court, their lawyer filing a motion for an order to move Sharon to the Nat G. Polinsky Memorial Rehabilitation Center at Miller-Dwan Hospital and Medical Center in Duluth for further testing. Jack Fena was now becoming more involved in the guardianship case even though Kevin Spellacy from Minneapolis was still the attorney of record in Sherburne County District Court. Fena's exchange with Thompson probably confirmed his suspicions that she was an opponent who potentially could disrupt his clients' lives and jeopardize the personal injury case. At Fena's recommendation, the Kowalskis also made a motion that Judge Douglas be removed from the case for bias, a type of relief that was very risky to request, since such a motion alerts all judges to the mistrust of the moving party. In response to these motions, Sharon's attorney, Tom Hayes, argued that the motion to remove Judge Douglas was untimely; the Kowalskis should have made that motion when the first hearings were held. He recommended the Sister Kenny Institute, the renowned rehabilitation center in Minneapolis, for Sharon's evaluation, but wanted their representatives to come to Sartell for the testing. Thompson's attorneys filed countermotions: first, to remove Donald Kowalski as guardian for failure to abide by the orders of the court concerning visitation and discharge, and, second, to have Sharon evaluated, if necessary, by Sister Kenny physicians.

Domestic relations cases — legal disputes over marriage, custody, guardianship — differ from criminal and other civil proceedings in many ways. In cases of custody and guardianship, the court maintains jurisdiction or the power to rule in a case even after it has made an order or decision. In other words, rulings by the court are not final because circumstances in family law matters are subject to change: a spouse may no longer need support, a parent may no longer be fit to visit, a ward may become competent. Unlike other lawsuits, where a trial leads to a final decision, irrevocable except by appeal, in domestic cases the

parties can continue to make motions as circumstances change, and each order
is subject to change by the lower court and appeal to a higher court. Domestic
relations hearings are also traditionally more informal, allowing relaxed rules
of evidence, including some hearsay. There is also a strong penchant for judges
to promote settlement through counseling, since family law matters are notorious for bringing out the most volatile side of the litigants. In court, family
values are often marked by vindication, violence, and vituperation.

Those values are not necessarily tempered by the adversarial legal profession. Witness a letter of August 27, a couple of weeks before the hearing on
having Sharon retested, from Jack Fena to Tom Hayes, stating that the former
did not agree with Hayes's recommendation that the testing take place at the Sister Kenny Institute. In that letter, Fena accused Hayes of being "biased towards
Karen Thompson" even though there was "substantial evidence, and I am again
putting you on notice that it exists, that Karen Thompson has been intention-
ally attempting to alienate Sharon Kowalski against her own parents and her
friends." Mr. and Mrs. Kowalski were "both presently under medical care for
extreme emotional distress," he announced to Hayes.

Fena's letter did not stop with the accusation of the possibility of the tort (a
civil wrong that allows the injured party to sue for damages) of intentional
infliction of emotional distress. It detailed the hardship the Kowalskis underwent, driving 171 miles to Sartell to visit their daughter, forcing them — because
of lack of funds — to stay at Don's brother's farm and drive "dirt roads" to get
to the nursing home. It stated that the Kowalskis believed Hayes was "squan-
dering the assets of the guardianship and using them to pay expenses for legal
services," causing Fena to divert all his time to the guardianship matter, "rather
than spending my time working on a dram shop action against the Blue Goose."[7]

Fena's letter to Hayes, the lawyer in the middle, was followed up by a dramatic handwritten missive from Don Kowalski to Sharon's counsel on August
29. Don, who had just come from Jack Fena's office, wanted Mr. Hayes to
"know that my daughter Sharon is in danger of losing her life in that nursing
home." The Kowalskis thought that Sharon was being fed improperly, was not
getting physical therapy, and was "lying in that nursing home with all those old
people in 100 degree temperatures in those diapers sweating and probably
under blankets." To her frustrated father, Sharon was "a frightened little girl"
who was not "making any progress at all" at Country Manor.

Don wanted to know why Hayes was "resisting" Sharon's move to the
Polinsky Center in Duluth. "You are hurting us and you are hurting Sharon,"
he stated, warning the ward's lawyer, "you had better believe we are angry
because you can't see this." He wondered why Hayes could possibly "want to
keep her there" in Sartell. "Is it because you are going to make big attorneys

fees by fighting our requests that she get better help and better medicine? For your information, there isn't that much money. . . . Other people are interested in Sharon because they smell money. We don't. We are interested in her because we love her and she is our daughter. Both my wife and I would be ready to die for our daughter." But they did not have "$100.00 per night to stay in hotels" in Minneapolis near Sister Kenny. "You might as well send her to Chicago," the exasperated Kowalski wrote. Even though Hayes didn't "seem to care" that they would not be able to see their daughter, they were not about to give up. "We feel we are saving Sharon's life. Why don't you call the Polinsky unit to find out what they have."[8]

Donald's letter was not an affidavit, a written statement made under oath before an officer of the court or notary public. Affidavits are often filed in legal cases in lieu of a person's actual appearance in court or as a supplement to that appearance. Their evidentiary value is not as great as that of a cross-examined witness at a trial, but the court often accepts them as sworn statements concerning a contested matter. The Kowalskis did write a joint affidavit on August 10 in anticipation of the motion. Since July 2, 1984, when Sharon was sent to Country Manor, it stated, Don and Della had made five trips to see their daughter and felt "the travel to the nursing home from their home north of Nashwauk is a hardship presently during good weather and will be even more of a hardship during the winter months."[9] In a supplemental affidavit written shortly before the hearing, Della related what happened during a visit on August 30, when they found Sharon sitting up in the wheelchair and after visiting with her for a while "put a piece of white, lined paper in front of her on her tray." Della put a pencil in her daughter's hand: "I then told Sharon to write anything that she wanted to write. Sharon took the pencil and she wrote on the lined paper the word Help, Ma, and under it Help me." Della then detailed how Sharon had wiggled her thumb in assent to the possibility of transferring to the Polinsky Center in Duluth. "As a mother," the affidavit ended, "I know that Sharon loves me and has faith in me and has trust in me."[10]

The affidavits that Karen Thompson's attorney, Beth Ristvedt, filed came not from her client but from third parties, mostly friends of Karen and Sharon. Two of the affiants, one the assistant director of academic studies at Ohio State University, Mansfield, corroborated Karen's account of the assault incident with Della on July 28. The alleged shove by Della Kowalski had taken place directly in front of Sharon, less than two feet away, according to Thompson's witness, and Don watched but did nothing.[11] In another declaration, a teacher at Big Lake High School, where Sharon had worked, stated that when she visited the nursing home, Sharon was able to "shoot balls into" the hands of her visitor's children, turn on the television, and operate the remote. "Affiant has observed a very positive change and improvement in Sharon since visiting her in the St. Cloud hospital," the document concluded.[12] Mary Wild, who described herself as a good friend of the two women, noticed Sharon on August 8 to be very "depressed and withdrawn" shortly after her parents finished a visit. After Karen asked some questions, Wild declared that Sharon disclosed that her parents had frustrated her, that she did not want to see them, and that she wanted Karen to stay with her. Wild testified that Sharon was mad at Karen for leaving her and was afraid Thompson would leave her because of her parents. Wild also swore under oath that Sharon had made "drastic improvement" since leaving the hospital, wanting to play chess and knowing where the pieces went and how they moved, whispering phrases such as "turn me" and "I'm cold" during outings with Karen.[13]

On September 13, 1984, at four in the afternoon, the parties found themselves in Buffalo, Minnesota, in the Wright County Courthouse, ready to hold the first courtroom hearing in the *Kowalski* case. Kevin Spellacy and Jack Fena appeared for petitioners Don and Della Kowalski; Elizabeth Ristvedt and Peter Donohue for respondent Karen Thompson; Thomas Hayes for the ward Sharon Kowalski; and Orrin Rinke for Country Manor Nursing Home. The lawyers and the judge had been discussing the case in chambers since before three that afternoon. Judge Douglas began by denying the motion to remove him as judge, which he called "untimely," assuring the Kowalskis that he had "no bad feelings against the person who filed the affidavit" against him. He then stated that, among all the motions presently filed, he was at this time prepared to hear only the one by the Kowalskis to obtain an order requiring a second medical opinion about Sharon's condition.[14]

Before Kevin Spellacy could proceed with calling witnesses concerning this motion, his cocounsel Jack Fena rose to read a stipulation or agreement that he had reached with Tom Hayes about the motion. It stated that even though Hayes continued to favor the Sister Kenny Institute in Minneapolis for his client's relocation, he "had studied the brochures of the Nat G. Polinsky Memorial Rehabilitation Center and has no reason to believe that said Nat G. Polinsky Center is inadequate for the purpose of Sharon Kowalski's evaluation." Ristvedt had no awareness of the stipulation, nor did her client, who after this hearing characterized Hayes's actions as a wavering about-face motivated by Fena's agreement to relinquish his opposition to the payment of fees to Hayes (*Why Can't*, 62–63). Later, in an interview, Hayes would call Thompson's assessment "a crock."

Spellacy's direct examination began by calling to the stand Donald Kowalski, who testified that he had spent $21,000 of his own money since the accident on hotel rooms, travel, and other expenses. About his daughter's

condition, Don testified that Sharon could answer their questions with an
alphabet board, knew the date of her birthday and the ages of her parents,
knew about the Polinsky Center, and had nodded "yes" when asked by Don if
she wanted to go there. On cross-examination by Ristvedt, Mr. Kowalski
admitted that Sharon had made "some" progress at the nursing home, but he
was adamantly opposed to day passes for Sharon. We "didn't feel that we
wanted to put Sharon on display in a shopping center in her condition" or anywhere "in public," he testified. Ristvedt continued with her cross-examination,
a mode of inquiry that, unlike direct examination, allows counsel to ask leading
questions, ones requiring only a yes or no answer:

> Ms. RISTVEDT: If we were to assume that Sharon is transferred to Duluth and
> she does not make progress there or respond to treatment there, would you
> believe that Sharon might not be making progress because of no longer hav-
> ing the contact with Karen Thompson?
> DONALD KOWALSKI: No.
> Q: Do you believe that Karen Thompson loves Sharon?
> MR. SPELLACY: I object to the relevancy of it, Your Honor.
> MR. FENA: What he believes—
> THE COURT: We are talking about evaluation and it is pretty hard for Mr.
> Kowalski to know that. I will sustain the objection. I assume, as I have from
> the first day we met, that all of these people have great concern for Sharon
> or they wouldn't be going to these great lengths.
> Ms. RISTVEDT: Your Honor, my reason for asking that is to get at the witness's
> opinion, and that opinion reflects on his whole attitude toward the situation.
> THE COURT: It is hard for him to know. I will sustain the objection.
> BY Ms. RISTVEDT: Are you aware, Mr. Kowalski, that the doctors and other
> medical personnel had indicated that Sharon gave more consistent responses
> and a greater degree of responses to Karen than to other persons?

Spellacy objected again. He thought the question lacked a foundation and was
vague. Which doctors was counsel referring to, and how could Mr. Kowalski
be qualified to know the value of their opinions? Eventually the court overruled him, on condition that the question ask about awareness only. Don finally
answered "yes"; he was aware of the medical opinion that Sharon was more
responsive in Thompson's presence.

On direct examination, the next witness, Della Kowalski, her voice cracking as she told the story, recounted the visit when her daughter wrote "Help,
Ma! Help me!" on a piece of a paper, which counsel submitted in evidence.
When Mr. Spellacy asked Della if she wanted to continue or take a break, she
stated that she wished to proceed, admitting that she was presently receiving
treatment from a doctor for stress and agreeing that the move to Duluth would

be easier for her. Over an overruled objection as to relevancy, Spellacy offered into evidence a letter from the Kowalskis' family physician, William Wilson, to support their contention that both Della and Don were being treated for stress and that the move to Duluth could provide relief to his patients.

Ristvedt's witnesses testified that Karen Thompson's geographic proximity was essential for Sharon's recovery. Kathi Sims, the social worker at Country Manor, told the court that Karen could always elicit a response from Sharon, while all others, including parents and medical attendants, had only sporadic success in doing so. When Ristvedt asked her witness if she thought it was unusual for Sharon to be unresponsive after a visit by her parents, Spellacy objected to the question as lacking a foundation. Examining counsel, he claimed, had not established his witness's credentials and ability to answer a question. Judge Douglas sustained the objection; it called for a medical opinion, he agreed. Sims was able, however, to testify that she had "discussed" the potential move from Sartell to another facility with the patient. "Sharon responded most consistently to me by either putting out her pointed finger, which is the index finger or her little finger. . . . I would say that she has consistently responded to wanting to remain in the St. Cloud area." Stephen McCaffrey, registered physical therapist at Country Manor, testified that Sharon responded more consistently during physical therapy sessions when Karen Thompson was present. "She does consistently better. She responds quicker. She responds to what she is asked to do. There are times when I've worked with her when she has not responded at all and she consistently responded when Karen is there." McCaffrey also testified that he believed Sharon could communicate reliably and had often communicated her desire to stay in the St. Cloud area, though the question, when he was present, was always posited by Karen Thompson.

Judge Douglas then called for brief closing arguments by the three attorneys, so they could preserve the record if an appeal was necessary. Spellacy emphasized the readiness of the Duluth facility: "As to the reports of the doctors that we have submitted, including Cowan, Pollard, Eckman, and Goff," he argued, they insist that "time is of the essence now, and that it is essential that Sharon be evaluated just as soon as possible, and in that regard, the Polinsky Center has a compelling advantage over Sister Kenny because they are in a position to take Sharon tomorrow afternoon and financial arrangements have been made." The other point he wanted to make was that Polinsky was "separate and apart from the influence of Dr. Larson, and particularly this theory of Dr. Larson's that Karen Thompson has had influence over and a magical connection with Sharon that her parents don't have." He contended that his physicians were better qualified in rehabilitation medicine than Dr. Larson. Finally, he spoke on behalf of his clients, who "have been just put through the worst possible turmoil the last eight months and their resources are drained and they are to the point where they have to receive medical help because of their condition, and I think it is about time that we show some deference."

Ristvedt made her closing argument quickly after Spellacy sat down, almost in rebuttal: "Your Honor," she began, "Mr. Spellacy is basing his argument on reports of doctors who have not seen Sharon, that have merely reviewed the record." She pointed out that Dr. Larson's opinion about a "special relationship" between Karen and Sharon was no unproved "theory" but an empirical observation corroborated by "personnel from the Country Manor Nursing Home" who "indicate to us that they see greater consistency of response and a greater level of response." After methodically summarizing the testimony, Ristvedt concluded that Sharon needed to be somewhere near Karen and that Sister Kenny was the best facility in Minnesota.

In his closing, Tom Hayes stated: "I recommended, Your Honor, Sister Kenny Institute, but I think there are some factors that the Court has to keep in mind beyond the mere recommendation of counsel here today." He pointed out, first, that there was "a bed available tomorrow" at Polinsky and not at Sister Kenny, which was "something that the Court has to take into consideration." Speed was important, Hayes admitted, given his client's need for rehabilitation. "I wish I could waive [*sic*] the magic wand and my client could just walk out and not worry about it," he commented finally. "I wish I could waive the magic wand and have the three parties, those who obviously care very dearly for my client, to be able to sit down and join forces and work together. I'm not going to assign any blame for failure to do that, but I just wish it could happen."

A trial court judge is not required by law to write an opinion that explains the legal reasoning for a decision. Some judges do; some do not. In 1997, when asked about his decision in 1984, Judge Douglas stated that he could not talk about the case because it was ongoing — the guardianship of Sharon Kowalski would be an open case for as long as Sharon was legally incompetent. Even though the hearing had lasted until 6:55 P.M. on the evening of September 13, the court order was issued the very next morning, as if in answer to the urgency pleaded by the moving party, the urgency that seemed to have swayed Tom Hayes. The order stated: "Sharon Kowalski shall be immediately transferred to the Nat G. Polinsky Memorial Rehabilitation Center, Duluth, Minnesota, for evaluation to see whether it is appropriate that she enter a course of inpatient rehabilitation, and if so, to evaluate where said rehabilitation should occur."

The Kowalskis had prevailed in the second round. Karen Thompson was devastated. On Friday morning, she heard from the director of the nursing home that the Kowalskis would be taking their daughter to Duluth within the hour. The Kowalskis came into the room and started packing while Karen was sitting at Sharon's bedside, trying to explain to her that they would not be separated, that the move to Duluth would be temporary. When Karen left, Jack Fena followed her into the hallway and recommended that she stay away from Duluth altogether (*Why Can't*, 65–66). "I don't want to talk to you. Leave me alone," the distraught Thompson told him. "I'll do everything I can to get you off this case. I don't think you're the type of person Sharon would want representing her. By fighting dirty you might wind up hurting Sharon's case." Fena retorted that Karen was the one who was hurting Sharon's case by insisting on their partnership and thereby jeopardizing her chances of a substantial reward from a jury. "You don't really care about Sharon," an angered Karen replied. "All you care about is your $200,000 out of the injury suit. You don't deserve a cent. . . . By the time your share and all the expenses are taken out, there won't be any money for Sharon anyway" (*Why Can't*, 66).

Karen turned and raced out of the nursing home, no longer able to hold back her tears. After class, she threw a few things into a suitcase and got on the highway northeast to Duluth, a two- to three-hour drive she would soon memorize. Upon arrival, she was pleased to discover the Kowalskis were not with Sharon but upset to notice that many items from Sartell were missing from the room at Miller-Dwan Hospital, a pale yellow building on a hill overlooking Lake Superior. The Bible that she had given Sharon was gone, along with pictures of the Briggs Lake house. Sharon's eggshell mattress and a lapboard for resting her arms in the wheelchair were also missing. For the next weeks, Thompson drove to Duluth every day after school, arriving at five-thirty and turning back to go home at ten-thirty. For the coming months, she would find herself walking the streets of this cool, windy city, watching the traffic lights swinging wildly from wires at intersections: red, yellow, green.

On October 9, 1984, Dr. S. K. Goff from the Miller-Dwan Hospital and the Polinsky Center wrote an evaluation of Sharon Kowalski, a month after her arrival in Duluth.[15] He described the patient during the examination as having her head lowered and to the right, both arms in "flexion posturing," making "spontaneous movements of the right" with marked "spasticity." Besides her "hyperreflexive" joints (i.e., her extended muscles), Dr. Goff found Sharon's progress during her stay at Miller-Dwan "unremarkable." Her "yes/no responses," he stated, "seemed unreliable." Her "auditory comprehension" was felt to be "severely impaired, meaning that her responses were inconsistent and spotty. She had limited expressive abilities which also limited evaluation of auditory comprehension."

Speech therapists and psychologists reported that they had tested Sharon by asking her for yes or no responses by head nods, finger pointing, and scanning, a method by which the examiner presents a series of response choices, pointing to each item in hopes of eliciting a response from the patient. The examiners felt that "responses to all modes of communication were inconsistent. The results tended to be different with the same question getting different responses." When they tested Sharon's ability to understand words, sentences, and paragraphs, they found "comprehension of common words using the scanning response system was 100% accurate," which "was the only consistent performance noted by the therapist during the entire examination."

In summary, the examiner "felt that the patient was able to inconsistently read and comprehend at the single word level" but that Sharon's "expressive communication" was "severely to profoundly impaired." Based on the color preference part of the Stanford-Binet intelligence scale, her cognitive functioning ability "would be below a 6 or 7 year age level," and "at a functional level, she was at a severe range of impairment." He felt, however, that "her actual cognitive function at times may be higher, which would be consistent to a head injury, when at times islands of increased function appear. It is likely that her judgment or ability to make decisions for herself would be severely impaired, significantly due to her difficulty establishing a reliable means of communication." The examiner also noted, "It is very easy to lead her responses, misinterpretate [*sic*] her gestures. This supports the opinion of the psychologist that she is not able to make judgments and decisions on her own."

Incorporating the findings of these others, Dr. Goff wrote a report that came to some serious conclusions about Sharon's behavior and adjustment. Although the ward seemed at times to be alert and at other times lethargic, he wrote, "there does not seem to be any pattern with this level of responsiveness." Overall, Goff agreed that there was a "severe level of impairment" that would most likely improve only a very little, since most cognitive improvement occurs within the first year after a brain injury. "The patient is incompetent to make decisions regarding her own welfare, and she is not able to make judgments or decisions on her own," Goff stated, though he did mention that "it was felt important by the therapists that a close follow-up be indicated, because of the difficulty of assessing the accuracy of this patient's responses." The Duluth doctor recommended that Sharon be placed in an ongoing rehabilitation program with daily physical, occupational, and speech therapy — Park Point Manor Nursing Home in Duluth was, in his estimation, the best facility.

Goff's report would become influential in the course of the ensuing litigation. The symptoms of Sharon's brain damage were physical: the loss of her ability to use her muscles to raise her feet and arms (the bilateral Babinski signs), her spasticity or stiffened muscles, causing awkward movements, the involuntary up-and-down movement of her eyeballs (vertical nystagmus), and the inequality of the diameter of her pupils (anisocoria) were physical signs that pointed to severe, widely distributed (diffuse) damage to the cortex, the thin layer or mantle of gray substance that covers the surface of the cerebral hemisphere. This outer layer, highly developed in humans, is responsible for the higher mental functions, as well as visceral functions (Sharon could not swallow and was fed by a tube into the stomach).

These tests showed that in the fall of 1984, at least, Sharon's ability to formulate competent decisions and communicate them was profoundly impaired. The intelligence sections, however, were hampered in their administration by Sharon's lack of attention and lack of ability or willingness to process information. She might have been able to hear the instructions, even understand them, but she was unable to form a cogent response at the time of the testing. On the other hand, this disconnection between comprehension of outside information and ability to express one's response was also typical of diffuse cortical loss.

In addition to taking advantage of Goff's findings, Jack Fena also hired his medical expert in his personal injury case to visit and evaluate the plaintiff. The elderly George Cowan, a veteran of courtroom expert testimony, interviewed Sharon Kowalski on October 4, after reviewing her chart. "Sharon was lying quietly in bed, appearing to be completely helpless," Cowan wrote to the plaintiff's attorney. "I attempted to interview Sharon but she was unable to speak." He concluded "at this point and in the immediate future she will require a great deal of tender loving care and parental love which is unconditional." Cowan's letter would also become part of the record for the next hearing.[16]

Karen herself admitted that Sharon's functioning had undergone a dramatic decline with her move to Duluth. Karen's sister Linda, in an affidavit attached to the October 18 motion to move Sharon back to St. Cloud, stated that she was "shocked at her appearance. Her whole attitude and demeanor were totally different than at Country Manor and at my home. She never moved her head, her eyes did not seem to focus, she had no facial expressions, and made either no response or inconsistent responses to questions."[17] Theophanis Hortis, a former professor and friend of Sharon Kowalski, reported that the first time he saw Sharon after the accident in St. Cloud she was "much more alert, was much more consistent in her responses, and aware of what was going on around her. She could do more things such as writing, brushing her teeth, playing checkers. She had facial expressions, she would laugh, would remain alert and concentrate for longer periods of time." In Duluth, he was "dismayed by her appearance"; she "never moved her head, her eyes did not seem to focus, she had no facial expressions and would not smile."[18]

Beth Ristvedt amassed other affidavits in her attempt to demonstrate that Dr. Goff's report in part reflected Sharon's regression after a disruptive move.

Nurses from Miller-Dwan in Duluth testified to Sharon's responsiveness to Karen, to the "special relationship and rapport" between the two women; one went so far as to state that Sharon was depressed about being in Duluth and was afraid Karen might not come back.[19] In contrast to the Polinsky report's finding that Sharon's reading ability "indicated a severe impairment," Joan Thralow, occupational therapist, declared, "Sharon was reading [at Country Manor] a paragraph consisting of five sentences and 42 words and taking a comprehension test consisting of five multiple choice questions the last time she was tested and had 100% accuracy. She was able to add and subtract one digit numbers."[20] A social worker, Kathi Sims, observed that "by the time Sharon left Country Manor, she was writing one to three word clusters, would say 'hi,' play checkers, could respond consistently when she wanted, and could move her right hand. For example, an okay sign, the 'I love you' sign, the 'thumbs up' sign. Sharon could voluntarily wave goodbye, wipe her mouth, smile and interact with people."[21] By marked contrast, the Polinsky report found Sharon's expressive communication skills "severely to profoundly impaired."

These dozen affidavits, Dr. Cowan's letter, and Goff's report were the main documents filed with the court in anticipation of the upcoming hearing in Buffalo, but the Kowalskis' attorneys had also procured some affidavits in an attempt to impugn Karen Thompson's character. Testimony in those sworn statements by Sharon's family and her friends on the Range portrayed Karen as controlling, moneygrubbing, and condescending. Sharon's sister testified that at the time of the accident, Sharon was thinking of leaving Karen and moving to Colorado, and Karen Tomberlin, Sharon's former coach, gave a particularly damaging description of Thompson's behavior at Sartell:

> She had Sharon opening her fingers, wiggling her fingers and things like that. She had Sharon moving some balls toward her chin and moving a ping-pong ball to a different colored ball and things of that sort. Karen Thompson then said to me now I would see the best thing that Sharon had learned to do. Karen Thompson turned to Sharon and said write the word "Karen". . . . She then put a marking pen in Sharon's hand and Sharon started to write. She wrote the word "help." Karen Thompson became very agitated and upset over this. She took the notebook paper and looked at it and said, "Sharon! You're writing the word 'help'! I am very upset about this!" . . . I felt that Karen Thompson was trying to cover something up. I was very uneasy and upset about this. . . . As a friend of Sharon's, I myself am very concerned. I fear for her safety and her well-being.

Tomberlin's affidavit gave another version of the "special rapport" that professional caregivers had described in their testimony.[22]

When Judge Douglas met with the parties on October 18, his first order of business was to sort out the pending motions and rule which one he would consider first. Originally, Karen's attorney had moved the court to return Sharon to Country Manor, where her progress was remarkable, but the attorneys for Country Manor were now refusing to accept Sharon as long as there was not one unlimited guardian; they were unwilling to put up with the acrimony of the shared rights under the present order. Ristvedt quickly revised her motion in favor of another nursing home in St. Cloud. The Kowalskis' attorneys were prepared with motions to amend visitation rights, establish Donald Kowalski as unconditional guardian, change venue in the case to Itasca County in Grand Rapids, transfer Sharon Kowalski to Park Point Manor, and have Sharon's property returned from her "landlady" Karen Thompson to the guardian. The judge ruled promptly that he was only going to rule on the proper location for Sharon's residence, a matter of pressing importance. The parties agreed to submit the motion based on affidavits, to forgo a hearing. and allow the court to make its decision based on the documents filed by both sides. The judge did, however, allow oral argument by the attorneys.

Ristvedt began. She reminded the court that in June the judge had ordered Sharon from St. Cloud Hospital to Country Manor over the objections of Sharon's parents. Within two weeks of the "transfer," the parents and their attorneys were seeking means to circumvent the court's decision. Numerous affidavits from health care workers at both facilities, she argued, demonstrated that "Karen Thompson is able to motivate Sharon into greater achievement than the various professionals in their fields. Removing Sharon from the extensive contact with Karen Thompson, available in the St. Cloud area, has caused regression in Sharon's condition. The only factor that has changed is Sharon's location. This distance can no longer be tolerated if the Court looks to the best interest of the ward, Sharon Kowalski, and provides her with her right to recovery."[23]

Kevin Spellacy rose from his desk with the specific intention of discounting Ristvedt's argument about the indispensable nature of Karen Thompson. He was backed by the weight of the Polinsky report, specifically its findings that any communication by the ward was unreliable, including any stated preferences she may have articulated prior to her arrival in Duluth. The report undercut "all of this lay evidence" about Karen's rapport with the ward, as well as Larson's opinion about "some magical connection." Sharon, Spellacy told the court, "now has the cognitive functioning ability which would be below a six or seven year old, so we are dealing with two different people, Your Honor, the person that Sharon may have been or was before the accident, and now we are dealing with a child. Therefore, all of this discussion about some relationship that may have existed, some friendship that may have existed between Sharon Kowalski and Karen Thompson, which somehow gives Karen Thompson the ability to evoke physical responses — hogwash! — because we have a five year old at this point." A five-year-old was incapable of maintaining a lesbian relationship.

Tom Hayes had read the Polinsky report carefully; he had come to some conclusions about the severity of his client's condition, and he made his argument accordingly. "There are some serious questions regarding my client's ability to express any kind of preference as to where she ought to go. That leaves us, by statute, with having to determine from outside forces, what is in her best interest. I don't think it is going to make a significant amount of difference whether my client is in Duluth, whether she is in St. Cloud, or whether she is in some place halfway between the parties involved in this case," he opined. He then spoke of how important Sharon's connection to her parents was "simply because they have the kind of love that can only be provided by a parent and I don't think there is any kind of love that is similar. Being a parent myself, and having experienced the love of being a parent; it is just unique." As he later recalled, he never wanted Thompson out of the picture, but he felt that when the chips were down, blood was thicker than romance.

The judge ended the hearing, informing the parties that he would have a prompt decision for them. The following morning, the court ordered Sharon Kowalski moved to Park Point Manor in Duluth. The judge based his decisions on certain findings of fact, which included the conclusions of Dr. S. K. Goff "that the ward's communication responses are inconsistent and variable, . . . that the ward's cognitive capabilities are quite limited and that she is presently functioning below a six or seven year age level."[31] Sharon would remain in Duluth for the foreseeable future.

When, in 1993, I came to the English department at the University of Montana, I decided to offer a course in law, literature, and politics again, but this time to a combination of graduate students in literature and law students. The former ended up on one side of the room — cynical, uninterested in reading cases, disdainful of false notions of justice; the law students on the other side were elated to read fiction, more exacting and literal in their applications of legal issues, and less trained in the slippage of signification. Before presenting the *Kowalski* case this time, I had found more references in law reviews, some published cases, a few newspaper articles. By this time *Baehr v Lewin* had ruled that the Hawaiian statute restricting marital relations to couples of the opposite sex was potentially unconstitutional sex discrimination. (The populace of that state had yet to pass a constitutional amendment requiring that marriage take place between man and woman.) Montana, however, was one of a group of remaining states with a "sodomy," or in this case a "sexual deviancy," statute on the books, a law making it a felony for members of the same sex to touch one another with sexual intentions. A case pending before the Montana Supreme Court had yet to overturn the statute on the grounds of a violation of the right to privacy, so homosexual sex was still a crime in Missoula. Students also became familiar with the anti–gay rights initiatives of the Oregon Citizens Alliance, which proposed eliminating homosexuality and discussions of it from schools.

Within this political and legal context, the *Kowalski* case study gave students the opportunity to investigate the ideologies — the dominant viewpoints — that prevailed in a contemporary narrative of same-sex love. The literature students were outraged at the "patriarchal" bias of a judiciary that had no sympathy for the cultural and social positions of the lesbian litigants in the case. For them law was politics wrapped in terms of art. The law students, on the other hand, understood the *Kowalski* case as one that was trying to set a new precedent, one that was working against presumptions that had developed historically and were subject to change only through political and legal action. Inside the law, the *Kowalski* case seemed plausible, productive, indicative of the kind of inertia that some lawyers spent their lives resisting, pushing courts and juries to a recognition of social reality; outside the law, the case seemed an instance of institutional prejudice against lesbians, against women, against the disabled, against equality. Between these positions lay the conflicting narrative versions of the history of the case, the particulars that the literature students wanted to ignore, but the law students saw as potential fodder for argument. By the time the course was completed, I realized that there were stories to be told about this case: stories that would convince and confuse; stories that would unfold biases against lesbians, the working class, the disabled, lawyers, and doctors; stories that would disturb those prejudices by weaving a web of particulars over the categorical imperatives that gained their certainty from the exclusion of particularities. I wanted to tell those stories.

My own story gave me the impetus: I was the son of a Polish-Irish father; I had struggled with coming out in my twenties; I was a lawyer turned literature teacher; I had tested positive for HIV in 1991 while finishing my dissertation; I was a gay man in a state that criminalized my lovemaking. I could find myself in this story, even if a woman's experience was alien to me, even if I was not a lesbian. I could still explore the importance of this case for queer rights. Had not feminists taught us that gender was as much a culturally constructed category as some essential subjectivity? Didn't the limitation of my identification in fact aid in telling the whole story?

FOUR

Injunction

> Society's discomfort with public acknowledgements of gay sexual
> orientation also is demonstrated by its treatment of gay relationships.
> Relationships are inherently public in nature. A couple in love wants to
> spend time together, to socialize together, to live together. Even if they don't
> discuss their feelings for each other in public, the constant proximity of a
> same-sex couple sends messages to the outside world. Discrimination against
> gay relationships often results from this public quality. It also can take the
> form of refusal to allow legal, and therefore public, recognition of the
> relationship.
>
> Marc Fajer, *Can Two Real Men Eat Quiche Together?*

By the middle of October 1984, Karen Thompson was physically exhausted.
The combination of a six-hour round-trip drive to Duluth, university teaching responsibility, and stress from dealing with an increasingly less responsive
Sharon was leading her to a point of serious questioning — not about her commitment to Sharon but about how she was going to manage her responsibility.
She spoke with her friend and colleague Julie Andrzejewski, who advised talking to the press about Sharon's case as a way of garnering the support of disability rights and civil rights organizations (*Why Can't*, 79ff). Karen took her
advice, believing that sooner or later the media would find out about the story
anyway. After she called the *St. Cloud Times* and spoke to its reporter, an article appeared in that newspaper on the very morning of the hearing that led to
Judge Douglas's decision to place Sharon in Park Point.

"Gay Issue Clouds Fight for Custody" read the front-page headline in the
St. Cloud Times (on October 18, 1984). Tony Kennedy told of the "ugly court
battle" between the "quadriplegic's" parents and Karen Thompson, "who
claims to have carried on a secret lesbian relationship with Kowalski for the past
four years." Thompson believed she would set a national precedent for homosexuals if she were designated Kowalski's guardian, the *Times* article noted.
"In our minds, we're married and are devoted to each other for a lifetime,"
Karen told the reporter. Kowalski's parents told Kennedy that no one could
love their daughter as much as they did. In a telephone interview, Don said

"there is 'no way' his daughter and Thompson have had a lesbian relationship." Thompson was "about as sick as they come," Don stated, claiming he and his wife were "worried that Thompson will sexually abuse their daughter if Thompson is allowed to continue visiting her."

In the article, Karen recounted how she was told what "trash I had written" and "how sick I was." The Kowalskis told her that she just wanted to see Sharon naked, and in one communication asked her, "Have you sexually abused our daughter today?" Karen told Kennedy she had avoided the press up to this point because she was afraid of losing her job by revealing her homosexuality, but now she had no choice. "The whole issue is us being gay," Thompson asserted.

After reading the article, Karen was extremely upset with the media's assessment of her situation, believing that the press was "as homophobic as the medical and legal institutions." The *St. Cloud Times* article was followed by pieces in the *Minneapolis Star Tribune* (October 26, 1984) and the *Duluth News-Tribune* (October 30, 1984), which relied on an Associated Press release that featured Jack Fena's opinion: "The Kowalskis claim Thompson's efforts are motivated by a desire to control large damage awards Kowalski may receive from a drunken driver who ran into her car last November. . . . We want her (Thompson) off the family's back and we want her off Sharon's back." Fena posed the question: "Where do you send a helpless child? Certainly not to her landlady" ("Disabled Woman's Parents, Professed Lover Battling in Court over Rights to Her Custody," *Duluth News-Tribune* October 30, 1984, sec. A, p. 2). A follow-up article in the *St. Cloud Times* on October 24 quoted Karen as stating that she was going public to gain the support of civil rights, gay rights, and disabled persons organizations. Judge Douglas, however, maintained that he had heard "no testimony or evidence related to gay rights" during the October 18 hearing. "My decision is not based and will not be based on those kinds of questions," the newspaper quoted Douglas as saying. *Those kinds of questions*, however, were the unstated subject of the dozen affidavits Ristvedt filed on behalf of Thompson.

When Karen Thompson talked to Ellen Rogers, a reporter for WDIO-TV in Duluth, the station at first expressed interest but then suddenly stopped calling. Thompson soon discovered that Jack Fena had written a letter to the station managers on November 1, thanking them for their "forbearance" in pursuing the Sharon Kowalski story, reiterating his belief that the use of the tape that Karen had delivered to Ellen Rogers represented "an invasion of Sharon Kowalski's privacy" and claiming "the whole entire story involving Sharon Kowalski to be libelous, slanderous and defamatory." In spite of the pressure the station was receiving from Thompson, Fena stated that his clients refused to go on camera. "Your television transmitter on the Range is 10 miles from my clients' house in Nashwauk and as I stated to you, all of these news releases and news stories disseminated by Karen Thompson had a terrible effect upon and have caused great mental anguish to my clients, Don and Della Kowalski."[1]

Fena's characteristic redundancies were designed to scare the television station into dropping the story for fear of legal action, an action that at best would be difficult to prove. He claimed that the potential story would be tantamount to libel, a civil wrong (tort) that involved a false or malicious publication printed for the purpose of defaming or injuring the good name of another. Defamation is a general name for either speech or writing that is potentially actionable if the statements made are false and cause damage. The publication must tend to expose a person to public scorn, hatred, contempt, or ridicule — homosexuality being the kind of attribution that is actionable because in the eyes of the so-called reasonable community, and therefore the eyes of the law, such a characterization exposes a person to hatred and scorn. Hence, the reference in the St. Cloud paper to Thompson's "claim" of a "secret lesbian relationship" was carefully reported as an unproved allegation. Truth, however, is always a defense to defamation, and if he were to go to court, Fena would have to prove by a preponderance of the evidence that Sharon was not a lesbian. The invasion of privacy that Fena added to his demand letter was an analogous tort that had grown out of defamation law but was broader in scope. Courts had ruled that persons have a right to be free, in some instances, from unwarranted publicity, regardless of the truth of the statements made.

Another legal action was afoot by the Kowalskis' attorneys as a direct result of the newspaper coverage of the case. Kevin Spellacy and Fena filed a motion for a temporary restraining order (TRO) to prevent Karen Thompson from visiting Sharon because of Thompson's disruptive conduct and use of the media. A TRO is a form of preliminary injunction that asks a court to order a party to refrain from doing a particular act or activity until the question of a more permanent form of relief can be adjudicated by the court. The moving party must prove that the status quo is in jeopardy of changing before the court will have an opportunity to hear and decide a pending motion.

In an affidavit attached to the motion, Spellacy stated that on October 25 he was informed by Donald Kowalski that Karen Thompson was involved in a "lengthy confrontation" with Park Point Manor Nursing Home over a request by Thompson to take Sharon to a volleyball game. Joann Susens, a nurse at Park Point, refused to issue the day pass without the guardian's approval; Dr. Goff, the treating physician, had given orders to that effect. According to Spellacy's declaration, Ms. Susens was also "upset about an article about this case

. . . in the *Duluth News-Tribune*" and "did not want the media on the premises, as the same could impair the privacy of Sharon Kowalski." Spellacy argued that publicity was jeopardizing Park Point's ability to give Sharon optimal care.[2]

Karen told a different story about her interaction with Park Point Manor. Her first visits led to discoveries that Sharon's feeding tube was detached from her stomach, that there was no wheelchair available for her, and that she was not being bathed except by sponge in bed. When the St. Cloud State volleyball team came to Duluth, Karen wanted to take Sharon to the game. While Thompson was calling her attorney from the nursing home, she noticed a memo on the wall entitled "Guidelines for Handling Karen Thompson," ordering that she was not to have access to medical records. Dr. Goff, she learned, had ordered that all visitation and outings were subject to Sharon's father's discretion. Thompson was outraged at the violation of the court order, but on inquiry the judge refused to override Goff's orders. Sharon never attended the volleyball game (*Why Can't*, 86–87).

On November 2, a joint affidavit was filed by Spellacy and Fena in support of both Don Kowalski's motion to become general guardian with unlimited powers and his request for injunctive relief. Fena claimed that "despite the Court's best efforts to protect the good name and reputation of Sharon Kowalski . . . Karen Thompson knowingly and deliberately took this matter to the press on the eve of the Court's last hearing" — a "cynical attempt" to "influence the Court's ruling." Fena quoted from a note written by Karen to the Kowalskis that in his eyes unequivocally demonstrated "Thompson's vindictive personality." The note from Karen read as follows:

> I would like you to return *my* white sweater (Sharon wore a lot of my clothes since she didn't have a very complete teaching wardrobe) and maroon sweater (they are Lady Garlands I believe) which you removed from our house. I would also like a complete accounting as to how any of Sharon's money has been spent and a copy of the present inventory on file.
>
> By the way, I hope you don't think everything is settled or over because I have in no way given up on my fight for Sharon's right to recover and live as high a quality of life as possible. Hope you're having no problems sleeping at night and living with your selves for the pain you are causing Sharon and the setback in progress caused by this move. Have a good week! Be seeing you.

Fena's affidavit continued with an anonymous letter he received from someone in St. Cloud, which he claimed "suggests that a serious backlash against Karen Thompson's 'gay rights' is developing." Exhibit 4 was dated October 24, typed in capital letters, and unsigned. "I was in a cardiac care unit when she [Sharon] was in the same," the writer stated, "and my wife met this so called Thompson, and the most vivid thing she remembers about her is that she seemed to be so overly concerned, that she left the impression on my wife that she was ad-libbing or just over dramatizing to a point where she was just sickening." Enclosing newspaper clippings, the anonymous letter writer speculated, "She could loose alot [*sic*] but, then why go public . . . unless one knew of the end result of getting more money than one would get from college teaching, like insurance or say a few million to live on easy street, for the rest of one's life. I suppose one might admit they were queer if it paid off hansomely [*sic*]." The former patient did not want to get involved in the case but volunteered that he had children attending St. Cloud State and had heard that some students were dropping out of Thompson's classes, intimating that she would soon need to "get her hands on some money." He and his wife found the Kowalskis to "be real nice people," and he was happy Sharon was in Duluth. "Find a way to keep Thompson away," the anonymous missive closed. Fena's affidavit continued by noting that Thompson was receiving a "considerable course of psychological therapy," that her conduct was "becoming more irrational," that her "bullying and intimidating conduct" was interfering with the efforts of the nursing home to carry out the mandate it received from the court.[3]

Karen Thompson answered these accusations with her own sworn statement that "none of the contacts which I have had with the press have hampered the efforts of Park Point Nursing Home to render proper treatment for Sharon. And I have never done anything to jeopardize Sharon's care and treatment." But Judge Kim Johnson, a member of the same district court as Judge Douglas, granted the Kowalskis' request for injunctive relief on November 7, issuing a modified restraining order that disallowed either of the parties to disseminate medical records to third parties, including the media; prohibited either party from bringing any visitors with them without the approval of the nursing home; eliminated all outings for Sharon Kowalski except those sponsored by the home; and enjoined all parties from "engaging in any disruptive conduct, confrontation or arguments with the personnel of the Park Point Manor or anyone else on its premises."[4] The order restricted Sharon's access to the outside world and prevented the public from gaining information about her condition.

Many motions were still pending for the court. The Kowalskis wanted to change venue in the case from its present location in Sherburne County near St. Cloud to Itasca County, where Nashwauk was located; they also wanted Donald given the full powers of guardianship, including the power to decide where his daughter should live and who should be able to visit her. Thompson counterfiled for a second evaluation of Sharon's psychological condition, for the right of Sharon to be present at hearings, and finally for the removal of Donald Kowalski as guardian for failure to act in the ward's best interest.

In an affidavit filed on November 28, Karen again attempted to refute some of the claims of the Kowalskis and their attorneys. To build her case for being Sharon's primary caregiver and de facto spouse, Karen also attached a copy of the life insurance policy they had filled out, making Sharon the primary beneficiary of $50,000 in the event of Karen's death. The policy was dated June 8, 1983. She submitted notes of support that she had received from the community, including professors from the counseling and human relations department at St. Cloud State. Her lawyers filed an affidavit from Dr. Stephen Vincent, a psychologist at St. Cloud Hospital who had seen Karen, Don, and Della in a joint consultation session. "Karen Thompson appeared very committed to Sharon," Vincent wrote, insisting that nothing had given him "the impression that Karen Thompson was in need of psychological treatment." He also cautioned that "it is risky to assign an overall age level to someone in Sharon's condition because there are differing developmental levels in different areas on different occasions."[5]

Thompson told the court she had seen the psychologist, Dr. Charles Chmielewski, only ten times for counseling and that most of those sessions dealt with the problem of overcoming the Kowalskis' reactions to her disclosure of her love for Sharon. An affidavit from Chmielewski himself stated: "It is my opinion based upon my contacts with Karen, that her commitment is sincere, had been there for a significant period of time and that Karen spoke of the commitment as a life long commitment." Regarding Sharon's mental capacity, Chmielewski agreed with Vincent that it was "very inappropriate to place an age estimate on someone in Sharon's condition based upon one subtest from one test." In his experience, "brain-injured patients typically respond with much more variability, and their performance differs greatly depending on the nature of the task being requested."[6]

Beth Ristvedt continued to make her case for reevaluation by filing affidavits describing the major downturn Sharon had taken since her move to Duluth. One of Sharon's students at Big Lake High School, Gail Romthun, noticed a marked change in Sharon at Park Point but testified that she was able to get consistent responses from Sharon to a number of questions, including positive responses to wanting to live in St. Cloud, attend court sessions, and have Karen as her guardian. Pat Larson, Sharon's supervisor at the Sherburne National Wildlife Refuge, testified that Sharon "talked with me sometime ago [before the accident] informing me that she was gay and in love with Karen Thompson." Pat attached a letter she received from Sharon in August 1983, before the accident: "Hi. How's your summer been?" Sharon's letter with a Garfield cartoon at the bottom began. "I went to summer school 2nd session to finish up my Driver Ed. Certification. It was a good experience for me. The only problem is that I've become a more verbal 'backseat driver.' Karen has threaten [*sic*] to make me walk a couple of times." The letter concluded with "a few fish stories" from a trip Sharon had just taken to Canada with Karen. "We haven't been camping all summer and the week we decide to go, it decides to rain! Anyway we did manage to get in a couple of days fishing. Karen had something (must have been 'Jaws') snap her line two different times. Needless to say she also caught most of the fish . . . disgusting [smiling face drawn]." Sharon's cheerful letter disclosed her willingness to talk about Karen as the main person in her life.[7]

November 19 through 23 saw a series of further affidavit filings. Other friends of Karen and Sharon testified to Sharon's pre-accident disclosure that she was gay, living with Karen, and committed. Pam Orrock, a former manager of the basketball team that Sharon coached at Big Lake High School, alleged that "Sharon had mentioned to me several times how she and her parents just didn't get along. On one occasion coming home from a weekend we had spent at their home, Sharon said, 'I just can't get along with them. I can't stand going there and staying more than a day.'" When Mary Wild talked to Sharon a week before the accident, Sharon told her friend about accepting a golf coaching position at St. Cloud State and mentioned how much she still loved Karen. These half-dozen sworn declarations that Sharon was in the process of coming out to friends before the accident, Ristvedt contended, revealed how central the issue of same-sex partnership was becoming in the case.[8]

Kathy King, a friend of Sharon's who had cerebral palsy, "wrestled with her conscience" before writing directly to Judge Douglas in November. "I have observed Sharon Kowalski for the past seven weeks," King wrote, and "I have also read the court transcripts, viewed a videotape, and have read articles in several papers throughout the state. During this time I have also watched Sharon regress to the point where she is most often uncommunicative and lies in bed in almost an embryonic position." King concluded that this case is "one in which a *handicapped* person's rights are being violated. In this instance, I know that of which I speak. I myself am handicapped, having cerebral palsy. I am very lucky to have always had supportive people help me through the rough spots. These people have been, by and large, individuals who are not blood relatives. It takes a person with real *chutzpa* to look past the handicap, find your strengths, and accept you for you."

King believed that Sharon's rights were being violated under Minnesota's Patients' Bill of Rights. Enumerating the four basic categories under the bill — the right to adequate health care, the right to information, the right to privacy, and the right to self-determination — King believed Sharon could "consistently communicate her wants and needs. The only thing is that one has to use her language or method of communication. From the records I've read, her method was not used in the evaluation process." King also believed that restrictions on visitation were violating Sharon's right to information and privacy. "My biggest fear for her is her being shut up in an institution against her will when she has a viable alternative. Many brain injured individuals have no alternatives. They are abandoned by their loved ones and shut away for life," King wrote.

Predictably, the social worker asked the judge to return Sharon Kowalski to the St. Cloud area — "the place she has told me that she wants to be." Having observed her with Karen Thompson, King declared that "Sharon responds to her like to *no one* else I've observed. With her type of injury and disability, I feel that this is her only real chance of survival." She concluded her personal letter with a troubling anecdote. Her own godson had died of an injury very similar to Sharon's at St. Paul Ramsey Hospital in 1976. "His death came after many months in the hospital — in fact, on the day he was to be discharged from one facility to another. Even after autopsy no medical cause could be found for his death. It was hypothesized that his death was a result of his loss of a will to live. I really fear that Sharon is also heading in this direction," King's letter concluded." King's unsolicited letter, not an affidavit, was sent to Judge Douglas instead of Kim Johnson, who was currently hearing motions in the *Kowalski* case. Judge Johnson had scheduled November 30 as the next court date to hear the extant motions of the party.[9]

In the meantime, Thompson's letter to the Minnesota Civil Liberties Union (MCLU) produced the first ostensible result of her decision to "go public." Two lawyers from the MCLU interviewed Thompson in November, saw the video of Sharon at Country Manor, and prepared an amicus curiae, or friend of the court, brief with Judge Johnson before the hearing. An amicus curiae brief is submitted by one who is not a party to the lawsuit to aid the court in gaining information it needs to make a proper decision or to urge a particular result on behalf of the public or a third party who might be affected by the court's resolution. The MCLU's brief stated that the motions before the court "raise fundamental questions concerning nursing home residents' and visitors' rights to free speech and association as guaranteed by the First Amendment of the United States Constitution." The brief reminded the court of its obligation to carry out the best interests of the ward and suggested that any action by the nursing home that is contrary to those best interests "may be the functional equivalent of state action violative of the constitutional rights of such ward."[10] The reference to "state action" — a term of constitutional law — suggested that the actions of the nursing home, if done under a court order, would be tantamount to an action by a government entity and therefore would fall within the parameters of the First Amendment, which prohibits the limitation of free speech by government or state action.

The court appeared to be affected by the amicus brief, perhaps as well by the stridency of the affidavits filed by Fena, including the lawyer's statements about the session with Dr. Vincent that were directly contradicted by the psychologist himself. For whatever reason, the ruling on November 30 was not wholly adverse to Karen Thompson. The court denied the Kowalskis' motion for change of venue, the visitation schedule was revised, and the motion for unconditional guardianship by both parties was postponed until May 2, 1985. The court also gave Thompson the power to have Sharon reevaluated at Thompson's own expense.[11]

A few days later, counsel for both parties held a telephone conference in which they mutually agreed to drop certain motions. During that conversation, Fena provided evidence over the phone that Della Kowalski had been hospitalized for a nervous breakdown, evidence that led to Ristvedt's agreement to withdraw her motion to remove Don Kowalski on condition that the Kowalskis withdraw their motion to revise the April 25 order and give Don unconditional guardianship powers. Della apparently was devastated by the publicity even in the local papers, the airing of their private lives on television and in all the major newspapers of her state. The agreement reached by the parties would turn out to be only temporary, as a follow-up letter by Ristvedt clearly intimated. "I certainly do not want Mrs. Kowalski to be misled that our withdrawal somehow means that the whole matter will go away," Ristvedt wrote to opposing counsel. Her letter proceeded to enumerate a few of the current ironies in the case. Even though Judge Douglas "recognized that the parties involved needed professional help back in April when in his order he recommended but did not order psychological help," the Kowalskis were attempting to exclude Thompson "on the basis of her contact with a psychologist" while at the same time "seeking action from the Court based upon Mrs. Kowalski's nervous breakdown and her failure to psychologically handle this entire situation." Both sides were under considerable stress, Ristvedt noted, and neither should be excluded for seeking professional help.[12]

In an attempt to confront some of her own concerns, Karen Thompson visited her parents in Ohio over Christmas in 1984, determined to come out to them and explain her ordeal. Her determination to tell her parents was partly motivated by a fear that newspaper reports had already reached Ohio or that someone had already "outed" her. She had in fact already told them she was filing for guardianship, but she did not assume that this disclosure would indicate that she was anything more than a good friend of Karen's (*Why Can't,*

105–6). The day after she arrived, she approached her father while he was in the garage leaning over the engine of a car. "I'd like to talk to you about some things, but I'm not sure you really want to hear them." Mr. Thompson looked his daughter in the eye and told her he knew everything, pulling an anonymous letter with a northern Minnesota postmark out of a drawer and showing it to her. Karen's father offered his support but asked that she not tell her mother. They agreed to keep the information about Karen's lesbianism from Mrs. Thompson, though upon returning home Karen feared that she was bound to find out and prayed she would not.

It was just a matter of time before many people knew about their relationship. Besides contacting the press, Karen, with the aid of Julie Andrzejewski, had set up the Karen Thompson Legal Fund and sent letters to friendly faculty and groups they thought might be supportive. Their first letter raised $650.00 to defray legal fees that were now close to $15,000. The letter was also sent to members of Presbyterians for Lesbian/Gay Concerns (PLGC), an organization that Karen had joined after her associate pastor, having read the articles in the *St. Cloud Times*, voiced his approval of her effort. He agreed that there was nothing in the Bible that condemned a committed, loving relationship with another human being, admonishments against same-sex behavior in Deuteronomy and Paul's epistles notwithstanding. This interpretation had also been Peg Chemberlin's. Karen found it comforting.

However, she did run into some trouble with her fellow parishioners (*Why Can't*, 106–8). A woman who had encouraged Karen's work with Sharon suddenly announced that she couldn't believe Karen was gay: "Don't you think you probably have just an agape love for Sharon where you love others in Christ? You must have allowed Satan to twist the love you had for Sharon into something else to try to get you away from Christ" (107). Karen defended herself, claiming that Christ never refers to homosexuality, and if he really condemned it, he would have stated it clearly. In her defense, she also mentioned the approval of the associate pastor, but that statement led to a reprisal. He later asked to speak with Karen and suggested in no uncertain terms that she not use his name when mentioning her lesbianism. Bowled over by the pastor's unwillingness to publicly support her, Karen decided to leave the church.

Thompson was buoyed by the support that came in the form of letters and small contributions. One gay man wrote to her about his partner, who was dying of cancer but from whom he had separated because of their fear of "coming out" to family and doctors. He thanked Karen for her public stance and shared with her his grief that when his partner needed him the most, he wasn't there. He said that he had lost the home and other personal possessions they owned together. After reading the letter, Thompson began to realize that her experience was not an isolated instance. She wondered how many others were struggling through similar tragedies (*Why Can't,* 108). Although she hardly mentioned AIDS in this part of her subsequent memoir, her interviews during this period showed some awareness of how this epidemic was affecting the lives of gay men, unable in countless cases to spend time together in intensive care units, unable to follow their lovers to their hometowns to care for them as they died, unable to claim the right to speak at their funerals, unable in the simplest of memorials to claim themselves as the lovers of the deceased in a fifty-word newspaper obituary.

One family wrote to Thompson about their gay son, whose homosexuality they, like the Kowalskis, at first found almost impossible to accept. They volunteered to write to Sharon's parents about their similar experience of initial shock and gradual acceptance, and Karen encouraged them. But the letter, from the Kowalskis' point of view, was another ploy by Thompson. They could not believe that she was circulating letters libeling their incapacitated daughter. They immediately turned such presumptuous trash to their attorney, with a shake of their heads. Their daughter's tragic disability — as if that physical state were not enough — was turning into the worst nightmare of their lives. Wasn't it enough to have to drive continually to Duluth to see Sharon, their athletic and fun-loving girl now bedridden in a nursing home? Della's breakdown was understandable under these circumstances: constant calls from the media, lawyer's fees, doctor's bills, hours in the car, and now mail from strangers asking them to accept the fact that their daughter was queer. Fena quickly dictated a letter to these misguided well-wishers, demanding that they cease harassing his clients.

The Kowalskis' lawyers were making other preparations for the upcoming hearing. In response to counsel's request, Dr. Julie Moller, from the Duluth Clinic, wrote to Jack Fena on December 20, 1984, about her examination of the ward. A veteran internist, she saw Sharon on December 13 at Park Point Manor and spent "at least half an hour" with her "trying to assess how easy it is to communicate with her, how well she comprehends and if she is able to make significant decisions." Dr. Moller's report would become an exhibit in subsequent hearings:

> She [Sharon] is severely impaired physically due to her closed head injury in 1983 and has only very limited ability to move her right hand and the fingers of her right hand. She is unable to speak or swallow. She is unable to move her other extremities. She has been given a small electronic computer printer which prints out messages on a strip of paper when she presses the letters with a pencil. This requires only light touch. She was able to spell the word cat. I asked her to spell her name Sharon but she only wrote SA. . . .

I presented her with a series of nonstructured statements or questions to which she could answer "yes" or "no" by moving her index finger or her thumb. . . . It appears to me that there was quite a bit of inconsistency in her answers. She is apparently not aware of the fact that she is at Park Point Manor in Duluth, but thinks that she is at the Country Manor Nursing Home in St. Cloud. She does not understand the word "parents," which apparently is too abstract for her. It appears that she likes her mother, her father, and Karen Thompson and enjoys their company. She thinks of Karen Thompson as a good friend.

I do not believe that Sharon Kowalski is able to make any significant decisions as to her future care. She had extensive psychological evaluation in October at Miller Dwan Hospital. At that time, it was felt that she was functioning mentally at a level below six or seven years of age and it is my opinion that she continues to function at this level. It is also my opinion that it is appropriate for her father as her parent to retain guardianship of his daughter.[13]

Catherine Anderson and Ryan Jagim, licensed psychologists, were hired by Karen Thompson to evaluate Sharon at Park Point after the first of the year. The judge had recommended that Karen not be present during the testing session, and the nursing home was intent upon enforcing that order. While Thompson was helping Anderson set up the testing equipment on the evening of February 6, a nurse came into the room and insisted that Karen leave as ordered by the judge. Anderson stated that the testing had not started yet. A few minutes later a nurse's aide arrived and made the same demand. Karen eventually did leave before the testing, but when Anderson emerged to inform Karen that Sharon's responses were erratic, that Sharon thought she lived in Nashwauk before the accident and did not know where she was living presently, a distraught and disappointed Karen tried rather vocally to defend Sharon in the hallway. She claimed the Kowalskis had "brainwashed" their daughter into believing she was in Nashwauk before the accident and attributed Sharon's disorientation to the refusal of Park Point to let her out on passes to see the city she was living in. "She's been like a prisoner here," Karen recalled telling Anderson.

The nursing staff at Park Point had a different version of the testing session, one that would later become evidence. The nurse's note from Ann Pellman, the head nurse, stated that Thompson was doing more than helping set up, that she was in fact "helping with the typing." Pellman heard part of Thompson's conversation with the tester in the hallway. "I couldn't hear much of what Cathy said, but Karen was agitated, stating, 'she's being held prisoner here' and various other things about this nursing home being wishy-washy and not taking a stand and Sharon is being brainwashed by her parents." Pellman's emotional note finished with a flourish: "I can't remember it all, but I found it extremely disgusting. Sounded like Karen is about to lose her marbles. Also is VERY VICIOUS." Pellman admitted that she was "angry," as "you can tell by the handwriting." Pellman's note was soon discovered by Jack Fena.[14]

In an affidavit prepared later at the request of Karen Thompson, Catherine Anderson attributed Karen's comments to frustration over Sharon's lack of orientation and unresponsiveness during the test. Anderson found nothing "vicious" in Thompson's comments and attributed the "prison" comment to Karen's feeling stymied by the ban on outings. A few days later, Anderson produced her written evaluation of Sharon's condition, concluding that the ward had in fact "exhibited some confusion on her current place of residence, on one occasion typing Duluth and on another occasion typing St. Cloud." Sharon's "time awareness was the most significantly impaired, with her getting both the dates and the day of the week wrong." She did show some evidence of "higher cognitive functions" and was able to perform several simple one- and two-step math problems. Sharon "was also able to identify and categorize familiar objects in her environment." Her long-term memory was relatively more intact.

When Anderson asked Sharon if she was depressed, Sharon typed "yes" and identified that emotion as "sad." Anderson noted that the patient "denied any suicidal ideation when asked. The only spontaneous affect which Sharon displayed during the evaluation was when, after discussing her present living situation, she hung her head and refused to interact any further for approximately three or four minutes." Anderson also viewed a videotape from 1984 that showed a much more capable Sharon. The psychologist concluded that Sharon was "currently experiencing a major clinical depression" and recommended counseling and medication. "Further assessment will be necessary to determine the degree to which her depression is precipitated by her separation from Karen Thompson, although that pattern does appear to be substantiated," she noted. Anderson also recommended that the patient be given every opportunity to leave the "confinement" of "the convalescent environment. Therefore, it is recommended that she be allowed out on passes on a much more frequent basis to facilitate her interaction with her environment."

Unlike Moller, Anderson made no conclusive statements about Sharon's capacity, level of intelligence, or ability to recover. Both experts couched their assessments in the noncommittal language of "I believe" and "it appears," revealing the inexact science of medicine and psychology that would continue to provide unanswerable questions about Sharon's capacity to make some of her own decisions while simultaneously providing in the eyes of the law an expert, objective determination of the "true" state of the ward.

Sharon also received visits from Kathleen T. Wingen and Carla M. Hansen of Tri-County Action Programs, Inc. (TRICAP), a handicap services organization located in Sauk Rapids. TRICAP worked to meet the needs of children and adults with disabilities in Benton, Sherburne, and Stearns Counties in Minnesota. Karen Thompson initially contacted the TRICAP office in October 1984, and the first visit took place for two hours on November 15, when the program's representatives found Sharon to be aware and alert, as well as "actively interactive." The second visit took place on January 24, when Sharon appeared angry that they had not visited her earlier but eventually agreed to talk.

TRICAP also concluded that Sharon had entered a state of depression and needed immediate psychological counseling to allow her "to come to terms with the fact that she is now, and probably will always be a disabled person." Insisting that Sharon was capable of conveying her wants and needs, the TRICAP representatives wrote to the court, "This individual should be allowed to provide input at court proceedings." They also revealed that Sharon had expressed to them how torn she felt between her parents and Karen Thompson. They believed that this conflict "had great bearing" on her rehabilitation and depression. They wanted the court to appoint a social worker familiar with disability and recommended as a start that Sharon get involved in the Ms. Wheelchair Minnesota Pageant scheduled for May.

In answer to the specific questions asked by TRICAP, Sharon consistently responded that she was gay and typed out "Karen T." as her lover's name. She also responded that she wanted Karen to take care of her. The TRICAP representatives directly contradicted Dr. Moller on questions of Sharon's ability to make decisions for herself. Not surprisingly, those specialists were influenced by their own positions — one a busy internist stopping by to evaluate a patient for thirty minutes and providing a quick assessment in keeping with the demands of an attorney seeking an expert opinion; the others, representatives of an organization devoted to the promotion of the legal and human rights of disabled individuals, in their eyes dismissed as "vegetables" and abandoned in nursing homes all over the country.[15]

As Thompson's troubles mounted on the medical front, Julie Andrzejewski and Peg Chemberlin decided to form the Committee for the Right to Recovery and Relationships, a diverse group of activists that focused on publicizing the negative coverage of the case in the mainstream press and raising money to defray legal costs. A list of gay and lesbian and disability rights groups was compiled, and an updated letter was sent all over the country. Within a few days, reporters from the alternative press began to call Karen. A gay bar owner in Superior, Wisconsin, just across the border from Duluth, found a place for Karen to stay when she came to visit Sharon and volunteered

his club for an auction that raised $1,000. Support for Karen's "cause" was
slowly growing.

As spring came about, Jack Fena wrote to Judge Douglas asking for per-
mission to allow the Kowalskis to bring their daughter home for Easter. "The
Easter holiday is an important religious holiday to the Kowalskis who are
Catholic and it is causing both Mr. and Mrs. Kowalski, especially the mother,
great mental anguish in not being able to have her daughter home for Easter."[16]
Sharon went to Nashwauk for Easter without any serious opposition, and
Karen also flew to her parents' home in Ohio for spring break. In the living
room, her mother outed her before she could broach the topic. "It really upsets
me when people keep things from me," Karen's mother stated. "You're a lesbian!" Karen confirmed her mother's suspicions and assured her she was happy
with Sharon. "Mom," Karen stated, "my choice was to be a workaholic all my
life and wonder what was wrong or accept my love for Sharon and start living
for the first time." Karen's "choice" was not the one her mother would have
preferred, but once she found out her daughter's secret, she was as supportive
as the rest of the family (*Why Can't,* 125).

My interest in the *Kowalski* case coincided with a growing concern about queer
issues in the academy, especially at an institution like the University of Montana, where lesbian and gay professors were largely closeted and undergradu-
ate students, with their private and anonymous Lambda meetings, were the
only visible evidence of lesbian and gay life on campus. By teaching the *Kowalski* case and writing about queer issues, I had taken a stand on coming out in a
place that arguably was still the frontier in issues of sexual orientation. The
state of Montana itself was a location reminiscent of the Iron Range, though
copper, silver, and now gold were the more likely minerals in this treasure state.
Both regions had the same cycles of exploitation, the same clear-cutting, the
same arsenic in the rivers, the same open-pit mines, the same underemploy-
ment. In many ways, this Rocky Mountain state, with its sexual deviancy code
and its legislature heavily indebted to the rhetoric of the Christian Coalition,
was more conservative socially than northern Minnesota, though Missoula was
certainly thought to be an oasis of tolerance. The university town had the
state's only gay bar, called Amvets, which was located in a smoky, low-
ceilinged basement. It served as a veterans' watering hole by day, a lesbian and
gay bar by night. "Don't ask, don't tell" appeared to be the motto of both sets
of strange bedfellows, the subterranean venue serving a clientele that fluctu-
ated between drag queens, alcoholic barflies, and big circles of women drinking beer and laughing.

Thinking more and more about the *Kowalski* case — its exemplary combination of legal, queer, and theoretical issues — I applied to the Center for Feminist Research (CFR) at the University of Southern California for a fellowship to research it for six months. I had written an article entitled "Making Justice" about the case that was coming out in a social policy journal and found that the CFR was happy to provide me with an office. My research leave coincided with the decision of my partner to go to graduate school in social work at USC, a move he had made with intentions that were more than academic. He found Montana stifling and, as I later discovered, had no intention of returning. I wrote a proposal to the CFR, explaining how the case raised issues of feminism, disability rights, and homophobia within a compelling narrative that I hoped to document. I also explained that I was in a committed same-sex relationship myself and so had firsthand knowledge of what it means to stay in the closet and what happens when one decides to come out. Yet my orientation was tempered, I told the CFR, by a commitment to unfold this narrative as objectively as possible.

In the spring of 1995, shortly before my trip to Los Angeles, I found myself with my partner, sitting in the old open-air trolleybus on the way to visit the Allerton Gardens on the Hawaiian island of Kauai. The tour guide spoke of the designers of the beautiful gardens as Robert Allerton and his adopted companion, John Gregg, referring to their connection as a loving "father-son" relationship. Driving past the maidenhair ferns growing out of the hillside, walking through the fields of flowering ginger, we dreamed of the paradise these men had created for themselves, the love they put into their plants, the Hawaiian culture of *aikane,* the name for a younger same-sex lover in native Hawaiian culture.

Robert Henry Allerton was born on March 20, 1873, the only son of a rich Chicagoan. To the chagrin of his father, he spent his life studying and collecting art and architecture, designing and planting gardens, avoiding marriage. In 1922, Allerton met a young architecture student at a Dad's Day dinner in the Zeta Psi fraternity house at the University of Illinois. They became paired for the rest of their lives. Years later, in 1959, after a change in Illinois law, Robert adopted John Gregg. In 1937, they bought one hundred acres on a sandy bay in Kauai, the garden island of Hawaii, and designed the tropical gardens now known as Lawai-Kai. The Allerton Gardens, where Robert and John spent the rest of their lives, were now a national botanical treasure. After Robert died on December 22, 1964, he was cremated, and his ashes were scattered on the outgoing tide in the bay at Lawai-Kai.

What our tour guide was not daring to name was a story of same-sex love, a history still hidden. Robert and John must have had their own encounter with domestic relations law. Why had Robert adopted John, and what was the change in the Illinois adoption law that allowed him to turn a man who (I assumed) must have been his lover into his son? How had this lifetime commitment, euphemized under the terms "protégé" and "father-son" relation, infiltrated the heterosexist channels of domestic relations to legitimize same-sex passion, expand the definition of family, and allow inheritance? How had the money Sharon and Karen did not have given Robert and John the power to create this paradise?

That afternoon, I rode the tiny waves in the shallow water of the bay where Robert's ashes had been scattered, dreaming of this famous *locus amoenus* between worries about my classes, about my research into the *Kowalski* case, about my partner's refusal to swim. Why would a professor of Renaissance literature want to get involved in a contemporary history of lesbian love? How did the compulsion of romance create a mandate for social change — through adoption, guardianship, marriage?

Baehr v Lewin, the Hawaii case of same-sex marriage, was making headlines in the local newspapers even as I hiked through Waimea Canyon and Robert Allerton's gardens that spring.[17] The legislature was preparing to take action against the state's judicial determination that disallowing same-sex marriage was unconstitutional sex discrimination. The plaintiffs' application for a marriage license that initiated the lawsuit had nothing and everything to do with the myths of sexual tolerance in Hawaiian culture (the *aikane* practice), Robert Allerton and his partner John Gregg, Sharon Kowalski and Karen Thompson, even me and my partner. United by same-sex love, we were disunited by culture, geography, law, gender, and history — pulled back together by our place outside the norm.

But private romance has its public consequences. Looking into the politics of same-sex marriage, I studied the national backlash that followed the 1993 Hawaii Supreme Court ruling. In the immediate aftermath, many state legislatures had considered or enacted laws restricting marriage to couples of different sexes. In September 1996, the United States Congress, legislating in a domestic relations area traditionally left to the states, overwhelmingly passed the Defense of Marriage Act (DOMA), a bill at first called unnecessary by President Clinton but then readily endorsed by him as the election approached. The vote was 342 to 67 in the House, 85 to 14 in the Senate. DOMA, which passed through Congress faster than any other legislation that session, was described by Senator Edward Kennedy as a "mean-spirited form of Republican legislative gay-bashing cynically calculated to try to inflame the public eight weeks before the November fifth election." But if the truth be known, it was really a bipartisan effort. Democrat Barbara Mikulski of Maryland voted for it and was outed as a lesbian as a result.[18]

The debate over DOMA turned the *Congressional Record* into a revival meeting, demonstrating the complex relation between literature, religion, politics, and sexual orientation, a relation that underlay the controversy over Karen Thompson's petition to become her lover's guardian. In debate, Congressman Steve Buyer of Indiana argued, "[W]e are a nation of people, a society based upon very strong Biblical principles. . . . God laid down that one man and one woman is a legal union. That is marriage, known for thousands of years." In response Congressman Jesse Jackson Jr. of Illinois remarked, "When I came to Congress, I placed my hand on the Bible and swore to uphold the Constitution; now I am being asked to place my hand on the Constitution and uphold the Bible." For Congressman George Gekas of Pennsylvania, "homosexuality is inherently wrong and harmful to individuals, families, and societies," while another congressman relied on the wisdom of William Bennett, who believed that recognizing same-sex marriage "would be the most radical step ever taken in the deconstruction of society's most important institution . . . the keystone in the arch of civilization."[19] The issue of same-sex marriage and the rights that attached to it was invoking the call of the deepest of social mythologies.

Hearing

Thus the ideal of impartiality generates a dichotomy between universal and particular, public and private, reason and passion. It is, moreover, an impossible ideal, because the particularities of context and affiliation cannot and should not be removed from moral reasoning. Finally the ideal of impartiality serves ideological functions. It masks the ways in which the particular perspectives of dominant groups claim universality, and help justify hierarchical decision-making structures.

Iris Marion Young, *Justice and the Politics of Difference*

Polish Independence Day, May 3, 1985, had begun the most extended round of hearings to date in the matter of Sharon Kowalski. Up to this point, Minnesota's Tenth District Court of Sherburne County had practiced the art of compromise. Over a year earlier, Judge Bruce R. Douglas had approved the settlement agreement that named Sharon's father guardian but gave Karen Thompson equal rights to visitation and medical information. When Sharon was discharged from St. Cloud Hospital in July 1984, the court initially ordered her to nearby Country Manor Nursing Home in Sartell over the protest of the Kowalskis. Two months later, Douglas agreed with Donald Kowalski's attorney that Sharon should receive further testing at the Polinsky Center in Duluth. In October, ruling against Thompson's motion to bring Sharon back to St. Cloud, the court ordered the ward to the Young Adult Rehabilitation Unit of Park Point Manor Nursing Home in Duluth, where she was presently residing.

Sitting down to his desk at eight o'clock that May morning, the heavyset Douglas perused the foot-high pile of papers in manila folders that the bailiff had placed on his desk. The clock on the wall was ticking relentlessly in his well-appointed chambers, replete with a darkly varnished desk and matching bookcase set off by a navy blue rug. Drifts of paper had accumulated at various strategic locations throughout the room: an empty chair, a tabletop, a vacant corner on the floor. The sequence of judicial orders in the Kowalski matter, summarized on a sheet of paper stapled to the inside of the top file, indicated that the middle ground taken in this dispute up to this point was proving more provocative than remedial. The previous November, in Douglas's absence, Judge Johnson had issued an injunction against both parties, restraining them from disrupting the nursing home. Now the five o'clock news and the *Minneapolis Star Tribune* were covering the story; Sharon had recently fallen into a clinical depression, and Park Point Manor was under investigation for unsafe and unsanitary conditions. The courtroom was filling up, and they were waiting for his arrival.

Since February, affidavits had steadily flowed into the clerk's office for the click-thump of a file stamp that made these written avowals part of a record that was growing exponentially. Opening one of the files, the judge quickly scanned an affidavit from Handicap Services that requested Sharon have input in the proceedings, citing Section 504 of the Federal Rehabilitation Act and the Minnesota human rights statute.[1] Unless a doctor would testify to the ward's physical or mental incapacity to attend or comprehend, this affidavit would require attention.

A recent affidavit from Don Kowalski claimed that his daughter, reduced to the cognitive powers of a six-year-old, did not even know what a lesbian was, yet he argued on the same page that Sharon's right to privacy was being invaded and she was being libeled by allegations about her sexual orientation in the newspapers. "Gay Issue Clouds Custody Fight," the front-page headline of October 18, 1984, from the *St. Cloud Times* article stared out, its contents detailing Thompson's claim of de facto marriage and the Kowalskis' allegation of fear of sexual abuse. Two legal angles were obvious: the law did not recognize same-sex marriage in spite of what was in Thompson's mind; and Donald Kowalski's allegation of sexual abuse was potentially libelous.

The judge had stated to the press that questions of sexual orientation had not entered into his earlier decisions, but highlighted yellow sections of Thompson's deposition were telling a different story:

> MR. FENA: You have, to my understanding, stated in some of these news articles that you did not consider your involvement in Sharon Kowalski's guardianship controversy a gay rights issue, isn't that true?
>
> KAREN THOMPSON: That I didn't consider it a gay rights issue?
>
> Q: Right.
>
> A: I said it should not be a gay rights issue. I said it's a human rights issue and Sharon had those rights.
>
> Q: Had you stated, though, to the contrary, that it is a gay rights issue?
>
> A: I have said that it should not be, but the underlying issue is that it is. If there were laws that two people could be married, we would have been married and this wouldn't be happening. So it does become a gay rights issue. . . .
>
> Q: In particular, do you deny the reference in Angie Workman's affidavit, the woman you spoke to in the waiting room at St. Cloud Hospital shortly after

the accident, do you deny the reference where she quotes you as stating that you are going to make this a national gay rights issue and take it national?

A: I did not say that in that context to her, no.

Q: What did you say it like?

A: I said I would appreciate your help in trying to discuss this with the parents. Maybe you could get through to the parents and make them understand that I don't want this to go to court. This could get blown up. This could become a national issue. . . .

Q: One of the news articles stated that after you met Sharon, you discovered you were gay, is that correct? Do you remember that article?

A: I think that came from the *Chronicle,* the college paper. You don't just discover you are gay. That was just his way of putting it. I didn't say it that way, no.

Q: You didn't say it that way?

A: No. It makes you go through the whole searching process and finally come together with who you are and what you are. . . .

Q: You don't agree with that part of it, that you discovered, where the article says, you discovered you were gay after you met Sharon Kowalski?

A: I came to grips with it that I was gay and, yes, I wanted to live a gay lifestyle. . . .

Q: Had you ever had a heterosexual relationship?

A: Yes, I have.

Q: And were you at one time pregnant?

A: Yes, I was, and I don't know what that has to do with this.

Ms. Ristvedt: I would object to anything further on that line. . . .

Mr. Fena: And that was your desire and Sharon's desire [to stay in the closet], isn't that true?

A: Sharon was more for coming out than I was. She was wanting to start doing things more publicly. . . . She took me to the Cities to a gay concert because she wanted to do things. . . . I can only speak for myself. I was scared to death about coming out of the closet.

Q: Sharon had not come out of the closet, had she? Yes or no.

A: Depends on what you call coming out.

Q: Well, Sharon had not told her parents, had she?

A: She told her work supervisor. She's told other people.

Q: Well, she hadn't told her parents, had she?

A: No, she'd gone public in some ways, but not others. She had not told her parents, no.

Q: And you had discussed, and you knew that she did not want to tell her parents, didn't you?

A: We had discussed it, yes.[2]

The judge's five-minute reprieve had turned to ten. He closed the plastic-bound deposition and remembered a memo from one of his clerks on the relevance of the "gay thing." Even if there was a special relationship between these two women, the law summary stated, the guardianship statute did not require or even suggest that a spouse become guardian; the criteria had to do with the best interest of the ward, including Sharon's preference (if she were capable of having one) and the guardian's commitment to the ward's welfare. The common law might create a presumption in favor of a spouse, but another presumption also lay with the family. Looking at the clock, Douglas decided to wade through the rest of this sea of words later.

The judge rose from his desk and walked over to the closet, pulling the robe off its wooden hanger and sticking his head into its blackness before finding the hole for his neck. "All rise," the bailiff growled. "The District Court of Sherburne County is now in session, the Honorable Bruce R. Douglas presiding." Once the judge had found his high-backed swivel chair, the bailiff stated, "You may be seated."

"In re the matter of Sharon Kowalski, ward," the judge called. Four attorneys and two clients (Karen Thompson and Don Kowalski) moved from their seats in the front row of the gallery through the swinging gate of the bar to the tables that were lined up before the raised dais. The aisle in the gallery split the north from the south: Della Kowalski, Debbie DiIorio (Sharon's sister), and some friends sat in the fourth row on the north side, staring at the judge; on the St. Cloud side were Karen's sister and brother-in-law. The case was a civil war of sorts, but in this one the north had more in common with the south — rural, working-class, rooted in traditional values that might be open to progressive economics but balked at the innovations of sexual politics. In the back, reporters from *Equal Time* (a gay and lesbian paper from the Twin Cities), the *Duluth News-Tribune*, and the *St. Cloud Times* sat with their notebooks open and ballpoints poised. Other strangers peppered the wooden seats, smoothed and yellowed from the wear and tear of anxious litigants awaiting their fate.

"Jack Fena for the petitioner Donald Kowalski," the former assemblyman announced. The other attorneys, Kevin Spellacy, Tom Hayes, and Beth Ristvedt, stated their appearances for the record. Besides the clerk, sitting at a desk between bench and bar, Ristvedt was the only woman among the officers of the court. The judge immediately ordered counsel into his chambers, where for the next ten minutes, off the record, he told them there was no way he could deal with all the filed motions during this hearing, that he was only prepared at this time to hear the April 1 motion requesting that visitation and contact by Karen Thompson be extinguished. He admonished counsel about existing restraining orders, looking at counsel, and pleaded with the lawyers to overcome their client control problems. Out they then marched to return to their positions in the courtroom. The Kowalskis were baffled, Karen suspicious, but the judge then explained to the audience that he was to proceed only on the motion for removal of Thompson's visitation rights.[3]

This ruling put Ristvedt at a disadvantage. The court was deciding if Thompson was unworthy of maintaining her already compromised position as nonguardian with shared rights of visitation and supervision of the ward. There was no offensive motion before the court to determine if Thompson herself should be guardian and not Donald Kowalski. This procedural decision also gave counsel for the Kowalskis the opportunity to present their witnesses first, and they capitalized on this opening by essentially monopolizing the hearing.

Although Jack Fena was hired by the Kowalskis to handle the personal injury case, the interference of Thompson made it necessary to become active in the guardianship dispute as well. In the usual course of legal events, his client Donald would be named as guardian of the person and estate of his daughter and then named as guardian ad litem in the personal injury action. The plaintiff's lawyer could then solely deal with the guardian in proceeding with personal injury litigation. Liability in the case was open and shut; Sharon was hit by the intoxicated Greg Yeager, who was cited at the scene. The difficulty arose in finding a deep pocket to pay the damages, in this case the insurer of the Blue Goose, the bar where the driver had gotten drunk. Under the so-called dramshop law, drinking establishments were exposed to liability for negligently serving obviously inebriated customers, especially if it was obvious they were about to drive. Sharon's injuries were so severe that Fena demanded the liability limits of both Yeager's and the Blue Goose's policies, which could bring the case over the half-million mark, leaving secure a substantial fee for the attorney, who was advancing all the costs of litigation.

Thompson's petition to become guardian and her insistence on her lesbian relationship with the injured plaintiff, however, were creating some serious roadblocks to a quick settlement of the personal injury suit. Juries from the Iron Range would be unlikely to give large sums of money to lesbians, especially those who "advertised," and insurance company lawyers were well aware of that fact. During settlement negotiations, all the parties would be factoring in "the gay thing," now plastered all over the evening news from Grand Rapids to Cloquet Valley. Fena wanted Thompson out of this case as soon as possible, and he was employing various legal tactics to achieve that goal. Claims of invasion of privacy, slander, sexual abuse, greed, and publicity hunting by Sharon's "landlady," as Fena liked to call Thompson, were part of a strategy of letting Itascans know that this pushy professor from St. Cloud was fabricating her gay story for her own aggrandizement at the expense of the silenced young woman from Nashwauk, reduced to wearing diapers by the negligence of a drunk driver.

"I'm going to call four witnesses for some hopefully brief testimony, Your Honor, relative to the issues in our motion," Fena told the court. First on the stand was Debbie, Sharon's younger sister, whose daughter had been killed on November 13, 1983, and whose son had suffered injuries from which he had now recovered. When Sharon came to pick up the kids on the Thursday before the accident, Debbie testified, her sister had complained that "there wasn't much opportunity in Minnesota for her job situation anymore." Sharon had been laid off, Debbie told the court, and was talking about moving back to her parents' house for a while or moving to Colorado. During that evening, Sharon told her sister that "she wanted to get away, that Karen was somehow becoming possessive and wanting to control things that she did in her life, and she didn't like being controlled by her," Debbie testified. Sharon thought of Karen as "a friend, someone to talk to" who gave her "financial help," but someone who "was trying to put her in place of the baby she had given up," Debbie told the court.[4]

The direct examination turned to Debbie's observations of Thompson's comportment in the hospital and nursing homes. Karen, she felt, had no respect for Sharon's family when they visited. "If we would be standing by the bed trying to talk to her, Karen would just come and interrupt, and if I would be standing by her, like holding her hand or something, Karen would come right in between and she didn't care if anyone else was there or not," Debbie stated. She recalled that Karen would come "right between us" and put her face "within inches" of Sharon's and "talk to her like a baby," aggravating the entire family when they were trying to visit.

Fena then presented exhibit 1, a set of photos of Sharon and her friends during a visit to the Kowalskis' home in Nashwauk last Christmas. Images of a happy Sharon with her family and male friends set the stage for a line of questioning about Sharon's depression, which Fena wanted to tie to Thompson's intrusive behavior. Debbie testified that Sharon was "withdrawn and unhappy" at Country Manor at Sartell, but "she would look very happy" and her "spirits seemed higher" at Park Point Manor in Duluth. "Whenever she went home, she would look so happy and you could see it on her and friends would come over and see her there and she was laughing," Debbie told the court. Fena then approached the "gay issue":

Q: Did your sister, Sharon, ever tell you she was a lesbian or gay?
A: No. . . .
Q: Now, have you noticed that in the last two or three months that Sharon has become depressed?
A: Yes.

Q: You have seen the news stories regarding your sister, Sharon, and Karen Thompson, . . . and these have been in the local press in Northeastern Minnesota, including the Range, right where your parents live — where you live?

A: Yes. . . .

Q: Have any of her friends or childhood friends, her high school friends, present Range friends, ever told you that Sharon was involved in any lesbian relationships with anyone?

A: No. . . .

Q: If that were true, do you think that Sharon would want you or your father or your mother to know?

A: Yes. . . .

Q: Are you saying, Debbie, that Sharon would want to tell her parents that she was gay, if she was gay, that she would have had the courage to do it?

A: Why don't you rephrase it? . . .

Q: Well, do you think Sharon is embarrassed by them [the news stories]?

A: Yes.

Q: Is your family embarrassed by them?

A: Yes.[5]

Jack Fena had no further questions. Taking notes, Judge Douglas had not objected to Fena's leading, compound, and vague questions, leaving that task to opposing counsel. The witness's testimony raised questions. Was Sharon about to leave her friend, and, if so, what did this say about their "significant relationship"? Why was Sharon currently depressed if her sister claims she was doing so much better in Duluth? In the middle of Debbie's testimony, Karen felt like jumping up and shouting, "That's not the truth," but she restrained herself, scribbling notes on a yellow pad she handed to Beth Ristvedt when the direct examination was over (*Why Can't*, 133–34). Her notes reminded her lawyer that Sharon had just accepted a job as assistant golf coach at St. Cloud State the week before the accident, that at the hospital she gave the Kowalskis all the space she possibly could, and that the publicity took place in October, well before Sharon's depression. Why had Beth not made more objections?

Ristvedt began her cross-examination of Debbie by asking her a set of leading questions about Sharon and Karen's relationship:

Ms. RISTVEDT: Are you aware that Sharon has consistently responded to several persons that she loves Karen?

DEBBIE DiIORIO: No. . . .

Q: Prior to the accident, were you aware that Sharon had moved three times with Karen Thompson?

A: Yes.

Q: And that she lived at various times in an apartment with her?

A: Yes. . . .

Q: And then finally moved in together into the home out by Briggs Lake?
A: Yes.[6]

After her brief cross-examination of the witness, Ristvedt sat down. Tom Hayes rose and followed with another line of questioning that pertained to the reliability of the witness's observations:

Q: In response to a question posed by Mr. Fena, you indicated you believe that Sharon has become depressed? . . . Would you please describe for us your basis for that opinion — what you observed.
A: Well, I have gone there after Karen has been there. I met her coming out of Sharon's room at one time, and whenever I have gone very recently, Karen has been there and she doesn't — she seems almost to hide from — like she will turn away and close her eyes and kind of curl up.
Q: How many times have you visited with Sharon immediately following a visit by Karen Thompson in the past three months?
A: In the past three months, probably once.
Q: In response to a question posed by Mr. Fena, you indicated that Sharon appeared to be embarrassed by some of the news stories?
A: Yes.
Q: What did you observe that led you to conclude that?
A: That she didn't want to look at anybody.
Q: How did you tie that into the news stories?
A: Well, they had been after the news stories had come out, and after all the arguing in court and stuff.
Q: Do you know whether or not Sharon had an opportunity to see or learn about any of the news stories?
A: I don't know for sure. She couldn't tell me if she did.[7]

Hayes sought to undermine Debbie's earlier testimony about Sharon's publicity-induced depression by eliciting the infrequency of her visits, as well as her inability to establish a credible link between Sharon's behavior and the press reports. Hayes was also reminding the judge that the allegedly stressful newspaper coverage of the lesbian component of the case had begun in October, when Debbie had testified that Sharon was supposedly improving after her move to Park Point in Duluth.

Fena's next witness, who had arrived during Hayes's cross-examination, was George Cowan, a practicing psychiatrist in Duluth and chief of psychiatry at Miller-Dwan Hospital, where Sharon had spent some time before being placed at Park Point. He was one of Fena's hired experts in the personal injury suit. Cowan had graduated from the University of Minnesota Medical School in 1936, had been a psychiatrist for the army during World War II, and was board-certified in psychology and neurology. "Doctor, can you hear me?" was Fena's first question. Fena then proceeded with the litany of credentials, establishing Cowan's authority as an expert in psychiatry if not, more appropriately, in rehabilitation medicine. Dr. Cowan first saw Sharon on October 4, 1984, at the request of Dr. Goff. "I attempted to talk to her. I got no responses. The nurse told me that she would probably answer my questions by blinking her eyes, one blink for yes and two blinks for a no," Cowan told the court. "Her replies to my questions were very inconsistent. She would reply to one question one time with a yes and later on the same question she would reply with a no. That is as much as I could get out of her." When Dr. Cowan visited Sharon again at Park Point Manor, he was not able to communicate with her at all. From his expert opinion, Sharon's "disability" was "permanent, total in permanence."[8]

Jack Fena then asked Dr. Cowan about his experience with "people who are gay or lesbians":

> MR. FENA: [T]ell the Court whether or not, from your practice, if you find that many gay people are concerned about the anonymity of being in the closet so-to-speak?
>
> DR. COWAN: Most of those that I have seen prefer to remain anonymous.
>
> Q: Well, usually, who are the main people that a gay person would not want to have that information made known to?
>
> A: To their parents.
>
> Q: Okay, now, I want you to assume something, and there is some "ifs" in my question: If Sharon Kowalski were gay, and if she had been in a lesbian relationship with Karen Thompson, and if she had discussed not telling her parents, and if Karen Thompson told Sharon's parents about their lesbian relationship, and then told Sharon: "I have told your mother and your father and I have issued press releases and I am telling the Court" — do you have an opinion as to what that would mean or how Sharon Kowalski would react to that?
>
> A: Yes.
>
> Q: What is your opinion of those circumstances?
>
> A: My opinion is that this would be very devastating to her.
>
> Q: In what way, Doctor?
>
> A: Well, I think it would cause her to withdraw and be depressed — be very upset. . . .
>
> Q: Do you have an opinion as to whether or not the disclosure of this lesbian relationship issue to her parents, to the public in the area where she lived, would have contributed to or caused her depression or her present depression?
>
> A: If we can assume she understood what was told to her, then, the answer is "yes" it would certainly aggravate any existing condition. . . .
>
> Q: How about the pain-injured [*sic*] persons like Sharon, do you have an opin-

ion as to whether family means something, or a lot, or is necessary, or what is your psychiatric opinion, based on your experience in dealing with these types of injuries?

A: I think family means everything to a person like this. . . .

Q: In your experience in this light as a doctor, as a psychiatrist for many years, would you equate or can you equate paternal love and weigh it against the love I might have for my wife, or my girlfriend or what have you?

A: I think that is a different kind of love.

Q: There are conditions on most kinds of love?

A: Well, let me put it this way. Some kinds of love they call it love, but it is this kind of love like if a woman tells her husband "that I will love you if you buy me a new mink coat," that is not love, but they call it love.

Q: Okay.

A: There should be no conditions with respect to love.

Q: Isn't parental love unconditional love in your opinion?

A: It should be. . . .

Q: Now, let's assume that Karen Thompson has told Sharon Kowalski that your parents only have you in the nursing home because you are gay, that she made statements to her that were negative against the parents, do you think that would have an effect on Sharon?

A: Yes.

Q: What kind of an effect?

A: Well, I hate to abuse the word, but I would say devastating. . . .[9]

Assuming everything that counsel had told him was true, Dr. Cowan gave his opinion: "If I were writing orders on Sharon, which I am not, if I were writing the orders, I would write an order forbidding Karen Thompson from visiting this gal."[10] Fena was done with his witness, having established, under his scenario, the urgent need to remove Karen Thompson from Sharon's care.

Ristvedt began her cross-examination, methodically reading prepared questions from her yellow pad. The seventy-five-year-old witness had testified for this well-known personal-injury lawyer, she elicited, on prior occasions and had made his second visit at the request of counsel. Cowan had seen Sharon Kowalski only twice. She continued:

Ms. Ristvedt: You have indicated that you have worked with lesbian persons on prior occasions?

Dr. Cowan: Yes.

Q: In working with them, have you found that lesbian couples can be as committed as married couples?

A: Some, yes.

Q: It would be like some married couples, some more than others?

A: Yes. . . .

Q: Have you found in your practice over the years that many brain injured patients suffer depression?

A: Yes. . . .

Q: Is it possible that persons who are brain injured get depressed when persons whom they are close to or loved, are no longer visiting or no longer around?

A: Of course, yes.

Q: If you assumed that Sharon is happy to see Karen, and requests that Karen Thompson visit her, and when requested by personnel, when given a choice, that she would rather have Karen do things for her than other persons, if you assume those things, and further assume that when Karen leaves, that Sharon then curls up and tucks herself into a fetal position, can you offer an opinion as to some of the possible causes of her withdrawing at that point?

A: Not really. It is hard to say.

Q: So there is a whole variety of reasons why she could be withdrawn?

A: Yes.

Q: And really, without having done a psychological testing, and really doing a thorough testing of Sharon, it would be difficult to find out the exact reason why she would be withdrawing or appear to be withdrawing?

A: Well, in that state she is in, I think it would be impossible to find out the reason.[11]

Ristvedt's cross-examination did not pursue its strategy as aggressively as it might have. Dr. Cowan was not reminded that he attributed, hypothetically, Sharon's depression to Karen's outing of Sharon to her parents and the press, even though he admitted the impossibility of determining causation. Cowan was not pressed by counsel on his beliefs about the unconditional love of parents as opposed to lesbian lovers, about how he would have reacted if Karen Thompson were a male. Ristvedt had established the psychiatrist as Jack Fena's hired expert, one with only a cursory familiarity with Sharon's case. Tom Hayes now approached the stand.

MR. HAYES: Tell me, Doctor, has there been some kind of controversy among psychiatrists nationwide on homosexuality in general in the past few years?

DR. COWAN: Well, to tell you the truth, I don't really know, but among our profession, there is controversy all the time about most everything.

Q: Okay, do you know whether or not homosexuality has, in the past, been characterized or classified as some kind of psychiatric disorder by the Psychiatric Association?

A: I think it used to be but not anymore.

Q: Do you know approximately when that opinion was changed?

A: Oh, probably since the end of World War II.[12]

Q: Do you personally subscribe to a psychiatric opinion as to whether or not homosexuality is a disorder or not?

A: Well, it is considered a sexual disorder.

Q: Do you consider it a psychiatric disorder?

A: Well, I would have to ask you what you mean by "psychiatric disorder"?

Q: Does the American Association or your national association of psychiatry have a listing of disorders, particularly psychiatric disorders?

A: Yes.

Q: Do you feel that homosexuals should be classed among that list?

A: Well, you didn't answer my question as to what you call a psychiatric disorder. I said it is classified among the sexual disorders. It is not considered a mental illness if that is what you are driving at.

Q: Do you ever seek to treat patients that come to you who are homosexuals for that homosexuality?

A: No, the homosexuals that I see come for other reasons. For example, I recently saw one that was very depressed because his lover rejected him. I suppose in a sense that is because of his homosexuality. I treated him for depression not for the homosexuality. I don't know how to treat homosexuality. Most of them — not all of them — don't want treatment. Sometimes they come in because they have guilt feelings about it.

Q: In your opinion, can psychiatrists offer treatment for homosexuals with status as homosexuals?

A: I don't know of any. . . .

Q: Doctor, if some of the staff members from Park Point Manor were to indicate to you that they had consistent success in communicating with Sharon Kowalski on very elementary terms, would you feel that possibly, given your knowledge or background —

A: Oh, sure, you can communicate with animals. . . .

Q: If Sharon Kowalski would consistently indicate that she wanted to visit with Karen Thompson, would that change your opinion as to whether or not Karen Thompson should be permitted to visit her?

A: Well, if she was consistent in that reply and all others, yes. . . .

Q: But it is your opinion at this point in time, based on the records, she was not consistent in all others?

A: That is right.[13]

Cowan told the court that if Karen Thompson were to refrain from discussing issues of homosexuality and issues of the controversy between her and Sharon's parents, he might allow visitation on "a neutral basis without discussion of a personal nature." Finally, Hayes elicited that the witness had spent only ten minutes with Sharon the day before the hearing but had talked to the nurse for twenty.

Because of time constraints, the Kowalskis' counsel, who had eaten up the morning hours with his witnesses, volunteered to submit the testimony of his other two witnesses — Don and Della — by affidavit. Ristvedt, in fact, was planning to call Don as an adverse witness anyway. Calling for a recess until one o'clock, the judge arose from his swivel chair behind the dais and went to his office to eat his lunch and comb through a snarl of discovery documents. The judge was beginning to realize this "hearing" was at some fundamental level inaudible; the case was becoming more contentious as more time passed. The need to appoint a sole and final guardian was becoming paramount — the animosity between these parties was growing more unhealthy by the hour. The choice might ultimately be an arbitrary one, but at least it would create some continuity to Sharon's life.

Karen Thompson slowly walked out of the courtroom, engrossed in conversation with her attorney. She had heard this so-called expert pass judgment on her (to whom he had never even spoken) and Sharon (with whom he had spent about fifteen minutes), and she noticed that her lawyer had not objected to any of Fena's ridiculously hypothetical questions. Sure, Karen told Beth, she had told Sharon what was going on in court, when Sharon said she wanted to hear, and, yes, she had read her the articles, when Sharon assented, but she had been doing as much since the beginning of the case. Beth tried to calm her client, assuring her that the judge could see through Fena's expert as someone without thorough knowledge of the case. The problem was Fena's attempt to turn Sharon into a completely incompetent child who was incapable of making decisions for herself and therefore in need of a return to the bosom of her biological family. That was his strategy, and if it worked, it would negate the ten or fifteen affidavits on file from nurses, therapists, and friends who stated that Sharon loved Karen and wanted Karen in her life. Yet even if the court saw fit to negate Sharon's capacity entirely, Ristvedt argued, it could not overlook Karen's devotion and success in working with Sharon, a success greater than that of family or doctor. Ristvedt's direct examination of her client would have to make that perfectly clear.

The Kowalskis must have been more than pleased with the performance of their lawyers, who had given their daughter Debbie an opportunity to tell their side of the story to a court of law and had found an expert who recognized Thompson's bad effect on their daughter. Fena reminded his client Don to just answer the questions on the stand, not to volunteer any information, and if he did not understand a question, to ask the lawyer to repeat it. Don must have been wondering why in the hell he was in this predicament. During the entire lunch hour the same question ate away at him — a retired man, living a quiet life on the Range, suddenly fighting to maintain the solidarity of his family in the face of so-called American justice.

"Please raise your right hand," the clerk droned after the group had reassembled in the yellowed halls of courtroom 6 at one-thirty. "Do you solemnly swear to tell the truth, the whole truth, and nothing but the truth, so help you God?"

"I do," Don Kowalski replied. Ristvedt was on her feet. She was calling Don as an adverse witness in part to try to prove his own incompetence as a guardian, his irrational animosity toward her client, and, by contrast, the overwhelming superiority of her client.[14]

Ms. RISTVEDT: Have you ever told her [Sharon] that you are seeking to have Karen removed from her life?

DONALD KOWALSKI: No, I haven't.

Q: Why haven't you told her that?

A: Because I think she has got enough to put up with without outside problems.

Q: Do you think that Sharon would be upset if she knew that you were seeking to have Karen removed from all contact with her?

A: I don't know.

Q: Are you aware that Sharon has indicated to Dr. Moller that Karen is important to her?

MR. FENA: This is going to be objected to. Are you quoting from some medical record?

Ms. RISTVEDT: The affidavit that you submitted [of Dr. Moller's exam]. . . . Mr. Kowalski, are you aware of any responses that Sharon has made to Dr. Moller regarding Karen Thompson?

MR. FENA: Your Honor.

Ms. RISTVEDT: I'm just asking if he is aware of any.

THE COURT: The question is, are you aware of any responses that Sharon may have made to Dr. Moller about Karen Thompson?

DONALD KOWALSKI: Yes, I read the medical records of Dr. Moller.

Ms. RISTVEDT: Are you aware in there that Dr. Moller thinks that Karen Thompson is a good friend?

A: No, I'm not. . . .

MR. SPELLACY: Your Honor, I'll object to this line of questioning on the basis that I think it is improper impeachment. Dr. Moller may have some observations and this witness has different observations. I don't think it is proper this witness be impeached by what another witness has said.

THE COURT: Overruled to this extent that she just asked whether he is aware of the report. It is appropriate since the guardian is in charge here and let's find out from him what he knows. . . .

Ms. RISTVEDT: Are you aware that Sharon has indicated to one of the nurses at Park Point Manor that Karen is a loved one? . . .

MR. FENA: I object to that and I think the witness should be given further foundation like who, when, where, and at least some little bit of help on it, Your Honor. It is a rather self-serving question.

THE COURT: I don't know if it is self-serving. He certainly can identify more specifically the number of nurses there. . . .

Ms. RISTVEDT: Have you read the depositions [of nurses Mary Kay Hewitt and Ann Pellman] and exhibits attached to the depositions?

DONALD KOWALSKI: No, I haven't. . . .

Q: Do you believe that Karen is a loved one of Sharon?

A: No.

Q: As a general statement, do you believe that loved ones are important in Sharon's recovery?

A: Yes.

Q: Would you agree that as Sharon's guardian, one of your responsibilities is to act in the best interest of Sharon?

A: Yes.

Q: Under what circumstances would you come to believe that Karen is important to Sharon? Is there anything that could convince you?

A: I haven't seen anything. . . .

Q: Since last fall you have brought three motions to remove contact between Karen and Sharon, is that correct?

A: That is correct. . . .

Q: If you are not successful today, will you continue to work towards that goal?

A: I will.[15]

Ristvedt had no further questions. Fena rose to cross-examine his own client, whom he and Kevin Spellacy had attempted to protect from exposure during opposing counsel's questioning. He began with questions about the deposition of Jane Russell, the nurse who wrote the note calling Thompson "very vicious," and recalled overhearing Karen say to the psychologist that Sharon was imprisoned in Park Point and "brainwashed" by her parents. Donald acknowledged reading the nurse's note by Russell and through a set of leading questions denied ever attempting to brainwash Sharon or denigrate Thompson in his daughter's presence. Don then proceeded to corroborate the testimony of his daughter Debbie, recollecting that Thompson became "so bossy" that he had to call her out of the intensive care room and tell her "for cripes sake! to quit irritating Sharon like that." He stated that the treating physician, Dr. Brix, volunteered to order Thompson out of the hospital, but Don decided at that point to allow her to stay even though "I had to ask her if she would let the family at least have a little time with their daughter alone, and she would not give it to us — never."[16]

Donald's assessment of his daughter's prognosis was, he believed, realistically pessimistic. The doctors, he stated, "don't feel Sharon is going to get any better and that she is in a state that probably she will stay in, but we pray all the time and hope that Sharon is going to get better and someday be able to make her decisions." He hoped that someday Sharon would be able to return to the family's forty-acre spread on the Range, where he had retired four years earlier from Hanna Mining Company. He had given plots on the property to two of his children and had hoped to give one to Sharon. After denying any knowledge of Sharon's contributions to the mortgage at Briggs Lake, where she was living with Thompson, Fena changed tacks:

> MR. FENA: Are you aware that nurses have testified under oath that Sharon is embarrassed when Thompson talked to her about being gay and makes comments about what kind of love they are going to have?
> DONALD KOWALSKI: Yes. . . .
> Q: I want to know if you are aware of it because Mr. Hayes asked you, or Ms. Ristvedt asked you if you would keep working towards that goal to ban Thompson, and you said "yes.". . . Are those the reasons?
> A: That is the reason.
> Q: Are you doing it just because she said she is gay? Do you really care?
> A: I don't care. It really doesn't mean much to Sharon now what she was.
> Q: Is she in diapers?
> A: She is in diapers. . . .
> Q: She is a totally helpless person?
> A: Totally helpless.[17]

Counsel had no further questions, but when Ristvedt announced that she had two more witnesses, Judge Douglas decided the court would stay in session in the evening, reconvening at five-thirty until the hearing was done. He told the attorneys to be back in fifteen minutes, ready to proceed, then stood and left the court. Douglas went back into chambers and began to peruse the discovery. He glanced at the deposition of Mary Hewitt, a licensed nurse-practitioner of twenty-five years, who had never heard Karen directly denigrating the quality of care at Park Point. But Hewitt did state that there had been confrontations between Thompson and the staff, and that Thompson was very critical of the type of wheelchair the home provided. Hewitt also heard Thompson say some "negative things" in Sharon's presence — particularly about the fact that the home was allowing Sharon to go on outings with her parents but not with her. When questioned about the issue of sexual orientation, Hewitt related that there were "times when I'll be in the room" when Karen "will make comments to the fact of being gay, or there was a time where she had made a comment about what kind of liberty she could take with her." Sharon, Hewitt testified, seemed "embarrassed" when Karen, right before bedtime, made some flirtatious comments about "how far" she would go with Sharon. "A lot of times when Sharon doesn't like what she's hearing or it bothers her, she closes her eyes and turns her head and that's what she did," Hewitt stated.[18]

Douglas also came across the deposition of Bruce Erickson, Sharon's nurse's aide, who had been an army medic. He stated that Sharon responded more favorably to Thompson than to anyone else. Karen was the only one who could get her to open her mouth for a toothbrush, and Sharon seemed to get mad when Karen left without taking her.[19] A former licensed nurse-practitioner, Joan Shelhon, stated in an affidavit that the young adult unit at Park Point was violent — fist fights between male patients, assaults on nurses, sexual advances on nurses, tearing of drinking fountains out of the walls. Shelhon declared that during her visit to Park Point Manor on April 27, 1985, Sharon had typed that "she wanted to make love with Karen Thompson" and "played scrabble, making small words" with herself and Karen, who was present. In the middle of their visit, Shelhon wrote, "there was an altercation right outside Sharon's door between a male resident and an orderly that frightened Sharon a great deal. She typed on the typewriter that this happens frequently and she is frightened by this."[20]

Karen Thompson spent the recess in tumult. During Donald's previous testimony, she had barely been able keep back her tears. She felt disrespected, demonized, denigrated, all because she was doing her best to take care of her lover. Was anyone going to stand up for Sharon's rights and insist that she receive optimum care from a first-rate, safe institution, or more advantageously, from a home that Karen wanted to make for her? Her lawyer again tried to calm her client, telling Karen that their case was just starting and they would have ample time to demonstrate how vindictive Fena was, how much Sharon loved her and wanted to be with her. Opposing counsel had painted a picture of her client — prejudicial and stereotyped though it was — as a borderline hysteric and control freak who was trying to keep Sharon from the bosom of her family. The overbearing lesbian was a stereotype that fit well into most people's mental frames for understanding difference by placing Karen on the margin of normalcy. Ristvedt would have to prove during the next round of testimony that Karen was socially reliable and capable in spite of the opinions of a judiciary that still failed to acknowledge ingrained homophobia.

Jack Fena and Kevin Spellacy probably left the courtroom quite pleased with the outcome so far. Debbie and Don had been salt-of-the-earth witnesses, demonstrating their genuine and solid concern for a member of their immediate family whom they wanted to protect from the machinations of a disruptive out-of-towner, someone who felt she could just steal Sharon away from her roots on the Range and turn her into a Cities lesbian. Fena told the Kowalskis they could head back home, that he could handle the rest of the hearing through cross-examination. He told Don they would submit further affidavits to fill in any gaps in the testimony, including the names of nurses he had talked to and what they had said. He was also planning to call Dr. Moller and have her write another letter.

In 1996, I had come to the Center for Feminist Research in Los Angeles as a teacher and lawyer wishing to write the kind of book that would show rather than analyze the dilemma of the Sharon Kowalski case. As I waded through documents related to the case, I began to realize that it was impossible to divorce my retelling from my own versions of justice. I also wondered how a literary critic would be able to present what happened without rising to the temptation of saying why. How could a gay man, raised in the comfortable suburbs of California, be able to understand the feelings of an Iron Range father who grew up working in the mines? How could the common ground of same-sex orientation be enough for a man to take the side of a woman? How many people really believed that gender was primarily a social construction, infused with myths of naturalism? Was it fair for an asymptomatic HIV-positive man to identify with the mental and physical disability of Sharon Kowalski? Over-reaching these concerns was my desire to tell a story that had embedded within its intricacies all the ethical dilemmas the social fabric of America was facing with laws like the Defense of Marriage Act (DOMA), with the alarming suicide rate of gay teens, with Exodus, the Christian organization that purported to convert homosexuals to lovers of Jesus.

Whose side, as a gay man, could I possibly take in this social debate? The answer to this rhetorical question itself presupposed a confluence between political and sexual orientation. Not every practitioner of same-sex behavior championed gay rights; in fact, there was a legacy of conservative gays who now were in the limelight of the alternative media, following in the footsteps of people like J. Edgar Hoover, Roy Cohn (right-wing lawyer and onetime McCarthy aide in the fifties), and Arthur Finklestein, the millionaire political consultant who lived with his longtime companion, Charley Manning, and their two children in an iron-gated estate in Ipswich, an exclusive suburb north of Boston. Finklestein had been instrumental in the reelection campaigns of Jesse Helms and Lauch Faircloth, as well as Bibi Netanyahu and Bob Dole, the very power brokers who championed the antigay agenda of the reactionary right.

There are many different kinds of lesbians and gay men in the world; perhaps this divergence could explain Karen Thompson's initial reluctance to talk to me on the phone after I had written her two letters. She treated me like yet another reporter in search of a story, trying to capitalize on the sensation of

Sharon's and her struggle to survive. And what was my motive anyway? Behind the sanctified vows of teaching tolerance and altruism, was there not an ego in search of publication, a professor in search of tenure? After considerable persistence, I finally managed to have a valuable discussion with Karen, whom I found personable and articulate, though cautious. She talked to me about her current struggles with health care, with reimbursement for disability, with federal and state bureaucracies. Karen told me that she wanted to write another book, this time about the travails of taking care of the disabled at home. Sharon, she related, was holding up fine, though as she asserted realistically, she sometimes was present and alert and sometimes was not — Sharon was Sharon. She had lost so much time in the protracted legal struggle that her condition was almost irreparable, but Karen still held out hope.

After a couple of calls, I talked Thompson into a bargain. A large majority of the medical and legal records in the case were presently at the foot of Potrero Hill in San Francisco in the offices of Deborah Chasnoff, the famous independent filmmaker *(It's Elementary)* who owned the rights to the story and had done lots of groundwork for an HBO special that never took place because it was deemed too controversial by executives at Time, Inc., when they bought the cable channel. I agreed to make a copy of the records and send them to Karen in exchange for access in San Francisco. Karen somewhat reluctantly agreed to allow me to travel up to Chasnoff's office.

I found other records — mostly periodical pieces — at the One Institute, the gay and lesbian archive in Los Angeles that was affiliated with the Center for Feminist Research. The archive, then housed on an alley in West Hollywood, was accessible only by yelling up to the second-floor window; the hours were variable, and the queers who staffed the crowded, dusty space made the steely Chasnoff seem like Mother Teresa. Eventually they got used to me, and I managed to find some mass mailings from the Committee to Free Sharon Kowalski that I wouldn't have located elsewhere.

My days were spent poring over records in the office space that was adjacent to the athletic track at USC. My nights were spent alone in a single bed in a rented room on Mount Washington, next to the Self-Realization Center in central L.A. Unrealized, my lover and I had broken up within a month of his moving to Los Angeles. I no longer knew what it was like to harbor the hopes of lifelong commitment, and though comparisons were indeed odious, I wondered how much weight the courts should lend to a four-year romance — lesbian or otherwise. How quickly lifetime commitments can crumble, how fragile the bonds of affinity through which we claim power and exclude others. Family, friends, partners, spouses — love's proclaimed but unstable connections — were the often flimsy foundation for disconnection and isolation.

SIX

Continued Hearing

Now in every matter they deal with, the laws aim either at the common benefit of all, or at the benefit of those in control, whose control rests on virtue or on some other such basis. And so in one way what we call just is whatever produces and maintains happiness and its parts for a political community.

Aristotle, *Nicomachean Ethics*

"Gay Friend, Parents Vie to See Patient," the *Duluth News-Tribune* entitled its front-page article on May 2, 1985. Described as a teacher who "claims she is the lesbian lover of Sharon Kowalski," Karen Thompson told the *News* that Sharon's recovery came to a halt as soon as she was moved from St. Cloud to Duluth. Before the transfer to the Nat G. Polinsky Memorial Rehabilitation Center, Karen insisted, Sharon "would try for me what she wouldn't try for anyone else" because "that's what love is"; now their separation made communication more difficult. But Jack Fena claimed Thompson's overbearing presence — not her absence — was the cause of Sharon's depression. The Kowalskis are "'strong, religious, deep-feeling people," the famous Iron Range attorney told reporters, whom Thompson has caused "the most excruciating mental anguish that anyone could describe." The adversarial legal system was giving the press ammunition for its dramatic storytelling, verbal fodder that was starting to produce as well as reflect the parties' rapid movement away from any conciliation.

As Judge Douglas sat in his office before the hearing reconvened, he glanced over a list of Sharon Kowalski's belongings, prepared by Karen Thompson, attached to the back of her lengthy deposition of April 22, 1985:

Honda motorcycle, Suzuki motorcycle, Tent, Sleeping bag, Tape recorder, Toaster, Jig saw, Ping pong table and net, Two pairs of cross-country skis and poles and boots (Linda Anderson had borrowed a pair of them from her before the accident), Bicycle, Two fishing poles and one-half fishing tackle, *Pool table, *Desk and chair and dresser set, Softball glove and ball, One leather jacket for motorcycle, Field guides (for wildflowers, edible plants, animal tracks), Garfield collection (six little ones and one medium), Three motorcycle helmets,

Igloo cooler, Rifle (or maybe it's a shotgun), Ski racks. (*Sharon bought these from me with the understanding that they would not leave the house. She wanted to own something since almost everything we have is actually mine, but if for any reason we ever separated, I would buy them back.)[1]

In many ways, this inventory told the whole story: the tragic irony of the permanent immobility of one whose life had revolved around mobility, the added twist that her accident did not occur, like so many of those suffered by athletes, during one of her sport pursuits but during a drive back to the place she did and did not call home — the Range. Karen Thompson's asterisks punctuated a relation of generosity and control.

That evening, when testimony resumed, Beth Ristvedt called to the witness stand Dr. Gail Gregor, a staff physician at Sister Kenny Institute in Minneapolis, specializing in physical rehabilitation primarily in cases of brain-injured patients, spinal cord injury, and stroke. The stocky, short-haired Gregor, who would become a major medical influence in the case, testified that she had worked with other traumatic brain-injured patients who had same-sex partners. "People get injured indiscriminately," she stated, and "it is not necessary to have blood ties to have a very significant beneficial effect on an injured person, and the converse is also true: many times family members are disruptive to the recovery process."[2] At Ristvedt's direction, Gregor concluded by focusing on Sharon's special relationship with Karen Thompson, which although in itself did not present an uncommon circumstance, was remarkable because of the extraordinary strength of the bond.

As Tom Hayes began his cross-examination, he discovered that Gregor had become involved in the case after being contacted by the Governor's Council for the Handicapped, the State Civil Rights Commission, and the Gay and Lesbian Legal Referral Service, all in a matter of two weeks. Board-certified in rehabilitation medicine since 1981, Dr. Gregor had never testified in court before, though she had given depositions. Although "usually tragedies like brain injuries" brought "people together of varying backgrounds and lifestyles," the doctor declared, "conflicts among family members or between loved ones related or unrelated can have a definite effect and a depression on someone with a brain injury." The usual medical model for overcoming such animosity was counseling, but "it sounds like we are all here today because that has failed or not been attempted," the doctor volunteered over Fena's objection as lacking foundation.[3]

The objection overruled, Hayes wanted to know whether or not it was beneficial to have one side or the other discussing the dispute on a consistent basis with the brain-injured person. Gregor answered that it depended on "how the information is being transmitted." She explained that a "brain-injured person's existence is as fragmented and disrupted, and those who recover enough to tell us what they remember of their experiences — it is very much like a dream state with memories out of sequence and out of chronological order with a very strong predominance of emotional reaction rather than fact." Gregor cautioned against trying to "eliminate conflict" or information, especially because interaction was crucial to avoid a deterioration of the injured person's ability to maintain relationships.[4]

On cross-examination, Mr. Fena elicited that Dr. Gregor had never interviewed the patient, though she had read some of her medical records. From what she could assess, Dr. Gregor was "having a hard time, after being here all day, understanding why family members would try to exclude a friend from visiting a friend." Fena proceeded to attempt to impeach the witness based on her familiarity with the case. She had not seen Dr. Goff's report but had seen other records and also requested information. At one point, Douglas was forced to interrupt the sparring doctor and lawyer as they argued over the availability of records: "Let me suggest this for both of you. Stop!" the court interjected. "I want one person to talk at a time." The examination continued:

MR. FENA: Now getting back to your statement where you could not imagine somebody wanting to exclude somebody, what is the effect, Doctor, in your judgment or experience of one of these so-called loved ones by making derogatory statements about the parents, and I am talking about Karen Thompson now making derogatory statements to Sharon about her parents?

A: I don't understand the question. Are you telling me that is a fact?

Q: I am asking you to assume that fact. Would that be significant?

A: It would be a concern.

Q: Right, and if you were the attending physician and the nurses on duty were to tell you that Karen Thompson was making negative — and giving negative messages to Sharon, would that also be a concern to you — yes or no, please?

A: That is not a yes or no question.

Q: Okay, go ahead and answer it the way you want.

A: As a physician — as a treating physician for a person such as Sharon with a brain injury, the information from the nursing staff about conflicts, or about negative information would be a concern and would need further investigation medically.

Q: Medically?

A: Uh-huh, because the treatment of a brain-injured person includes all significant others, so I would be concerned about the nature of those communications, where it is coming from and what else is going on in that person's life.[5]

When Fena asked Dr. Gregor about the possible adverse effect on Sharon if Karen Thompson told her that her parents were keeping her prisoner and that she was in a nursing home only because she was gay, the expert replied that she would have a greater concern "about the professionalism of the nurse communicating that information." Fena told Gregor that the nurse provided the information "under subpoena like you are here testifying in court to tell the truth," but Dr. Gregor stood her ground. She was as concerned about the "the nurse making those observations" as she would be about whether "the loved one was having some difficulty with the adjustment and needed help."[6]

Sword-crossing continued over Fena's questions about the Christmas photos he had entered into evidence as exhibit 1 when Debbie Kowalski was testifying. Counsel wanted to know if Dr. Gregor saw "depression" in the photos of Sharon smiling. "I cannot make a diagnosis or an assessment of depression on the basis of a photograph," Gregor insisted, while Fena maintained that "those photographs show Sharon having a good time, relaxed." The doctor refused to use "those adjectives," and the arguing continued without objection from opposing counsel:

> MR. FENA: Come on, you are a doctor, you treated these people. What do you see in those photographs.?
> DR. GREGOR: I see a brain-injured person in a family portrait visiting with people and neighbors at a Christmas party.
> Q: Happy?
> A: There are smiles on Sharon's face, yes.
> Q: I didn't ask you if there were smiles on a face. Does she look happy?
> A: Yes. . . .
> Q: She doesn't look depressed to you, does she?
> A: No, but you can't tell by looking at a still picture whether a person is depressed or not. It is a behavioral diagnosis. . . .
> Q: Doctor, counsel [Dr. Cowan] said that he thought it would be devastating for Sharon to hear her parents condemned by Karen Thompson. Do I take it you don't agree with that?
> A: I disagree.
> Q: Yes or no.
> THE COURT: She is trying to answer. Let her give her answers.
> MR. FENA: All right, the lawyer asks her questions.
> A: I think I would disagree with the previous medical expert on the cognitive abilities of Sharon and the cognitive abilities of Sharon are the necessary medical information to determine a devastating reaction, or any reaction to sensory input, social or informational.
> MR. FENA: I move it be stricken as not responsive.
> THE COURT: Denied.[7]

On redirect examination, Ristvedt asked Dr. Gregor whether she would eliminate Karen Thompson's visitation even if all of Fena's assumptions were true. The answer, of course, was no, that a loved one like Thompson should be worked with. On further cross, Hayes elicited from the doctor that Sharon's preferences for visitors and for places she wanted to live could be expected to be variable. "One of the most consistent things about brain injury is inconsistency," she stated. But such questions are not futile, she continued, and need to be asked again and again in order to assess the trend of the answers. After the doctor stepped down, the court ordered a short recess for all to regroup after the contentious testimony.

Karen Thompson's direct examination on May 3 began with an open-ended question from her attorney Beth Ristvedt about whether Karen had any idea why the nursing home personnel at Park Point (Mary Kay Hewitt and Jane Russell) felt that some of the subjects that Karen discussed in front of Sharon were having a negative impact. Nervous but confident, Karen stated that she thought none of the "things" she was telling Sharon were "negative." Karen believed it was all "a matter of interpretation" of the "facts." When she met Sharon in the room, Karen testified, she typically oriented her by asking questions such as "Sharon, do you know where you are?" Sharon sometimes gave a correct response and sometimes did not. Occasionally, Sharon would ask, "Why am I here?" and Karen would tell her that she was there because the court order placed her in Duluth and that had come about because her parents wanted her to be there. Sharon often told Karen to "take me out" or "please get me out of here," and Karen responded by explaining again that "there is an order preventing me from being able to do that."[8]

Thompson's frustration in dealing with her partner's desire to get out of the nursing home was now commonplace. When Sharon would type "take me home" on her machine, Karen patiently had to explain again that she was doing everything possible to take her home, which the petitioner understood to be St. Cloud. But Sharon continued to be frustrated, sometimes typing or handwriting, even when other people were in the room, "Karen, make love to me." When Thompson was forced to "reject her" partner, Sharon invariably became "very upset with me. My hands are tied. There is little I can do with Sharon in that nursing home." Thompson told the court that she had "constantly told Sharon she needs the love and support of her parents and of her family," but Sharon continued to be concerned about choosing between people and thought Karen was leaving for good every time they said good-bye. "Generally speaking, she grabs hold of my hand so tight that I literally have to pull my hand out of hers and normally [when] she does that, when she grabs hold, she will turn her head away and she then won't respond to anything else I am saying."[9]

Thompson's testimony was then interrupted by the judge, who had an appointment and continued the hearing again until May 9. In the meantime, at the behest of Hayes, Spellacy, and Fena, the court ordered that the videotapes and photo album held by the court as exhibits not be released from the clerk's office under any conditions. The judge's concern about the release of images to the press mirrored the alarm Jack Fena and the Kowalskis had shown over the increased media spotlight. Fena had complained about and attached to his own declaration copies of a recent *Duluth News-Tribune* series entitled "Making a Life Together: Gay Couples Share Same Dreams as Heterosexual Couples" (Laurie Hertzel-Schleppenbach and others, March 25, 1985, sec. A, p. 5). As part of their coverage of gay life in Duluth, the staff reporters for this feature had juxtaposed an article on Karen and Sharon with a longer piece entitled "Being Gay Is No Big Deal to Trucker," the story of an anonymous gay man in Duluth who had moved "from San Francisco three years ago" and "shatters the limp-wristed image of a big-city homosexual."

Bill's pseudonymous story was not Sharon's, but there were similarities. "At 25, the burly trucker finds Duluth a nice place to be," the feature writers began, "despite the outpourings of hatred he's seen toward gay people, especially last fall during debate over the human rights ordinance proposed and later defeated here." Unemployed, Bill did not want his own name to be used "because publicity could make it harder to find a job." In spite of the hatred, he wanted to stay in Duluth because of "the slower life." He didn't like "life in the fast lane" in San Francisco. "It's pretty here, it's cheap to live and (there isn't any) AIDS." Duluth could be a "tough town for a gay person who looks the part," he told the *News-Tribune*. "You can't flaunt it. You just can't walk around in lavender shorts. It just doesn't cut it."

Born and raised in Philadelphia, Bill was the only child of strict Baptists. At an early age he knew he was different — he "liked the father on (the television show) *Lost in Space*" — and by high school realized he was gay, "but kept it secret until he joined the Navy." He complacently informed his interviewers that the Navy knew about his orientation: "If you don't make a big deal, they don't care," he said. But when Bill started to make a big deal — marching in parades and speaking out — he was discharged; soon after he left San Francisco, in part because he "was starting to act too gay. It wasn't me. It was like I copied people around me. But I watch the Super Bowl. I eat at McDonald's. I'm just like anybody else. I just like to go to be with men," Bill stated.

His story was typical of gays and lesbians, like Sharon and Karen, all over Middle America. Bill's parents, he reported, still didn't understand him. "Everyone said, 'Tell them, tell them, it's great to be gay.' My mother threatened to commit suicide. They're Baptist. Fundamental Baptist. They blame the

Navy. They blame San Francisco. They made me go see a psychiatrist. They still try to fix me up with pretty girls when I go home," Bill complained. In the next breath he told the *News-Tribune*, "Being gay isn't your whole life. It's just your preference for sex. It's not that big a deal. It's nobody's business. I don't feel it's that different."

In a column adjacent to Bill's story in the Duluth paper, "Custody Case Tests Laws on Relationships" discussed Sharon's case as an example of the legal problems lesbians and gays face in legitimizing their relationships. "With scant legal documentation of their relationship, Thompson has a problem that could eventually confront many unmarried couples living together." She had been forced as a result of Sharon's sudden disability to reveal "deep secrets about their personal life," in part because the state does not permit same-sex marriage. The revelation of such secrets, moreover, led to the charge by the Kowalskis that Thompson's bid for guardianship was endangering the physical and moral safety of a daughter reduced to the capacity of a six-year-old. "It's about a person who's totally helpless trying to be controlled and taken over under some demonic claim," Fena told reporters (Laurie Hertzel-Schleppenbach and others, "Custody Case Tests Laws on Relationships," *Duluth News-Tribune*, March 25, 1985, sec. A, p. 5).

When court resumed at one-thirty on May 9, Jack Fena was present but Kevin Spellacy was not; the latter had officially withdrawn from representation of the Kowalskis for reasons that were never articulated. From this point forward, Fena would remain counsel of record in both the personal injury and the guardianship matter.

Ristvedt resumed the direct examination of her client. She wanted Karen Thompson to explain why she felt the environment at Park Point was "combative." Thompson testified that "there have been loud disruptions where somebody walked into the room when I have been there and it has happened dozens of times where somebody walked into the room right up to within a couple of inches of you and even grabbed hold of you and/or yelling incoherent types of things to you." When Karen was there, she was able to send them out of the room with a firm warning, but she worried about "what happens when Sharon is there by herself." Thompson categorically denied having told Sharon that she was in a "violent environment" or that "her life was in danger," questioning opposing counsel's hypothetical assumptions in previous testimony.[10]

Thompson's testimony about communication with Sharon also belied the experts. She used the "hand method," in which Sharon moved her hand to answer yes or no, as well as a little lap typewriter. Karen claimed she talked with Sharon about everything from "A to Z." Ristvedt then steered the examination toward a central issue:

Q: Have you and Sharon ever discussed the issue of being gay?
A: Yes, we have.
Q: Were you present in the courtroom last Friday when Sharon's father indicated that based on information that he had from the doctors and his personal information, he did not feel that Sharon was capable of knowing what that meant?
A: Yes. . . .
Q: Have you and Sharon ever discussed the meaning, and do you feel she knows what she is talking about when she refers to the word "gay"?
A: Yes, I do believe she knows what it means when we use the word "gay." I think it has been very important for me to establish whether or not Sharon understands that and exactly where Sharon and I are. I will ask Sharon what our relationship is and she will either type "gay" or she will type "lovers." On different occasions and like if she types "lovers," then I will ask her "are we gay?" Then she will say, "yes." Then I would say, "what does it mean to be gay?" Then normally her response to that is "us." Then I will say, "okay, we are gay, what does it actually mean?" On two or three different occasions, Sharon typed the word "queer." Then I said, "do you really believe we are queer, Sharon?" She types, "no." Then I said, "so can you actually define it for me, Sharon? Tell me what it means to you?" What she has consistently responded has been "lovers, same sex."
Q: Is this something that is fairly recent that you have discussed with Sharon?
A: I discussed it again last night.[11]

Karen had been discussing the case and their sexual orientation since the accident, so Sharon's depression could hardly be attributable to such disclosures, she reasoned. Ristvedt's concluded direct examination had established Karen Thompson as a formidable, thorough witness, dedicated to Sharon with a zealousness that was both admirable and potentially overwhelming. Karen's long, methodical answers served as indications of her desire both to tell the whole story and to make sure that her side of the story was perfectly clear. She ascribed to Sharon a clarity of mind that by some accounts might be oversanguine, but her optimism was not uncorroborated.

When Hayes began his cross-examination, his focus provided an insight into how he was approaching the case. He saw the evidence of a "very vicious" Thompson by the Park Point nurses, even if already contradicted by Karen, as the major sticking point to her credibility. Thompson insisted that she had no problem with the staff at Park Point. When asked about the truth of the depositions of Ann Pellman and Jane Russell, she replied, "I did not agree with what they were saying. My interpretation of what is negative and theirs obviously differ. So if you are saying, did I think what they are saying was true, no, I did not, but I think it was open to their interpretation versus mine." Thompson refused to state that the nurses were lying but speculated that "homophobia runs deep in our society and I don't know where they stand in relationship to their feelings on Sharon's and my relationship, and how that might influence or how they perceive different situations."[12] Hayes's questioning had sharpened the focus of the conflicting evidence, which the judge would have to evaluate for credibility.

The coast was now clear for one of the first major courtroom confrontations between two of the strongest personalities in the case: Jack Fena, Iron Range ex-legislator and litigator, and Karen Thompson, women's sports coach and born-again lesbian. Fena began by discussing the complaints that were now mounting about the quality of care at Park Point. Initially, Karen admitted that she had talked with Arnold Rosenthal at the State Department of Health about conditions at Park Point, including the missing emergency string for Sharon to access—a patient's right under the Handicapped Bill of Rights. She also spoke to him about other problems at Park Point, claiming that her discussions were confidential. Ristvedt made no objections. Fena then handed Karen Thompson a copy of guardian's exhibit 3, a note that Karen had sent to Sharon's parents after the move to Duluth:

MR. FENA: Is that your writing?
A: A long time ago, yes.
Q: Did you tell things such as you wrote on this yellow piece of paper to Sharon about her parents?
A: I would have to read that again to know exactly what is there.
Q: Having in mind that you testified that you discussed everything with Sharon, do you tell her things like you wrote on that paper?
A: Well, this here was concerning clothing removed from our house. No, I have not talked to her about that. . . .
Q: "Hope you're having no problems sleeping at night and living with yourselves for the pain you are causing Sharon?" [reading from the exhibit]
A: Why—
Q: "And the set-back in progress caused by this move?"
A: I am terribly frustrated. They wouldn't talk with me in person so I left them that note—
Q: Well, wait until I finish: "have a good week." Is that what your attitude towards these parents that you tell Sharon or you claim to tell Sharon to love them, and is that typical of your attitude toward them, Karen?
A: No.
Q: That is just something that you wrote out of frustration, I suppose?
A: I wrote that to them trying to hope I would get a response that we could sit down and talk, but they wouldn't talk with me. . . .
Q: Okay, are you aware that Dr. Moller has recommended that your visits are

> not in the best interest of Sharon Kowalski and that she is a highly vulnerable adult and that your visits are disruptive and harmful and you are aware of that, are you not?
>
> Ms. RISTVEDT: I object to that question. The reports have not been admitted in evidence and I am going to object to their admittance. Perhaps we should take care of that issue first.[13]

Jack Fena was attempting to introduce two new medical reports on opposing counsel unannounced. Although he had spoken to Ristvedt the day before about Dr. Moller's letter, he had not yet informed the other side about Dr. Goff's letter of May 8. With good reason, Ristvedt objected to the admission of the medical reports into evidence; she was given little or no time to review the documents or depose the witnesses who made the statements in them. The production of documents at the last minute violated the rules of discovery in civil procedure, which required that both sides disclose all their documents well in advance of trial to allow each party to "discover" or be apprised of the evidence against them *before* the trial, thus often obviating the need for court proceedings — in theory, anyway. Ristvedt also claimed that the reports were unreliable. Goff's report was based on Cowan's report, which relied on nurses' notes and not firsthand observations he had made. Cowan, she argued, was basing his opinions on statements he had no way of verifying. "I think clearly this is a grandstand approach to get doctors who are obviously under Mr. Fena and the family's control to come up with an opinion that supports their opinion," Ristvedt told the court.[14]

The court reminded counsel that these doctors, Goff and Moller, had been treating physicians for some time and were not necessarily Mr. Fena's hired guns, suggesting that Ristvedt could have deposed them earlier. Douglas then asked for Mr. Hayes's opinion about this late introduction of medical reports by the treating physicians. Hayes believed that the court should accept them with the proviso that the parties understand that they were not made under oath, were filed late, and had not been subject to due process, namely, the right to cross-examination. Hayes suggested that Fena have the reports turned into sworn statements or affidavits and then allow Ristvedt to present counteraffidavits.

Judge Douglas decided to take a ten-minute recess to look at the reports. By getting these unquestioned documents in front of the judge, Fena had struck a major blow to Karen Thompson's case. No doubt the "relaxation" of the rules of evidence in domestic relations cases made that judge's decision to consider all evidence, no matter how procedurally tainted, justifiable, but the content of the reports was strong and condemnatory. In his letter, Dr. Steven K. Goff, doctor of physical medicine and rehabilitation, wrote that he had "discussed" the situation of Sharon Kowalski at Park Point Manor with Dr. Cowan, Dr. Moller, and the head nurses at Park Point.[15] "Doctor Cowan," Goff stated, "reported that he had indeed documented negative responses on the part of the patient to statements made specifically by Karen Thompson. We are both in agreement," he continued, "that the current cognitive status of Sharon does not allow for any sophisticated interpretation on her part of statements made to her by others." Based on his own assessment and those of the other two physicians, he concurred "that accessibility to Sharon on the part of Karen Thompson should be eliminated."

Dr. Julie Moller wrote a less Orwellian piece that nonetheless came to the same conclusion. As a staff doctor, she saw Sharon briefly once a month. "On my visit May 6th, 1985, she was noncommunicative and appeared depressed. I conferred with the nurses who take care of her; they tell me that after Miss Karen Thompson's visits with the patient she seems more depressed and curls up in a fetal position. The nurses consider Miss Thompson's visits as abusive to a vulnerable adult." Dr. Moller wrote to Fena, "In my opinion, the visits of Miss Karen Thompson are disruptive and harmful and therefore not in the best interest of the patient."

After reading the documents, the judge quickly returned to the bench, reconvened the hearing, and announced that he had overruled Ristvedt's objection, allowing the documents into the record with the proviso that Thompson's attorney had the right to depose the physicians in the future. Fena then resumed his questioning by returning to the issue of gay rights, which the two had discussed in Karen's deposition:

> MR. FENA: Maybe this will be my last question. You have said on occasion, Karen, this contest or trial here is not a gay rights issue, isn't that true?
> A: I had tried to say it should not be, yes.
> Q: Yes, and you are not — you agree with me that you are not asking the court to decide this case on a gay rights issue, are you?
> A: No, I am asking it on the basis of what is medically best for Sharon.
> Q: But it is not, just so we understand?
> A: I believe that I should have certain rights.
> Q: I understand, but —
> A: Based on our relationship, I would hope that it doesn't make it a gay rights issue.
> Q: Can we agree, or do you agree with me, you heard me say it is not a gay rights issue? . . .
> A: I don't know. In fact, if that is just some way people are dealing with things.
> Q: Forget the others. Can you and I agree that this really is not a gay rights issue, that it makes no difference if Sharon is or is not gay, it makes no difference if you are gay or not?
> A: I believe it does make a difference if Sharon is because that means who might be important to Sharon, who might be important for the recovery process.

Q: And then you feel then that it is because —

A: We can't eliminate who we are. . . .

Q: Well, which do you lean more to, that it isn't a gay rights issue, you said that, or —

A: It is a human rights and handicapped rights issue.

Q: We can leave it at that, that it is a human rights issue?

A: We can leave it at that, yes.

Q: We can forget that it may or may not be a gay rights issue, can we have that here?

A: I don't know that it can be totally forgotten. There are issues that involve Sharon and Sharon's care.

Q: Have you been trying to make that into a gay rights issue?

A: No, I have not.

Q: Actually you do agree with me that this is not and should not be a gay rights issue?

A: To an extent, yes, I do.[16]

Thompson and Fena's tug-of-war over the issue of gay rights highlighted the conflict over competing portrayals of Karen's relationship to Sharon — lesbian partner or roommate? Thompson's reluctant agreement to subsume the primacy of their same-sex love under human rights — however principled — allowed the court to overlook their de facto marriage.

The closing arguments that followed were brief. Fena requested that his client be appointed unlimited guardian of his beloved daughter; Hayes argued that Donald continue to be guardian but that visitation by Thompson continue with the proviso that discussion of the litigation in front of Sharon be prohibited. Beth Ristvedt asked to submit a trial brief as closing argument rather than do so orally. She wanted to comment on the discovery gathered after depositions of Goff and Moller.

As it turned out, a flurry of other testimony arrived by affidavit in the time between the end of the second hearing on May 9, 1985, and the date of Douglas's decision on July 23. An affidavit from Donald Kowalski, again appearing after his testimony on May 5 and without cross-examination, stated that he was present at the hearing when "Thompson quoted my daughter as saying 'make love to me.' I and my wife Della now not only have the continuing and even deeper fear that Sharon will be sexually abused by Karen Thompson, but we both believe and know that our daughter Sharon would be totally incapable, due to her severe brain injury, of having such thoughts and would never make such a statement."[17] This affidavit was supplemented by a declaration from Kenneth Krossen, forty-five-year-old patient at Park Point whose profession was heavy equipment operator and truck driver. Injured in an auto accident himself, Mr. Krossen stated that on "Sunday, May 12, 1985, I observed Karen Thompson take Sharon Kowalski into the bathroom at Park Point Manor and close the door. Thompson gave Sharon a bath. I could see this had happened when they came out. They were behind the closed door for at least thirty minutes and I stayed and observed all the time Karen Thompson had Sharon behind the bathroom door. I will state to the Court that I have read about the Karen Thompson dispute and I along with other nursing home patients at Park Point are concerned for Sharon Kowalski's safety and her vulnerability to sexual abuse."[18]

Ristvedt countered with an affidavit from Dr. Gregor, who stated that "based upon my experience and education it is normal and natural for a brain-injured person to make their sexual desires known particularly to those who may have been former lovers. Brain-injured patients often have a disinhibition regarding sexual matters and their comments and action may or may not be socially appropriate action or responses."[19] Karen's lawyer also provided deposition testimony of the two doctors in an effort to undermine the credibility of Goff's and Moller's letters. Julie Moller, an internist who attended over one hundred Duluth Clinic patients at Lakeshore Lutheran Home and Park Point Manor, saw each patient approximately once a month for a few minutes, "entailing primarily speaking with the nurses about care, finding out if there are any problems as far as they're concerned in any way, and then seeing Sharon and talking briefly." Moller admitted she based her opinions on the nurse's assessment: "Ann tells me that following these visits by Miss Thompson they feel that Sharon is more withdrawn and appears — appears more depressed."[20]

Goff admitted in deposition that Sharon received benefits from Karen, that there was very good interaction between the two of them, and that Karen provided stimulation, caring, and good nursing care. His decision about "elimination" of Thompson was based on an acceptance of the statements of Dr. Cowan, which he did not investigate. Dr. Goff also indicated, Ristvedt pointed out, that he would not normally recommend that a husband or wife be excluded without first having given that person an opportunity to discuss the situation with him, though in this case he had never talked to Karen Thompson.[21] Furthermore, the opinions of Dr. Cowan were based on nurses' statements that themselves turned out to be speculative. Jane Russell, one of the nurses claiming "negative impact," could not recall any specific derogatory remarks, and Mary Kay Hewitt only recalled comments made about the court situation to Sharon.

Ristvedt argued finally that Donald Kowalski "cannot accept Karen Thompson as the loved one of his daughter, and hence his actions as a guardian are clouded by that failure." Although his stated goal was "to sever all ties" between the two women, "he has not even discussed this matter with his daughter whose life he is seeking to dramatically alter." Ristvedt found Don's refusal unsurprising, since "[h]e argues on the one hand she wouldn't understand it, but on the other hand that she is devastated by the publicity. If she understands one, she understands the other," Ristvedt reasoned.[22]

Thompson's lawyer had filed her closing argument on June 17, but the lawyers' communication with Judge Douglas did not stop with the submission of final arguments. Fena continued to send letters to the judge claiming that Karen Thompson was endangering Sharon at Park Point and fomenting a rally that took place outside the nursing home after an investigation of a number of health facility complaints. Ristvedt wrote back denying that Karen was the instigator of the rally, insisting that her client did not even attend it, though she was aware of its occurrence and had talked to the organizers. The rally was held by local disability groups that were anxious about the levels of violence and lack of care at Park Point.

Meanwhile, the Minnesota Civil Liberties Union became involved in the case. Sharon had signed a statement in November asking the MCLU to represent her, and the organization had filed an amicus brief on her behalf after the hearing. On May 30 and June 12, lawyers from the union came to visit Sharon again. One of them was Amy Bromberg. By the time I interviewed her in 1997, Bromberg had become an intellectual property lawyer working on the eleventh floor of the Rand Building in downtown Minneapolis, but in 1985, while working for Faegre and Benson, one of the city's largest civil litigation firms, she came across a memo that announced the need for a pro bono lawyer in a guardianship rights case. She and another lawyer "jumped on it" — she being, by her own admission, a "knee-jerk liberal" from way back.

As Bromberg recalled in her later interview, the firm at first was interested not in working for the MCLU but in helping Tom Hayes in his representation of Sharon. (Discussing the quality of some of the lawyers in the case, she shook her head and mumbled something about low handicaps and golf courses.) Actually, everyone was in over his or her head in the case, she recalled. She was pleased to be out of litigation, she admitted, and named the Kowalski case as one of the factors that got her out of the courtroom.

Initially Sharon's case interested Bromberg because it raised the question of disabled persons' rights and capacity to retain counsel. Did they have it? Could they be restricted from access to potential lawyers? After she had an initial interview with Sharon, she recalled that Fena tried desperately to keep her from Park Point Manor and later from Leisure Hills, where Sharon was eventually transferred. The Faegre firm joined the MCLU only after the court refused to allow it to represent Sharon on its own. Faegre was a big Minneapolis firm with a reputation beyond reproach — full of liberal do-gooders from the Twin Cities — and the Kowalskis did not want it to have anything to do with their daughter. On June 20, Bromberg and the MCLU had requested the right to represent Sharon Kowalski and also asked the court to have Sharon tested again before reaching a decision based on the May hearings.[23] Their motions were denied as untimely — the court stating that the record was already closed and the matter under submission.

In Bromberg's view, the record in the case is "appalling." For her, its darkest elements reflect a homophobia fueled by the cultural conflict between the socially conservative Iron Range tradition and gay-lesbian lifestyles, as well as by passionate personalities on both sides. On the one hand, she believed that Thompson — even before she'd come out and become politicized — had been a highly assertive and deeply committed partner with a clear and unwavering vision regarding what was right for Sharon. Bromberg, however, acknowledged that such a strong affirmative vision may have crowded out other viewpoints, which undoubtedly displeased some individuals.

On the other hand, Bromberg seemed impatient with the pervasive influence of Iron Range culture and norms in this case. The Kowalskis, themselves deeply rooted in that culture, obviously struggled to come to terms with the reality of their daughter's sexual orientation (and disability) and feared that Sharon might be subject to sexual abuse. That fear was brought into the courtroom and clearly colored the court's early deliberations and decisions. As a consequence, in Bromberg's view, Sharon's own wishes were ignored, which precluded her from getting the kind of timely care that might have facilitated and even accelerated her rehabilitation.

Besides important issues about the rights of the disabled to freedom of association, including the right to have sex, for Bromberg the case also raised larger questions about the nature of prejudice or hate. There was no ground zero of neutrality in this case, or in any other, she philosophized; from the beginning there was no place of pure particularity where people existed without generalizations attached to them. People did not learn to stop hating — especially in domestic cases, in which blood ties seemed to give people the liberty to justify their own belief that they were the only ones who were right and that they could hide their prejudice under a cloak of "privacy." For Bromberg, the invasion of privacy or outing issue was dubious at best, not only because Karen Thompson was never a gay activist until the role was thrust upon her but also, and importantly, because the privacy issue would be moot if whether one were lesbian or not was not a hot point for hatred. She did not know how to stop prejudice, though this case surely brought her to the brink of wondering why law often perpetuated what it was designed to prevent.

As the summer of 1985 was passing without a decision from Douglas, the case continued to garner minor media attention. Besides the state coverage in papers such as the *Duluth News-Tribune* (May 2 and 4, 1985), the lesbian and gay media — both local (*Equal Time*) and national ("Father Moves to Bar Lover," *Washington Blade*, April 26, 1985, and *Advocate*, June 25, 1985) — wrote about the story along with its pervasive coverage of a new epidemic that was sweeping through the gay male community. The press had not grown interested in Sharon's case solely because of the story's compelling narrative. Julie Andrzejewski and other friends of Karen Thompson had been busy issuing press releases, announcing that "a group of St. Cloud citizens has formed the Committee for the Right to Recovery and Relationships to provide support for Sharon and Karen."[24] The committee planned to publicize the case through videos, photos, and testimonials of Karen Thompson. Its goal was to defray the mounting legal expenses that the case had generated, but the group also wanted to shine a national spotlight on Sharon and Karen's plight.

At first, help came from the MCLU, TRICAP Handicap Services, and the United Handicapped Federation in St. Paul, the latter sending a copy of a unanimous resolution passed on May 9 to Judge Douglas, which recognized "the importance of persons with disabilities having access to significant others, particularly in times of physical and emotional stress." The gay and lesbian community in Minneapolis had been slower on the uptake; the story of northern Minnesota lesbians was not one that immediately mobilized the urban gay community, but eventually the Minneapolis lesbian and gay paper *Equal Time* (J. C. Ritter, "Woman Fights for Right to Care for Partner," April 3, 1985) sent one of its reporters to cover the case. J. C. Ritter's first article in April reported that "Thompson has been shoved out of the closet as a lesbian to her parents and co-workers at St. Cloud." Thompson told reporters, "When you've spent four years hiding a relationship, it's hard to prove it really existed. It would have been better if we had talked with our parents ahead of time. It was hard for them to find out this way." Ritter told the coming-out story with precision and completeness, but he also emphasized Thompson's romantic commitment. "I won't quit," Thompson declared. "We're entitled to a chance to make it. I love her. She's my world. She taught me how to laugh and play, how to take a walk and how to listen to birds." *Equal Time* followed up with articles on May 15 and June 12, quoting Jack Fena as stating, "The family is the bedrock of our civilization in this country, of all of our philosophies, and all of our religions" (Jane Lansing, "Lover, Parent Relationships Debated in Two-Day Hearing," May 15, 1985). The June article reported that more than $5,000 had been raised for the Karen Thompson Legal Fund by the patrons of the Main Club in Superior, a St. Cloud fund-raiser, Minnesota Gay and Lesbian

Legal Assistance, and donations from organizations as far away as Brown University (Duane Graves, "More Than $5,000 Raised for Thompson," June 12, 1985). Thompson still reported $25,000 in additional attorney's fees.

Those financial costs paled beside the shock Thompson experienced on July 23 when Douglas handed down his order appointing Donald Kowalski as "guardian of the person and estate of Sharon Kowalski . . . with all the powers enumerated in Minnesota Statutes 525.56 (3) and (4) without limitation or condition." The order explicitly gave Sharon's father "the power to determine who may visit Sharon Kowalski, and the times and duration of such visitation," but it stated that in making those decisions he was to consider "the best interest of the ward and any reliably expressed wishes of the ward, both of which may change from time to time." The judge made clear that "the guardian shall also consider regarding visitation, the recommendations of medical and health care personnel and the needs and desires of the institution wherein the ward resides."

Douglas's findings of fact that accompanied his order may have provided some clues to the basis for his decision, which relied heavily on the medical testimony of the physicians from the Duluth Clinic. The court found that "the ward lacks sufficient understanding or capacity to make or communicate responsible decisions concerning her person"; that "Donald Kowalski is the most suitable and best qualified among those available and willing to discharge the trust"; that "the ward's ability to respond or communicate had been inconsistent and, at times, unreliable, which situation may or may not improve"; and that "the ongoing conflict between Don and Della Kowalski and Karen Thompson adversely affects the welfare of Sharon Kowalski at the present time; and elimination of that conflict and its adverse effect on the ward is in the best interest of the ward at the present time."[25]

What prompted Judge Douglas, who previously had recognized a "significant relationship" between Karen and Sharon, to seek now by fiat an elimination of that relationship for the time being? For Douglas, the Kowalski matter as it was presented to him was not about gay rights; it was about providing some stability in a situation where power sharing was having a deleterious effect. Only speculation would call forth the common-law presumption in favor of relatives, as well as a reliance on the late but categorical statements of Drs. Moller and Goff as reliable reasons for recognizing how Douglas was leaning in the case. He probably had no idea at the time how disruptive the consequences of his effort to provide stability would become.

From May 20 to June 2, 1997, I conducted interviews and collected documents about Sharon Kowalski's case in Minnesota, using grant money I had received from the University of Montana for summer research. I arrived in Minneapolis on a beautiful blue May morning, rented a car near the Mall of America, and traveled north after negotiating a maze of highways encircling the Twin Cities. Soon I was in farm country: flat, green, interspersed with stands of pine. Heading north, I watched Dodge pickups with silver canoes pass me.

I had scheduled about a dozen interviews with doctors, lawyers, journalists, and, I hoped, Sharon and Karen, though aspirations for the latter had received a setback a day earlier. I was told shortly before I left that Karen had decided not to talk to me in person about the case. My previous conversations with her suggested she was interested in having the story retold from a legal perspective. But Patty Bresser, Karen's partner, informed me when I called that they were leery of my investigation and that they were writing another book, and so thought it was best not to speak to me in person. Their suspicions about a gay professor writing a legal history of the case still struck me as quite perplexing, but the more I discovered about the personalities in the case, the more important their refusal became. Though upset at not being able to interview the principals in the case, I had seen so many letters and declarations and statements and videos that an interview might also have been anticlimactic.

Unable to reach Beth Ristvedt on the phone in Missoula, I pulled over at a rest stop near Blue Fin Bay on Lake Superior, a resort that sign described as "relaxing yet exhilarating." When I finally spoke with Karen's first attorney, she told me she was having ethical problems about talking to me and asked me to call back after she found out whether or not she would violate attorney-client privilege by granting an interview. Attorney-client privilege creates a shield of confidentiality between a lawyer and his or her client around their conversations, but it usually is used to prevent testimony in court. I called back ten minutes later to discover that she was sorry, but her former client insisted that she not talk to me. She said the best she could divine was that Thompson and Bresser were writing another book. In an effort to change her mind, I told her about my other scheduled interviews. Needless to say, I was disappointed by my failure to secure the interview with Ristvedt and, more generally, by my evident failure in gaining Thompson's support for my own exploration of this important case.

After checking into a Duluth motel, I walked along the shore of the dark blue waters of Lake Superior. I was neither relaxed nor exhilarated. It had hit me that I would have to become much more aggressive if I wanted to go beyond a superficial retelling of a landmark case in lesbian and gay law. I wondered, of course, if Karen was simply being wary of what she perceived as yet another slipshod reporter or was vigorously exerting what she may have considered her proprietary right to tell this story. Certainly, Ristvedt's comment seemed to suggest the latter. Of course, both may have been true, too. I simply didn't know for sure.

Karen herself had called for a "real investigative report" on the case and yet seemed resistant to a gay man undertaking that very task. Perhaps that resistance was also entangled with the angry and controlling feminist persona that had either been adopted by Thompson or foisted upon her by the insensitive media covering the story. Either way, my gayness apparently did not provide sufficient common ground for Karen to take me into her confidence, which suggests that the values that underpin gay rights are not always shared by the individuals most concerned about those rights. That deeply saddened me and, obviously, made my efforts far more challenging and problematic than I'd anticipated. They did not, however, persuade me to end my quest to understand and write about such a crucial story in the gay and lesbian experience.

SEVEN

Appeal

A trial by or in a community is also a trial of that community.
Robert Weisberg, "Proclaiming Trials as Narratives,"
in *Law's Stories: Narrative and Rhetoric in the Law*

Temporary Restraining Order

"Lesbian Bitter over Decision," the headline read the morning after Douglas's decision (*St. Cloud Times*, July 24, 1985, sec. C, p. 1). "[I]f Sharon and I were a man and a woman, we'd be married and this couldn't happen to us," Karen Thompson told reporters, dismayed that the court saw fit to see Sharon "as a vegetable" by ruling her incapable of choosing her visitors. Uncertain about the possibilities of future visitation, Thompson assured the *Times* that she would be seeking an appeal. Jack Fena retorted that Thompson wanted to be guardian for financial reasons, to get her hands on part of the personal injury judgment. He reported that his clients were very happy to get "back to a normal life" with their helpless daughter under their "care, custody, and control."

Twenty-four hours after Donald Kowalski became unlimited guardian, Park Point Manor notified Beth Ristvedt that visitation had been restricted to all but family members and a few friends. Karen Thompson, Tom Hayes, the MCLU, and disability rights groups were specifically excluded. On July 25, Sharon was transferred from Park Point Manor in Duluth to Leisure Hills Nursing Home in Hibbing, about a fifteen-minute drive east of Nashwauk. As Karen was later to write, she was devastated. She saw no justice or logic in the decision, especially in the conclusion that Donald Kowalski was qualified as a guardian of Sharon's social needs. "Was it because the court thought that, as a man, he could handle the financial end better?" Thompson and Julie Andrzejewski later speculated in their account of the case. Karen was further anguished by the *St. Cloud Times* story, which had the gall to print Fena's claim that she was interested in money. Julie quickly replied to the article in a letter to the editor, reminding the *Times* that Thompson had filed for guardianship of the person, not the estate, and therefore could not gain from the lawsuit as

Fena insinuated. The use of the term "bitter" in the headline, Andrzejewski added, was "homophobic" (*Why Can't*, 157–58).

Thompson was also outraged by the mainstream media's representation of her as the "woman who claims to be Sharon's lover." Such language, Karen noted, was used to skew a poll that the *St. Cloud Times* took in August concerning the outcome of the case. James Makepeace, the *Times* pollster, asked the following of 209 adults: "Some time ago, a St. Cloud woman was disabled in a car accident. She now requires permanent care by a guardian. The court appointed the woman's father as guardian rather than a female homosexual friend who claims she had maintained a marital-type relationship with the disabled woman. In cases like this, do you think the guardianship should be awarded to the father or the relationship partner?" The poll's results showed that 48.8 percent voted for the parents, 25.8 percent voted for the "homosexual friend," and 25.4 percent were undecided. In September, a disability rights activist, Paul Reichert, wrote to the paper protesting Makepeace's use of the word "claim," stating that "it is a matter of fact, and of court record and testimony, that Karen and Sharon are lesbians who had set up a long-term, permanent relationship with one another." Reichert's rhetoric echoed the growing sentiment among the disabled and lesbian and gay communities, which were slowly finding out about the denial of visitation rights by the guardian.[1]

On August 5, the MCLU, now fully involved in the Kowalski case, moved Judge Douglas for a temporary restraining order that would lift the guardian's visitation prohibitions pending an appeal to be filed. The motion was continued until August 7, the day before Sharon's twenty-ninth birthday, the same day the MCLU filed its appeal in the Twin Cities. Since an appeal usually stays or suspends a lower court order until the higher court's decision, Karen Thompson and Paul Reichert decided to travel to Leisure Hills the next day with a copy of the appeal and a birthday present for Sharon. When they arrived, the nursing home in Hibbing turned them away, claiming that Sharon was not there. Thompson returned the next morning, to be turned away again because the administrator was gone for the week. A verbal confrontation led to the home's officials threatening to call the police. Frustrated, Thompson left and called her lawyer, who advised her to go home to St. Cloud and wait until she could investigate.

A complicated set of legal maneuvers ensued among the litigants in the case. Both the motion for the TRO and the MCLU appeal filed on August 7 claimed that Sharon Kowalski's civil rights had been violated by Judge Douglas's July order because it failed to give the ward the "least restrictive" conditions of guardianship as required by statute. They also argued that giving Donald Kowalski complete power over visitation essentially violated Sharon's right of association. Both documents sought to lift the guardian's ban on visitation as soon as possible. But Jack Fena in response took the extraordinary action of telephoning the Court of Appeals to get a continuance on the restraining order hearing until August 23. The Court of Appeals granted Fena the extra time, but the appeal filed on August 7 still should have suspended the visitation order. A round of telephone calls on August 13 among the MCLU, the Attorney General's Office, Fena, Donohue (who was now acting on Ristvedt's behalf), and both the lower court and the Court of Appeals clarified the situation, leading to a reinstatement of Thompson's visitation rights until a decision was made on the TRO.

On August 14, Karen Thompson held a press conference in St. Cloud before leaving for Hibbing to visit Sharon. John Ritter from *Equal Time* reported that she "challenged Donald and Della Kowalski to meet with her for the sake of Sharon's well-being." Thompson said that as long as Sharon was treated like a six-year-old, she would not demonstrate her mental capacity. "I'd welcome the opportunity to sit down with Donald and Della and a counselor," said Thompson. "I'm more than willing to meet with a mediator. What's to lose? Only time? Everyday time is lost for a lifetime. They're condemning her to a lesser quality of life." For Thompson, the case was now about spousal rights. Her attorney Peter Donohue concurred: "The court does not recognize same-sex relationships," and for that reason the dispute, he contended, should be of major concern to gays and lesbians across the nation (*Equal Time*, August 21, 1985, p. 1).

When a now more outspoken, more political Thompson reached Hibbing on August 14, she found two friends of the Kowalskis stationed in the room; they refused to talk to her but remained the entire time. The nurse noted that when Thompson arrived at 5:45 P.M. with companion Paul Reichert, "[p]atient was sitting in wheelchair. . . . Patient showed recognition. Face was flushed, eyes watering." Sharon, the note continued, "responded with finger movements of yes and no to Thompson's questions." The nurse came into the room every fifteen minutes, finding "conversation appeared deep and intense and excluded other parties in the room. Karen held her hand and looked in her eyes a lot. Resident appeared to accept the attention. Resident did not appear exuberant or depressed." At 7:30, Karen was informed that her visiting hours were complete, according to the schedule, but she insisted that the court order allowed her to stay as long as she wanted. "Ms. Thompson," according to the nurse, "left the building at approximately 8 P.M.," telling Sharon before she left, "I might come back or not. I have to make a phone call. I want you to know, Sharon, that I haven't broken any rules to see you."[2]

When Thompson visited during the next four days, she was often able to find Sharon alone. By Karen's own account, the staff was amazed at Sharon's transformation when she was with her because the patient had been almost completely nonresponsive since her move (*Why Can't*, 161). Apparently, Sharon had not been to physical therapy since her arrival three weeks earlier. Karen spoke with the staff and demonstrated the kinds of exercises she had been doing with her. Sharon's short-term memory, Thompson remembered, was at a nadir. If Karen left the room even for a drink of water, upon her return Sharon would not remember that she had just been there. When Karen had to leave on Monday night to return to her summer class, Sharon seemed panicked and typed, "Help me. Get me out of here." It was the most difficult parting Karen could remember. Neither was aware it would be the last time they would see each other for more than three years.

Thompson was planning to return to Hibbing in two days, but on August 20 her attorney called to inform her that based on a doctor's order, her visitation would no longer be allowed. Even though Karen legally had the right to visit, the nursing home was bound to follow the orders of the treating physician, in this case William L. Wilson, the family doctor of the Kowalskis, who took it upon himself to eliminate Thompson's visitation. Dr. Wilson had treated Della for her nervous breakdown after the litigation had begun, and he had firsthand knowledge of the effect the loss of the Kowalskis' grandchild and injury of their child had upon the family. He wanted to do everything he could to protect them. When he was approached by the Kowalskis' attorney, Jack Fena, Wilson took it upon himself to investigate the matter.

In his letter to Fena, Dr. Wilson stated that he had conducted "an extensive review of her medical and psychological evaluations," and "[a]ccording to affidavits and statements from individuals who have observed this interaction at Park Point Manor, it has come to my attention that Karen Thompson has been involved in bathing Sharon Kowalski behind a closed door for a prolonged period of time. It has also come to my attention that Ms. Thompson has alleged a sexual relationship with Sharon Kowalski that existed prior to the accident." Based on his knowledge and best medical judgment, he felt "that visits by Karen Thompson at this time would expose Sharon Kowalski to a high risk of sexual abuse" and "to recurrent bouts of reactive depression that have greatly impeded her recovery in the past." Wilson directed the staff at Leisure Hills "to not allow Karen Thompson to visit Sharon Kowalski under any circumstances."[3]

In addition to Dr. Wilson's letter, Jack Fena arranged for Donald Kowalski to file an affidavit with the court explaining his decision to eliminate Karen's visitation. Donald stated that he "cut off Karen Thompson's visitation based upon these expert opinions." He also recalled that Karen had previously testified that she had a conversation with Sharon in which Sharon stated that she wanted to go out with Karen first to the Ground Round for a strawberry daiquiri and then wanted to make love to her. "Said statements," Donald declared, "are ludicrous in light of the fact that Sharon would choke on a strawberry daiquiri; she has the mental abilities of a six-year-old, is in diapers and has to be turned every two hours, and is totally incapable of making such statements."

Donald's affidavit also voiced his strong opposition to the entrance of the MCLU into the case. "[B]y no stretch of the imagination," he stated, "should any group along the spectrum from the Civil Liberties Union to the American Nazi Party be allowed to step in and act on their own, for their purposes, where a party is incapable of hiring them." The guardian believed that Karen Thompson not only had literally "brainwashed" his daughter but also was the source of the statements Sharon allegedly had made to Janlori Goldman and Amy Bromberg, attorneys for the MCLU. "I feel that they are in fact representing Karen Thompson and would respect them more if they would stand up and admit they represent Karen Thompson." Finally, Sharon's father thought that Thompson had betrayed the trust of the court by going "public with many and numerous press conferences and coverage in the radio, newspapers and television all over the State and all over the Country," when Sharon was "unable to confirm or deny in any rational manner all these statements."[4]

Donald Kowalski's declaration supported Fena's contention that Thompson was defaming and invading the privacy of the ward by using the press to publicize her case and "outing" her incapacitated lover. The privacy claim would gain increasing sympathy both with the courts, ever wary and antagonistic toward the media, and with many others who felt Sharon should not be outed under any circumstances without her consent, or at least that Karen could have negotiated the disclosure of her affinity to Sharon without sensationalizing it. This argument was founded on the premise that the disclosure of homosexuality continued to be a potentially harmful speech act, both economically and emotionally.

Thompson characterized Wilson's letter as "homophobic" and "ridiculous," especially in light of nurses' notes that documented Sharon's "high motivation" in the presence of "her former roommate" and "nonresponsiveness" in her absence—notes that Wilson's letter ignored (*Why Can't*, 163). Meanwhile Peter Donohue slowly drafted and then sent a five-page letter to Dr. Wilson, asking him to reconsider his decision, but Thompson was growing increasingly impatient with such methodical approaches to what she saw as an emergency situation. The letter took nine days to write, and Sharon was sitting in Leisure Hills without any information about Karen the entire time.

Fed up with the lack of results by her lawyers, Thompson contacted the Minnesota Office of Health Facility Complaints and asked it to investigate

Sharon's rights to visitation under the Minnesota Patients' Bill of Rights, which gives hospital patients the power to choose their own visitors. A special investigator for the Office of Health Facility Complaints of the State of Minnesota, Peter S. Collinson, made an unannounced visit to Leisure Hills on September 11. Collinson reviewed Sharon's medical record and care plan, interviewed staff, and visited and interviewed the patient. In a discussion with the patient, he noted that Sharon indicated by her raised thumb and a message on her typewriter that she did want to see Karen Thompson. The investigator concluded that Leisure Hills was in violation of the Patients' Bill of Rights and gave the facility five days either to rescind the order denying Thompson's visitation or to provide "adequate documentation" for why an order stopping visitation was necessary (*Why Can't*, 166–67).

The September 11 write-up was never acted upon, for on September 13 the Minnesota Court of Appeals made its first ruling. By this date a number of appellate procedures were under way — four, in fact. The MCLU had, as noted, filed its notice of appeal on August 7 on behalf of Sharon Kowalski (File No. C1-85-1502). On August 22, it filed another notice of appeal in conjunction with Tom Hayes, Sharon's court-appointed attorney who had associated the MCLU (File No. C1-85-1595). On the same date a petition for discretionary review was filed by Karen Thompson's lawyers (File No. C2-85-1590), arguing that the trial court had abused its discretion by appointing Donald Kowalski. On September 3, Thompson's lawyers also filed a notice of appeal (though this notice would be dismissed in December by motion of Thompson's counsel).

In civil practice, any party has an opportunity to appeal to a higher court when it feels that an injustice or error has been committed by the lower court. Appellate courts review the record of the trial court and hear arguments, but they reverse the judgment only if they find a clear abuse of discretion or misjudgment by the lower court or find that the lower court judge made an error in an application of law to the facts. Appellate courts are generally loath to second-guess decisions of a domestic relations judge, who has had the advantage of having firsthand experience with the often subjective evidence. Winning an appeal is difficult unless the trial judge made a clear mistake of law.

In its September 13 ruling, which was in fact made public on September 19, the Court of Appeals dismissed both the MCLU appeal on behalf of Sharon Kowalski (File No. C1-85-1502) and Thompson's petition for discretionary review (File No. C2-85-1590). The appeal by Hayes and the MCLU (File No. C1-85-1595) was ordered treated as an appeal solely by the ward's attorney. The MCLU was allowed to file an amicus brief, and Karen Thompson was permitted to assert her position in this appeal. The Court of Appeals also lifted the stay on Douglas's order of July 23, expressly giving that order of unlimited guardianship force and effect until the appeal decision was made. The court first ruled that the MCLU did not have standing to act as Sharon's lawyer because she did not have the capacity to consent to an attorney other than the one who was appointed. Second, the court ruled that Judge Douglas did not abuse his discretion in disallowing the MCLU to become cocounsel with Hayes because the union's request was tardy. Finally, the court ruled that in spite of Minnesota Statutes Section 525.714, which suspends operation of a trial court order "until the appeal is determined or [the appellate court] orders otherwise," Judge Douglas's order should continue in place, effectively upholding Donald Kowalski's right to eliminate visitation for Thompson.

A three-judge panel of the Court of Appeals made the decision, with one of the three, Judge Doris Huspeni, dissenting. The chief judge of the Court of Appeals, Peter Popovich, himself an Iron Range native, was both a personal friend of Jack Fena and the jurist who would play a major role in the first set of decisions by the Minnesota Court of Appeals, himself writing the first published opinion in the case. Both Popovich and Wozniak, another Iron Ranger, would later be criticized for cronyism by Karen Thompson and others. Although this September decision was not a published opinion, Judge Huspeni stated in her brief dissent that the "trial court did not find the ward was endangered by liberal visitation and I discern nothing in the record before us to support a finding that operation of the statute (staying the order) will endanger her. I would apply the statute and suspend operation of the July 23 order until resolution of this appeal." The two majority judges, Popovich and D. D. Wozniak, would continue to hear Kowalski matters for the remainder of the 1980s.[5]

In response to the ruling by the Court of Appeals denying its representation of Sharon, the MCLU filed writs of prohibition and mandamus to the Minnesota Supreme Court. These so-called extraordinary writs sought immediate relief from the highest court of the state because of a compelling need for judicial action. The MCLU's writ argued that the court was proceeding without recognizing Sharon's constitutional right to an attorney of her choice. But the MCLU's writs, like a majority of such appeals, were denied by the Minnesota Supreme Court on November 4, as was its subsequent motion to reconsider.[6] Undaunted and hoping to get a higher court to recognize what Bromberg and her colleagues saw as a basic Fourteenth Amendment due process right, the MCLU took its appeal to the next highest court, the Supreme Court of the United States, which hears appeals from state court decisions that potentially violate federal constitutional law.

The September decision by the Court of Appeals effectively meant that Karen was not going to be visiting Sharon in the near future, at least until the court heard and decided those appeals that remained pending. Ironically, the finality of this decision gave those who were opposed to it added momentum. Karen began to try every means possible "to bring the case to other people's attention." She called disability rights groups, lesbian and gay organizations, and feminist activists. With the help of Julie Andrzejewski, she made the decision to switch counsel, seeking lawyers versed in human rights law who were also more aggressive. Karen later stated, "We [Karen and Julie] reasoned that maybe we should hire a nice white male who would be more acceptable to the system we were dealing with. But that reasoning went against everything I believed in and my beliefs were all I had left" (*Why Can't*, 167). The once conservative and Christian Thompson was learning from her colleague that sexism, sexual harassment, racism, and handicapism were all related forms of oppression. Karen decided to retain Sue Wilson and Toni Pomerene as her new attorneys — both Twin Cities lawyers who had worked on lesbian custody cases in the past.

As media coverage began slowly to expand beyond local newspapers and the gay press, which were now reporting the case on a monthly basis (*Equal Time, Advocate, Gay Community News, Washington Blade*), Karen received letters of support and small contributions. Amy Bromberg wrote an article for the *Civil Liberties News*, stating that when she visited, Sharon was able "to respond to questions of both an objective and subjective nature." Bromberg reported that Sharon told Janlori Goldman that her favorite bird was an eagle, that she was physically handicapped, that she was gay, and that she wanted to be represented by the MCLU. *Ms.* also published an article in September entitled "The Right to Care," with a companion piece called "Benefits for Gay Couples" about a West Hollywood ordinance that allowed couples to establish domestic partnership by registering with the city clerk for a fifteen-dollar fee. Sharon and Karen's case would be linked in the future with the domestic partnership movement.[7]

Motion for Contempt

Don and Della Kowalski were trying to settle down after the tumult of litigation and publicity. With Sharon fifteen minutes away at Leisure Hills and Thompson ordered to stay away, they hoped to return to a semblance of the life they led before the accident had hurled them into tragic loss, enormous attorney's fees, and endless car trips to Duluth and St. Cloud. They got an unlisted telephone number to avoid the media and referred all their problems to Jack Fena, who at this point they felt was protecting them as well as possible.

Frustrated by legal setbacks, Karen Thompson, on the other hand, began reluctantly to speak out, first at St. Cloud State classes on human rights, then at a Take Back the Night rally in Minneapolis. Personally, she struggled with anguish and depression, remembering Sharon's face as she left her unbeknownst for the last time. She visited Peg Chemberlin, her pastor in the United Ministries, and tried to arrange some form of mediation through the Kowalskis' priest, but there was no response. She survived as best she could on the routine of teaching, but she suffered from headaches and bouts of nausea, wondering what her lover could possibly be thinking had happened to her.

Karen's new attorney, Sue Wilson, knew her way around the domestic relations courts of the Twin Cities. Undoubtedly aware of how nasty they could be, she had learned to maneuver through restraining orders and mediation sessions, through visitation schedules and arguments over the value of community property. The short, blonde barrister with a striking, sincere face dealt not only in the law of romance gone bad but also in the constructive end of lawyering: drawing up adoption papers for lesbians and shared property agreements between women living together, fighting for the rights of women to have children on their own. The *Kowalski* case came to her and her law partner Toni Pomerene at a time when she had the expertise to reverse what was from her viewpoint an outrageous outcome that separated two lovers at their time of greatest need.

Sue Wilson's first strategic plan, besides working to prepare the appeal of the July 23 ruling, was to bring another motion in district court, one of contempt against Donald Kowalski for not obeying the court's directive to take Sharon's social interests into account as guardian, as ordered by Douglas. The barring of Karen, she would argue, was a breach of Donald's duties as guardian. Before bringing the motion, however, she needed more information about the validity of William Wilson's professional assessment and the decision-making process of the guardian. She subpoenaed both Dr. William L. Wilson and Don Kowalski for depositions. Jack Fena objected, claiming the matter was closed and calling the subpoenas harassment, phoning Judge Douglas and the Court of Appeals. But the order and the appeal did not technically prevent discovery in the case because guardian matters were never closed as long as there was a ward under the jurisdiction of the court. Sue Wilson agreed as part of the negotiations to travel to Duluth on October 7, 1985, to take the deposition of Dr. Wilson, but when she got there, the physician was not present. He did not feel he had to honor the subpoena, he stated on the phone from the Range. Sue Wilson called Judge Douglas, patiently detailing what she no doubt took to be Fena's obfuscation. The parties then agreed to drive to Hibbing to take the deposition that afternoon.

The deposition of William Wilson turned into an ordeal. For an hour and a half, five attorneys, a court reporter, and Karen Thompson caravanned to the heart of the Range. The testimony itself could not help but be anticlimactic. William Leslie Wilson was born in Baltimore but currently resided in Chisholm, Minnesota, one of the Range towns. In his forties, he had received his medical degree from the University of Minnesota in 1974 and was board-certified in family practice, a field of general medicine that includes pediatrics, obstetrics, gynecology, and internal medicine. He had not taken any specific courses in rehabilitation medicine, was presently working at the Adam's Clinic in Chisholm, and was also the Kowalskis' family physician.[8]

Dr. Wilson admitted there had been a meeting between Donald, Jack Fena, and himself before he wrote the letter in August denying Karen access to Leisure Hills. "I believe," the deponent continued, "he [Donald] did mention things about her [Thompson] being belligerent with staff at the nursing home [Park Point], that things had been apparently allegedly said negative about the parents, about care that she had been receiving at various nursing homes." Karen's attorney — the other Wilson — tried to pin down the witness about the "problems" Donald had mentioned, but the doctor balked, claiming, "I don't recall exactly." Sue then asked him about what records he reviewed to write the letter, specifically court records. One of Dr. Wilson's sources was newspaper articles: "I think it's extremely important," he emphasized, "when somebody's intimate, psychological, social, personal life is exposed in such a manner, I think that's extremely critical." When asked how the newspapers specifically affected Sharon, the doctor said he was worried that the articles "could be discussed with her perhaps." As a family practitioner, Dr. Wilson was concerned about the "entire family," about the "devastating effect on the subtle interactions between loved ones," including, of course, "a vulnerable adult who relies so much on the love and care of her family." In this context, the doctor was defining loved ones as Sharon's "parents mainly."[9]

Dr. Wilson stated that he saw Sharon only twice before writing the letter and could not remember whether he asked her about visiting Karen before or after he wrote it. "I wasn't then and I'm not now convinced that she could give meaningful input," he stated categorically. He did admit that nurses at Leisure Hills had not mentioned any major problems with Karen's visits, and that he had overlooked occupational therapists' notes in his report. His main concern in banning Thompson was prevention, given the past history of the case. He had read the declaration of Kenneth Krossen, the patient from Park Point who swore he saw Karen stay in the bathroom with Sharon for a long time, but he was not relying entirely on that affidavit only. "That was just more or less an 'antidotal' [*sic*] thing representing a situation that I believe could occur. Even if it didn't actually occur, I can see it occurring."

Ms. Wilson: But what you're saying — are you saying that every single person who's been in a sexual relationship and is then injured is at risk of being sexually abused by the person they were involved with?

William Wilson: I think the potential definitely exists.

Q: For example, if your wife, god forbid, were injured in an accident and was disabled, she would be at high risk of being abused by you sexually?

A: I think the potential is there, yes.

Q: So you would be concerned that you would abuse her?

A: No, I didn't say that. I can speak for myself, as far as what my actions would be. I can't speak for — the potential in the situation exists.

Q: Let's assume this awful situation — which will not happen and we hope would never occur to any of us — but your wife is injured. You're saying that the potential exists for you to sexually abuse her. Then would you say that she should have restricted rights to see you, let's say, only with the door open, with someone else there?

A: Possibly. . . .

Q: Did you in writing this letter assume that there had been a sexual relationship between Sharon and Karen?

A: I assume that there was, you know, a good likelihood, yes. I have no way of first hand knowing that.

Q: When there is an injured individual, doctor, what type of involvement do you usually recommend for the significant other of the injured party, in their treatment?

A: What do you mean by significant other? I don't understand.

Q: Let's say someone that they were living with or married to.

A: That depends on the situation. I mean, a roommate in college might not have any involvement whatsoever. The impact of such an illness is so great that my biggest concern would be on direct family members and their interaction.

Q: When someone marries, do you believe they create another family as part of their family?

A: Yes.

Q: Now if someone is a lesbian, do you know whether they can marry?

A: I don't believe they can.

Q: If that's correct, do you believe that the emotional, that emotionally the person they're involved with is significantly different from the emotional relationship they'd have with a spouse if they were heterosexual?

A: There may be some differences, yes.

Q: Can you tell me what those differences are?

A: I said there may be differences. I have to deal with the specific case, I guess. . . .

Q: What are your personal feelings about lesbians, doctor?

A: I think it's something that — it's a choice of sexuality. It's something that's probably—there's a biological and a social component. And individuals who are homosexual have just as much right to express as adults, in a free society, to express their sexuality as anybody else.[10]

At this point Jack Fena asked for a short break. He then went to the telephone and called Peter Popovich, chief judge of the Court of Appeals, who immediately ordered an end to Wilson's deposition and all other scheduled depositions until the appeals were adjudicated. Everyone at the table was astonished to hear of this ruling—an appellate court judge orally interrupting discovery was a rare, almost unprecedented, legal action. As Sue Wilson opened her briefcase and picked up her pencil, yellow pad, and notes, she was shaking her head in disbelief. She also knew she was confronting a resistance greater than she expected in the "progressive" state of Minnesota. She was beginning to realize that this guardianship battle would require all her available resources. Popovich's order came down on October 11, stating that even though the trial court had orally ordered the deposition to proceed, Sue Wilson had failed to bring a formal motion before the district court detailing why she wanted to conduct discovery while the case was on appeal as required by Minnesota Rule of Civil Procedure 27.02.[11]

As legal fees on both sides continued to mount, Sue Wilson's office researched and prepared its motion for contempt, which was filed in the district court on December 13. In addition to seeking a court order against the guardian and the right of further discovery, Thompson's lawyers, in an extraordinary pleading, requested that the attorney for Donald Kowalski, Jack Fena, be removed as counsel for the guardian because of a conflict of interest. The conflict, Wilson argued, arose from his position as lawyer for both the guardian's interest and that of the plaintiff, Sharon, in the negligence lawsuit. As personal injury advocate, it behooved Fena to argue that his client was maximally incapacitated and a reproductive heterosexual in order to make a jury disposed to award an optimal judgment in damages. As lawyer for the guardian, on the other hand, Fena had a duty to see that his client act in the best interests of the ward, which would include providing her with every opportunity to get well and maximize her social exposure—including visits with her same-sex partner of four years.[12]

Wilson and her client also filed a complaint against Fena with the Lawyers Professional Responsibility Board, alleging the same conflict. Gary Bloomquist, chair of the Twentieth District Ethics Committee, and member of the Range bar, was asked to investigate. But he decided to resign instead and sent an exasperated letter to the board, complaining that "Karen Thompson and her wacko relationship with the poor girl who is the subject of all of this has filled my stomach to the brim and I cannot digest anymore" (*Why Can't*, 178). The board eventually informed Sue Wilson that it would defer to the district court on the conflict-of-interest issue. The district court eventually denied Wilson's motion, and on appeal, in a Catch-22, Judge Wozniak would later rule that the conflict-of-interest issue was moot because the Professional Responsibility Board had made no finding.

Affidavits by Jack Fena, Dr. Wilson, and Donald Kowalski challenged the arguments of Thompson's new attorney in her motion for contempt. Fena vehemently opposed another test of Sharon. "To spend what would be thousands and thousands of dollars of Sharon's money to have an evaluation for Thompson's purposes, not Sharon's purposes," he stated, "would be a travesty and would be totally against Sharon's best interests in the long run."[13] Donald Kowalski flatly denied that he asked Dr. Wilson to end Thompson's visitation, even though he "totally" agreed with the decision. Thompson, he declared, had orchestrated her own exclusion. On December 15, 1985, Don wrote in his affidavit, he and his wife had asked Sharon a series of questions during a home visit after reading to her some of the newspaper clippings. Sharon indicated "no" on the typewriter when Don asked her if she wanted Karen Thompson to visit her. "On that day my wife and I also asked Sharon the following questions: Are you a lesbian? Answer: 'No.' Was Karen Thompson your lover? Answer: 'No.' Was Karen Thompson your landlady? Answer: 'Yes.' "[14]

Just as Karen Thompson's attitude changed with the adoption of her new attorney, Sue Wilson, and her close association with Julie Andrzejewski, so too the position of the Kowalskis was increasingly filtered through the strategies of their attorney, Jack Fena. Playing upon the inconsistency of Sharon's responses, Donald was contending that Sharon saw Karen as her landlady — an assessment no professional opinion up to this point corroborated. The nature of the affidavits in these motions from both sides had become more vitriolic, more ad hominem, and therefore by some accounts more litigious, stretching the capacity of the adversarial system to function as a method of arriving at a fair dispute resolution.

Conference Call

By stipulation of the parties, the motions came before a different district court judge, Judge Douglas's colleague Kim Johnson, through a conference call on December 20, 1985. Sue Wilson's motion for contempt, which was supported by both the MCLU and Tom Hayes, proceeded from the premises, first, that a guardian by statute is "subject to the control and direction of the court at all times and in all things" (Minnesota Statutes Section 525.56, subd. 1) and, second, that an individual may be found in constructive contempt for disobeying "any lawful judgment, order, or process of the court" (Minnesota Statutes Section 588.01, subd. 3[3]). Wilson argued that Donald Kowalski had violated Judge Douglas's order when he eliminated Karen Thompson from visitation four days after the ruling was issued without considering either Sharon's "best interest" or her "reliably expressed wishes" as required. The subsequent letter by Dr. Wilson, solicited by and sent to Jack Fena, was, according to Karen's lawyer, "engineered" in a way that "contravenes the wishes of the ward." In regard to Fena's conflict of interest, Wilson noted "the extreme prejudice to Sharon Kowalski" of a situation in which "it benefits the father's position in the guardianship action to allege that Ms. Kowalski has the mental abilities of a six-year-old, and is incapable of making consistent statements" rather than treat Sharon as an injured adult capable of choosing her friends and loved ones.[15]

Mr. Fena in reply maintained that his client was acting in Sharon's "best interest" by keeping Karen away. He claimed that neither he nor Don Kowalski asked Dr. Wilson to order Thompson off limits at Leisure Hills, even though he did supply Wilson with records and did meet with the doctor and Donald. As to the reliably expressed wishes of the ward, Fena reiterated that the court had found Sharon "totally incapable of making decisions as to who can visit her." He assured the court that the opinions of four experts are clear: Thompson should not visit.[16]

Tom Hayes, during the telephone hearing, argued "that there ought to be some specific provisions at this point in time granting visitation with Sharon Kowalski, the ward, with any party that she has had any kind of relationship with in the past — be it familial or simply on a friendship level." Hayes found no credible or consistent evidence in the record of "a situation where Sharon Kowalski has indicated a reluctance to visit with Karen Thompson." His argument ended with a critique of Fena's experts. "As a matter of law," he felt, the doctors' reports "do not contain sufficient information to justify a complete prohibition of visitation by any single individual," especially given Sharon's need for stimulation from outside sources.[17]

On January 3, 1986, Judge Johnson summarily denied all of Sue Wilson's motions. "There is no evidence," Johnson stated, "that the Guardian, Donald Kowalski, did not take into consideration the best interests of Sharon Kowalski and any reliably expressed wishes of Sharon Kowalski regarding the allowance or arrangements for visitation between Sharon Kowalski and third parties." Johnson stated that Sharon should be evaluated annually, but there was also no evidence that Donald had failed at this point to comply with that requirement. "Such evaluations should specifically address the ability of Sharon

Kowalski to reliably express her wishes as to visitation."[18] Johnson's express establishment of a requirement for an annual evaluation that addressed the issue of visitation would come back to haunt the guardian in the future.

Long Briefs

Sue Wilson appealed the decision immediately. There were now two district court decisions on appeal, the July 23 ruling by Douglas (File No. C1-85-1595) and Kim Johnson's December ruling (File No. C6-86-176). The appellate briefs in the second appeal were sharper and more strident than the first. Counsel on both sides had received ample opportunity to restate their case, such repetition honing Jack Fena's skills in presenting a set of facts that argued for victimization of his client and the necessity of his strict visitation schedule. Karen Thompson, he argued, "has repeatedly held press conferences on this matter, and during times she had visitation with Sharon Kowalski she continually bombarded Sharon with negative messages," causing Sharon's medical doctors to conclude that Thompson's visits have been "harmful." He continued:

> While the [first] April 25, 1984 order was in effect, new developments began to occur. Karen Thompson became unthoughtful and insensitive to Sharon when she wrote letters to Sharon's parents claiming a gay relationship. Karen Thompson became unthoughtful and insensitive when she fought tooth and nail to keep Sharon in a nursing home with an 87-year-old roommate who chanted 24 hours a day in temperatures that soared to 94 degrees without air conditioning. Karen Thompson became unthoughtful and insensitive when she made numerous motions in court to oppose Sharon receiving optimum medical care at the Nat G. Polinsky Memorial Rehabilitation Center.[19]

Fena continued his inimitable style of mixing rhetoric and objectivity in his statement of facts: "This is not the gay rights issue which Karen Thompson continually characterizes it as in the press; it is a medical issue," counsel stated. "If Karen Thompson were a male, Donald Kowalski would still follow the medical advice and provide for his daughter's safety and well being." For Fena, "the bottom line in this matter is that Karen Thompson continues to harass Mr. Kowalski. She continues to bring appeals which are without merit. She continues to cost the estate of Sharon Kowalski a great deal of money through these frivolous actions." Finally, he maintained, "Karen Thompson has repeatedly stated that she and Sharon are as husband and wife, despite the fact that Minnesota does not recognize such a marriage. In *Baker v. Nelson* 291 Minn. 310, 191 N.W.2d 185 (1971), the court looked at Minnesota Statutes Section 517.01

and determined that the terms 'bride and groom' and 'husband and wife' would not allow for a same-sex marriage."[20]

Sue Wilson's response argued that the guardian failed to ascertain the "best interests" and "reliably expressed wishes" of the ward *after* the order that appointed him guardian was made. The banning of Karen four days subsequent to Douglas's order evidenced that the guardian made no effort to ascertain the ward's wishes or to obtain medical evidence that Thompson's visits must be curtailed to improve Sharon's health. The letter by Dr. Wilson, upon which the guardian subsequently relied for his ban of Karen, counsel argued, was not based on reliable medical evidence but "in large part on his conclusion that any visits would put the ward at a high risk of sexual abuse." Counsel then recounted Dr. Wilson's interrupted deposition testimony during which he "admitted that there would be a high risk that he would sexually abuse his own wife if she were injured." Dr. Wilson, the petitioner's lawyer wrote, could cite no medical or psychological literature on which he based his "astonishing" and "absurd" opinion, especially because "absolutely no evidence of Karen Thompson sexually abusing Sharon Kowalski exists in the record."[21]

Sue Wilson also asserted that none of the physical therapists or psychologists had ever recommended discontinuing her client's visitation. The reports of Drs. Wilson, Goff, and Moller were like a house of cards, all dependent on the assessment of Dr. Cowan, which, counsel reiterated, was itself based on two short visits and no psychological testing. She concluded, "Is it any accident that almost all of the 'medical reports' relied on by Respondent to deny all contact between the ward and Karen Thompson begin 'Dear Mr. Fena:'? Why would a medical report be written to anyone?" Dr. Wilson, moreover, denied visitation without even speaking to Thompson. "The problem," as Karen's counsel saw it, was that "one attorney has hired the doctors, shown them what he wants them to see, and then used their letters to him as 'medical reports' purporting to bear some relationship to the truth." Ironically, she argued, the hiring attorney in question was the guardian's attorney and not the ward's attorney. "Does it make a difference that the ward's other attorneys have opposed the guardian in virtually every court conceivable, and on virtually every possible issue?"[22]

Oral Argument

In January, the Court of Appeals held its hearing on the appeal of Douglas's original order (July 23, 1985, File No. C1-85-1595). Karen's convalescence after a necessary hysterectomy was cut short by her insistence on attending the hearing in Anoka. Six days after surgery she was lying on the back seat of Julie's car on her way to the courthouse (*Why Can't*, 179–80). At the appellate hearing, the MCLU's Amy Bromberg, on behalf of Sharon as a friend of the court, argued that the order of July 23 had violated Sharon's constitutional right to freedom of association, a fundamental part of citizenship under the penumbra of privacy protection implicit in the Bill of Rights and the Fourteenth Amendment. She first cited Justice Louis Brandeis: "The makers of our Constitution undertook to secure conditions favorable to the pursuit of happiness. . . . They sought to protect Americans in their beliefs, their thoughts, their emotions and their sensations. They conferred, as against the government, the right to be let alone — the most comprehensive of rights and the right most valued by civilized man" (*Olmstead v United States*, 277 US 438, 478 [1928] [dissenting]). Citing contraception *(Griswold v Connecticut)*, abortion *(Roe v Wade)*, and other cases dealing with privacy rights, the MCLU contended that the right to choose whom to see, talk to, and love was also a fundamental right that must be carefully guarded in cases of incapacity.

Referring to the reasonable preference of the ward under Minnesota law, Bromberg explained that only a clear finding of medical need could serve as a compelling reason to abridge the freedom of association. Minnesota law contained a four-step evidentiary process for finding a ward incapacitated, she outlined. First, there must be clear and convincing evidence of medical need (Minnesota Statutes Section 525.551, subd. 3). The second step required the court — if it found medical need exists — to explore "available alternatives" that were "least restrictive" of the rights of the patient. The third step is the "substituted judgment" standard: the court must ascertain the preference of the incapacitated person. Courts should not decide what most people would do or even what appears wise, but rather what the ward would do if she were competent and "understood all the circumstances including her present and future competency." The fourth step required the court to make specific findings of fact (Minnesota Statutes Section 525.551, subd. 5).[23]

Bromberg argued that the probate court failed to make any specific finding other than the need for "elimination of conflict" between the parties, which, she maintained, "in and of itself, is not a legally sufficient basis upon which to infringe significant personal liberties." There was no finding by the court that such elimination of conflict was medically necessary, that less restrictive alternatives had been explored, or that the predisposition of Sharon was the elimination of Thompson. "There was no doubt what Sharon Kowalski would have done. She would have continued to see Karen Thompson."

Bromberg's most passionate arguments came in discussing the double bind of the disabled patient. Once declared incapacitated, she argued, wards were often subject to "gross condescension" and "treated without dignity." Sharon

Kowalski was a case in point. "Her guardian and the court below presume that she is unable to decide whether or not she wants to see her friend, and have given no weight to either the decisions she made while fully competent or the wishes she has expressed since the accident." As a result, the ward has become "subject to the whims of her guardian, including the guardian's prejudices and private biases," in this case Donald Kowalski's "deep-seated prejudices against homosexuals." Bromberg concluded, "While we cannot control such prejudices, neither can we tolerate them." One of the most basic of constitutional rights was the right "to choose whom you talk to, whom you visit, whom you befriend, and whom you love."[24] Many of Bromberg's arguments about incapacity were probably applicable to homosexuality as well: "gross condescension" and presumptions about a lesbian's inability to know what she really wants — a man — were part and parcel of the cultural backlash against same-sex orientation. Driven into the closet and silenced, lesbians and gay men are also treated with indignity and subject to the whims and private biases of their guardians — heterosexuals in power.

The arguments of Gary Pringle (Tom Hayes's associate) and Sue Wilson were similar to those of the MCLU, but they focused on the legitimacy of spousal ties as a criterion for guardian appointment and, as a corollary, the equivalency of same-sex partnership to marriage. Citing divorce cases in which "cohabitants" had a "logical expectation" of sharing child custody in the case of separation between nonmarried couples, Wilson argued that the probate court made no specific finding in this case with regard to why the "spouse" Thompson was not better qualified to be guardian than Donald Kowalski. In her constitutional argument, Wilson maintained that "homosexual relationships should not be afforded any less protection than other relationships merely because they do not conform to the societal 'norm.'" Wilson cited Federal Circuit Court of Appeals cases that upheld students' rights to form gay organizations on university campuses under the First Amendment's protection of freedom of association. By analogy, she argued, "The Probate Court's July 23, 1985 Order flagrantly disregards the relationship between Sharon Kowalski and Karen Thompson and denies them their fundamental right of association, a right which courts have an obligation to guard zealously."[25]

As the final lawyer to argue at the hearing, Jack Fena hammered home his main point that Drs. Moller, Goff, Wilson, and Cowan agreed that Sharon had been effectively reduced to the capacity of a six-year-old child who did not have the judgment to make decisions for herself. He also argued that before the accident Sharon had been planning to leave Karen and that Karen had cost Sharon thousands of dollars by outing her. As a result of Thompson's violation of Sharon's right to privacy, Fena argued, he was no longer able to argue in the personal injury action that the accident had deprived Sharon of the capacity of having a husband and children, an argument that was translatable to substantial monetary damages in that pending case. Fena's position indicated how important the values of reproduction are in the legal system.

The court had ninety days to make its decision after hearing oral argument. Meanwhile, that winter the Kowalskis continued to hope some closure would come to this sad chapter of their lives, seeking to live as best they could with the condition of their disabled daughter, her medical bills, and the loss of their savings. Thompson, on the other side, continued to worry about the precious time lost at Leisure Hills, where Sharon was clearly not getting the rehabilitation therapy that she needed to make progress. The law's delay in this case was having a real effect on its helpless victim. Meanwhile, Karen's friend Julie continued her fervent work on the Committee for the Right to Recovery and Relationships and the Karen Thompson Legal Fund. She wrote press releases and letters to the editor and set up speaking engagements for Karen.

On January 17, the *Washington Blade* reported the imminent Court of Appeals ruling, quoting Thompson as stating, "This will be a gain for everybody" if the case is won. The article continued, "She [Thompson] refers to letters she has received from Lesbians and Gays across the country, people who have lost partners through illness or accident and have been denied the right to have a say in their treatment or, in many cases, even to see their partner in the hospital" (Shelley Anderson, "Til Catastrophe Do Us Part . . . A Minnesota Woman Fights for Her Injured Lover's Best Interests," *Washington Blade,* January 17, 1986, p. 1). Jack Fena told reporters he agreed that it was "a heart-rendering [*sic*] case; I feel sorry for Thompson," but he insisted that "she brought it on herself" by comparing Sharon's situation to "being in prison" and making "unfavorable" statements about Sharon's parents, thereby making Sharon depressed (Stephanie Poggi, "Disabled Rights Issues Raised in Kowalski Case," *GCN,* February 15, 1986, p. 1).

J. C. Ritter's article in the Minneapolis *Equal Time* ("Karen Thompson: Still Fighting, Despite Stress," February 19, 1986, p. 9) also reported Karen's side of the story. It began: "Karen Thompson was teaching class at St. Cloud State University when a sheriff's deputy delivered the legal notice. She was being sued for $31,000 by her former attorneys for nonpayment of her bill." The article discussed the $72,000 in legal fees Karen was attempting to defray through fund-raising. Her main source of stress, however, was the ever-diminishing window of opportunity for Sharon's recovery through rehabilitation. "Experts say two to three years for motor relearning in cases like Sharon's. We're pushing the upper end," Karen told Ritter, implying that Sharon was on rehabilitative hold as long as she remained at Leisure Hills.

Ritter was also interested in the larger ramifications of Sharon's case for other gays and lesbians. Constitutional issues concerning freedom of association were doubly important when a culturally marginalized lesbian became even further classified by a handicap. "Implications of disability issues are even greater for gays and lesbians," Ritter reminded his readers, many of whom were HIV positive and aware that "AIDS brings homophobia to the hilt," as one legal specialist in Minneapolis told the reporter. Thompson was credited with at least making the judiciary recognize the existence of queers.

In the *Lesbian Inciter*, a local San Francisco publication, Thompson was quoted as saying, "I won't call it the justice system, because it isn't justice," referring to the lack of legal protection for gays. In a now familiar refrain, she called on everyone to come out, "I see hope, and I know that it's less threatening to be out of the closet. All of this loving support coming from the people I'd feared for so long." The article concluded that "this is a very complicated case, made so by Lesbophobic misogynist parents, lawyers, and laws that protect the Lesbian hating" (Mariel Rae Burch, "Lesbian Couple Torn Apart by the Court: Help Needed from Lesbian Community," *Lesbian Inciter*, February/March 1986, 12–15).

Decision

On March 4, 1986, the Minnesota Court of Appeals handed down *In re Guardianship of Sharon Kowalski*, a unanimous decision of three judges written by Chief Judge Popovich (Wozniak and Sedgwick, concurring).[26] This was the first of three published decisions about the guardianship case in the permanent records of the State of Minnesota. Popovich ruled that Judge Douglas neither abused his discretion in making Donald Kowalski guardian nor erred in giving Kowalski full authority to determine visitation.

The Court of Appeal relied on factual findings whose sources, the justices believed, had been tracked carefully. The shaping of the decision around these findings pointed to the art of shaping law through careful selection of evidence. Under its section called "Facts," the court stated that Sharon's communication skills were "limited to hand and face signals, pointing to written words, one-finger typing on an electric typewriter, and physical displays of emotion." Her responses were "inconsistent," and she "was burdened with a child's mental capacity between four and six years of age." Reviewing the medical evidence, Judge Popovich found that Dr. George Cowan, a "psychiatrist of numerous qualifications," had, along with Drs. Moller and Goff, recommended that "Thompson be prohibited from visiting the ward because the ward enters a detrimental, depressed state after Thompson's visits."[27]

The court also reported as fact that the relationship between Kowalski and Thompson "was uncertain." Even though they had been "roommates for four years prior to the accident, had exchanged rings, and had named each other as beneficiary in their life insurance policies, [p]rior to the accident, Sharon had closed their joint bank account and had also told her sister she was considering moving to Colorado or moving home and that Karen Thompson was becoming very possessive." Thompson's claim of a "lesbian relationship with Sharon Kowalski" was countervened by evidence that "Sharon never told her family of such a relationship or admitted it prior to the accident."[28] Curiously, the testimony of Debbie Kowalski became controlling, while the "uncertain" designation for Karen and Sharon's relation ignored the district court's finding of a "significant" relation.

In his "Analysis," Popovich began by carefully stating that appellate courts would not interfere with the exercise of the district court's discretion except in the case of clear abuse, the court citing a presumption in the law in favor of family ties. He quoted Cowan's opinion that a father's love "is unconditional." Popovich continued, "Any preference of the ward regarding guardianship is unreliable. The best interests of the ward were served by Kowalski's appointment" because contact with Thompson "upsets the ward and results in her depression."[29] The court also found no error in the decision to give Donald the full power of guardianship, discrediting the MCLU's argument that the "least restrictive" mode of protection was not enacted for Sharon, who should have some say in her visitation schedule. The court continued by noting that the right to free association was not absolute and must give way to the "compelling state interest" of "protection of the ward's well being by the State acting as *parens patriae.*" Sharon's lack of capacity rendered her a ward of the state, which in effect became her parent and had the power under that authority to make decisions for her. "Regulation of visitation" *was* "least restrictive of her rights," the court concluded, given that Sharon's "moodiness" followed Karen's visits, even if they were productive of responses. The court reasoned that the government and the guardian's restriction on the ward somehow freed her from the oppression of Thompson's overwhelming presence.

When faced with the question of the "preference of the ward," as articulated in the statute, the court also relied on Debbie Kowalski's testimony, which it found highlighted in Jack Fena's appellate brief. "At present, the ward's responses to questions are inconsistent. She has expressed interest in visiting with Thompson. Thompson claims the ward has clearly indicated to her the ward's preference to maintain their visitation. The guardian claims he is acting consistent [*sic*] with the ward's preference to move away from Thompson based on Thompson and the ward's relationship just prior to the accident."[30] The confidential relationship between Karen and her partner, relied upon repeatedly by Wilson, was held to be secondary to the parent-child relation of trust, which is "even stronger when the child has been incapacitated to a four-to-six-year-old mental ability."

The Popovich decision did fall within the parameters of appellate practice, which traditionally refuses to second-guess a lower court about evidentiary findings, though in this instance it did change the description of the Kowalski-Thompson lesbian relationship from "significant" to "uncertain." The court also saw fit to allow Donald to introduce what it called "quietude" into Sharon's life, at least for the time being. This was the peace and quiet that the Kowalskis had sought, but for Karen it must have seemed much more like the vegetative state that she had so adamantly opposed.

On May 24, 1997, I woke up in the Chalet Motel on London Street in a rainy Duluth, facing a long Memorial Day weekend that had closed down many of the libraries I needed to visit for research. I had completed five interviews and scheduled at least three more, despite Karen Thompson's apparent effort to dissuade potential interviewees from talking to me. Her strong opposition to my efforts continued to strike me as inconsistent with her stated desire for a thorough (and, presumably, objective) investigative report and as bewildering in light of my own ideological sympathy for her cause.

That night I went downtown to Eighty-second Avenue North looking for the Northland Gay Men's Association in an old brownstone with huge halls, wide staircases, and carved banisters. The dark corridors told me that the scheduled Friday night open house was not happening. As an alternative, I tried to see *Liar Liar,* the Jim Carrey comedy about lawyers, but it was playing only in the distant suburbs. I finally settled for sleep in a smelly hotel room. It was one of those eventless Friday nights when I was prone to self-questioning, this time asking myself why exactly I was stressing over some witness taking her phone off the hook, why I was pursuing the past in the middle of America, trying to tell a story that many did not want me to tell. I told myself I was doing it because I didn't give up easily, because I found out one day that my lover had delivered a deadly virus into my bloodstream and my heart skipped too many beats and I looked into the abyss for a second and said to myself, "You're not going to be here for very long—what matters to you?" So I ended up in Act Up in Buffalo, handing out condoms and clean needles, and started teaching queer books and thinking about how I might contribute to telling the story of lesbian and gay discrimination in a way that would make a few people get over it, in a way that might show how complicated and simple it is, how unreasonable and passionate. So I stumbled across a story about same-sex love that grabbed me, and I decided to grab it and wrestle with it.

For one thing, exposing the myth of a fundamentalist Republican sports coach turned radical feminist lesbian was allowing me to revisit my own biomythology — straight trial lawyer turned liberated gay professor. I was still talking about the law after leaving it, still single, unhappy, frustrated by roadblocks to writing. Coming out and becoming a teacher had not changed my status as workaholic, loner, and romantic, though it had made me more of an activist, made me aware of prejudice and the need to challenge it. Had Karen Thompson's history changed her status as competitor, coach, whistle-blower? Doubtful. Everyone had to either persevere or surrender. But under the struggle to write rights lay the same insecurities, the same clutching for recognition that had become the trademark of Sharon's case.

By May 25, I was sitting on the bed in a small room at the gay Hotel Amsterdam in downtown Minneapolis on Hennepin Avenue, the Market Street of this town, wide and seedy. That day I had visited the Quatrefoil Library, a lesbian and gay archive in St. Paul, and procured copies of articles covering the case in the local press — *Equal Time, GAZE.* That night I danced at the Gay Nineties, the Mall of America of bar scenes, where under one roof I got to choose from a leather bar, a drag bar, a stripper, and a heavy metal dance bar. Nothing happened; I danced by myself.

I walked back to the hotel on Hennepin and started thinking about the case again. It seemed troubling that the fight for rights of domestic (though perhaps undomesticated) same-sex partners emphasized coupling as opposed to copulation as the bottom line, as if the couplet — the avowed lifetime commitment to connubial bliss — would somehow legitimate the sodomite (male or female), somehow homogenize the homo as just like everybody else: a human with rights instead of the wavering, ungrammatical, nonprocreative, unmentionable other s/he had become over the annals of time. Shouldn't the emphasis, I thought, be not on our couplage, as if we were everything Ozzie and Harriet were except for anatomy (which may be true), but simply on our copulation, our behavior — lesbian or gay — which in itself among consenters was just an act of pleasure or affection?

Those who hated our "unnatural and unnameable" acts were the actual culprits — their condemnation was obscene. Was I any less legitimate as a queer because I was alone, celibate, uncoupled, because I hadn't exchanged rings, taken out insurance policies, made vows on the banks of the Blackfoot River? Did I need a lifetime commitment that cloned the sexist and sometimes violent institution of marriage in order to gain respect? Whether or not Sharon was in a relationship, she had a right to see her gay friends, to be a lesbian, just as Karen did. And in an ideal world her guardian would be the best person for the job — not a spouse or a parent who did not have the stamina or the skills to negotiate. If Karen and Sharon were legally allowed to marry but as a spouse Karen was not a good caretaker, then a legal presumption in favor of her appointment would also be unfair. It seemed to me that same-sex marriage — while an option that I wanted to have — was not the answer to preventing hatred of our copulation, which when I did it seemed natural and kind and worth naming. The *Kowalski* case was about caretaking and same-sex love. They were not mutually exclusive, but they were not isomorphic either.

While spinning my wheels through Memorial Day 1997, in Minneapolis, commemorating those who invented "don't ask, don't tell" in order to keep the armed forces — a hotbed of same-sex activity — in the closet, I found myself drinking coffee and ruminating in Barnes and Noble. Society, it seemed, was more concerned about whether or not we *said it* than whether or not we *did it*. Karen's transgression was arguably a verbal one. A quotation from a book by Judith Butler I was perusing happened to confirm my current opinion: "The line that demarcates the speakable from the unspeakable instates the current boundaries of the social. Could the uttering of the word [homosexual] constitute a slight, an injury, indeed, an offense, if the word did not carry the sedimented history of its own suppression?"[31] The offense of Karen's act of speaking the love that dare not speak its name was exacerbated by Sharon's imposed silence. Karen was the bad lesbian who talked; Sharon was the good lesbian silenced by incapacity.

Later that afternoon, I took a walk around Lake Calhoun. Minnesota has lakes even in the middle of cities, even if some of them are rather scummy. I sat on the lawn and watched the couples stroll by the shore — some of them runners with sweatbands, others pushing babies in strollers. A few hours north, these strangers could have been the Kowalskis, strolling with their elder daughter and her friend around a water-filled open-pit mine. Trauma had interrupted that vision, but what had made it unresumable — what kept Sharon from wheeling around the lake with her parents and Karen? Was it the law or love? The laws of love and then the love of law had raised walls around the parties and led them into the sorrows of disaffinity, disaffection, and disdain. I was looking for clues to the way our legal system functioned in domestic relations. It seemed to work to unrelate, to undomesticate, to polarize in many cases.

The case was coming into focus for me as I talked to more people and read more articles. There was the Duluth–St. Cloud coconspiracy, which was really not a conspiracy at all but a number of well-meaning, liberal judges and lawyers and journalists who ruled against Thompson for reasons that they were hiding behind — theories of invasion of privacy and control and protection of the culture of the Iron Range and its inherent bigotries as something that was ingrained in their society and therefore in need of preservation. On the other hand, Thompson's personality had gotten her into trouble — not so much because she was defiant but because she was self-righteous, potentially overpowering. As one judge stated, custody cases are often about control — about power and its abuse. There was a disconcerting element of Karen's personality that had nothing to do with sexual abuse and everything to do with overprotection. Both sides appeared to be hiding behind their own weakness in the face of the tragedy that had befallen Sharon — and them. In some ways more than for Sharon, the events were forcing them to come to terms with their own failings — whether bigotry, homophobia, or, on the other hand, a kind of incompatibility. Hamartia — some lack of grace under pressure — infused all the characters.

I began to wonder what I would do if my lover were injured and his parents kept me from him, refusing to recognize my devotion to him, refusing to let me visit him. Or, more plausibly, how would I feel if I were lying in a hospital dying from Kaposi's sarcoma or internal herpes, demented and wasting, as I had seen my best friend and as I often imagined myself? What if I were in Sharon's spot, though Sharon was not dying from AIDS but living with a disability, and semantically I was also *living* with this fatal disease, too? What if I were secluded somewhere in a suburban home or a rest home or a halfway house, barred from seeing my lover, from holding his hand or hugging him or hearing him talk, standing over me or sitting with his feet up on my bed and his golden retriever curled up at the foot of my bed? What if I couldn't say good-bye to him? What if . . . ?

EIGHT

Publicity

If anyone were allowed to fall in love with *anyone*, the word "homosexual" would not be needed.

Judy Grahan in Karla Jay, ed., *Out of the Closets*

"High Court Rejects Appeal from Lesbian, Set to Hear Sodomy Challenge Monday," read the headline in the *Washington Blade* on March 28, 1986. The United States Supreme Court had declined without comment to hear the Minnesota Civil Liberties Union's appeal on behalf of twenty-nine-year-old Sharon Kowalski, rejecting the contention that Kowalski's constitutional right to an attorney of her choice had been violated when Minnesota courts refused to allow MCLU attorneys to represent her. Janlori Goldman called the court's action a "terrible, terrible tragedy." Although Tom Hayes would continue to represent Sharon Kowalski in the litigation, Goldman told reporter Lisa Keen that the MCLU would be limited to filing amicus briefs in future motions. In the same article, Keen noted that "what many legal observers consider 'the perfect case' for testing the constitutionality of state laws prohibiting homosexual sodomy goes before the U.S. Supreme Court Monday." The case, *Bowers v Hardwick*, involved an Atlanta gay man, Michael Hardwick, who was arrested in his own bedroom. "Hardwick seeks to have the Georgia sodomy statute — which prohibits both heterosexual and homosexual sodomy — thrown out," Keen stated, "as a violation of the right to privacy under the U.S. Constitution" (*Washington Blade*, March 28, 1986, 1).

The dismissal of a case about the constitutional right to counsel for the handicapped and the acceptance of a case about the constitutional right of privacy between consenting adults had converged in the spring of 1986. Both had in common the same-sex orientation of the person whose rights were allegedly violated; Sharon Kowalski and Michael Hardwick were part of a growing field of gays and lesbians who were struggling to make the law accountable for their civil rights. An adjudication of "incapacity," however, had put Sharon outside the parameters of the civil rights laws that formed such a large part of the legal arguments against Donald's guardianship. That finding had rendered Sharon a ward, unable to make decisions for herself, including the decision to hire a lawyer.

On March 24, the Associated Press had issued its own headline,"U.S. Supreme Court Denies MCLU Appeal" (*St. Cloud Times,* March 24, 1986, sec. B, p. 1), signaling the heightened scrutiny by the media of the *Kowalski* case, coverage of which was already occurring with some frequency in the Minnesota, gay and lesbian, and feminist media. Julie Andrzejewski's letter to the editor in response to the *Minneapolis Star Tribune*'s coverage outlined the contentions of Karen's supporters. "Two major questions are raised by this case," she wrote, "Is Sharon being denied the right to recover as much of her physical and mental capabilities as possible because of the homophobia of institutions and individuals? Do constitutional rights (of association and representation by the counsel of one's choice) extend only to the able-bodied and heterosexual populations?" (Julie Andrzejewski, "The Trampled Rights of Sharon Kowalski," *Minneapolis Star Tribune,* March 25, 1986, sec. A, p. 19).

In spite of the Kowalskis' insistence on their own right to privacy, their attorney Jack Fena was well aware of the public strategy of Thompson and her cohorts; he also no doubt realized that in spite of his appellate victories, the guardianship dispute continued to be a thorn in his side. He wanted to counter the "issue-smelling" that he believed characterized the MCLU's and Thompson's tactics. In answer to their publicity, he sent letters to some of the local media, targeting first the campus newspaper at St. Cloud State, the very heart of Karen's support base. In the *St. Cloud State University Chronicle,* Fena told reporters that the relationship between these women was never "welded in iron"; in fact, evidence showed that Sharon was thinking of moving home at the time of the accident. Bringing in the lesbian issue was "a red herring," Fena said. "She's been given more rights than a man would have gotten. Was it Thompson's right to come out and talk about the nature of the relationship?" Fena asked. "What's more private than a person's sexual preference? I think Thompson has inflicted grievous harm." He insisted that a third person had no right to disclose another's sexual preference, especially to that person's parents. He felt the gay community had been "brain-washed in this case by Ms. Thompson and I believe if they were to view the medical records thoroughly they wouldn't give Ms. Thompson five cents to continue these attacks on Sharon Kowalski and her family" (Brenda Guderian, "Attorney Wants Other Side of Story to Be Heard," *St. Cloud State University Chronicle,* April 1, 1986, 3).

Ironically, Fena was using the same right to privacy to accuse Thompson that Michael Hardwick was using to justify his bedroom sexual practices in Georgia. This irony was lost on Thompson, who in disbelief read the article in her own school newspaper as if it were an April Fools' Day prank. Why was the press willing to believe Fena without any investigative reporting? she questioned. "Even some lesbians in Minnesota became convinced by the articles that there was no evidence that Sharon and I had indeed had a relationship," Karen would later write (*Why Can't,* 184).

But shortly after the publication of these depressing articles, Karen got a call from Richard Schmeichen and his partner, David Hoagland, the former a coproducer of the Academy Award–winning documentary *The Life and Times of Harvey Milk,* the story of the political rise to power and assassination of the gay San Francisco supervisor. The filmmakers were appalled at what was happening to Sharon and discussed the possibility of making a docudrama. "While I couldn't imagine our personal lives being portrayed on national television, I was desperate to get the story out to the public. To make such a decision was particularly scary because I knew I really couldn't control whether the story would be sensationalized. I decided to wait until the appellate court decision before answering," Karen later wrote (*Why Can't,* 184). Desperation for publicity and control over sensationalism would not always be compatible in the future.

Others in the lesbian and gay community were starting to come alive over Sharon's plight. Judy Fjell, a lesbian folksinger from Montana, volunteered to write a song for Sharon and Karen. Her song about AIDS, "Love Is a Dangerous Promise," struck a strong chord with Thompson, who kept hearing the refrain "Will you be there for me?" The song became part of her stump speech: "Now love is a dangerous promise, what a risk it can be / When you say you'll be there for another you never know what that might mean." When the concerned Fjell asked Thompson to come back to the Bay Area to give a talk, Karen found herself six weeks later under the bay on BART going to her first major speaking engagement, one that gave rise to the inaugural Committee to Free Sharon Kowalski. Less than three weeks after she flew to Boston to speak to gay and disabled activists and, while relaxing at a lesbian clambake, came to the realization that there were lesbian women like her all over the country. For the first time, Karen began to feel emotionally connected to the women's movement. A workshop followed at the Michigan Women's Music Festival that summer, the still guarded Thompson uncomfortable at the sight of topless and bottomless women asking her questions about guardianship. When she accidentally ran into one of her attorneys at the festival, the latter stated, "The problem is, you're just overdressed for the occasion, Karen" (*Why Can't,* 187).

Thompson's mettle was about to be tested further. In late May, Sue Wilson had argued the second appeal before the Minnesota Court of Appeals in St. Paul. Sharon's guardian was not following the visitation guidelines outlined in the court order of July 23, she argued, and therefore was in contempt of court. Sharon clearly wanted Thompson to visit, counsel reiterated, but the guardian would not permit it, ignoring the requirement that he take into account the ward's wishes and best interest in relation to visitation. After oral argument, the waiting game began again. Karen quietly put her hopes on the chance that the appellate judges would recognize how unfair it was to keep her from Sharon, just as many of the people she spoke to had come to realize.

But when Thompson returned from Michigan later that summer, her new-found popularity and support were mocked by *In re Guardianship of Sharon Kowalski,* the second published unanimous decision in the case, this time written by Judge Wozniak with Judges Leslie and Foley, concurring.[1] Wozniak's short decision demonstrated that the Court of Appeals was not inclined at this time to countenance any of Thompson's claims in spite of her attempts to garner support in the media. The judge ruled that the trial court had not abused its discretion in refusing to find the guardian in "contempt of court for terminating the visitation rights of the ward's former joint guardian and roommate, where the record indicates that this visitation has a detrimental effect on the ward." The court also ruled that the Minnesota Patients' Bill of Rights (Minnesota Statutes Section 144.651 [1984]) "imposes duties upon health care facilities and not upon guardians" and thus did not apply to Donald Kowalski. Wozniak also ruled that appellant Karen Thompson was "not entitled to conduct further discovery in this matter" and that "no conflict arises" from Jack Fena's "representing both the ward in her personal injury action and the guardian."[2]

In his factual summary, Judge Wozniak described Sharon as a "physically and mentally impaired" person who was "burdened with a child's mental capacity between four and six years of age." He described Thompson as the "former roommate" of Sharon's and stated that "serious animosity exists between Thompson and the Kowalski family. There has been extensive litigation between the parties." Wozniak's opinion did not mention lesbianism once, and the court decided on its own initiative to address the issues of discovery and the Patients' Bill of Rights. The tone of the short opinion was clearly "enough already" — exactly that of Jack Fena's statements. Wozniak also felt that the previous ruling had set the matter to rest. "All four of Sharon's attending physicians have stated that Thompson's visits were having a negative effect on Sharon's improvement," he stated, adding that "this court has already held that Donald Kowalski's termination of Thompson's visitation was in Sharon's best interest."[3]

The court ignored Sue Wilson's critique of the medical testimony, which echoed Tom Hayes's original argument at the December hearing; instead, it relied on the Popovich decision to declare the medical issue closed. "In light of this previous determination by this court [that 'medical testimony supported termination of Thompson's visitation']," the court concluded, "Thompson's argument that Donald Kowalski is in contempt of court for denying her visitation is without merit." The court was not interested in the necessity of a new determination of "expressed wishes" after the order nor in discussing the record concerning the "substituted judgment" of Sharon. As Wozniak made perfectly clear, "At that time [the time of the first opinion], this court was aware that, immediately after being appointed guardian, Donald Kowalski had terminated Thompson's visitation."[4]

News of the Court of Appeals decision took the wind out of Thompson's sails. A year had passed since her last visit with Sharon; she had spent close to $90,000 to discover that the denial of her right to see Sharon was within the parameters of the guardian's and the district court's discretion. The case would be appealed, Sue Wilson assured Karen, but the chances for Supreme Court review at either state or federal levels were slim at best. For one thing, there were more questions of fact in this case than questions of law: the case had boiled down, first, to a determination of Sharon's capacity to voice her desires, which the Duluth medical professionals found lacking, and, second, to a determination of the best interest of Sharon, which the medical profession judged to be the elimination of the outspoken and contentious Thompson. To what degree could these experts tie Sharon's depression to Thompson's assertiveness? Were they inclined to dismiss a lesbian lover in favor of a Catholic family from the Range? Did they really believe Thompson was too disruptive for their patient at this point? Or were they convinced by the colorful and popular Jack Fena?

While the Kowalskis saw their victory as an expensive price for peace from the harassment of media, politics, and the law, they could now, they hoped, put this bad dream behind them and pursue their retirement. Thompson, on the other hand, slipped quietly into depression After some reticence she agreed to visit a counselor, Elizabeth Baraga, who helped her "grieve" the loss of her sense of the world as she knew it. Thompson later reminisced, "I grieved the destruction of my faith in the judicial system. . . . [I]t was obvious to me that the courts could do anything they wanted regardless of the law. It didn't matter what the facts were" (*Why Can't*, 190).

Karen grew closer to Julie Andrzejewski, the activist lesbian who was working on her case. Julie was an atheist, however, and Karen associated primarily with Christians. One day Julie began a sarcastic critique of televangelists, many of whom, Karen suddenly admitted, she watched while riding her exercise bicycle in the morning. Julie told Karen to tune in to their political message, to the way they used homophobia as a pitch for donations. After long debates and discussion, the two colleagues decided to write a book — about Sharon and Karen, about facts and feelings. It would be a story of an evangelist turned lesbian activist, a story in direct opposition to the Exodus narrative the media had been covering since that gay conversion group's inception in 1976. Exodus was a Christian organization that sought to convert lesbians and gay men by teaching that freedom from homosexuality is possible through faith in Jesus Christ. Its business was turning lesbians into evangelists. The born-again Thompson was undertaking a different kind of exodus.

"I'm a little frustrated at this point," Karen told *Philadelphia Gay News* in a telephone interview on September 5, 1986, by what she called the "old boys' network" in the Minnesota courts. Judge Wozniak, she said, came from the Iron Range. Sue Wilson told reporter Emily Kahn, "The problem with judicial homophobia is that if you're homophobic you don't know it, and there's no way to explain it to them." Karen's lawyers were pessimistic about prevailing on appeal but had begun a letter-writing campaign to two judges on the Minnesota Supreme Court who were thought to be sympathetic to lesbian and gay civil rights (Emily Matilda Kahn, "Minnesota Court Rejects Another Thompson Appeal," *Philadelphia Gay News*, September 5, 1986, 5).

Mark Kasel, a reporter for the local Minneapolis gay press (*GAZE* and others), had followed the *Kowalski* case from the eighties through all its twists in the nineties. When interviewed in 1997, he was still acting as one of the unsung chroniclers of lesbian and gay life in Minneapolis, a bespectacled young man in his late twenties or thirties (it was hard to tell) managing the Kenwood Apartments East and West, no-frills brick rectangles perched on green hillsides near the expressway. Writing articles for almost no pay about the Minneapolis queer community (they came from farm towns as far away as eastern Montana), Mark lived in a crowded basement apartment, where he took me after I bought him dinner at Rudolph's Bar-B-Que on the corner of Franklin and Lyndale, a dark, big-boothed fifties affair, rather empty when we were there sloshing our way through weak coffee and greasy patty melts. Skinny, well-spoken, and slow-eating, Mark, who had grown up in St. Paul, took me into his apartment, chatting prosaically about all the "A-gays" in the "community" in his matter-of-fact manner. He had a copy of a videotape of Karen Thompson in Washington giving a tearful speech about same-sex marriage to a gathering of GLBTs. Mark had nothing negative to say about Karen Thompson and attributed any dissension in the ranks to internalized homophobia, though he conceded that she was hard to get to know at first. His articles had kept Minneapolis lesbians and gay men informed about Sharon Kowalski's ordeal.

The well-respected *Gay Community News* in Boston also followed the case closely. After noting that "legal avenues may be nearly exhausted for a lesbian who has been fighting to visit her disabled lover for over a year," staff writers reported that Thompson now planned to pursue more public routes of action. "It's obvious the system is not going to deal with this case," said Thompson, "unless an awful lot of pressure is brought to bear." The article reported that local organizing efforts had begun around the country: a San Francisco group distributed ten thousand leaflets at the Gay Games and sold "Free Sharon Kowalski" T-shirts and buttons. A national newsletter was forthcoming, and Karen Thompson was slated to speak in Washington, D.C., on September 24 and in New York in November (Stephanie Poggie, *GCN*, "Thompson Seeks Publicity to Pressure Minnesota Courts," September 14–20, 1986, 1).

Karen published her first editorial — entitled "Why Can't Sharon Kowalski Come Home?" — in October (*Sojourner*, October 1986, 21). Her book would take the same title as this editorial, excerpts of which were widely disseminated in flyers at rallies across the country. It was in fact a transcription of a speech Karen had given in Boston and would later deliver at colleges, gay organizations, and law schools around the country. The famous stump speech spoke simply and directly to issues Thompson cast as wider than "the homophobic court system and medical profession" that "would rather declare a person totally helpless mentally and physically than deal with the issues of this case, and every single human being should find that threatening." Although she believed she would not be fighting this battle "if we weren't gay," Thompson insisted that there were "key human rights and disability rights issues involved." The case was setting a precedent that a human being could "be denied the right to be present when her future is being decided upon, that a human can be kept from having any say in what's happening to her even though she can type words, phrases, sentences. This is appalling and frightening." The precedent could be used against straights and gays alike, she told audiences. "In one split-second any of us could become Sharon Kowalski. We could be disabled through accident or illness, and this case could be used to take our rights always from us."

Karen spoke about how her relationship with Sharon had "very much been made an issue in this case, with the Kowalskis claiming that I'm a sick, crazy person who made it all up." Ironically, Thompson admitted, she had "been forced to prove a relationship that we spent four years trying to hide." Before the accident, Karen "hadn't even used the word 'gay'" and "had been scared to death when Sharon told me she wanted to tell her work supervisor about our relationship." She finally came out because she "needed power" and "finally realized that as long as I was scared and invisible, I would be vulnerable; I was much more vulnerable in the closet than I am out." Thompson understood that "by not being willing to come out and take a stand," lesbians and gays were admitting that "there was something wrong" with them (Karen Thompson, "Why Can't Sharon Kowalski Come Home?" *Sojourner*, October 1986, 21).

Karen's moving rhetoric brought many, including herself, to tears through its evangelical sincerity reminiscent of the young female Methodist in George Eliot's *Adam Bede*. Thompson also began to give regular interviews, stating in one with Anne Phibbs of the *Gay Community News* that she soon learned how impossible it was going to be to take care of Sharon by herself. She realized she "needed more people power and more political power. I also came to understand that I couldn't carry this struggle alone on a personal level, either," referring to the support she got from gay and lesbian people in St. Cloud. Phibbs then broached the sexual question: Were Karen and Sharon able to carry on their relationship as lovers after the accident? Thompson equivocated, asking, "Just because Sharon's disabled, does that mean she's quit feeling or needing things? My attorneys think I will be clobbered, that I'll be shot down with that type of information on the stand right now. But the idealist in me makes me feel that the disability rights group should be able to fight for Sharon's rights to have a relationship." If Sharon could type out "I want to make love," Karen stated, why couldn't she? Phibbs then asked Karen about Donald Kowalski's charges that she would sexually abuse Sharon if allowed to visit her. Karen replied that the doctors had never observed anything to substantiate their fear; what is more, the doctors were, on the one hand, saying there was no sexual relationship and, on the other hand, claiming that if there were, there would be potential for abuse. "That's the logic of our medical profession."[5]

Wherever Karen went, she had two strong recommendations for whomever she addressed: come out and legally protect yourself. "As long as we're in the closet, as long as we're segmented into couples like Sharon and I were, and as long as the gay men and lesbians keep split, then we will never gain any rights." Karen's advocacy had led her to the realization that romance and gender can create their own closets, allowing two people of the same sex to feel they can shut out a world that is a step away from separating them. In *On the Issues* (November 1986, 4), Thompson revealed that she had come out "nationally before I came out to myself." It had been "a very humanizing, humbling experience" for her. "The gay rights groups were the first to offer me support. The very groups I didn't want to be labeled part of and that I was as homophobic about as the straight population. And that's really sad," Karen told her interviewer, lamenting her earlier internal homophobia. "I believed that Sharon and I were 'normal,' we weren't like 'them,' whatever 'them' is. Now, I've had the opportunity to meet many 'thems' and found out that they're very much like us. It's been a real eye-opening experience" ("The Crusade of Karen Thompson," *On the Issues*, November 1986, 4).

In November, Karen spent three nights in New York City, speaking to enthusiastic audiences and forming another Free Sharon Kowalski group. Sponsored by the Gay and Lesbian Community Center, Lesbian Feminist Liberation, and the Gay Women's Alternative, Thompson lectured not only about homophobia, sexism, and handicapism but also about the need for gay and lesbian couples to sign durable powers of attorney — notarized and witnessed documents that give one's partner the right to handle all financial affairs, all medical decisions, as well as visitation and living facilities in the case of incapacity. If Sharon and Karen had signed one of these documents, they would probably be together today, she was often quoted as saying.

Karen also met with producers at *60 Minutes*, who seemed extremely interested in the press package she had supplied them. They told her they would contact her in a few months (*Why Can't*, 193 ff). The *60 Minutes* interview began a series of dealings between Thompson and the network shows over airing a story about Sharon's case. Karen was exhilarated at first, with the thought of national coverage of her plight giving her hope, but there were several false starts. After the people from *60 Minutes* called to tell her they would begin filming in February, she called them back to find out they were overbooked and were not sure if they could get to her story. Inquiries followed from *West 57th Street* and *The Phil Donahue Show*, both of which had heard about the case from a producer at *60 Minutes*.

When contacted by these producers through their attorney Jack Fena, the Kowalskis adamantly opposed any media coverage. Not only were they very private people opposed to sensationalizing their daughter's hardship; they also felt that the press had no understanding of their situation and had shown no sensitivity to their position in the case. Jack Fena faithfully voiced the concerns of his clients to the producers of the shows, in one case visiting New York to talk with *West 57th Street*. The networks were professionally committed to telling both sides of the story, and if one side would not cooperate, their task was made more difficult. *West 57th* told Karen to wait; they would look into another way to tell the story. CBS would delay another year before contacting her again. The *Donahue* show almost came to air. The producers called Karen and told her the Kowalskis had agreed to appear; a date was set, but the airing was canceled when Don and Della found out that Thompson was to be on the same show. They flatly refused to be in the same room as Thompson and decided at the last minute that even splitting the show with Karen would be too risky. They had seen what the media could do to their message and remained wary.

Finally, in March 1987, Karen was offered a half-hour time slot by Sally Jesse Raphael in St. Louis; she would share the time with a transsexual who had been separated from her son. Interrupted by Sally at the outset of her five-minute, memorized introduction, Karen found herself caught off guard, unable to compete with the audience, the transsexual, and Sally. She was not able to make the points she wanted as the show descended into gross overgeneralizations about acceptable "lifestyles." Thompson left St. Louis discouraged about television, deciding that the best way she could have "some control over the format" was to concentrate on speaking engagements and her book. Invitations to speak, which she rarely turned down, continued to increase. At the National Gay and Lesbian Health Care Providers Conference in Los Angeles, she spoke on homophobia in medicine, coming face-to-face with the first people with AIDS she had ever met.

When she returned from Los Angeles, Thompson opened an invitation asking her to be a grand marshal at the New York City Gay Pride Parade. With fear, she accepted. At this point in her life, her spring weekly routine began Monday through Thursday with teaching quietly at St. Cloud; then, from Thursday through the weekend, she would transform herself, flying all over the country to speak, to receive the Long Distance Runner Award from the Minnesota chapter of NOW, to the Gay Pride Rally in Washington, D.C., in anticipation of the October 11 march on Washington. At every gathering Karen said a prayer to a god about whose gender and denomination she was now uncertain. In an interview with *Minnesota Women's Press*, Thompson declared, "I believe in God. One on one, my personal relationship with Christ tells me there is a bigger picture, that I don't hold all the pieces. But religion is frightening. I found that it may be another institution that I have to re-evaluate, that my perception may be totally wrong" (Amy Lindgren, "Nightmare Leads Karen Thompson into Struggle for Rights, Reunion," *Minnesota Women's Press*, May 12, 1987, 1).

In June, Thompson returned to St. Cloud to discover the *St. Paul Pioneer Press* (June 14, 1987, sec. D, p. 1) had published "A Silent Ordeal," a feature-length article by Nancy Livingston with full-color photos on the struggle of the Kowalskis to take care of their daughter. On the cover of the Sunday Morning section, a photo showed Don and Della with Sharon, head tilted, between them in a wheelchair. Don, his large, metal-rimmed glasses and big forehead accenting a receding hairline, sat with a smile on his face. Della, her head tilted, too, rested her chin on the back of Sharon's chair, her hair in a stylish bouffant, her manicured hands stretched out on her daughter's shoulders. Sharon looked out from the wheelchair with a surprised, almost tearful, look on her face. In bold, the article began: "Karen Thompson has made her custody battle for accident victim Sharon Kowalski a nationwide gay rights issue. Now, consider the other side of the story, the anguish of parents Don and Della Kowalski, who have won in court, but lost their peace of mind." Livingston's article sounded a tragic note: "The historic case has pitted parental rights against gay rights and the rights of the handicapped. At this point, Sharon's parents, Don and Della Kowalski, have won, but it has cost them their life savings and their happiness. Meanwhile, Thompson refuses to let the issue die."

Karen Thompson, thirty-nine, "in her sensible shoes and no-nonsense clothes," the feature stated, "radiates authority. But when she watches a videotape of her former lover struggling to bring a cup of water to her lips, the starch goes stiff on her spine." Livingston wrote of the "national" support Thompson was garnering through stories that portrayed her as a "heroine," while the Kowalskis "have borne the emotional burden of their daughter's paralysis. Their savings, their peace of mind and their plans for a leisurely retirement all have been lost." The *Pioneer Press* wanted to give readers an insight into Don and Della's suffering as "week in and week out, they have known despair as they dutifully travel the 10 miles back and forth to the Hibbing nursing home, where their eerily silent daughter lies trapped in her twisted body." Unlike the media-savvy Thompson, the Kowalskis had "resisted media attention," even though they have "chafed at the 'oppressor' image that has been thrust on them."

Now they felt "compelled to share their story with Minnesotans," feeling they had "been portrayed as mean-spirited, narrow-minded people who are holding their daughter prisoner because they disapprove of her sexual preference." Because Don and Della "do not believe their daughter is a homosexual, they can't understand Thompson's motives," Livingston reported, describing the excruciating questions that continued to torture them. "Why? Why doesn't this woman leave Sharon in peace? Why won't she leave us in peace?" The Kowalskis did not think of their daughter as anyone's "lesbian lover." They never knew her in that role. "To Don and Della, their eldest child was a basketball star, skier, nature lover, motorcycle rider, fun-loving daughter and thoughtful aunt to her niece and nephew." Beyond the relentless intrusions of Thompson, the Kowalskis faced some medical, legal, or media reminder almost every day. "A good night's sleep" was "a distant memory." Don Kowalski detailed the random thoughts that careened "through his unconscious":

> What is Sharon thinking, sitting in that nursing home? Does she remember the accident? Does she feel sad? How did she really feel about Karen Thompson? Why does Karen want Sharon now? Is it money? What would she do with Sharon if she ever did get custody of her? What am I going to do now that my $30,000 savings is gone? . . . Why did all this happen to a retired miner from Nashwauk who has worked hard all his life, raised a family and put enough money away to live out his life in modest comfort?

The article ended with a description of Sharon's attendance at Debbie's wedding to her second husband, where the Kowalskis' elder daughter was "surrounded by smiling relatives." Della told the *Pioneer Press* that Sharon looked as though she wanted to cry when she had to depart. " 'Sometimes it's so hard to leave her,' Della says. And then Della starts to cry." The Kowalskis said "hope" was "thin" that Sharon would ever recover or that their lives after these "legal and ethical crises" would ever be the same. " 'God Almighty is the only one that has the answer,' " the article ended, quoting Donald Kowalski.

The *Pioneer Press* feature sent Karen into another "tailspin" (*Why Can't*, 204). Julie wrote a reply instantly, but it was never printed. In it she voiced the concerns of disability groups about the stereotypes promoted by such language as "their eerily silent daughter lies trapped in her twisted body"—turning the disabled into scary and repugnant subhumans. The "Silent Ordeal" was really Sharon's, the letter stated, since she has been silenced by the medical and legal professions—cut off from those she loved before the accident because of discrimination against the disabled and lesbian communities. Karen's reply, which she drafted carefully, was published, with considerable emendations. In it, Karen called for professional mediation of her dispute with the parents and reiterated her love for Sharon (*Why Can't*, 205).

The *St. Paul Pioneer Press* also published a letter from Jack Fena, in which he ironically wanted to "set the record straight" — a record that seemed as straight as his clients could hope from the press. "Karen Thompson, as Sharon Kowalski's instructor at St. Cloud State University, used her position of power and authority to take Sharon over and influence her and dominate her," the attorney told readers. "It is common knowledge that teachers have power over their students. For some reason, this never appears in the press. If this were Johnny Thompson instead of Karen Thompson and Johnny had entered into a sexual relationship publicly with a student, what would the effect be then?" (Jack Fena, letter, *St. Paul Pioneer Press*, June 28, 1984).

After two months of negotiation with the *Pioneer Press*, Sue Wilson was finally given permission to print her reply to Fena's letter. She pointed out that Sharon and Karen made a commitment to one another, initiated by Sharon, two years after Sharon had taken a class with Thompson. "The real issue in this case is whether or not a young lesbian woman, who had never told her parents about her sexual orientation, should be denied the right to continue to see a person significant to her recovery and to continue the relationship she has chosen, simply because she was disabled by a tragic accident," Wilson insisted. "The precedents set in this case have sent a shock wave through the gay, lesbian and handicapped communities. Concerned people report to me their horror that the First Amendment right of free association seems to have been so flagrantly violated in this case. It appears to me that they are right" (M. Sue Wilson, letter, *St. Paul Pioneer Press,* August 8, 1987).

In contrast to the *Pioneer Press* article by Nancy Livingston, Mike Salinas told the same story from a different side in his feature that appeared in the *New York Native,* the gay and lesbian paper that served Manhattan. "Right now a young woman lies trapped in an institution, unable to provide effectively for her considerable medical needs, 24 hours a day in bed and in diapers, forcibly separated from her beloved," Salinas began. "For over two years she has been deprived by her keepers of the special instruments she needs for basic communication, deprived of the care of her loved one, deprived of therapy which would keep her from sinking further into inexorable decay and death. Her tragic story has been ignored by state officials who could alleviate her suffering," he continued. "Her name is Sharon Kowalski, and she is a lesbian. Because of that, she lies day after day imprisoned, without the simplest of rights granted to even the most despised American prisoner. Kowalski is held against her will in a nursing home in Hibbing, Minnesota. A drunk driver took away most of Kowalski's abilities; it took the American justice system to take away her rights."

Salinas continued with a historical background for his New York audience, describing the upbringing of Sharon Mary Kowalski, born August 8, 1956, a strong and healthy baby with brown hair and hazel eyes, who grew up as "a good example of the hardworking Poles from whom she is descended, outgoing and popular with a crowd when she wasn't indulging in her secret passion for long walks alone in the woods." Sharon's parents, much like other families in Hibbing, had married young and started their family immediately, her father joining the other men in town in the iron ore mines, "while her mother tended to the house and the three children, as was expected of women in the area."

Salinas wrote of the "overt sexism" of Iron Range culture, in which Mark Kowalski, the favored son, received special treatment, while a "quiet resentment" grew in the outgoing Sharon, who wanted to go to college and live a life different from that of her mother and sister. Sharon did, "against all odds, and against all advice," achieve her dream of earning a college degree and simultaneously realized another dream when she met one of her teachers. Salinas told the story of Sharon and Karen's clandestine relationship. "Homosexuality was an unmentionable topic in Polish Catholic communities such as Hibbing and although Karen came from the relatively more liberal New Concord, Ohio, it was still not a palatable subject for her to discuss with her parents," the feature explained. "It never seemed necessary, anyway. Everyone seemed to accept the relationship on the terms the two women described: that Sharon was Karen's tenant."

The feature-length article progressed through the chronology, detailing the conflicting reaction to Sharon's condition from Thompson and Sharon's parents. When asked about the claim that she was sexually abusing Sharon while bathing her, Karen replied to the *Native*, "Have you ever bathed a person with a brain injury? As if I have enough hands to sexually abuse her! If you've ever worked with a person with spastic movements, putting them in a tub full of water, you know that if you took one hand away to sexually abuse them they'd fall into the water and drown." Karen continued, discussing how Donald could hardly stand "touching her let alone massaging her, bathing her!" He did not take his daughter out on day trips because *he* did not want to be embarrassed, the article noted. "And yet," Karen stated, "the court found him to be a better guardian than me. I'm not an elitist, but he's a retired miner with a sixth-grade education and I'm a specially trained therapist."

Salinas's feature also reviewed the legal maneuvers in the case and the "old-boy network" of the Minnesota courts. "Court of Appeals Judges D. D. Wozniak and Peter Popovich are both from Hibbing; they play hockey with Fena regularly, and Popovich served in the legislature with Fena," Salinas reported, noting finally that Governor Rudy Perpich was also from Hibbing. State-sanctioned homophobia was central to this tragic case, a prejudice that left unheeded Sharon's signature plea at Leisure Hills: "Help me. Get me out of here" (Mike Salinas, "Free Sharon Kowalski!" *New York Native*, April 6, 1987, p. 1).

The summer of 1987, in spite of its ups and downs, was a season of mobilization for Karen Thompson. The original Committee for the Right to Recovery and Relationships in St. Cloud continued its campaign, while another coalition of disability, lesbian and gay, feminist, and civil rights groups in the state formed a committee called Bring Sharon Home, organizing petitions to legislators, meetings with state officials, demonstrations, and press releases. Karen and Julie worked on their book, which had an August deadline. After speaking to NOW groups in Philadelphia and Florida, Thompson identified herself as a lesbian feminist activist without reservations. In July, NOW adopted a resolution in support of Thompson's right to visit Sharon.

In a speech at Take Back the Night in Minneapolis, the once reserved Thompson declared: "I've had a crash course in understanding our rich white heterosexual able-bodied Christian male system that oppresses *anyone* who is *different!* This system oppresses Sharon and me because we're women, we're lesbians and Sharon is disabled." But Thompson insisted she was telling her story "not to depress but to empower." She refused to let her pain eat her up but instead told audiences that she could channel "that pain and anger into a constructive outlet and become an agent for change." Karen's speech ended with a warning: "If we don't answer the question 'Why can't Sharon come home,' if we don't win this case, the question tomorrow might be, *why can't you come home?*" (*Why Can't*, 214–15).

By the middle of my stint in the North Star State during May of 1997, I found myself driving around in circles — Minneapolis, St. Cloud, Virginia, Duluth, Minneapolis. My travels eventually brought me to Mille Lacs, between St. Cloud and Hibbing, to take photographs, visit the accident site, and stop at Garrison, home of the Blue Goose. As I approached the location of the accident fourteen years after its occurrence, the highway was divided ten miles from Onamia, roads following either side of the lake. There were two lanes going north on Highway 169, the west fork. I passed Chico's Place, Kwadna Bar and Restaurant, and Eddie's Lake Mille Lacs Resort, with launch fishing and boat rentals. Walleyes were big here. It was cloudy but not going to rain — just a thin layer of sixty-two-degree nimbi. My fear was that I myself might get into an auto accident as I retraced the route. If I were rendered unconscious, how would I keep people away from my blood? Universal precautions.

The lake was huge — I could barely see the other side. Econolodge was on the left, Cozy Cove Resort on the right. There was a lot of slashing and burning going on; highway workers were unearthing trees and then burning them. I wondered about the logistics of the accident itself, given the clear and maneuverable condition of the roads. Proceeding north to Garrison, I stopped at the Izatys Historical Marker, which read: "In this vicinity stood the great Sioux village of Izatys where Duluth planted the French Coat of Arms on July 2, 1679. The settlement was visited by Father Hennepin in 1680. About 1750 the Chippewa moving westward from Lake Superior captured the village and in this decisive battle drove the Sioux permanently into Southern Minnesota." I went through Garrison and took a picture of the Blue Goose Inn, which had been reconstructed. Next to it was an off-sale liquor store. Anglers were welcome. I decided not to sit down in there — it was only 11:55. I drove on, past Tame Fish Road, Bennetville, and Highway 11.

The terrain was open, the roads were wide and straight, and as I headed up to the Iron Range town of Virginia to interview Judge Gary Pagliaccetti, I started to think about the case. What was it about, anyway? Sameness and difference? Power? Ethics — or, as dictionaries phrased it, the science of ideal human character? Custom? Boundaries? Morality? Who, I asked myself, decided the way we must be to be together, the way Sharon and Karen must live their lives, the Kowalskis theirs? What standard generalities — what laws — applied to all particulars? The ideal of justice within legal systems was administered through a set of rules that codified existing customs, including religious beliefs and individual predilections, making philosophical notions of an objective and fair standard of law almost always tainted by subjective positions. Under this inevitability, how could the historical bias against gays and lesbians not tip the balance of the scales in Sharon's case?

Even more than the codes we lived by, epistemology itself, the methods of thinking — the ways of understanding the world — seemed to have embedded in them processes of categorization that discriminated, judged, condemned, and excluded. These categories applied to both queers and Christians and those in between — to Julie Andrzejewski, Judge Popovich, and Tom Hayes. Not only was objectivity elusive, but the mind itself worked to inculcate difference and rank it.

On the other hand, maybe ignorance, not ways of knowing, was the problem in the Kowalski case. Maybe the case illustrated a lack of exposure and experience that proved morality was not just a matter of blood or chromosomes or icons or geography or capital, that judgment based on such categories was in fact unethical. Had Sharon come out on the Range, would the Kowalskis' generation have been ready for it? Would the Kowalskis have joined love of their daughter with a vague inkling of tolerance to accept her? Ethics might be about tolerance of everything but intolerance, as Marcuse said, everything but ignorance, blissful though it might be, everything but irrational discrimination.

Maybe I was looking for reasons behind behavior where there were none. Was fear explainable — Sharon's fear of the Range mentality, Don's fear of Thompson? Fear found its social mitigation in security, ownership, blood, religion, sexual orientation, gender, shared oppression — ties that were binding, that connected and, in connecting, disconnected from others. As each of us filled our own sense of lack with the promise of group fulfillment, with the promise of identity, with the promise of god, those outside our armor were threatening to expose the emptiness it was hiding — the fragility of life, an exposure we tried to react against. With what? Aspersion, nonrecognition, denial, animosity. Definitions, certainty, assurance (the Range "mentality," the gay "agenda") kept us from the boons that chaos might confer — the openness, uncertainty, doubt, and anxiety that could come from change. Even history and its emanation in legal precedent also defined and confined — condemned or taught. This authority was another form of stability, another form of power, another way of avoiding principle again, avoiding some ideal like equality in difference, some mandatory freedom, some shot at fairness, some respect for everything but disrespect. Some philosophy.

NINE

Petition

God gave them up unto vile affections: for even their women did change the natural use into that which is against nature: And likewise also the men, leaving the natural use of the woman, burned in their lust one toward another.

Romans 1:24–27

Decisions of individuals relating to homosexual conduct have been subject to state intervention throughout the history of Western Civilization. Condemnation of those practices is firmly rooted in Judeao-Christian moral and ethical standards.

Bowers v Hardwick, 478 US 168

Assuming that romantic friendships and lesbianism are historical variants of the same thing, Faderman asks: "if these romantic friendships were in the quality and intensity of the emotions involved no different from lesbian love, why were they so readily condoned in earlier eras and persecuted in ours?" . . . What produced the change in attitude, she believes, were reactionary responses to the demands of first-wave feminism, and—even more emphatically—the increasing tendency [in the nineteenth and twentieth centuries] by sexologists to pathologise female homosexuality.

Lillian Faderman, Surpassing the Love of Men

Almost a millennium after Saint Paul wrote his epistles, and within a year of the pronouncements of the chief justice of the United States Supreme Court and one of the most eminent lesbian historians of our era (Lillian Faderman), Karen Thompson's lawyer filed a petition for an order restoring Sharon Kowalski to capacity and other relief in the Probate Division of the Sixth Judicial District, County of St. Louis, on September 16, 1987.[1] Sue Wilson was facing an archive of erasure and condemnation from discourses as varied as religion, law, biology, psychology, and medicine. Her client was a homosexual; her job was to legitimate that designation in the face of a history of opprobrium. A change of venue in the case did not make the task any easier; the Kowalski case had been transferred from St. Cloud to the northern district that included both Duluth and Hibbing, where Sharon was currently residing at Leisure Hills.

Under Minnesota law, a petition for restoration to capacity like this one could be brought by any person, but the petitioner must prove at a hearing by a preponderance of the evidence that the ward is no longer incapacitated. Sue Wilson's motion alleged that Donald Kowalski, the present guardian, had not complied with either the January 3, 1986, order of Judge Johnson or Minnesota Statutes Section 525.58, subds. 2–3, both of which required annual reevaluations of Sharon in order to keep the court advised of her condition. Wilson was asking the court to allow her client, petitioner Thompson, to reenter the litigation — conduct discovery, depose witnesses, subpoena records — to meet the burden of proving Sharon's capacity. She also requested that the medical evaluation take place at the Sister Kenny Institute in Minneapolis, the only rehabilitation facility in Minnesota with a special brain-injury unit that included social workers. Finally, since Thomas Hayes had recently resigned as Sharon's court-appointed lawyer, Wilson put forth the name of Brian O'Neill as a replacement, the attorney from Faegre and Benson in Minneapolis who was familiar with the case from previous amicus briefs he filed for the MCLU and who was also willing to take the case on for free (pro bono).[2]

Jack Fena's short memorandum of law in reply to Wilson's new legal maneuver made an argument of res judicata, a legal doctrine that declares once a case comes to judgment in a court of competent jurisdiction, that judgment is conclusive upon the parties in any subsequent litigation involving the same parties and the same cause of action, thereby preventing relitigation of cases already decided on the merits. This doctrine usually does not apply to guardianship cases, where the action remains legally open until the guardianship is over. As part of his argument, Fena listed and exhibited the nineteen separate appeal orders and decisions from the Minnesota Courts of Appeals and Supreme Court, as well as the United States Supreme Court, that the dispute had amassed.[3] But, as the decision bore out, the sheer volume of litigation is not determinative in a guardianship case, where the factual circumstances are subject to change and the court is established to monitor those changes.

Fena also filed affidavits. In his capacity as the plaintiff's attorney in Sharon's personal injury suit, set for trial on January 4, 1988, he set out in his own declaration that further testing of Sharon at this juncture "would have a bad and detrimental effect on the outcome of Sharon Kowalski's personal injury and dram shop case." Harry A. Sieben of Minneapolis, whom Fena had associated in the negligence case, concurred, stating that "any further medical or psychiatric examinations of Sharon Kowalski would result in additional expense and delay to the Plaintiff." Fena also claimed that Karen Thompson was on the witness list for the defense in this personal injury suit against the Blue Goose. Fena called Thompson's petition "nothing short of harassment" and characterized the petitioner as a "stranger" without standing "to meddle into the guardianship," claiming her pleading was part of a campaign to invade the Kowalskis' privacy.[4]

Included in Fena's affidavit was another letter from Dr. William Wilson, who reiterated his opinion that Sharon had "very limited ability to communicate effectively her desires and needs." Wilson still considered Sharon a "highly vulnerable adult" who could easily be subject to "sexual abuse." Dr. Wilson also reported that Donald Kowalski had recently undergone "repeated coronary angiography" because of unstable angina. The stress of the legal battles with Karen Thompson was, according to the physician, a "direct causative factor" of his patient's heart condition, and Wilson recommended that Don stay out of court for the next six months. The physician's letter was the first public notice of the guardian's health problems.[5] The *St. Paul Pioneer Press* had documented Donald's stress; previous records had detailed Della's nervous problems; and even Thompson had openly discussed her own emotional traumas and the help she sought for them, though her physical condition had not yet suffered. For both parties, the media spotlight on the case had brought a new dimension of daily anxiety, adding an element of harassment to the already risky and expensive business of litigation — in Donald's case the mind was taking its toll on the body.

But for Thompson and her followers the media had become the message, publicity their one avenue of pressure in a case that had exhausted its legal appeals. On October 11, Karen was a featured speaker at the National Gay and Lesbian Rights March on Washington, addressing an estimated two hundred thousand people. The *Village Voice* reported that an uneasy Thompson marched in the banner-holding front line between performer Kate Clinton, a lesbian comedian, who "took care of her," and Harvey Fierstein, the author and star of *Torch Song Trilogy,* whom she had never heard of. Backstage, Karen rehearsed her speech over and over, but her turn to speak was interrupted by the arrival of Jesse Jackson in a "staccato flash of cameras." Distracted, Thompson finally found herself before a microphone in front of a rapt audience as she delivered her message. When done speaking, the *Voice* reported, she went backstage crying over having left out the part about living wills, the sobs preventing her from hearing the crowd "out front shouting, 'Bring Sharon Home! Bring Sharon Home!'" (Alisa Solomon, "Activist by Accident," *Village Voice*, October 20, 1987, p. 29).

More copy came on October 26, when the *Minneapolis Star Tribune* (M. L. Smith, "100 Rally at Capitol to 'Free' Brain-Damaged Woman," October 26,

1987, sec. B, p. 1) and the *St. Cloud Times* (Debra Olson, "Supporters Rally to 'Free' Woman," October 26, 1987, sec. C, p. 1) described protesters "bundled up against a biting wind" to demonstrate in St. Paul on the steps of the capitol. To the beat of a solo drum, demonstrators carried a large, black wooden wheelchair to the steps as three others dressed in black judicial robes read excerpts from various court proceedings (John Ritter, "Rally for Sharon Kowalski, Supporters Urged to Call Officials," *Equal Time*, November 11, 1987, p. 1). Rally organizers collected 130 signatures, which they sent to Governor Rudy Perpich along with petitions from other states asking him to review the case.

In a telephone conversation with reporter Debra Olson of the *St. Cloud Times*, Donald Kowalski gave his side of the story. He had spent thousands of dollars protecting his daughter, and the appeals had gone all the way to the Supreme Court. "If the court is satisfied, who is she (Thompson)?" Kowalski asked. "Is she above the court? There is nothing that will ever stop her. If she doesn't get exactly what she wants, there's no use talking." To verify Donald's point, Olson quoted Thompson as stating that even civil disobedience might at some point be necessary: "Someday, I might walk in and see Sharon and, if they want to arrest me, they can arrest me," said the frustrated professor.

With the coverage in the *Village Voice*, other progressive media began discussing the case. On November 8, in an article entitled "Lesbian Supporters Campaign to Bring Sharon Kowalski Home," Leslie Feinberg, the transgendered author-to-be of *Stone Butch Blues*, reported for *Workers World* that "wide-spread fund-raising efforts of groups nationally, and Thompson's tireless campaign" had raised all but $30,000 of Thompson's $110,000 legal bills. Feinberg reported that a birthday card campaign by Rainbow Women, a disability rights group, had resulted in the collection in August of over a thousand cards, but Governor Perpich reportedly refused to deliver them to Sharon (Leslie Feinberg, "Lesbian Supporters Campaign to Bring Sharon Kowalski Home," *Workers World*, November 19, 1987). Sharon's case, ironically, had brought together the socialist Feinberg and the onetime Reagan Republican Thompson.

Another reporter, Mark Stodghill, a staff writer for the *Duluth News-Tribune*, was an unlikely candidate to stay up until one in the morning interviewing Karen Thompson on a chilly night in November 1987. But he and Thompson had some things in common. Stodghill was a hundred-miler and used marathons to train for those grueling races. Like Thompson at one time, he was also a self-styled conservative in the conservative town of Duluth. He grew up dirt poor in the Twin Cities and went to school to eat his lunch and play ball, mostly hoops and baseball. About the same age as Thompson, Stodghill also long knew that he would be involved in some kind of sports and coached for a while in the Twin Cities before moving to Hibbing. But he left coaching, he commented, about the time that coaches were asked to relate to their players instead of the other way around. He spent the first seven years at the *Tribune* on the sports desk, but after he started having kids, he put in for a change because sports means working weekends. He was not sure how he got assigned to the Kowalski case. He had been covering murder trials at the time and knew little or nothing about civil law, but he was beginning to write features, and the case had an emotional appeal. It dealt with a Range lesbian being outed against her will.

Stodghill's opinion about gays and lesbians might be characterized by some as "don't ask, don't tell," with all the implications of the Uncle Tom assimilation that this policy promotes, but his attitude was in many ways more complex. Later, in 1996, when the *Tribune* had given him his own column called "Northern Lights," he wrote a story entitled "Ellen's Sex Life Is Not My Concern." The reporter began by declaring that he was not one of the forty-two million people who the ABC television network says "celebrated" the coming out of Ellen DeGeneres's sitcom character on prime time. "Don't call me a homophobe — I have no fear of homosexuals," Stodghill explained, but you "can call me a prude." He neither condoned nor condemned "the gay lifestyle" but simply did not want it "shoved" in his face, by either "TV show or parade." He also resented "the inference that there was something wrong with him" because he was "not prepared to jump on the gay bandwagon of fashionable liberal enlightenment."

The article ended with a revelation. "You have to be pretty ignorant not to know that homosexuals are our political leaders, our bosses, our teachers, our sons and daughters, or in my case — my only living brother. I don't call him my gay brother or my homosexual brother. He's my brother." For Stodghill, sexuality was a private issue, one that called for modesty and respect (Mark Stodghill, "Ellen's Sex Life Is Not My Concern," *Duluth News-Tribune*, May 11, 1997, sec. E, p. 1).

"Did Karen Thompson have a right to out Sharon Kowalski?" Stodghill asked me during an interview in 1997. "What choice did she have given the circumstances?" A few years after Stodghill had interviewed Karen in 1986, he heard that she had "badmouthed" him during a lecture at the University of Minnesota at Duluth; he wondered why, because he thought he had given a pretty fair account of the case. But Thompson was competitive, he reflected. She played sports, and like all good players she played to win and was willing to do anything to come out on top.

From the reporter's perspective, the Kowalski case was about invasion of privacy. He felt conflicted about writing the story because he knew the Kowalskis would be upset, but like a good reporter he put aside his mixed feelings and did his job. He liked Della more than Don, who was blunt and constantly saying things that demonstrated a lack of education. But he felt sorry for the Kowalskis because the case depleted them, drained them of their health, their money, their peace. They happened to have chosen the most colorful, outrageous, and popular character on the Range for their lawyer — Jack Fena, who at loggerheads with Thompson and her attorney, Sue Wilson, turned the case in a direction that prevented Sharon's "best interests" from remaining paramount.

"Karen Thompson says she spent four years in a secret lesbian relationship — and has spent the last four years trying to prove it existed," Stodghill began his first article on the Kowalski case. He was, unfortunately, unable to talk to Don, Della, or Sharon Kowalski then. "They don't know and they don't care," he quoted Jack Fena concerning the Kowalskis' attitude toward their daughter's lesbianism. Fena told the reporter that Thompson would walk a mile barefoot over crushed glass to talk to a person carrying a pen or a camera. "This woman has manipulated the press to cause all this g—— grief over nothing," Fena told Stodghill. "Thompson should start an advertising firm. She'd be the world's biggest success. She can manipulate the media and the press. She's got to be the greatest. Merrill Lynch should hire her."

"Fena's got a point," the article continued. "Thompson has been traveling all over the United States 11 of the past 13 weeks spreading a message she calls 'Free Sharon Kowalski.'" Thompson was happy to spread the word to Stodghill. "When Karen Thompson wants to make a point she thrusts out her left hand with fingers curled," he wrote, detailing the three faces of Karen's case: sexism, handicapism, and homophobia. If Karen were a man, if Sharon were not described as "an eerily silent daughter trapped in her twisted body" ("Since when are disabled people eerie?" Karen asked), if people did not hate her for proclaiming her lesbian love in court, Karen stated, the case would be over, and she would be guardian. Thompson appeared neither emotionally nor physically vulnerable, Stodghill wrote, as she voiced her discontent at the "rich, white, heterosexual, able-bodied, Christian male system that oppresses Sharon and me."

Stodghill's article concluded with a summary of his interview with Karen. Until August 1987, he reported, Thompson — if she could have — would have snapped her fingers to become a heterosexual, but in Florida last summer she finally accepted herself as a lesbian and a feminist. About Don's physical condition, Thompson said she felt sorry for "these people if this is true that he's had a heart attack. And, yes, I can question whether or not it's true because they will say or do whatever they need to do at the time." Thompson said she felt bad for Sharon's parents, but she had been trying to go to counseling with them since the case began, yet they continued to refuse (Mark Stodghill, "Custody," *Duluth News-Tribune,* November 17, 1987, sec. A, p. 1).

Thompson's new petition was destined for the bench of Robert Campbell, a Duluth judge all too familiar with the ins and outs of family law on the Range. The now-semiretired jurist (interviewed at lunch on May 23, 1997) had spent twenty-seven years in Duluth as a probate, juvenile, and, for the last seven years, civil judge. Before becoming a judge, he had practiced on the Range for three years. As he peered at me with his piercing black pupils, the judge ate pancakes covered with cream and eggs while he recollected when he got the case: 1987, after the first two appeals. He did not ask for it; it was transferred to him when the new petition was filed. It was a bit of a circus, he remembers. Fena — a Bible-thumping former assemblyman from Hibbing — and Sue Wilson, who brought a busload of Free Sharon Kowalski activists with her from the Twin Cities for the first hearing, which the judge held in Hibbing. Though Duluth was the county seat, Campbell was an old-fashioned circuit judge, moving around from place to place, holding court in hospitals and the backs of pickups when necessary. During that initial hearing, conservatives sat on one side of the aisle, liberals on the other — he remembered that much. He had already been to Leisure Hills to visit the ward before the first court date. Sharon had been well taken care of there, he stated quietly, in a manner that cultivated calm in what must have been a career of maelstroms.

Campbell had graduated from Carleton College; he had lesbian friends. The Range, he explained, had a culture of its own, made up of blue-collar union "liberals" when it came to workers' rights, Roman Catholic conservatives when it came to social issues. For example, Campbell put forth, the Range had voted for Paul Wellstone for U.S. Senate. Yes, he admitted, the Kowalskis were unlearned, but they were products of their background, which does not excuse them. But what can the law do to change cultural contexts? He was not sure it could or should do anything. Campbell remembered one summer bringing back a friend from college to the Range — a black exchange student from Ghana. The two of them were going to work in the mines together for the summer, but the African did not last two weeks — the prejudice was more than he could handle. He announced he had to leave, and Campbell got his first grown-up dose of Range culture at the moment he saw his friend get on the bus.

During the judge's visit with Sharon, her attention seemed to him intermittent, remembrances of the past bringing a renewed gleam to her eye, especially recollections of athletic events. Most of Sharon's friends were lesbian athletes from the Range, many of whom were sharply divided about the case, including the judge's own friends. In fact, most of the Duluth community was disturbed and divided about the litigation. He had received a lot of hate mail regarding the case, he mentioned in passing. Most of the lesbians on the Range were threatened with being outed if they testified against Karen Thompson, he said, and that kind of tactic angered him.

One of his main concerns about the case was Karen Thompson's "control" problem. If she was as controlling and difficult in her relations with others besides Sharon, how would that reflect on her treatment of the ward? Campbell had taught at the Domestic Abuse Center in Duluth for many years and had lectured regularly on the dynamics of family law disputes. Control and power were the common terms in most abuse cases, and he did not necessarily mean physical control; the judge noted that a large percentage of abuse was not necessarily physical. He worried about this issue in relation to Karen Thompson even though he found her absolutely dedicated to Sharon in every respect. That dedication could border on intransigence, that single-mindedness on an unwillingness to compromise.

Once the relationship was ruptured by the large-scale outing of Sharon by Karen, positions became even more entrenched, and there was little chance of going back to the status quo ante. The judge grew rather exercised when asked about the invasion-of-privacy issue. The other behavior that made him nervous about Thompson was the way she put Sharon on display, a display that had nothing necessarily to do with sexual orientation. For him, the invasion of privacy was the turning of Sharon's disability into a spectacle, without regard for her own cultural milieu, her own previous life as a private, nature-loving, softball-tournament lesbian from the Range. Closeted lesbians on the Range had a right to live their lives as they did. So did Sharon, he thought.

The first hearing on Thompson's petition came before Campbell on November 18.[6] Toni Pomerene, Sue Wilson's partner, argued for the petitioner Thompson while Jack Fena and Harry Sieben appeared on behalf of the guardian. The ward had no attorney at this time, but Kristin Siegesmund appeared on behalf of the proposed attorney, Brian O'Neill. Pomerene argued Thompson's case: the guardian statute required the court to set a date for a hearing on restoration to capacity whenever a person filed a valid petition. She had an affidavit from the defendant's attorney in the personal injury suit stating that contrary to Fena's declarations, an evaluation of Sharon Kowalski in the Twin Cities by an adverse medical examiner (the defendants' expert) was already scheduled for December. Roger Roe, attorney for the defendants in the personal injury case, in fact had agreed to allow Sharon to be evaluated for competency at the same time as his medical expert examined her. The coordination of these two examinations in the Twin Cities would meet the statutory requirements efficiently, she argued. Finally, Pomerene recommended that the court take advantage of the services of Faegre and Benson, one of the biggest firms in Minneapolis, by appointing Brian O'Neill attorney for Sharon Kowalski on a pro bono basis.

"If it please the Court and counsel, I want to make a brief statement about the facts of this case because a personal injury case is important here," Jack Fena began. His lengthy opening statement started as a rehearsal of the upcoming jury trial, beginning with a chronology of "a two-car collision which occurred at about 3:40 o'clock P.M. on November 13, 1983, six miles south of Onamia, Minnesota." By the time Fena was informing the court that Wayne Marks and Mr. Yeager had "consumed little or no alcohol that weekend while at the cabin, instead concentrating on their hunting," Judge Campbell interrupted, wanting to know how much further counsel was "going to go with this" rehashing.[7]

At this point, Jack Fena became too excited to continue his extensive narrative and revealed to the court his discovery that Faegre and Benson had represented Yeager, the drunk driver, in defense of the case. Although actually Yeager's insurance company had the firm on retainer and Faegre had dropped the case within two months of receiving it, Fena dramatically waved a letter he had discovered that proved at one point the law firm of the proposed attorney for the guardian, Faegre and Benson, was working for the defendants in the personal injury case. This conflict of interest, which "appalled" counsel for the Kowalskis, combined with the appearance of Thompson on the defendant's witness list, evidenced a conspiracy to undermine the personal injury lawsuit that was of utmost importance to Sharon's financial future. "She's [Thompson] going to be the star witness for the defense and now she wants to be able to have her examined and Mr. Roe, who is defending another insurance company involved in this case, Your Honor, has offered to help pay the expenses for that examination."

Coaxed by the court to continue with his substantive argument, Mr. Fena was anxious to set the record straight about visitation. In the face of Karen Thompson's repeated statements to the press about "Mr. Donald Kowalski prohibiting her from visiting Sharon," counsel felt compelled to tell "the true facts" about how the petitioner lost her right to visit when the case was before Judge Douglas. "[W]hat happened down there was that Karen Thompson wrote a couple of letters to the parents, Don and Della Kowalski, and said — she talked about her relationship between the two, and I know exactly what the Court did down there," Fena stated, relating the inside story to Judge Campbell. "The Court and her then attorneys wanted to protect Sharon. They didn't want this stuff out in the public like it is now. Who would want that out about any member of their family? Nobody. Nobody. But she blackmailed her way into visitation rights by the threats of going public."

For Fena, "the goal has been clear from the beginning." Even "when Sharon lay dying in that hospital, [Thompson] kept running up to Kowalski with bills, rent, rent, utilities, utilities, telephone, telephone, credit cards, credit cards, and he is writing checks." For counsel, Thompson's actions spoke "louder than words and it's been money, money, money, money from the beginning, and she has carried her saga from one coast to the other in this country, putting Sharon Kowalski's name and the Kowalski family's name all over the country." Fena's version of the truth continued by recalling Dr. Cowan's testimony that "the last person in the world a gay person wants their lifestyle disclosed to is their parents. . . . That's who they fear most might find out," he insisted. "As a matter of fact, I read in the press that Ms. Thompson's mother was not told about her lifestyle, but she didn't bother to worry about Sharon's parents." All of this, he argued, had "damaged Sharon Kowalski, not only in her lawsuit, forget that, Your Honor, that's only money, but it's damaged her reputation." Initially, Fena restated, the guardian settlement was made to "protect Sharon," and if "I were the attorney at that time I would have done the same thing because my interest, too, would have been to keep this garbage out of the public eye."[8]

Fena's last comment must have brought considerable unrest to the courtroom, for Judge Campbell suddenly interrupted him and asked that counsel address the specific legal issues at bar. When Fena finally arrived at his legal argument, he introduced the tenuous ground of res judicata as the basis for dismissing the petition, claiming the case had already been decided. He tried to argue more broadly that the petition was frivolous and "vexatious," claiming that Thompson and her lawyers were "working with the insurance companies that are defending drunk drivers and rotten bars that serve people booze when they're drunk, and they're working hand-in-hand." Fena told the court he would relish the opportunity to cross-examine Ms. Thompson and destroy "her credibility." The court again admonished counsel to stick to legal arguments, and Jack Fena again repeated "res judicata" before launching once more into his inimitable mode of argument. "They know they can't restore Sharon Kowalski to capacity. They know that. This is a way to get their foot in the door because they want to take her over," counsel warned. The Kowalskis' attorney then alluded to the audience:

> And I saw the pens here and the T-shirts and the Free Sharon Kowalski Committee. I love it. I join it. But I would like this Court to free Sharon Kowalski from this evil that's upon her. That's what I would like to free her from, and that family, I would like to free them from this. This has got to end somewhere. Thompson has threatened civil disobedience. She has sent people in with false names up to that nursing home. She's become the greatest celebrity in the

world. She appeared on a talk show that I saw sitting next to a person who had a sex change talking about Sharon Kowalski. How would she like it if somebody did that to her? I don't think she would .[9]

Fena finally argued that the Minnesota statute allowing "any person" to petition for restoration to capacity must be limited by the right to privacy and that Karen Thompson, who had no legitimate interest in bringing the petition, was invading Sharon's privacy by pursuing this action. "[W]e Americans," he closed, "cherish our right to privacy as much as all other rights that we have, maybe more. We like to be secure in our homes. We want to be bound with our families, and that's a private right. The fabric of the family is a private right protected by the constitution of this country, I hope. I know, I believe, and to allow now this assault on that unit to come in under this statute, any other person, is flawed under the fundamental law of the constitution of our state and our federal constitution."

Once Fena concluded his "brief" remarks, Judge Campbell asked Toni Pomerene if she had any response, reminding her that if she did respond, opposing counsel would have an opportunity to talk again. Pomerene, aware of that opening, nonetheless wanted to make clear that their motion was based on a statutory requirement and that a reevaluation, even if it found Sharon's capacity to be greater than it was considered to be at that point, would not lessen her damages in a personal injury case; in fact, if she were capable of some self-care, the amount of money it would take to provide for her mobility might increase her damages. Pomerene did not see how the cost of deposing the medical examiners was a great enough burden to outweigh the need to have Sharon evaluated in a timely fashion so that her quality of life could improve if possible. She reminded the court that Thompson had been subpoenaed by Mr. Roe and had nothing to do with the defense in the personal injury case.

Fena then rose to his feet to respond. Referring to his upcoming personal injury trial, in which counsel had a large stake, the Kowalskis' attorney argued, "They're going to inject, Your Honor, or try to inject in this case the lesbian issue, and I was not going to talk much about that, but I guess I owe a duty to Sharon Kowalski to remind the Court that there is a great deal of prejudice in this world and in this country." He did not think it took much of "a stretch of the imagination to think about a rural county like Mille Lacs County where that sort of lifestyle is not very prevalent, one might say, or may be not even tolerated or appreciated, and there are people, we are steeped deep in our society from the beginning of the founding of the republic in the belief of God." Roger Roe, the defense attorney, was undoubtedly "going to want somebody that wouldn't like a lesbian person. They might think if they could find one and pick up the Bible and read Chapter One of Romans of what it says, that juror could conclude that Sharon Kowalski shouldn't get any money because she is a lesbian."[10]

The main part of Fena's speech concluded, Judge Campbell himself spoke to the court about his own visit to Leisure Hills, where he found the ward "had made some progress" in relation to the "motion of some legs." The judge then detailed the security check he himself was forced to undergo at the hands of Dolores Paull, the social services director at the nursing home, in part because of a previous incident in which a woman by the name of Judy Lindquist of Lutheran Social Services showed up at Leisure Hills seeking physical therapy. Later Ms. Paull found Lindquist talking to Sharon, called the Lutheran agency, and discovered it employed no one by that name. The woman, upon questioning, said she worked at McDonald's in downtown Hibbing, but Hibbing had no McDonald's. Paull asked Lindquist to leave and later discovered that she may have been a member of a Free Sharon Kowalski Committee. The judge asked Ms. Pomerene to look into that breach of security and do what she could to prevent such intrusions in the future. He then told the court that if there were no further questions, he would take the petition under submission and render a decision within two weeks. Court was adjourned.

While Thompson's petition was under submission, Judge Campbell probably did not read syndicated columnist Cyra McFadden's assessment of the case as "a grim little immorality play, the immoral part how the law has failed these two [Sharon and Karen]" ("Karen and Sharon and the Spirit of the Law," *San Francisco Examiner*, November 29, 1987, sec. E, p. 1). The judge's "order" was reported in the *Minneapolis Star Tribune* ("Judge Chooses Guardian for Injured Woman," December 4, 1987, sec. B, p. 14). Campbell had decided to take time out. The hearing on competency testing was postponed until February 5, and the judge, eschewing the pro bono offer of Minneapolis's Faegre and Benson, appointed a Range lawyer, Gary Pagliaccetti of Virginia, as Sharon's new attorney. Pagliaccetti had some experience with the disabled; his daughter had cerebral palsy. The judge asked him to interview the ward and report back at the hearing on February 5. Campbell also postponed the testing day to avoid the conflict with the personal injury case, slated for trial on January 4. As it turned out, however, like many civil trials, the Blue Goose case did not come to the bench on schedule, and Sharon did not go to Minneapolis for an adverse medical examination in December. Negotiation in that case continued, but February soon arrived, and Judge Campbell again was faced with the ongoing disposition of Sharon Kowalski. He called first for an oral report from the new attorney for the ward.

By the time he was interviewed about the case in the summer of 1997, Gary Pagliaccetti, like Tom Hayes before him, had also become a judge. He sat on the bench in Virginia, one of the main towns on the Range, east of Hibbing. Judge Pagliaccetti, a conservative Democrat, really did not want to talk about the Kowalski matter. He had called the Professional Responsibility Board before the interview and learned that he could speak generally about the case but not about the particulars. In his late forties with graying hair, he had an office that looked like Cooperstown. Pictures of Don Drysdale and Sandy Koufax adorned the pristine walls of the chambers of this avid fan. Pagliaccetti remembered being given the case by Judge Campbell, but before that he had not heard of it. He did not read the paper and was not particularly interested in the law outside of performing his duties efficiently. He came across as a law-and-order family man happy with the comfortable norms of Range life, norms that excluded homosexuality from the ambit of coffee shop conversation. Virginia was a Democratic Labor town, yet socially it was as traditional as one could imagine. Minnesota, he mentioned, was 6 percent nonwhite, and 90 percent of that 6 percent lived in the Twin Cities. There was almost no diversity on the Range except for a holdout of old Polish immigrants who refused to speak English or leave their homes to die. There was no gay community in Virginia, though he knew of a lesbian "presence" in the town and was acquainted with some lesbian women.

The case was an unusual one, Pagliaccetti commented, analogous to a custody case but in many ways not "dream-upable." The courts, he intoned, did their best with the disabled given their limited resources, though there definitely should be more regular evaluation of those adjudicated incapacitated. The judge had a daughter, now seventeen, with cerebral palsy. When parents had a disabled child, he warned, their first and foremost instinct was protection, doing what they believed was right, as the Kowalskis did. But taking care of a handicapped person could be very frustrating and discouraging for both the caretaker and the patient. Pagliaccetti recalled that though the parties tried to make a sexual orientation issue out of this case, his job was to try to discern the preference of the ward for a guardian, not just her sexual preference. Being appointed attorney for a disabled person presented some very difficult legal problems for counsel, Pagliaccetti continued. How could an attorney advocate for a client he or she did not understand? How could counsel assess the whole situation without access to a working communication with the client? This dilemma made discovering the ward's preference very tricky. Sometimes the preference could not be discerned, and the attorney had to allow the court to decide the ward's best interest.

Pagliaccetti was an unlikely candidate to become the "liberator" of Sharon Kowalski, but when Sharon's new lawyer came to court on February 5, 1988, almost ten years before being interviewed, he brought with him some unexpected opinions. He told Judge Campbell he had met with Sharon four times for about thirty to sixty minutes on each occasion. When he explained the court notices to Sharon, it was his opinion that "she understood what I was talking about. It's my opinion that she understands the nature of these proceedings. It's my opinion that she, Sharon, understands a lot of things." Sharon's counsel felt that in many cases Sharon's "failure to react was because she didn't want to react."[11]

Two of their visits were productive, two less fruitful. They talked about Sharon's nieces and nephew, about Pagliaccetti's children, about the Super Bowl. Eliciting head nods from his client and sometimes a letter board yes or no, counsel discovered that Sharon, like most residents of nursing homes, felt she was receiving adequate care but preferred not to live there. "I have yet to meet anyone that I have talked to in a nursing home that didn't want to get out of the nursing home, but that was her response," Pagliaccetti remarked.

He told the judge that he had asked Sharon the same three questions on his first and second visits. "I asked her if she didn't want to stay in the nursing home, did she want to stay with her parents, and she stated, yes, she did. I asked her if she wanted to live with Karen Thompson, and she stated yes, she did." Both counsel and the attendant nurse, Terry Daniels, were surprised by Sharon's verbal response to the last question: "I asked her who she would pick between the two, and she spoke the word 'parents.'" Sharon, the nurse told Pagliaccetti, spoke only on rare occasions.

Mr. Pagliaccetti concluded that Sharon had "potential," but he was not "sure she's reaching that potential." He wanted to see his client "reach her potential" and for that reason he was "going to support an evaluation." Even though he believed that Sharon wanted everybody "to go away and leave her alone," Pagliaccetti insisted that the best interest of his client required that she be "pushed to her potential." Instead of Sister Kenny Institute in Minneapolis, however, counsel recommended Matthew Eckman in Duluth for the evaluation.[12]

Pagliaccetti's opinion was a surprise to most in the courtroom, especially the Kowalskis, and Judge Campbell sought to soften the blow by addressing the guardian directly. He asked Donald point-blank if he disagreed with any of the "factual information" the court-appointed lawyer had presented. Mr. Kowalski had misgivings about the recommendation. "I agree, you know, that Sharon knows what's going on and she's gained somewhat," Don told the judge, "but the thing that bothers me is no matter what she says today she don't remember. Tomorrow she won't remember that Gary was there or what was said to her. This is the — this is the problem that I have with this and this evaluation."[13]

Campbell then heard more testimony from Jack Fena, who again pleaded with the court to postpone the test while the personal injury matter was under way. The defendant Blue Goose had declared bankruptcy, throwing another wrench into the settlement negotiations. The judge finally had to deny Fena's request to make further comments. The judge ruled from the bench that the failure to have Sharon evaluated did in fact violate the January 3, 1986, order of Judge Johnson, and that an evaluation should take place. The court gave the parties two months to prepare information about the testing parameters, location, and participants in the evaluation and ordered that none of the attorneys or the parties except Pagliaccetti contact the doctors who would be chosen to examine Sharon.

"Lesbian Wins One Round in Custody Battle," the *Washington Blade*'s Lisa Keen reported on February 19, noting that Campbell's order was the first favorable outcome for Thompson since June 1984, a period of almost four years. Thompson was cautiously optimistic: "This is the start of blatant injustices being turned around," she stated. "It's the first movement in the right direction but it could go either way. We want to make sure valid testing is done" (Lisa Keen, "Lesbian Wins One Round in Custody Battle," *Washington Blade*, February 19, 1988). Pomerene compared Sharon Kowalski's maltreatment by the legal system to that suffered by parties in the 1800s as portrayed in Dickens's novel: "We have been in Bleak House; we have been in the worst legal system, but I am hopeful the course is changing now" (Mark Kasel, "Judge Rules Kowalski to Be Tested for Competency," *GAZE*, February 11, 1988).

Not by chance, a week earlier the *Blade* had run a story about a "San Francisco man who had cared for his lover for more than six months as he fought a losing battle against AIDS" but who "was not allowed to see him for the last two weeks of his life after the lover's family checked him into a hospital." Jay Wilson was caring for his partner, Michael Fasano, "who suffered from Kaposi's sarcoma" but "had been in relatively good health until he went to stay with his parents during Christmas. When he returned, he was so ill that he had to be transported in a wheelchair by his sister." Although Fasano had reportedly asked to spend his last remaining days at his home with Wilson, Fasano's family checked him into a San Francisco hospital on January 5. After two days of visitation, Wilson "was forced to leave by a family member and was told that only Fasano's immediate family was allowed to see him." Fasano died on January 18. The *Blade* noted that Wilson had no legal recourse under San Francisco law, which provided no legal protection for gay couples. Supervisor Harry Britt of San Francisco was expected to introduce a domestic partners bill, similar to the one vetoed by former mayor Diane Feinstein in 1982 (*Washington Blade*, February 12, 1988).

As Sharon's case continued to parallel family law developments related to AIDS, other media events took place in early 1988. Karen and Julie's book, *Why Can't Sharon Kowalski Come Home?* had been accepted for publication at

Spinsters/Aunt Lute, a women's press in San Francisco. On February 19, the Reverend Jesse Jackson, running for president, stood next to Karen Thompson as he addressed the Metropolitan Community Church in Minneapolis, laying out his policy on gay and lesbian rights. Jackson, speaking to a capacity crowd of a thousand, said other candidates had avoided making appearances with gay and lesbian groups. "They were afraid that being close to you would make them look unpresidential," Jackson stated (Debra Olson, "Woman Keeps Up Kowalski Fight," *St. Cloud Times,* February 20, 1988, sec. C, p. 2). He called for an end to discrimination based on sexual orientation and issued a press release: "I wish to express my support for Karen Thompson and Sharon Kowalski. Ms. Thompson is to be commended for her dedication and courage in seeking the best possible care for Sharon Kowalski, her life-partner. Ms. Thompson has been infinitely patient — but there comes an end to patience with a system that is unfair and unjust. We question the wisdom of any legal ruling which seeks to separate mutually consenting adults who have made a life commitment to each other."

The Jackson statement added momentum to the seventeen Committees to Free Sharon Kowalski now established across the country. The committees had raised $80,000 to offset Karen's legal bills of $115,000 and held a national meeting in Minneapolis in February. Fund-raising, outreach, media, and direct action committees were formed, each with its own set of tasks. By March 1988, Mark Kasel reported that the National Committee to Free Sharon Kowalski, with a mailing list of over three thousand names nationally, was pursuing a strategy of grassroots organizing to culminate in rallies across the country on August 8, 1988 — Sharon's birthday (Mark Kasel, "National Free Sharon Kowalski Committee Meets in Minneapolis," *GAZE,* March 10, 1988). Thompson's speaking schedule in March, he noted, included venues like the Universities of Massachusetts, California (Boalt Hall), and Vanderbilt, in addition to addresses at three national conventions. The Boston Gay Pride Committee selected Sharon Kowalski as a grand marshal in absentia, and the *Gay Community News* (May 13–19, 1988, 1) featured Sharon in a front-page article by Caroline Foty: "Judge Orders Tests for Kowalski: First Legal Breakthrough Comes as Activists Meet to Organize Nationwide Action." Thompson called the decision heartening but was saddened by the length of time it had taken to reach the point of ordering testing: "He [Pagliaccetti] is saying all the things I've been saying for years," she said, "and no one listened to me. Now they appoint this man to be Sharon's attorney, and suddenly people are listening. Meanwhile, look how much time has been lost for Sharon."

The loss of time was becoming a major issue in Judge Campbell's decision-making process. By June, almost ten months had elapsed from the initial filing of the petition to restore capacity; the court had still failed to appoint the examiners. Not until July 6 did Campbell select the all-male and all–northern Minnesota group of Drs. Matthew Eckman and Clyde Olson of the Duluth Clinic and Dr. John Hatten of the University of Minnesota (Duluth) to conduct the evaluation. "If in the opinion of either examiner it would aid in his evaluation to observe Sharon Kowalski in the presence of Karen Thompson," Campbell expressly stated, "then any restrictions on visitation imposed by this Court or the Guardian or Leisure Hills are waived for the limited purpose of the examiners' observation." The order authorized moving Sharon to Miller-Dwan Hospital in Duluth only (not to Sister Kenny) but left open the possibility of further evaluation at another location. Besides assessing Sharon's physical and mental well-being, the examiners were asked to answer the question, "Does she have the ability to reliably express her wishes as to visitation?" The judge set the testing date at July 31.[14]

For Jack Fena, the timing of the order, not to speak of its contents, was extremely detrimental to the settlement negotiations in the personal injury suit. He called the Court of Appeals and in an ex parte oral motion requested that the order be stayed until he had time to file a writ of prohibition, which would, if successful, nullify the order. The Court of Appeals granted the temporary stay for two weeks, giving Fena time to file the writ and the opposition, Sue Wilson and Gary Pagliaccetti, one week to respond. But, in the meantime, on July 19, the Seventh District Court in Mille Lacs County suddenly issued an order approving a settlement of the negligence action. The $330,000 agreement provided $119,000 in attorney fees for Jack Fena and Harry Seiben, $125,500 to offset a state lien for medical expenses, $65,000 for Donald and Della ($38,000 of which was to reimburse them for lodging, meals, telephone expenses, and mileage and $26,000 earmarked to buy a van for transporting Sharon). The remainder, approximately $20,000, was assigned to Sharon's estate.[15]

Both Wilson and Pagliaccetti immediately petitioned the guardianship judge to put the settlement funds in escrow pending the outcome of the capacity hearing. Campbell ruled that he had jurisdiction only over the $20,000 in Sharon's estate but agreed to allow none of that money to be spent without his approval. Sue Wilson expressed her disappointment with the size of the financial benefits available for Sharon's rehabilitation. "It looks like the purpose of the suit," she told Mark Kasel, "was for everyone to make money from Sharon's injury except Sharon herself" ("Kowalski Personal Injury Suit Settled," *GAZE*, July 20, 1988).

In spite of the settlement, Fena, having already acquired a stay, used the threat of a protracted appeal of Campbell's testing order to negotiate with the probate court. On July 29 he filed another affidavit from Dr. William Wilson, which recommended that Sharon should not be moved and that Karen should not be present during the evaluation. Fena agreed to withdraw his appeal if Judge Campbell would reconsider his order in light of Dr. Wilson's opinions. A hasty conference call was arranged for Wednesday, August 3, resulting in an agreement among the parties. Fena agreed to drop his appeal in exchange for Judge Campbell's express order that neither Karen Thompson nor any other nonmedical person be present at the initial testing of Sharon, though the testing was still to take place in Duluth. In the *St. Cloud Times* ("Professor Barred from Evaluation," August 4, 1988, sec. C, p. 1), Fena hailed the judge's decision: "The Kowalskis . . . did not object to having their daughter tested, but they did not want her moved and they did not want Thompson present during testing." Campbell, in the same article, stated that the evaluators could request that Thompson visit at some point in the future, but "she (Thompson) can't be there without another order of the court."

These legal machinations coincided with the first burst of national attention the case received from the established media. Between August 5 and August 8, the *Los Angeles Times, New York Times, Washington Post, USA Today,* and *Minneapolis Star Tribune* ran separate stories on the case, while the National Committee to Free Sharon Kowalski held a series of birthday rallies on Sunday, August 7, to benefit and draw attention to Sharon's position, dubbing it Free Sharon Day. Vigils, birthday cakes, street theater, and processions took place in Washington, New York, Boston, Los Angeles, Colorado Springs, Madison, and Tallahassee—a total of twenty-one venues across the country. "Accidental activist" Thompson and her supporters called for a Justice Department investigation into the "Sharon and Karen Case," the guardian dispute that had now separated the lovers for three years.

Debra Olson ("Interest Grows in Battle over Rights of Gay, Disabled," *St. Cloud Times,* July 30, 1988, sec. A, p. 3) was instrumental in bringing increased scrutiny by the national press. She in fact reported that Thompson had been interviewed by the *Times,* the *Post,* and *Newsday,* in addition to taping a program with television talk show host Geraldo Rivera that was to air later in the summer. CBS News was in St. Cloud that spring shooting a *West 57th Street* segment that was slated to air in the beginning of 1989, and Thompson had also appeared on *People Are Talking,* a nationally syndicated television program that originated in San Francisco. During her investigation, Olson was also able to interview a once reluctant Don Kowalski. At first, he stated, he avoided interviews in order to protect his family's privacy, but "it got to the point I don't really give a damn," he said. "If they want my opinion, I'll give it to them. We got sick and tired of her (Thompson's) lies and filth on TV and in the newspapers," Don stated matter-of-factly. "Sooner or later, our side's going to get out. As long as I'm here, I'm going to protect our kid." Don stated bluntly that Thompson was after two things: money and publicity for her book. "She better remember we can write a book, too," Kowalski told Olson.

Betty Cuniberti's "Just Whose Life Is It?" in the *Los Angeles Times* (August 5, 1988, p. 1) described the new heights of animosity that the participants had reached that summer. She wrote of a "vicious, four-year court battle" between Sharon's father and "a woman who says she is her lover." In an interview, Donald Kowalski called Thompson "an animal" who had put his family through "hell." The soft-spoken fifty-seven-year-old detailed depression, sleeplessness, weight loss, lack of energy, and chronic anxiety as symptoms both he and his wife had experienced. Whether or not his daughter was a lesbian was irrelevant, he told the *Times*. "What difference does it make, in Sharon's condition? I don't believe in that life style but I would not disown our daughter [if it were true]. The good Lord put us here for reproduction, not that kind of way. It's just not a normal life style. The Bible will tell you that."

Thompson's public campaign had infuriated the Kowalskis, Cuniberti reported. Sharon's sister Debbie bitterly noted that Thompson admits she had an abortion years ago. "If she killed her own baby," she said, "what would she do with Sharon if she found out Sharon wasn't everything she thought she could be?" Reacting to that statement, "Thompson's words flowed in rapid bursts of frustration and anger." She called Don part of a "rich, white, heterosexual, able-bodied, Christian, male system, which oppresses anyone who's different," and accused the Kowalskis of "attacking me physically and verbally" for five years. The *Los Angeles Times* had captured the vitriolic turn the case was now taking (Betty Cuniberti, "Just Whose Life Is It?" *Los Angeles Times,* August 5, 1988, p. 1).

The *Washington Post* also shed some light on the Kowalskis' frustration with Karen Thompson's organized struggle. In her interview with Donald, Joyce Murdoch reported that he felt Thompson had destroyed his daughter's dignity by talking about her in sexual terms. "As far as I'm concerned," Don told the *Post*, "they should have locked her up a long time ago." He also stated he would never believe his daughter is a lesbian unless Sharon herself told him. "On the farm and in the Army we called them queers and fruits, not gays and lesbians," he said. Thompson will never be granted guardianship, he said, because, "there ain't a law in the United States that allows a lesbian relationship." Jack Fena, the article stated, accepted responsibility for not having Sharon tested on a yearly basis, the statutory and court-ordered requirement that had led to Campbell's decision. Fena called the evaluation requirement a technicality that he was at first unaware of and then thought unnecessary. But Sharon's new attorney, Gary Pagliaccetti, the article reported, had a different view. He expected the tests to show that Sharon Kowalski was capable of instructing her attorney as to her wishes, but he wanted the evaluation to establish that capacity (Joyce Murdoch, "Fighting for Control of a Loved One: Guardianship Dispute Pits Disabled Woman's Partner, Family," *Washington Post*, August 5, 1988, sec. A, p. 1).

A day later, on Saturday, the *Minneapolis Star Tribune* presented its own account, briefer but also revealing. Allen Short reported that Sharon had received an earlier settlement in the personal injury action of another $330,000, but that money was placed in trust for distribution after Sharon reaches fifty — in 2006. Don again bristled at the accusations that he "dislikes homosexuals." " 'As long as they keep it to themselves,' " he was quoted as saying, " 'I don't give a damn what they do. . . . We're not trying to shove nothing on them. I wish they wouldn't try to shove nothing on us' " (Allen Short, "Sharon and Karen's Bitterly Sad Story Is National Cause," *Minneapolis Star Tribune*, August 6, 1988, sec. A, p. 1).

"There are other cases that pit blood relatives against loved ones, but there is no other case that approaches this one in symbolic importance," Tom Stoddard, director of the Lambda Legal Defense Fund, told the *New York Times*. For Stoddard, the case "has touched the deepest fears of every gay person: a fight among loved ones and denial of personal wishes." And Nan Hunter, director of the ACLU's Gay Rights Project, called the case unique in its intensity: "I don't think we've had any case that is so dramatic, or in which the conflict has been so extended. But there have been many instances of tension between surviving partners of men dying of AIDS and their family members." Reporter Nadine Brozan interspersed her quotations of New York professionals with comments from the principals. Karen repeated her account of the pre-accident status of her closeted relationship: "We never discussed being gay, never said the word out loud." For the Kowalskis, that silence was an indication of heterosexuality (Nadine Brozan, "Gay Groups Are Rallied to Aid 2 Women's Fight," *New York Times*, August 7, 1988, "The Nation," p. 26).

In Minneapolis, the August 7 rally took place in Loring Park, where a crowd of lesbians, gay men, feminists, disabled persons, and curious passersby gathered to celebrate Sharon's birthday and spend the afternoon enjoying birthday cake and refreshments and buying T-shirts and buttons ("Sharon Will Wheel Free," read one). In reference to the recent publicity in the major newspapers, Thompson, interrupting the solicitation of signatures on a giant birthday card, told the gay press that the case was now "blown wide open," that "Minnesota is being watched now," and that "we won't have the off-the-wall court decisions that we've had." Disabled rights activist Jaime Becker declared, "We are asked to let you rest in peace, Sharon, but you are not dead. You are alive! and next year you will be free." In New York a dozen protesters placed a wreath labeled "Free Sharon Kowalski" inside St. Patrick's Cathedral before they held a mass across the street—an outdoor service that protested the Roman Catholic Church's policy on homosexuality. Mayor Ed Koch of New York sent a telegram; Mayor Art Agnos proclaimed August 8 Sharon Kowalski Day in San Francisco; and Molly Yard, president of NOW, addressed the crowd in Washington (Mark Kasel, "Saying 'Happy Birthday Sharon' and Going for One Happy Return," *GAZE*, August 11, 1988, p. 1).

Judge Campbell had rescheduled Sharon's testing for Monday, September 12. While supporters were gathering for a rally in Minnehaha Park in Minneapolis and an all-night vigil at St. Paul Reformation Lutheran Church, she was in transit from Hibbing to Duluth to spend five days with the medical team at Miller-Dwan Hospital, headed by Matthew Eckman. A specialist in physical medicine and rehabilitation, Pagliaccetti's recommended examiner was a balding, married, highly intelligent medical professional. Timid but talkative, he wore red horn-rimmed glasses and when interviewed, he was not interested in being quoted, though most of what he said was confirmed by other sources. Dr. Eckman subscribed to the restoration theory in rehabilitation and believed the courts should more explicitly adopt it. Patients, he believed, to the degree possible should be restored to the life they were leading before the accident.

While Sharon was staying at Miller-Dwan, the staff was nervous. The building was closely guarded because of concern about paparazzi, even bomb threats, given the national publicity the case had garnered. This quiet hospital in northern Minnesota breathed a collective sigh of relief once those initial five days elapsed. The staff found Sharon Kowalski to be a very difficult patient, even by rehabilitation standards. She was surly, erratic, moody, and stubborn. She refused to swallow, even though her swallowing function was intact, for example. Because most brain-injured patients were risk takers (motorcyclists, mountain climbers), they usually had fairly strong and often difficult personalities, but some turned out to be delightful patients. Sharon Kowalski was not one of these; she was a handful and during her visit was found to be both not very nice and severely impaired. Even under these circumstances, the physicians visited with Sharon regularly, questioned her consistently, and gained insight into her mental capabilities.

Observation and questioning led the examiners to the conclusion that Sharon was in the closet for good reasons; she had a dominant, homophobic father and grew up in a male-dominant, homophobic culture. Thompson, the examiners noted, was wary, polite, angry, and frustrated, though she was clearly dedicated to this difficult patient and had a hands-on approach to her care that the parents were just incapable of.

Dr. Eckman maintained a very philosophical attitude toward caregiving in brain-injury cases. If Sharon's parents were less capable of taking care of Sharon than Karen was, they could not be blamed or judged as loving their daughter any less. Most brain injuries involving a married person end in divorce simply because the injured person's spouse does not have the "capacity" — the patience, the perseverance, the temperament — to provide the difficult care that such patients need. What made this case extraordinary was not that it presented a classic battle between a "fairriage" (as one person called gay marriage) and parental surveillance, but that two parties were actually willing to spend time and money fighting over taking care of a brain-injured person — when in most cases it is often impossible to find anyone willing and able to provide care. "Could you take care of your brain-injured spouse or partner?" one physician asked. "Could I?" the same doctor reflected. This kind of care takes a certain kind of personality, and rehabilitation specialists never cast aspersions on anyone who feels he or she has to walk away. So Thompson was an unusual case — someone who, in spite of her coolness and public campaigning, did quite well with Sharon on a one-to-one basis, though many wondered what it would be like to be married to her.

After questioning and evaluating Sharon over a period of days, the physicians determined that they wanted her to undergo a more thorough period of testing for at least two months. In the middle of October, thirty days after the initial testing as required by the court, they reported their findings to Judge Campbell. Once their recommendations were made, the case was out of their hands, though they were well aware that the law's delay was causing serious problems in this case. Sharon Kowalski was approaching the fifth anniversary of her injury, and the chances of her rehabilitation were already seriously compromised by posttrauma permanence.

Jack Fena had fought hard to avoid allowing Thompson's reemergence into the Kowalskis' lives, but when the settlement of the personal injury case in July left him with a fee of over $50,000, the climate changed. As attorney of record for Donald Kowalski in the guardian case, he continued through early August to represent his client, taking extraordinary measures to put off the testing and attempting to ensure that Karen Thompson would not — initially anyway — be present. But on August 17 Fena sent a letter to Don and told him that he was withdrawing from the case. Jack explained: "Frankly, I feel very hamstrung and feel that you are very angry with me. As I have told you many times I cannot take away Thompson's attorney's typewriter, I cannot nail a 2 by 10 across the Courthouse door, I can't stop Thompson from making press statements and I can't stop newspapers and television people from having shows." Even though he fully understood Don's "feelings and frustration with the justice system," he was forced to withdraw.[16] Fena's departure was a major turning point in the personality composition of the case.

The Kowalskis' position was at this point experiencing other eclipses. *Publishers Weekly* announced the upcoming November date for publication of Karen Thompson and Julie Andrzejewski's book, stating that twenty thousand copies would be printed. The women's press was also "examining eight offers to buy television and film rights" to the case. "Chronicling Thompson's uphill struggle against the sexism and homophobia that permeate this country's institutions, this controversial work reveals one woman's personal journey from closeted lesbian to feminist activist while reconciling her Christian beliefs with her own sexuality," *Publishers Weekly* reported ("Spinsters/Aunt Lute Publishing November Book on Sharon Kowalski," September 16, 1988, p. 28). Thompson, who had appeared on *Geraldo* with other gay and lesbian couples on August 15, went to Washington in September to collect an award from the Human Rights Campaign (a lesbian and gay lobbying organization in Washington) and was negotiating with the producers of *The Life and Times of Harvey Milk* for movie rights to her story. Her fame was growing.

In spite of good reviews from *Publishers Weekly* and the *San Francisco Chronicle*, Thompson's book was described in the *St. Cloud Daily* as "incomplete" and one-sided. "At various times, the media, doctors, lawyers, judges and even the clergy become villains in the story. At some points in the book, Thompson would seem to be the only one in the world who truly cares for Kowalski. That seems doubtful" (John Hughes, "Book Gives SCSU Instructor's Side of Kowalski Custody Fight," *St. Cloud Times*, October 6, 1988, sec. B, p. 1). Andrzejewski immediately dashed off a letter to the editor in reply, pointing out the inaccuracies in the review. "Contrary to 'identifying villains,' we have tried to explore some of the pressures that make responsible people remain silent or take the easy way out rather than confront prejudice directly," Julie wrote in defense of her book, which was "impeccably documented," according to the *San Francisco Chronicle* (Julie Andrzejewski, letter, *St. Cloud Times*, October 19, 1988, sec. A, p. 4).

On Monday, December 12, the parties were back in court. Campbell had received the report of Dr. Eckman and his cohorts and ruled that he would follow their recommendation that Sharon could benefit from further physical and mental rehabilitation at Miller-Dwan for two months. The judge stated that he would order the ward's move after the first of the year but ruled that the parties were not allowed to discuss the evaluators' specific findings with the press. Thompson told reporters she was "extremely pleased with the finding" but could say nothing else, while Donald refused to talk at all (John Myers, "Kowalski Case Decided: Judge Orders Treatment for Disabled Woman,"

Duluth News-Tribune, December 13, 1988, sec. A, p. 1). Campbell himself issued
a press release the next day, summarizing the medical findings without quoting
them exactly. The medical evaluators, he reported, concluded that Sharon was
able to express her needs to others directly but that her mental and communication skills required further testing. Kowalski's "present level of social and psychological well-being is quite low, related to the difficulty of the social situation,
as well as the chronic nature of her current placement in a nursing facility." The
judge's press release continued, "The evaluators' opinion is that with increased
communication skills in a safe setting, Ms. Kowalski could reliably express her
wishes concerning visitation" (Lisa M. Keen, "Kowalski, Thompson May Be
Reunited Next Month," *Washington Blade,* December 23, 1988, p. 3). Although
the evaluators apparently asked that Sharon be immediately transferred, Campbell granted the Kowalskis' request that Sharon come home for Christmas before
the transfer, also giving them time to appeal his decision. Campbell's decision
also gave Sharon and the hospital staff the right to choose who would visit as
long as the medical team believed Sharon had expressed her wishes reliably, but
the judge put no restrictions on visitation by her parents.

Karen Thompson eventually disclosed to reporter Candace Renalis that
Sharon had already made her desires known to the medical team ("Former
Roommate Confident Kowalski Will Want to See Her," *Duluth News-Tribune,*
December 14, 1988, sec. A, p. 4). "She made it clear in the evaluation," Thompson told the *Tribune.* "The issue (of my visitation) has already been dealt with in
the report." In an interview with the *Gay Community News* (Jennie McKnight,
"Big Break in Kowalski Case," December 18–24, 1988, p. 1), Karen directed
her anger at Judge Campbell, who had met the parties for five hours on December 12 to discuss the report but then failed to make the evaluation public.
Instead, he released a cover letter that was totally "lukewarm" compared with
the report, Karen stated.

Campbell, though working slowly, had carefully negotiated Sharon's move
to a rehabilitation facility, yet he could not avoid the consequences of his action
from the now-vociferous Thompson or the angry, beleaguered Kowalskis. The
latter promised an appeal. They rehired Fena, who in January asked for another
extension. The judge again accommodated his Iron Range constituency, delay-
ing Sharon's move until January 17. An affidavit from an irate Dr. William
Wilson stated that he was never consulted by the medical evaluators during the
week of Sharon's testing. Wilson claimed that Sharon did not need to go to
Duluth to learn how to communicate her desires because, he stated, "she did
not want to leave Leisure Hills and . . . she was very happy there." Yet in spite
of Sharon's emphatic clarity about her location, Dr. Wilson continued to insist
that his patient's "decisions must always be reviewed by a concerned, appro-

priate guardian."[17] Sharon's clarity of intention continued to be a filter through which the parties and their experts established their own viewpoints. The stage set for a standoff between medicine and law, Campbell, who had already delayed the move twice, decided to oversee the transfer personally, given Dr. Wilson's intransigence. When the Kowalskis' promised appeal and stay of the transfer order never materialized, the judge called Leisure Hills and told them of his order, stating that the transfer was mandatory. Wilson was finally forced to acquiesce when the van arrived with a copy of the judge's directive on January 17, 1989.

By February 1 Karen Thompson was on a list of visitors that the medical team determined Sharon capably requested to visit. In fact, the findings of the September evaluation indicated that Sharon wanted to see Karen, even though she was aware that her father would not be pleased if she did. The February 4 reunion was arranged at Miller-Dwan by psychologist Dorothy Rappel, one of the hospital's team of evaluators (Tony Kennedy, "Kowalski Visited by Friend Fighting for Custody," *Minneapolis Star Tribune*, February 6, 1989, sec. B, p. 1; Debra Olson, "Kowalski, Thompson United," *St. Cloud Times*, February 6, 1989, sec. B, p. 1). Prior to the visit, Rappel asked Sharon why she thought Thompson had not visited her for so long. Kowalski's response was "too far?" Rappel explained that Karen had not been allowed to visit, and said Sharon "got tears in her eyes" when she saw Thompson for the first time (John Ritter, "Separation Ends for Kowalski and Thompson," *Equal Time*, February 15, 1989).

"I'm elated," Karen told *Equal Time* reporter John Ritter. "It was highly emotional. I had tears streaming down my face, though I had vowed to remain calm. I had never dared hope Sharon would respond as well." Karen stayed the weekend and participated in Sharon's therapy sessions. "Sharon is not angry," Karen also reported, "but she doesn't understand why I've been going out of town (so to speak) and why so many people are interested in her. But she's very excited by it." Karen brought with her one of the huge birthday cards made at the rally the previous August. "It was very clear and very consistent that she thinks of me as her partner and wants to come live with me," an excited Thompson told reporters.

The Kowalskis responded swiftly and seriously to the reunion. Donald told the *New York Times* that he flatly did not believe his daughter was happy to see Thompson. He refused to believe they were lovers. "I've never seen anything that would make me believe it, and I will not change my mind until Sharon is capable of telling me in her own words" ("Woman's Hospital Visit Marks Gay Rights Fight," *New York Times*, February 8, 1989, sec. D, p. 25). Later he would be even more candid with the Associated Press's Tony Kennedy, who in a story entitled "Battle over Kowalski's Guardian Rages On" (*St. Cloud Daily*, February 12, 1988, sec. B, p. 1) reported that this retired couple was "spending their golden years at war with a lesbian professor." "I hate her (Thompson) with a passion," Donald was quoted as proclaiming, and "I can't picture an end to this." He accused Campbell of legalizing a lesbian relationship, even though Thompson "has no legal standing under any law in any state in the union." He also reported that he could no longer afford to fight legal battles over his daughter. "I have no lawyer and I can't afford one," he told the *Times.* An angered Dr. Wilson reasoned, "She (Thompson) used this whole business to deal with her own homosexuality and that's great, but she has used Sharon in the process."

Karen visited Sharon from Thursday through Sunday and again on Tuesday night, driving back from St. Cloud to Duluth through a snowstorm. Thompson did not mention Sharon's parents the entire weekend and spent most of the time holding hands with Sharon while both were shedding tears. It was the sound of Karen's voice and not her face that triggered Sharon's recognition, Thompson recalled: "I walked up to her, I don't think she — I have curly hair now and it wasn't before, I had on glasses and I used to always wear contacts — but as soon as she heard my voice, her eyes, they really did light up" (Lisa M. Keen, "Kowalski Sees Thompson for the First Time in Three Years," *Washington Blade,* February 10, 1989, p. 1).

At the end of 1988, the Human Rights Campaign asked Karen Thompson to write a fund-raising letter for its growing organization. The HRC, which made some controversial decisions in the 1990s to back Republicans instead of Democrats (in one case a gay Democrat) in senate races, raises money to convince politicians that gays and lesbians are just like everybody else. "I used to be what you'd call 'a-political' — until my lover was taken from me by the laws which govern our country," Karen's letter began. "Sharon and I lived quietly in a small Minnesota town. We never thought of ourselves as part of a 'movement' or even as members of the 'gay and lesbian community.' We were just 'Karen and Sharon,' and we believed we were safe from harm as long as we minded our own business."[18]

"Now," Thompson told the people of the HRC mailing list, "I realize just how *unsafe* we were, and how quickly and cruelly our rights could be stolen just because we loved each other." Now Karen was no longer apolitical, and she understood that the only security that lesbians and gay men could ever have was in political strength. Her cautionary missive told other members of the community not to "make the same mistake" she and Sharon had made. "Protect yourself and those you care about by supporting the Campaign Fund with a gift today," Thompson advised, adding a postscript: "P.S. Great news! Just as I finished writing this, the court allowed me to renew my visits with Sharon. So it does pay to be political."

As I passed at thirty miles per hour through Taconite (population 310) and Marble (population 116) on my way to Virginia for an interview, the Iron Range presented itself, on the one hand, as generic America, replete with Kmart, Kentucky Fried Chicken, Goodyear Tires, Jo-Ann Fabrics, and Dairy Queen, but, on the other hand, as a geography marked by huge amounts of ruddy iron slag built up on the side of the highway, occasionally blocking the view of rolling hills as far as the eye could see. There was rock everywhere, and the trees seemed stunted.

I had found Donald Kowalski's address in the Nashwauk phone book, but he said he did not want to talk to me unless there was a miracle that made his daughter better. I decided to send him a note later. On the other side, Karen Thompson, in spite of earlier statements, apparently did not believe the civil rights of gays and lesbians were very important — not that I was a spokesman for those rights, though certainly a proponent.

Even if I were able to interview the principals, I asked myself, would I really be able to discover some deep, dark truth hidden inside them — some revelation about hatred, oppression, prejudice, fear? Or would I find nothing but a person struggling to hold on to an identity, a value, a code, and not let go? Was there some miracle of immediacy — some magic in presence — that would make the mysteries of the Kowalski case, fueled by ideologies and demands for control, suddenly unravel and, like the end of an episode of *Perry Mason,* make the guilty confess and be punished, so we could point self-righteous fingers at the offending culprits? *People's Court* neglected to remind us that the law was often an ass, as Oliver Wendell Holmes remarked. It was also a reflection of ourselves, our beliefs, our principles.

Downtown Hibbing was bypassed by the main highway now. A Hibbing Co-Op Credit Union attested to the Democratic bent of this blue-collar region. But in spite of a history of labor activism, many Iron Rangers still held a less than egalitarian attitude toward divergent lifestyles. For some reason, the labor ideal of economic equality did not necessarily extend to other forms of equal protection, especially for lesbian activists. Did the once-oppressed masses, a select group in terms of gender, ethnicity, and sexual orientation, have the capacity to be oppressive themselves? How long could Sharon Kowalski have ranged freely on the Range? Like Montana, northern Minnesota seemed like closet country.

The space of social geography contains some curious political paradoxes,

I thought. Small minds are said to live in towns that are located in the middle of nowhere under the vast expanse of the wide-open country with ironically broad horizons. But more open perspectives are cultivated in hallowed halls and ivory towers of enclosed academies or enclaves, hotbeds, or ghettos of liberalism. I wondered why living in the outdoors under the big sky was not conducive to Rainbow Coalitions, to being out of the closet. Why couldn't Sharon Kowalski ever be home on the Range again? Why couldn't Sharon Kowalski come home to Hibbing? The prodigal daughter, I realized, had transgressed the boundary waters of common decency. She was now a rare bird gone permanently south because she fell in love — with a woman. Homogenized though the Range had become, some folks just were not welcome.

TEN

New Trial

I want to argue that a lot of the energy of attention and demarcation that has swirled around issues of homosexuality since the end of the nineteenth century, in Europe and in the United States, has been impelled by the distinctively indicative relation of homosexuality to wider mappings of secrecy and disclosure, and of the private and the public, that were and are critically problematical for the gender, sexual, and economic structures of the heterosexist culture at large, mappings whose enabling but dangerous incoherence has become oppressively, durably condensed in certain figures of homosexuality. "The closet" and "coming out," now verging on all-purpose phrases for the potent crossing and recrossing of almost any politically charged lines of representation, have been the gravest and most magnetic of those figures.

Eve Kosofsky Sedgwick, *Epistemology of the Closet*

Television

It is February 25, 1989. CBS is airing its prime-time news magazine, *West 57th Street*. Karen Burnes, a tall, long-haired brunette with a slow, emotional voice, narrates one of the featured stories.[1] The backdrop, she announces, for the case known as Thompson v. Kowalski is "the bleak, unyielding border of northern Minnesota called the Iron Range." The camera cuts to a windswept snowfield flattened by the harsh elements of brute nature. A male voice-over talks about "the Range," a place where "boys are boys and stay boys," while viewers focus on a group of hunters in orange camouflage fatigues drinking coffee. An image of a town in a snowstorm shows bundled-up couples moving down the street, holding children between them. "On the Range, men are men and women are women," the male voice continues, children are expected to graduate from high school, get a job, work hard, marry young, and have a family. People up here are very particular about the way things ought to be.

Cut to Karen Thompson on a couch, wearing a dusty pink blazer, white blouse, and black bow tie. A close-up frames her as she tells Karen Burnes that she did not want to be different; she always wanted to fit in. Cut to Thompson coaching volleyball, whistle around her neck. "I wanted to get married and have children," her voice sounds over. For thirty years she tried to do what she was supposed to do. A snapshot of Sharon Kowalski fills the screen — she wears an orange tank top, blue jeans, and a fishing hat. "Sharon didn't choose to be who she is," Karen states as the camera focuses on the big modular at Briggs Lake, beige, in the trees, near the lake. Burnes speaks of Sharon's and Karen's pre-accident lives — heavily closeted, fiercely private, guarding every look — as the camera pans the blue lake, interspersing snapshots of Karen and Sharon holding up a string of small fish. Sharon in an orange jumpsuit leans back in the aluminum canoe.

From a low angle, heat rises from a highway's pavement. "In one split second, everything changed," Thompson states, as we see a black-and-white snapshot of the Toyota in a gully — the left side of the front end ripped open, the hood creased. As Burnes describes the five-month coma, the segment features shots of Sharon, lying in bed, sitting in a wheelchair, her face pale, her head leaning to one side.

The camera cuts to Burnes interviewing Donald Kowalski. He is heavier and seems more formidable than he appeared in "The Silent Ordeal" photo. Donald has a Minnesota voice — friendly, homey, employing lots of "you knows," lots of understated inflections of emotion. His pain finds its outlet in a slight rise of a vowel sound, a slight whine in tone, a slight move in the steady mouth. "She can't do anything for herself," he states in a monotone. "She needs to be turned every two hours; she's in diapers." Sharon is "downright helpless, you know."

In a long shot of the courtroom, Burnes talks of the intensified emotions, the allegations of sexual abuse, Karen's commitment to legal redress. Brian O'Neill, the Faegre and Benson attorney who had volunteered to represent Sharon, is shown next — a heavyset man seemingly in his late twenties or early thirties. A loosened tie and shaggy haircut frame his round, rather pugnacious, aspect. He is feistier than anyone else on the segment. What more basic right is there, he asks, than the right to choose whom you want to see, whom you want to be your friends? It's so basic it is rarely articulated. This right was what the *Kowalski* case was really about, though that subject was completely avoided by phrasing the facts in a different way. Practically speaking, no matter what the legal briefs said, the question before the court was not the right of friendship but "should a father have the right to protect his daughter from sexual exploitation by a lesbian?" How is a court going to answer a factual question framed in this manner, O'Neill asks, in his effectively sarcastic tone.

A series of short interviews create a counterpoint history between Don and Karen. "I couldn't believe it," Don declares with absolutely no irony, referring to his daughter's sexual orientation. He speaks an emotional truth, expresses an inability as well as a creed. Thompson counters that she expected the Kowalskis to understand her love. Don never uses Karen's name, nor does Karen use his. Shifting pronouns serve as placeholders of animus.

The camera cuts to Karen at a podium talking about coming out, then to her at a gay and lesbian formal champagne reception (a Free Sharon Kowalski button appears on her lapel). Burnes tells us Thompson has raised over $100,000. Don speculates that Thompson wants money. He and his family, he reminds Burnes, "never asked for anything. We don't want anything. We want to be left alone to take care of our daughter." Don gets somewhat emotional in the next set of frames. "I'm still her dad — they can't take that away no matter what." Karen tearfully replies that "it is time to put aside fears and prejudices, to realize that we have all lost, but Sharon has lost the most, and we need to look out for her best interest."

The final shot shows Sharon being wheeled down the halls of Leisure Hills, pale and a little uneasy. Burnes gives an update. On February 2, 1989, Karen was granted the right to visit Sharon again. The long legal battle continues, Burnes concludes with a pregnant pause.

Evaluation

A Ph.D. in psychology, Dorothy Rappel specialized in treating people with strokes and head injuries. She was part of the Duluth team that evaluated Sharon in 1988 and 1989. When interviewed almost ten years later in 1997, this blonde, bespectacled woman in her fifties started the discussion by stating that Sharon had a severe head injury and as a result did her best in the here and now, though she was still able to recollect the color of her motorcycle and certainly remembered Karen Thompson when she finally was allowed to see her after three and a half years. The reunification was an emotional experience to witness for Rappel, who had never seen a case like this one before, in part because the circumstances surrounding it were highly unusual. Usually, she stated, it was impossible to find a home for severely disabled head injury patients — no one wanted them, and they languished in nursing homes, which did their best but were usually financially strapped and understaffed. The psychologist could not understand why a court would restrict access of anyone who wanted to care for a disabled person, especially someone with Thompson's dedication. Karen, Rappel stated, had on numerous occasions tried to reconcile with the Kowalskis, but in her view, the parents, whom she had visited on the Range, would not budge.

The Kowalskis told reporter Mark Stodghill that they remained deeply skeptical about the chance of their daughter's rehabilitation or ability to make decisions for herself ("Parents, Doctor Want Sharon Returned to Hibbing," *Duluth News-Tribune*, February 12, 1989, sec. A, p. 1). "You never give up on your kid and I believe in miracles, but now it's been over five years. You have to face reality," Della Kowalski told Stodghill as she began to cry into her cupped hands. Della and Don had made three visits to Duluth since Sharon's transfer in January but still held out hope that she would come back to Hibbing; they felt she was getting good care there under the supervision of Dr. Wilson, who told the reporter that Sharon's transfer was "an insult to the health care facilities and professionals of the Iron Range." Karen Thompson, however, was now a regular visitor. She added ten hours a day to her regular work schedule in St. Cloud — six hours driving to and from Duluth and four hours visiting Sharon.

The case was still gaining broader media attention. In a long op-ed piece in the *New York Times,* Tom Stoddard wrote that the tragedy of the *Kowalski* case underscored the injustice of the law's refusal to recognize same-sex marriage. Reprinted in the *Minneapolis Star Tribune* on March 7, Stoddard's editorial began: " 'In sickness and in health, 'til death do us part.' With those familiar words, millions of people each year are married, a public affirmation of a private bond that both society and the newlyweds hope will endure." Yet Karen Thompson, who had "pledged lifelong devotion" to Sharon Kowalski, had been denied the right to visit her partner for almost four years in large part because her "home state of Minnesota, like every other jurisdiction in the United States, refuses to permit two individuals of the same sex to marry."

"Thompson and Kowalski are spouses in every respect except the legal," Stoddard argued; moreover, the refusal to grant them the right to marry was tragic proof that marriage was "not just a symbolic state. It can be the key to survival, emotional and financial. Marriage triggers a universe of rights, privileges and presumptions. A married person can share in a spouse's estate even when there is no will. A spouse is typically entitled to the group insurance and pension programs offered by the other spouse's employer, and enjoys tax advantages. A spouse cannot be compelled to testify against the other spouse in legal proceedings." Like Sharon and Karen, millions of gay and lesbian Americans were being denied the individual right to marry, Stoddard wrote. While marriage was traditionally a heterosexual institution, he conceded, "history alone cannot sanctify injustice. If tradition were the only measure, most states would still limit matrimony to partners of the same race," since "as recently as 1967, before the Supreme Court declared miscegenation statutes unconstitutional, 16 states still prohibited marriages between a white person and a black person." The *Kowalski* case demonstrated that "sanctimonious illusions" about correct forms of love have led "directly to the suffering of others. Denied the right to marry, these two women are left subject to the whims and prejudices of others, and of the law." The refusal to allow same-sex marriage, Stoddard concluded, was a denial of "equal protection of the law" and a "monstrous injustice" (Thomas B. Stoddard, "Gay Adults Should Not Be Denied the Benefits of Marriage," *Minneapolis Star Tribune*, March 7, 1989, sec. A, p. 11).

"There Are No Clear-Cut Answers in the Tragedy of Sharon Kowalski," Eve Browning Cole's editorial was entitled (*Duluth News-Tribune*, March 2, 1989, sec. D, p. 10). This assistant professor of philosophy and women's studies at the University of Minnesota at Duluth steered a middle course in her hometown paper, speaking of our "hankering for heroes and villains, for clear moral contrasts between good and evil" in a case in which issues are "larger than the individual human relations in question." Browning Cole lamented that counterproductive "accusations of 'isms,' such as sexism, handicapism, and heterosexism, have been liberally flung about, mostly in the direction of the Kowalskis." The move of Sharon to Duluth, she opined, raised its own issue of "regionalism," with its implied insult to the health care community of the Iron Range.

Reviewing "all the ingredients of drama" the case contained, Browning Cole reviewed Jack Fena's "fondness for invective and disposition to talk like a Raymond Chandler character ('It's over. Finito. Sayonara, as they say')," providing a vivid contrast to "the cool urbanity of Thompson's Minneapolis counselors." And Thompson had her "flair for publicity, her controlled and articulate self-expression," which contrasted sharply "with Donald Kowalski's plain-spoken simplicity." While the professor noted that the case had become "a rallying point for interest groups supporting gays and lesbians, feminist issues and the rights of the disabled, . . . far less attention has been paid to the issue of parents' rights to care for and about an injured child." Out of an "urgent feeling of protectiveness," she argued, "the Kowalskis have acted in good faith" and "do not deserve to be peppered with numerous 'isms.'" She concluded that the *Kowalski* case pointed to a need that we "as a society get much better at speaking to each other and hearing each other, even when what is being said is unwelcome or upsetting."

In the midst of this public debate, under a secret May 18 order from Judge Campbell, Sharon was transferred from Miller-Dwan to the Ebenezer Caroline Center in Minneapolis, a transitional place for rehabilitation until a more permanent position became available at the extended care facility called Trevilla of Robbinsdale. The judge specifically enjoined all parties from discussing the details of the move in order to avoid press coverage at the Minneapolis center, but Thompson, who accompanied Sharon in the medical van, told reporter

John Ritter that the transfer to Trevilla would help create a more "stimulating environment" for Sharon's rehabilitation. Sharon, who now had a speech synthesizer to help her vocalize and a motorized wheelchair, continued to be inconsistent in her motivation to employ these devices. "Sometimes she chooses not to communicate, but she has made progress," Thompson told reporters. "She can operate a motorized wheelchair but it is frustrating when she chooses not to" (John Ritter, "Sharon Kowalski Moved to Mpls. Rehabilitation Center," *Equal Time*, May 22, 1989, p. 1).

The move made Thompson's life easier. The trip to Duluth from St. Cloud was more than twice as far as the trip from Minneapolis to St. Cloud, and Thompson found herself frequently traveling to the Twin Cities airport for flights to her various speaking engagements, including most recently to Washington, where she received a $3,000 contribution from the Human Rights Campaign Fund to help retire her legal fees, which now totaled more than $150,000. Featuring Gloria Steinem, the HRC reception was held the evening of the National March on Washington for Women's Equality, Women's Lives. Steinem stated that helping Thompson's legal battle has been "one of the best investments we can make. It's a horrendous and undeserved debt."

Events in the case began to take a further turn in Karen Thompson's direction. On June 12 Sharon was finally moved to Trevilla, a facility that provided rehabilitation and transition to less structured care. The March medical report, finally filed in court on May 22, contained the recommendations of Dr. Eckman's team, which specifically prescribed the transitional living program at Trevilla of Robbinsdale. The evaluators recommended that Sharon's ultimate goal be "to return to pre-morbid home environment." Eckman's cover letter stated, "We believe Sharon Kowalski has shown areas of potential and ability to make rational choices in many areas of her life. She has consistently indicated a desire to return home, and by that means to St. Cloud to live with Karen Thompson again."[2]

Judge Campbell kept close watch, however, over the dissemination of the Miller-Dwan information. Two gag orders in June prevented interested parties from discussing the case with the public, one of which had specific impact on Karen's presentation at the annual Twin Posts Gay/Lesbian Pride Week at the University of Minnesota in Duluth. In an order dated June 21, 1989, Campbell specifically enjoined Thompson from talking about Sharon's sexuality or her treatment.[3] Revising her planned remarks, Karen used Sharon's case as an example that illustrated the need for gays, lesbians, and disabled people to come to terms with themselves and fight for their rights. Campbell's attempts to prevent the release of information would lead to trouble in the coming months of litigation.

Wheels of Justice

In June, Sue Wilson reported that the petition to restore capacity was temporarily in abeyance, pending the outcome of two developments. The first was Sharon's rehabilitation: Would she be able to regain her own capacity, thus obviating the need for a guardian? The second was the imminent resignation of Donald Kowalski as guardian, which Wilson had recently discovered. Don apparently had asked Campbell to terminate his guardianship, "because if he can't do it his way he doesn't want to do it," Wilson stated in a press release from the National Committee to Free Sharon Kowalski dated June 18, 1989. After reading the March medical examination from the Eckman team, the Kowalskis, lawyerless and fed up with the medical profession, refused to attend any medical or legal meetings regarding Sharon's care. Their frustration with the process had reached a critical point as they watched their daughter moved even farther away from their home. In spite of this development, Wilson remarked, Campbell was not ready to turn the guardianship over to Thompson.

The news of Donald's surprise resignation hit Duluth's *News-Tribune* and St. Cloud's *Times* in the first week of July. "I have nothing more to say," Donald told Mike Nistler of the *Times* from his home in Nashwauk. Thompson told reporters that Judge Campbell was seeking a third person to become Sharon's guardian on an interim basis. "He felt that it would be too abrupt to go from Donald Kowalski to me," Thompson stated, but Karen still intended to bring Sharon home with her eventually and be her guardian. "I'm holding it up," Thompson told reporters, referring to her legal challenge to the appointment of the proposed third party (Mike Nistler, "Kowalski to Get New Guardian: Father Gives Up 6-Year Fight to Keep Disabled Daughter," *St. Cloud Times*, July 2, 1989, sec. A, p. 1; "Kowalski's Dad Won't Pursue Guardianship," *Duluth News-Tribune*, July 3, 1989).

Sue Wilson and the lawyers for the *Minneapolis Star Tribune*, meanwhile, had filed a writ of prohibition appealing Campbell's order of June 21, which prohibited disclosure of information regarding Sharon's care, treatment, medical condition, and sexuality. Judge Campbell argued that he was trying to protect Sharon from emotional distress, but the Court of Appeals ruled swiftly that the prevention of emotional distress is not sufficient to restrain the First Amendment freedom of public comment. In fact, the Court of Appeals argued, the order prohibited disclosure of information already made public, served no governmental interest, was not narrowly tailored, and failed to establish a compelling reason to make public information private. Campbell was also required under law — if he did restrict access — to inform the media and allow them time to object.[4]

On July 19, 1989, John Ritter published a long article in the Minneapolis gay paper *Equal Time* entitled "Protecting Our Rights," focusing on the *Kowalski* case's legal "legacy" for gays and lesbians in the age of AIDS. "Karen Thompson doesn't consider herself a hero," the article stated, "she simply did what she could to be with the woman she loves." Ritter retold the story of the couple's tranquil, private life in the country, when Karen dreaded even mouthing the word "lesbian," avoided associating with lesbians on campus, and voted twice for Ronald Reagan.

"The splinters from Karen Thompson's closet door are still flying. When the next chapter in the history of the gay rights movement is written, Thompson's efforts will be recorded as one of the first major triumphs in a fight for rights for same-sex relationships," Ritter's article began. He compared Thompson to Harvey Milk and Georgia activist Michael Hardwick, noting that the *Kowalski* "case was cited in a recent New York ruling upholding a gay man's right to the apartment lease of his deceased partner. The case also has been discussed as domestic partners legislation was passed, and later challenged, in San Francisco and debated in other places." Emma Hixson, an open lesbian and executive director of the Minneapolis Department of Civil Rights, told Ritter the case had created broad awareness of the pitfalls of not having legal protection for relationships. The case, however, had changed nothing legally. "The law sees us as being outside of the (heterosexual) structure," another Minneapolis attorney told Ritter. "They don't want us to see our lovers in the hospital or allow us to bury our dead. The only way for us to circumvent the law is to go to a gay or lesbian attorney and find out how you can fit into the heterosexual system. We can use the laws created for heterosexuals and fit them into our lifestyle" (John Ritter, "Protecting Our Legal Rights," *Equal Time*, July 19, 1989, p. 8).

In spite of the Court of Appeals ruling, Trevilla of Robbinsdale continued to guard its new patient's privacy with intensity. For the balance of the year and well into 1990, Sharon's rehabilitation records remained private as Thompson's attorneys prepared to renew their petition for guardianship. Karen continued to visit Sharon on a regular basis and receive passes to take her out on weekends. Sharon had also undergone major surgery in February on her leg tendons, which had atrophied in Hibbing. Tendons on her left wrist, shoulder, and finger were also surgically unflexed, and by February 12 she was recovering rapidly at the Sister Kenny Institute, an affiliate of Northwestern Hospital in Minneapolis, where the procedure occurred.

During the surgery approval hearing, Campbell also revoked a previous order requiring a staff person from Trevilla to escort Sharon on any outings, and he allowed increased visitation from others. Thompson told Kasel, "The judge is pleased at the progress Sharon has made using the van and the speech synthesizer," both of which Karen bought with money raised by her speaking engagements. Although Karen said the judge was "now clear on the point that I'm not publicizing and fundraising on this case," she simultaneously emphasized the need to return to such efforts in order to defray legal expenses and the cost of a motorized wheelchair for Sharon. To Kasel, Thompson seemed particularly optimistic at the beginning of 1990. Sharon "certainly is communicating more consistently with me," Karen continued, "although not always with the professional people" (Mark Kasel, "Surgery Marks Medical Progress in Kowalski Case," *GAZE*, February 22, 1990, p. 1).

The increased visitation with Sharon had recently required Karen to curtail her speaking engagements. In August 1989 she accepted the Humanitarian Award of the American Psychological Association and was a keynote speaker at the U.S. Student Association National Congress. One weekend in December, she spoke at eight separate engagements in New Jersey and New York City. "I want to keep pushing on the issues; I'm a confirmed activist," Thompson commented. "As I've grown and changed, so have my speeches. They've developed from that of purely social activist to a more political context. I've moved from where I was in 1988 when I was reluctant initially to endorse Jesse Jackson for President because it was political." Thompson had recently joined the board of directors of the Lambda Legal Defense Fund (*GAZE*, February 22, 1990, p. 1). In an important speech on May 11, 1990, at the University of Minnesota's West Bank Union Auditorium, she told her audience: "People who do not actively fight for human rights are guilty of passive oppression." Her solution for lesbians and gays: come out. "How can we develop our self-esteem in a glass closet? And it certainly is a glass closet, many people see into it anyway. And it's a very fragile closet . . . as long as we are closeted, as long as we are invisible, we are vulnerable" (Tom Cushman, "Karen Thompson: 'People Who Do Not Actively Fight for Human Rights Are Guilty of Passive Oppression,'" *GAZE*, May 17, 1990, p. 1).

By May 1990, however, Thompson's optimism had waned for reasons that she was not yet willing to disclose. Not only had her renewed petition not yet been granted, but she also reported that Sharon suffered from continued depression. Karen called this period "the hardest of all. It's hard to see Sharon and all the changes. . . . I don't know what our relationship will be anymore. It's been really, really hard." Karen was clearly not the person Sharon knew before the accident. "Sharon is in love with a memory, and I can't go back to being that person, not even for Sharon." Thompson stated plainly that Sharon had lost a lot of motivation during the seven years of protracted legal struggle. "Physically, she looks good now. Mentally, the price has been far greater,"

Thompson lamented (Susan Krajac, "Karen Thompson Will Not Be Silenced," *GAZE*, May 17, 1990, "Lesbian Pages," p. 1).

In the first weekend in July, Karen made the bold move of flying Sharon to San Francisco to jointly accept the 1990 Woman of Courage Award at the National Organization for Women's conference in San Francisco. The court had authorized the travel on June 14, and the event received plenty of media attention, again putting the spotlight on the case and more particularly on Sharon. The Associated Press circulated an unflattering photo of Sharon in her wheelchair, with her head leaning down on her right forearm and a sad look on her face, Karen standing next to the chair in pants and a NOW T-shirt, wearing an expression of pride. "People want to make this a gay rights issue," Thompson stated in her acceptance speech. "But it's really about sexism because people think women need to be protected from their own decisions. And it's about society's inability to deal with the rights and wishes of the disabled" ("Kowalski, Thompson Honored," *Duluth News-Tribune*, July 2, 1990, sec. B, p. 1).

The NOW conference in San Francisco, however, was very much concerned with gay rights, especially issues of rapprochement between lesbians and other feminists. Karen and Sharon were featured as the exemplary same-sex couple. Supervisor Angela Alioto proclaimed July 1 "Karen Thompson and Sharon Kowalski Day," and Molly Yard, NOW president, stated, "We often talk about the power of love in trivial ways. But I think that you have demonstrated the power of love and what it will achieve." In an ironic twist to the charge of invasion of privacy Thompson was defending herself against, delegates also passed a resolution against outing as a political technique. After heated debate, the convention adopted language that both foregrounded gay and lesbian issues as important for the feminist organization and frowned upon the very practice that brought condemnation of Karen Thompson from Iron Range lesbians and others. "NOW recognizes the frustration of lesbian/gay rights/AIDS activists who consider that exposing the sexual orientation of closeted Lesbian and Gay politicians and celebrities is an effective means of achieving a raised public consciousness," the resolution stated, but "the rights to privacy, self-determination and self-definition are basic feminist principles which exclude such 'outing' as a feasible or acceptable strategy."[5]

By the summer of 1990, the media were anticipating an end to the six-year struggle. "Custody Dispute Involving Gay Rights, Disabled Nears Close," the *Duluth News-Tribune* headlined on July 30, as it previewed reaction to the unopposed petition. "I see no basis not to have it happen this time," said Sue Wilson. "I rarely go into court with no opposition." Her assessment was technically correct, but the balance of the article reported that opposition to

Thompson's petition had not vanished. Although Don and Della Kowalski declined to discuss the case, their former attorney remained an outspoken advocate. Jack Fena wanted the public to know that Sharon's parents had not "abandoned" their daughter; these "working stiffs" had just been worn down by the tragedy and ordeal of the battle being waged by the "bucks-up" Thompson (Candace Renalis, "Custody Dispute Involving Gay Rights, Disabled Nears Close," *Duluth News-Tribune,* July 30, 1990, sec. A, p. 1).

Judge Campbell had made decisions for the ward himself for the past year in the absence of Donald's participation or success in finding a neutral third party to succeed him. "At some point, the judge cannot act as guardian," Sue Wilson told reporters (*Duluth News-Tribune,* July 30, 1990). Campbell had also been keeping a tight lid on the case, postponing hearings and adopting a wait-and-see posture in order to monitor Sharon's possible rehabilitation. But he could not delay indefinitely. He named public defender Fred Friedman of Duluth as Sharon's new attorney and Margaret Grahek her social worker, but he stopped short of naming a temporary guardian. Sue Wilson's motion for a hearing on guardianship, originally filed on November 27, 1989, was not scheduled for a court date until the following February but even then was continued until the summer, giving Sharon time to recover from her surgery.

In July, Campbell finally decided to schedule a hearing for August 3 at the facility in Robbinsdale, but upon his arrival that day he again ran into First Amendment problems. Operators of the Trevilla nursing home refused to admit reporters into the building, so Campbell in accommodation ordered the hearing closed. *Star Tribune* attorneys immediately contacted the Court of Appeals, and Judge Wozniak phoned Campbell at Trevilla, directing the lower court judge to either move the hearing to a public courtroom or cancel it and allow the attorneys to submit written arguments instead. Predictably, Campbell gave Friedman and Thompson's attorney until August 9 to submit written arguments, promising to make a decision by the end of August or early September.

Softball Lesbians

Fred Friedman, son of Jewish immigrants who originally lived on the High Line in northeastern Montana, had grown up in Chicago but attended law school in Minnesota and now counted himself local Duluth stock. He was named Sharon's attorney by Campbell when Pagliaccetti was appointed a judge in 1990. When interviewed in 1997, Friedman presented himself as a likable, extroverted, swarthy, funny, convincing lawyer. He spoke with some knowledge about the continuing fight against anti-Semitism in Montana and saw himself as a liberal in a socially conservative but friendly town. He liked the sidehill lie of Duluth, liked its streetlights swinging in the wind off the lake, liked the old brownstones. In fact, Friedman, as a member of the local bar as well as the community, knew all the major players: Campbell, Douglas, Stodghill, Eckman, and others. Both Campbell and Douglas, he stated, were themselves liberals in the tradition of Eugene McCarthy and Justice Douglas.

Friedman had strong feelings about the *Kowalski* case, insisting that it was not about homophobia but about outing, rights of privacy, and Karen Thompson's intransigence in the face of the Kowalskis' old-world ways and Sharon's cultural commitment to a contented closet. The public defender had lesbians in his office who worked for him, and he called Sue Wilson a friend. But Thompson, in his opinion, was aggressive, insensitive, political, emotional, especially in her remarks to Sharon's sister, Debbie. He did agree with Karen's treatment ideas and had no argument with her conclusion that the court made a big mistake in allowing the guardian to put Sharon in Leisure Hills, a nursing home that had been cited a couple of times by the health department since Sharon left.

The public defender found his appointment as Sharon's lawyer difficult because of the amount of travel time and Sharon's inability or unwillingness to communicate. Serious difficulties also arose when he began to get phone calls from lesbians on the Range who stated they did not want Thompson to become guardian. He wanted them to testify, but many were unwilling to divulge their sexual orientation in the courtroom even if the judge promised to prevent questioning in that direction. One, Rose Jones,[6] did testify; in fact she filed an affidavit in August 1989 against Thompson, whom she knew prior to the accident from trips with Sharon. Friedman reminded me that being outed in Duluth was an act of greater consequence than in New York City. He respected the need for many of these women — schoolteachers, small-town administrators, plant workers — to remain in the closet. The other woman who filed an affidavit in August against Thompson was Karen Tomberlin, a well-known Range teacher and track coach, who had since died of cancer. She was Sharon's athletic mentor and a friend of the Kowalskis. Friedman was impressed by her reputation in the Coleraine community and her closeness to Sharon.

Friedman's carefully composed letter to Judge Campbell written on August 14 evidenced the dilemma the case presented for him.[7] "If the ability to turn commitment into hard work, loyalty and energy is the test, nobody could meet the test of the guardianship statute better than Karen Thompson," Friedman wrote to Judge Campbell. But Sharon's family and many of her friends remained opposed to the appointment, he equivocated, and all "used the word 'controlling'" to describe Thompson, whom they perceive as a "smooth talker

and a hustler for various causes including handicapped rights, gay rights, resolution of homophobic hang-ups and other causes." They felt that they would
be unwelcome "with Karen running the show." But those who opposed the
petition had no alternative, and none of them were able to assume the responsibility. "Karen Thompson meets the statutory test but lacks the approval of
the Kowalskis," Sharon's lawyer told the judge. "If the Court finds this essential, she should not be appointed guardian. If it is not, then she is best qualified.
The issue is who is best able to provide for the care and needs of Sharon
Kowalski, including insuring the involvement of all of Sharon's family and
friends in Sharon's life."

Friedman's letter hedged most clearly in its final statements in which he
stated that Karen was best qualified unless parental approval was "essential."
He then claimed that the cares and needs of Sharon included assured "involvement of all of Sharon's family." Clearly the Kowalskis had no intention of ever
becoming "involved" with Sharon at the new handicap-accessible home Karen
had recently built on the banks of the Mississippi in Clearwater south of St.
Cloud, but clearly the Kowalskis had not involved Karen when they were
guardians. In the end, the decision was Campbell's to make.

Two other letters came to the court in August unannounced, though only
one was extant in the records. Both Karen Tomberlin and Rose Jones wrote in
opposition to Thompson's petition. Karen Tomberlin, who had filed an affidavit in the case as early as August 1984, introduced herself as a "close personal
friend of Sharon Kowalski's for 20 years," who wanted the court to know first
that Sharon was "a person . . . not a cause. Gay rights should never have been
allowed to become the issue," she declared. Although Tomberlin believed a
parent's love to be "unconditional from birth until death," Don and Della, she
admitted, were "spent—emotionally, physically and financially." Her sugges-
tion? Return Sharon to Leisure Hills, "where her parents could visit, take her
to ball games" where she could watch her beloved nephew Michael "compete in
football, basketball and baseball games for Nashwauk-Keewatin High School."
She suggested that a neutral third party like Fred Friedman become co-guardian
with a personal friend like herself. Based "on 13 years of sharing confidences
in letters, phone calls and private conversations prior to the accident," Karen
Tomberlin's conviction was "that Sharon's primary concern, loyalty and love
(previous to and at the time of the accident) went to her immediate family."[8]

Rose Jones, a Range lesbian and friend of the ward, also wrote to request
that Sharon be returned to her quiet life on the Range with her softball friends,
claiming Thompson's guardianship would preclude the interaction Sharon
shared with this close-knit if closeted group. When interviewed about the
Kowalski case in 1997, Rose Jones was close to forty, only three years older than

Sharon. Rose worked in one of the small towns on the Range and had a master's degree in education. She was guarded at first and insisted on anonymity, even though she was one of the only ones to testify in court. Sharon was a great athlete and a lot of fun, Rose remembered, having met her in high school. Sharon would often take off on her motorcycle by herself and sometimes dreamed about moving back up to the Range to start a motorcycle driving school. Rose had seen Sharon in the week before the accident when she was coming back to pick up Debbie's kids because her sister's marriage was breaking up. Rose knew the Kowalskis, knew how much anger both Mark and Debbie harbored about the case. She sympathized with them — a family caught up in a media event generated by people who had no respect for the Range mentality, one which she realized was guarded and private but one which, after moving from Duluth, she had learned to accept.

Jones had comforted her friend during her growing pains. When Sharon was drinking in the seventies, she would come over to Rose's house and spill her guts until two in the morning until Rose finally had to kick her out and tell her not to come back unless she was sober. Actually, Sharon had at one point professed her love for Rose, but the older woman knew it was just a teenage crush, even though Sharon did threaten suicide in one crazy moment. After that, they did not see each other for two years. Sharon finally got her "shit together," went back to school, did well at St. Cloud State, and came back to thank Rose. They took a long walk down the tracks from Grand Rapids to Calumet one summer after a softball game. Sharon gave her a motorcycle helmet as a present, and later Rose and her partner went with Karen and Sharon on camping and cross-country skiing trips.

The problem with the struggle, as Rose saw it, was Karen's personality — controlling from the beginning, refusing to let people in the hospital room without her there, wanting to see every medical record. Thompson went ballistic after the accident; she was loud and adamant about Sharon's care, not compassionate or in tune with the Kowalskis' mind-set. Karen was also a loner; she went through a fervent Bible-reading stage and relaxed only intermittently during the fishing trips they took together. Sharon looked up to Karen and thought Karen could bring her out of her shell, but Karen was not exactly the life of the party. She was possessive, questioned everything, and always focused attention on herself.

Rose truly believed Sharon would be better off with her family. Putting herself in the same situation, she felt family was more important, more long-term, more committed. She did not believe the case presented a gay issue; Karen made it one in part because she had to. Even if Sharon and Karen were legally married, Rose still did not think Karen was the right person to be guardian. Many others on the Range felt the same way, she stated, though they were afraid of losing their jobs if they came forward to testify. Rose was scared, too, and her parents were none too happy to learn of her involvement in the case. But she had to do it for Sharon.

Many of the members of Sharon's softball team, which Sharon could watch from Leisure Hills when they played in Hibbing, felt the same way as Rose about Sharon and the Range. They felt that Sharon's picture and name should not be in the media. Rose was incensed at the exploitation of the disabled that occurred when Sharon was taken to marches and put on television. If Karen Thompson wants to march, Rose declaimed, that's fine, but she had no right to take Sharon, especially when Rose believed that Sharon never wanted to come out, that she was happy with her quiet life on the Range, especially after her wild days had passed.

When people come out, Rose asked, what purpose does it serve? Coming out only creates friction and makes things harder because an issue that has been quietly tolerated must be addressed openly. Rose never came out to her parents, but she knew they knew. She also knew that the Kowalskis knew about her and probably about their daughter. Rose visited the Kowalskis often with her significant other, and they were always happy to see her. The problem with Karen Thompson was that she did not respect that way of doing business. Jones was a proponent of the open secret, that way of doing gay and lesbian business that avoided confrontation and accepted a cultural space of unspoken tolerance — don't ask, don't tell — which had allowed the subculture of Range lesbians to flourish within the circumscription of the benign dominance of heterosexuality.

The counterpoint to Jones's earnest discomfort with Thompson's petition was illustrated by a feature article in the *St. Cloud Times* by John Welsh, a cub reporter who came to the Kowalski story late after joining the staff of the paper in February 1990. "Karen Thompson took her friend Sharon Kowalski fishing again last month," the article began. "Fishing was once a favorite activity, but the two had not done it since a November 1983 automobile accident left Kowalski a quadriplegic and severely limited her ability to communicate." Karen told Welsh that Sharon was as content and peaceful as she had been since the accident. "The two didn't catch any walleyes during their outing on Big Sauk Lake," the article continued, "but they did nearly capture something more precious — a sense of normalcy."

Welsh's homey fish-story opening was followed by some interesting revelations about the changes currently taking place in Karen's life, changes that would complicate the case as much as Rose Jones and her cohorts would. "Sharon's and my relationship is very much in doubt," Thompson told the *Times.* "Whether I care for Sharon as a friend who loves her . . . or whether we find our way back to being lovers and partners . . . we don't know. . . . Sharon wants me to be the person I was four years ago. But I can't go back to being that person for anyone. Not even for Sharon." Sharon herself had been through changes, including a diagnosis of clinical depression and the development of disturbing habits that Thompson calls "coping mechanisms." Often Sharon rubs the fingers of her right hand before her eyes and goes into a trancelike state that can only be broken when someone grabs the hand away from her face, Welsh stated.

In the companion article on inspiration, Welsh spoke of the way the case had changed gay and lesbian outlooks on legal and ethical questions. More and more couples were signing durable powers of attorney, and in 1989 the Minnesota legislature approved a living will statute that allowed people to designate not only what kind of care they want to receive if incapacitated but also their preferences for who should make those decisions. Brian Coyle, a Minneapolis City Council member, was sponsoring a domestic partners proposal for city employees in part because of dramatic stories like Thompson's. Maury Landsman, an associate clinical professor at the University of Minnesota Law School, said that although some of the opinions in the case may have lasting legal ramifications, "the real legacy will be social and political. It tells people it's possible to win long-term fights. Karen Thompson is a kind of beacon to people who think about giving up the fight on controversial issues" (John Welsh, "Thompson-Kowalski Case Gave Inspiration to Others," *St. Cloud Times,* August 5, 1989, sec. A, p. 10).

Fifteen days later, the *St. Cloud Times* ran an Associated Press story that responded pointedly to Welsh's article. "Custody Battle Drains Kowalski's Parents" spoke of Don and Della's fear that they were on the verge of losing their thirty-four-year-old disabled daughter to her professed lesbian lover. "I'll never believe in our court system again. No matter what," Donald Kowalski told the reporter over the phone from his rural Nashwauk home. Donald stated that he had decided to break his media silence because he was tired of reading and hearing that he would no longer fight for his daughter. "I don't think you can ever give up on your kids, but you do give up on the system," he said. "It's just too much pressure, and Thompson and all those groups who support her will never give up as long as we are guardians. I think she is out to get us more than anything" ("Custody Battle Drains Kowalski's Parents," *St. Cloud Times,* August 20, 1990, sec. B, p. 1).

Finally, on August 31, Judge Campbell issued his surprising ruling that he was not willing to grant Thompson's unopposed motion. After reading the letters from Tomberlin, Jones, and Friedman, the judge determined he wanted to conduct a full hearing, now set for October 10, before making his guardianship decision ("State Judge Denies Guardianship Request," *Duluth News-Tribune*, September 1, 1990, sec. A, p. 2). Friedman said he planned to call no witnesses. "It's like bitching about a candidate without have another candidate," he said. "The people who care about her haven't come up with an alternative solution. The question is essentially that Sharon's parents and sister can't get along with Thompson." A frustrated but determined Sue Wilson said she planned to call fifteen witnesses to ensure an adequate record for appeal, emphasizing that increased litigation costs (estimated now at $750,000) represented funds that would not go to Sharon's rehabilitation (John Welsh, "Denial Only Temporary," *St. Cloud Times*, September 8, 1990, sec. A, p. 1).

Della told reporters she was pleased with the ruling but would not comment on the upcoming hearing. The Kowalskis had not attended the last few hearings and by their own admission were not likely to go to court again. Thompson and her attorneys remained officially philosophical, confident that the evidence in the hearing would be sufficiently overwhelming to award Karen guardianship. Unfortunately the amassing of that evidence was estimated to cost $20,000. In a telephone interview with David Anger of *Equal Time,* an emotional Karen stated, "I'm just so furious. It's a setback, but a temporary one. We will win, whether it is at this stage or in appeal." About the letters from Jones and Tomberlin, Karen said, "I'm being eaten up by this. We live in fear of some homophobic person talking against us." Sharon's lawyer, Fred Friedman, reiterated the "tragic" aspect of a case in which a lot of well-meaning people "can't or won't get together for the sake of Sharon." It was now obvious, Friedman told reporters, "that Sharon had a lesbian relationship and it's obvious that she kept it from her parents for what appears to be good reasons" (David Anger, "Judge Denies Thompson Guardianship: New Hearing Set for October 12," *Equal Time*, September 14–28, 1990).

Although Campbell had previously approved Sharon's participation in the NOW conference in July, he apparently had a change of heart in the wake of the Associated Press photo in San Francisco and the curiously professional letter from Tomberlin decrying the outing of Sharon. In September he unequivocally denied a request by Karen that Sharon be allowed to accompany her to Boston to the National Disability Pride Day on October 6, the judge stating it was not in Sharon's "best interest right now" to be allowed to attend the event. The vice president of NOW, Rosemary Dempsey, called the ruling "outrageous," "arbitrary," and "insensitive." In *GAZE*, a strident Thompson stated, "The irony is that Sharon is not being allowed to be with other disabled people, celebrating their diversity," because "[i]t's not in *his* best interest right now for Sharon to be out in public." Paula Ettelbrick, legal director for Lambda Legal Defense and Education Fund, criticized Campbell for "the travesty of waiting so long to appoint a guardian" and putting Sharon in a "legal limbo" (Mark Kasel, "Kowalski Denied Right to Attend National Disability Event; Pre-hearing Set for Oct. 10," *GAZE,* October 4, 1990, p. 1). Ettelbrick's admonishment, if it came to Campbell's attention, did not deter his deliberate course. The October court appearance led to a scheduling of two sets of hearings, one in Duluth in the first week in November and another set in Minneapolis for December 5 through 7. "Justice delayed is justice undone," the adage proclaimed, but Campbell was acting cautiously, giving his constituency an opportunity to be heard on Thompson's motion.

Peter J. Nickitas served as a law clerk for Judge Campbell in 1990. One of his assignments was to research the most relevant questions the court must ask of all potential guardians of Sharon Kowalski. The result was a memo dated October 19.[9] The statement of facts revealed not only that Mr. and Mrs. Kowalski were "hostile toward Ms. Thompson" and found "their daughter's putative sexual orientation, and that of Ms. Thompson, offensive," but also that Sharon Kowalski had "never 'outed' herself to her parents," even though, the clerk's memo continued, "Ms. Thompson . . . has 'outed' Sharon publicly to the court and members of the broadcast media on TV, radio, and publishing. Whether Ms. Thompson did this with Sharon's undisputed permission is unclear." Nickitas also noted, "Ms. Thompson, by her own admission, has other women friends with whom she shares the affection and comfort that she claims to share with Ms. Kowalski," alluding officially for the first time to Karen's involvement with Patty Bresser, the nurse from Connecticut whom Karen had started dating. Karen's two rings would become an issue as the hearing progressed, complicating the precedent the case was setting for same-sex partnership.

Finishing his statement of facts, the clerk proceeded to review the law, namely, Minnesota Statutes Section 525.539, subd. 7, which enumerates the factors that determine the "best interest" of the ward, including the statement that "kinship is not a conclusive factor . . . but should be considered to the extent that it is relevant to the other factors." In one of the cases cited (*Schmidt v Hebeisen,* 347 NW2d 62 [Minn App 1984]), the court resolved a family dispute over guardianship by selecting a neutral third party; another case cited the presumption in favor of the natural parents. Other cases stated that the existence of "ancillary liaisons" did not in itself justify denial of a petition, but if there was evidence that "from these liaisons flow harm to Sharon's emotional health, detraction from the healthy social interaction with other nurturing persons or degradation of Karen Thompson's 'current understanding' of Sharon Kowalski's condition," then the court, Nickitas advised, should view the petition with reservation. Thompson's relationship with Patty Bresser was now a factor.

Discovery

In anticipation of the November hearing, Sue Wilson scheduled the depositions of Rose Jones and Karen Tomberlin, the two women who had come forward to object to Karen's petition.[10] On November 2 she talked first with Jones,
the thirty-eight-year-old teacher, who remembered that Sharon still held the
state women's discus record. In the early eighties, Rose and her partner had
taken skiing trips with Karen and Sharon. The line of questioning continued:

> Ms. WILSON: You don't doubt therefore that Sharon was lesbian, do you?
> Ms. [JONES]: I don't doubt they had a relationship.
> Q: But you don't think —
> A: I've never doubted that. Whether or not she was lesbian, I don't know if
>   I'd go that far.
> Q: Did she go that far?
> A: No. . . .
> Q: Were Karen and Sharon closeted, as far as you know?
> A: Yes. They were very discreet, private. . . .
> Q: Is it a fair statement that it's basically — in the area that she grew up in, the
>   area that you're familiar with, that it's pretty much not okay to be a lesbian,
>   that you don't really — you don't get to say that or talk about it?
> A: We — I wouldn't broadcast it, put it that way, advertise. There are a lot of
>   people up there that are lesbians.
> Q: But they're pretty much closeted?
> A: Closeted and I think just discreet in their relationships with people.
> Q: Okay. For example, if you were a day-care worker or a school teacher, you
>   wouldn't want anybody to know you were a lesbian because people would
>   try to get you fired probably?
> A: That's pretty correct.[11]

Jones reiterated her belief that Thompson was "controlling and dominating"
and had violated Sharon's rights by exhibiting her in the media "across the
U.S." She felt Thompson was more committed to winning the case than to
Sharon's rehabilitation, especially because she had taken another partner. She
wanted Karen Tomberlin and a neutral third party to become guardian.[12]

The deposition of Karen Rae Wright Tomberlin, forty-six, of Coleraine
took place the same day. She was also a physical education teacher and had met
Sharon in that capacity when the latter was a sophomore in the neighboring high
school. They became friends when Tomberlin drove her to state track meets.
Sharon stayed in close contact after graduation, writing letters, calling, and stopping over for a lot of late-night sessions "where I'd keep popping popcorn and

we'd just sit around and talk." Before the accident Tomberlin had never met Karen Thompson. Sharon never "verbalized" her involvement with Thompson, but Tomberlin suspected — though she "didn't probe." Tomberlin did not see Sharon after the accident until January 1984, when she witnessed Thompson was treating Sharon "like a trained animal," making her do tricks with balls in a way that in Tomberlin's estimation just embarrassed and belittled Sharon.[13]

Wilson suddenly changed the subject, asking, "Do you believe that Sharon is a lesbian?" If she was, Tomberlin answered, she "was very discreet" about it before the accident, but not necessarily because the Kowalskis were intolerant. "I know it's something that Sharon didn't verbalize," Tomberlin tried to explain, "but probably in their hearts they understood, you know, as I probably did too, you know, the relationship Sharon had with Karen."[14] Sue Wilson was making some effective if subtle arguments about the parameters of "knowledge" and the open secret the Kowalskis had denied acknowledging since the inception of the case.

Uncontested Hearing

The case came before the court on November 8 in Duluth as scheduled. In her brief opening statement, Thompson's lawyer told the court, "This is a statutory proceeding, and the legislature has given us very specific guidelines in Minnesota Statutes 525.539 subd. 7 as to whom the court should name as guardian of an individual who is in need of a guardian." Wilson outlined the "three pronged test. The first is the reasonable preference of the ward. The second is the interaction between the proposed guardian and the ward. And the third is the interest and commitment of the proposed guardian in promoting the welfare of the ward in a number of categories, including physical and mental status and needs." Karen Thompson, she proposed, was the most qualified person in all three categories.[15] Counsel then proceeded immediately to her witnesses, most of whom were part of the team of health professionals at Miller-Dwan that observed and reevaluated Sharon in 1988 and 1989.

Matthew Eckman was the lead witness, board-certified in physical medicine and rehabilitation since 1976. "We evaluate and manage patients with a variety of neuromuscular, skeletal, physico-social problems," he stated, explaining his work at Miller-Dwan. During his initial evaluation of Sharon on September 14, 1988, at the court's request, Eckman "noted that she had limited communication, that she was considerably spastic, that she had some contractures, that she had a feeding gastrotomy, and was very dependent in her activities of daily living and needed a great deal of assistance with her physical care." After three months of evaluation, Eckman stated, "we concluded that she was able to reliably indicate the people she would wish to see." The March 10, 1989, report concluded that Sharon Kowalski had "shown areas of potential and ability to make rational choices in many areas of her life," and she had "consistently indicated a desire to return home. And by that she means to St. Cloud to live with Karen Thompson again. Whether that is possible is still uncertain as her care will be difficult and burdensome. We think she deserves the opportunity to try." Eckman thought "Sharon had some awareness that this process resulted in some stress for her family," who, she was also aware, "had traditional reservations about her returning to her previous lifestyle." There was no question in Eckman's mind that Sharon and Karen had prior to the accident "lived in the same facility," as he put it—that they were in a lesbian relationship.[16]

Dr. Eckman explained that Sharon had traumatic encephalopathy. "She has got a considerable degree of brain damage and this results in a variety of manifestations, including cognitive dysfunction; including memory loss, incoordination, motor problems affecting her posture, balance, arms, legs, trunk, and so she has considerable residual deficits." One of those deficits was a difficulty in recalling recent events:

> A patient with that [encephalopathy] can ordinarily recall items out of the distant past and they can at times respond to an immediate recall of giving them a number and they can recite the number back to you. But they will typically have problems recalling further instructions or, I mean, recalling instructions that they are given, what they did the day before or over a time frame. That varies. They will have problems with orientation, where they are and what the day, date, month, year, that kind of thing, depending on the degree of it.[17]

Eckman believed that in spite of Sharon's deficits, she consistently indicated an innate desire to return home, to return to where she was living before the accident.

Eckman's testimony completed, Campbell ordered a five-minute recess, giving the media permission to move around from their designated area in the jury box. The next witness was Dorothy Rappel, clinical psychologist at Miller-Dwan Hospital in the Polinsky Center since 1970. Rappel did "intellectual and cognitive evaluation," as well as "cognitive retraining, attempting to get people back to as close [to where they were] prior to their injury." She also did "disability counseling, helping people to adjust to the long term deficits of their disability." Rappel was responsible for attempting to see "whether or not Sharon was able to make any kind of a statement as to a future course for herself." Although her methodology was somewhat intuitive ("I know that I did not chart every single one of those times. I am hoping I did some place"), Rappel first established a rapport with Sharon and then asked her over a number of occasions about her preferences. "I can't remember my exact words," she testified, "but I tried to make that an open-ended kind of question . . . like if you could go any place at all to live after you leave here, where would it be? And she always said, St. Cloud with Karen, and that was consistent." Sharon regularly informed the psychologist that she was in a lesbian relationship.[18]

Dr. Rappel also stated that she had communicated to the Kowalskis her wish that they reach some form of accommodation with Karen Thompson, but "it was not something they saw as a possibility at that time." Judge Campbell at this point made a number of inquiries of his own. He wanted to know how often Sharon talked about her past before St. Cloud, whether Sharon knew if Missy was dead, whether Sharon was a private person. Dr. Rappel could recall few specifics about the first questions, but she did answer the last question: "My best guess would probably be that she would be a fairly private person, but I think she had a really good sense of humor. I think in that sense she would be pretty outgoing."[19]

The next witness was Rachel Komarek, manager of the Adult Rehabilitation Division of the Polinsky Center. She testified that she evaluated Sharon's communication skills. When Sharon was given a Wolf voice output command system, a synthesizer that picked up pressure from voicing mechanisms in the patient, she was able to point to letters and to spell words but was not able "to exert enough pressure to make that system — the synthesized voice part of the system — work." Asked about Sharon's sexual orientation, Komarek reported, "During one of the sessions I had with her, I was asking her to make a choice about what to do during therapy that day. She was not responding. She was not indicating to me what she wanted to do. So I asked her if she had had her choice of anything in the world what would she want to do and her response was, make love to Karen." Sharon had typed this response on a Zygo machine, a handheld keyboard writer. The court elicited through its own questioning that Karen was in the room at the time, but Komarek testified that Karen did not try to take over the rehab sessions or tell Komarek what to do.[20]

At this juncture, the record showed that Judge Campbell decided to recall Dr. Rappel for further testimony.[21] The judge proceeded with a line of questioning about the doctor's interaction with the ever-present Thompson. He wanted to know whether Rappel had discussed the lesbian relationship with Karen, and the doctor was "sure" she did "in general terms." She more specifically asked Sharon about the relationship. "So you don't know, or do you know, whether she and Karen had any commitment to one another?" Campbell asked the medical witness. "I certainly know that my feeling was that Sharon had this commitment with Karen," she replied. "I know that she was willing to say to me that she did have a lesbian relationship. I guess maybe that implies a lot of commitment to me, but I don't know what she said." The judge wanted to know if what Sharon told the witness implied a "lifetime commitment," and Dr. Rappel stated "not necessarily." Campbell pressed on. What if Sharon and Karen had a lifetime commitment, and "then Karen terminated the lifetime commitment to Sharon and took other partners, would that affect Sharon?" Rappel thought that it might "have an effect" on the ward, but "a friendship could still remain" that would be most "important to Sharon." The judge then questioned the psychologist about Sharon's parents. Had she asked Sharon to tell her parents? Rappel had not, but she "probably asked whether or not [Sharon] would be willing to do that." The ward had responded with an unequivocal no.

Sue Wilson followed up with questions about Sharon's capacity to be an adult and to carry on "an intimate sexual relation." Dr. Rappel answered that the question was more difficult than one would think. She finally stated, "I think — I certainly think that Sharon is still a sexual person. Just because she is disabled, you know, but that's up to her to decide or to do with what she wants to do with that. But just because she is disabled certainly does not make her asexual." Dr. Rappel was dismissed, and court adjourned until the following day.

Two press headlines on November 9 demonstrated the subjectivity of the archive. "Witnesses Say Kowalski Shouldn't Have to Choose," Candace Renalis of the *Duluth News-Tribune* reported, mentioning Dr. Eckman's comment that making Sharon decide to be with either Karen or her parents would be like "Sophie's choice, a forced decision to choose between equally loved ones" (November 9, 1990, sec. A, p. 2). Renalis did not report Eckman's testimony that Sharon had consistently expressed a desire to live with Karen. The Associated Press story was headlined in the *St. Cloud Times* as "Kowalski Should Have Choice, 2 Doctors Say." It began, "Two of Sharon Kowalski's former doctors have testified that the accident victim wants to live with her lesbian lover and should be allowed to do so" (November 9, 1990, sec. A, p. 3).

The Sunday before the hearing was set to resume in Minneapolis, a feature article by John Yewell came across the kitchen table of many Minnesotans — "After Tug of War Ends, Sharon Kowalski Is Sure to Be the Loser" appeared on December 2 in the *St. Paul Pioneer Press*. The article began with an allusion to the coming-out motif that was driving this narrative of homosexuality: "Like many children, Sharon Kowalski had a secret she was afraid to tell her parents. She never got the chance to tell them herself what millions now know." The theme: outing; the secret: lesbian love. The article gave a brief history of the case — its status as a "rallying point for homosexuals everywhere," Thompson's success on the "lecture circuit," the admiration of her book, "at least from afar" — but then proceeded with its in-depth observations. "And yet when people get close to Thompson, another picture emerges," Yewell wrote. "It is a picture of a combative, domineering woman who may be her own worst enemy, no matter how well-intentioned she is. Further clouding the picture is Thompson's admission that she has taken female lovers and would not rule out taking others were she to be named guardian."

After discussing the legal progress in the case, Yewell revealed his information about Karen Thompson's domination and promiscuity — motifs familiar to the mainstream media coverage of lesbians and gay men, especially the coverage of the St. Paul paper whose earlier piece ("The Silent Ordeal") had sought to give the Kowalskis' side of the story. Fred Friedman, Yewell reported, believed "Sharon does not fully understand that Thompson has had relationships with other women since the accident." In his investigation, the reporter also discovered two Rangers from Sharon's past who were willing to talk. Marge Netland, who was Sharon's best friend in high school, remembered her as very independent. "If she knew what was going on today, there's no doubt in my mind she would tell Karen Thompson where to get off," Netland insisted.

Becky Muotka, who had known Sharon since ninth grade, agreed with Netland. In high school, Muotka and Sharon ran together in a group of girls who participated in athletics on weekends. Muotka knew the family well, but as a lesbian now living in the Twin Cities, she also understood Thompson's position. "I didn't like Karen Thompson," Muotka explained her reaction during her initial visits to Sartell after the accident. "It was like she was clocking me: 'Your two minutes are up' — that sort of thing." Muotka asserted that her friend had no control over becoming "a gay symbol," and may well be miserable inside. This account jibed "with numerous accounts of other family members and friends," Yewell stated, adding that Thompson had been characterized as "manipulative and alienating," by some of her closest allies. Many who spoke to Yewell agreed that "if the parents are in denial about their homophobia, then Karen Thompson is equally in denial about her domineering attitude" (John Yewell, "After Tug of War Ends, Sharon Kowalski Is Sure to Be the Loser," *St. Paul Pioneer Press*, December 2, 1990, sec. E, p. 1).

Motion in Limine

The Minneapolis hearing on December 5 began with a legal maneuver that reflected the way the secrecy of same-sex love continued to pervade the issues of these public hearings. Fred Friedman had made a motion in limine, a pre-hearing procedure that requested the court to limit questions about witnesses' sexual orientation.[22] He began his oral argument by enumerating the frequent phone calls and letters he had received about the case, which he felt to some degree were his responsibility to bring before the court. These potential witnesses stated that they would not testify if they were forced to answer questions about their same-sex relations. Friedman thought that questions of sexual orientation were not relevant enough evidentially to justify the loss of valuable testimony that would be available if such questions were prohibited. He noted that in criminal cases, questions of sexual orientation were irrelevant to somebody's credibility as a professional witness, and the same rule, he noted, applied to civil law, though an exception was carved out for custody cases. Sharon's was not a custody case, Friedman reasoned, but a guardianship one, "and there is not a case on all fours" or directly applicable to sexual orientation and guardianship.[23]

Sue Wilson reacted with a tone that disclosed a new tack that appeared to recognize that the court was now her opposition. Disturbed that individuals were contacting the ward's attorney and the court without her knowledge, Wilson wanted to know the nature of those ex parte contacts and if the "Court was talking to witnesses" without giving her client an opportunity to be heard. While concerned about due process, Wilson stated she was not interested in routinely asking witnesses about sexual orientation, especially experts, but if someone has spent time with Karen and Sharon and her own partner, her sexual orientation could be very relevant, especially to conduct "before the accident" that might clearly prove Sharon's "lesbianism." For three and a half years Wilson had worked to establish the validity of Sharon and Karen's lesbian partnership; how could she now relinquish the opportunity to elicit evidence of that relationship because a few witnesses were afraid to disclose their own lesbianism?

Judge Campbell responded swiftly. " If you look through the file you will probably find more, as much, or more information from gay organizations, disabled persons representing disabled persons, either organizations, individuals, whatever, also contacting the Court," he told counsel. "It was a constant stream of correspondence, telephone calls, and I treat them the same as I treat anything else. That it has to be on the record. I can't consider it." The judge ruled from the bench that "witnesses should be able to inform counsel that they wish to or do not wish to have their sexuality divulged. If they wish to, there is no problem. If they do not wish to, I will order that counsel refrain from questions that will put their sexuality in issue or bring it out." But Sue Wilson wanted the ability to ask the witnesses who had been present at get-togethers, what activities they undertook; she wanted leeway to set the women-based scene. The judge granted her that parameter but then added an anecdote that suggested how he, as trier of fact, might interpret such testimony. Campbell took his fishing partner of twenty-five years as an example. "We go a lot of places together," he told the court. "He's single and we have no sexual relationship . . . and if I was involved in a similar suit similar to this I don't believe that somebody should have the right at that point to ask me that question." The judge would allow evidence of the activity but not testimony about the type of relation that existed.[24]

Sharon's Day in Court

After the agreement on the motion to protect the closet, Judge Campbell announced that Sharon Kowalski had just arrived in the Hennepin County courtroom, accompanied by a nurse from Trevilla. The announcement signaled the first court appearance of the central focus of this litigation since its inception seven years earlier. Sue Wilson was in the middle of calling Mary Connell, a licensed practical nurse, to the stand. Connell had been working with Sharon for a year and a half and was testifying that the patient was often unresponsive and withdrawn, but when Karen was around "she is always smiling. She responds better. She will cooperate better if there is something that needs to be done. She does use her communicator, her talking box, when Karen is around, not when she is not around." Karen, according to the witness, "was extremely concerned with everything with Sharon," but her concern was neither disruptive nor controlling.[25]

Fred Friedman, during his examination of Connell, pursued a line of questioning about Sharon that elicited a sense of some of her habits. He wanted to know how Sharon conducted herself when Thompson was not present. "A lot of times Sharon will just sit and be very quiet, doesn't want to — she does not use her machine," Connell responded, noting that Sharon was reacting the same way in court at that moment. Sharon also had the habit of covering her head with her sweatshirt, which Friedman noted she was also presently doing. Even when Thompson was present, Sharon sometimes withdrew in this manner. Friedman then asked Connell to communicate with the ward:

> Ms. CONNELL: How are you feeling today, Sharon?
> KAREN THOMPSON: She whispered good.
> THE COURT: Is that what she whispered, Mr. Friedman?
> MR. FRIEDMAN: I couldn't tell anything at all.
> KAREN THOMPSON: Can you type it on here, Sharon?
> MR. FRIEDMAN: Let me do it, please. For the Court's record, she spelled G followed by roughly a half a dozen O's and then a D.
> MR. FRIEDMAN: Thank you. That's all the questions I have, Ms. Connell.[26]

After Sharon's first statement to the court (with Thompson's assistance), Sue Wilson moved to her next witness, Kathy King, current staff development coordinator at Trevilla of Robbinsdale, who had first met Sharon at the Polinsky Center in 1984 and just happened to be in the employ of Trevilla when Sharon arrived recently. Because of her unusual position of having had previous contact with Sharon, Fred Friedman wanted her to compare Sharon's condition now to her state in 1984. "Actually, I was the person that admitted her [to Polinsky in 1984] so I remember her fairly well. Basically speaking, she was much more physically able at that time. She could pivot transfer. Her limbs — her left arm wasn't as tight. She was taking things by mouth. She didn't have the thrush." King did state that the communication equipment that was now available gave Sharon more opportunities to express herself, but her deteriorated physical condition made those devices more difficult to use. "What I am saying," she told the court, "is that as this process has occurred, at some point in the supposed rehabilitation, she didn't have rehab."[27]

Anita Johnson, another nurse, admitted "it takes Sharon a while to get to know somebody," but she had been able to get her to laugh in the past three months. When Karen comes in, Sharon is "a different person." Then Friedman asked Ms. Johnson to talk to Sharon:

> Ms. JOHNSON: Sharon can you look at me? Hi. Do you know me, from one Polack to another, do you know me? See, I can get her to respond to Polish jokes because I know she is Polish and I can get her to talk and laugh that way and talk about drinking beer and stuff.
> MR. FRIEDMAN: Gee, neither of you look Polish.
> Ms. JOHNSON: Our noses give us away, don't they?
> Q: Can you get her to use a communicator in any way? Or ask her if she is hungry, you know, whatever.
> A: Sharon, can you say how you feel today. How do you feel right now? Do you feel happy? Would you type that out for me?
> THE COURT: From your experience, Ms. Johnson, what does the pulling of the blouse or shirt over her head mean? Is she, you know, from your experience?
> A: What we have concluded that it's lots of times that she is depressed about things . . . or upset. . . .
> THE COURT: And while you have been here, have you heard her make a sound like a crying or a moaning sound in this courtroom today?
> A: She does that frequently.
> THE COURT: And does — does she make that sound or does that sound accompany her pulling her shirt over her head?
> A: Yes, lots of times.
> THE COURT: And do you feel that that means that she is sad or depressed?
> A: Right.[28]

Having reached an impasse, Judge Campbell called for a lunch recess. Jackie Nelson, the nursing assistant who took care of Sharon five days a week, took the stand at one-thirty. Sharon, she testified, was almost always more responsive when Karen was present. Nelson described Sharon's different reactions to her parents and Thompson:

> Ms. NELSON: Okay. Karen walks in the door, I mean, right away Sharon is just ear-to-ear smiles. She has her head up, stares at Karen. With her parents, she just doesn't react like that. I mean, she's just glowing when Karen walks in the room, she's so happy to see her.
> THE COURT: Just a minute, before you go on. Would you tell me what's happening right now with Sharon, if you know?
> THE WITNESS: What's happening? She probably just had a spasm in her legs.
> THE COURT: While we're on that subject, what happens when she has a spasm in her legs, what does that cause her to do?
> THE WITNESS: She cringes and she goes down, you know, you can tell. She like contracts.
> MR. FRIEDMAN: Can I have a moment, please, your honor? Does your leg hurt right now? Would you ask her, Karen, if her leg hurts right now?
> KAREN THOMPSON: When Sharon is having sort of a spasm, you're not going to get her to talk.
> MR. FRIEDMAN: Just answer my question, please. Ask her if her leg hurts.
> KAREN THOMPSON: Sharon, does your leg hurt right now? No? Now she's okay.
> MR. FRIEDMAN: Were you reacting to your leg or were you reacting to what Ms. Nelson just said? All right. Go ahead, please, okay.
> Ms. WILSON: Do you remember the question?
> THE WITNESS: Yes. When Karen comes in, like I say, she glows and when Karen asks her a question, she right away answers her, just like now. With her parents, they really don't talk to her like Karen does. I mean, they don't ask her questions. They just talk to her. They don't ask her anything.[29]

Mr. Friedman then attempted to get Sharon to respond to some questions Jackie addressed to her, but the answers were few and far between, and eventually Sharon pulled her shirt up again. When the judge started asking the witness about staff meetings and Sharon's attendance at mass, the patient began to moan.

The hearing continued, in spite of the ward's obvious stress. Jenette Adamski, a speech pathologist, was seeing Sharon three times a week to help her communicate more, whether by voice, speech pack, alphabet board, or head nods. Sue Wilson asked Adamski about communication with Sharon concerning the friends she would like to visit. She had never asked to see Karen Tomberlin or Rose Jones, Adamski testified, and when the pathologist started to talk about Sharon's friends on the Range with whom she "used to like to party a lot," Sharon often reacted in the negative when asked if she wanted to see them. On cross-examination from Friedman, Adamski stated that she believed Sharon almost always understood her questions even if she did not answer them, including the conversation presently transpiring in the courtroom. Friedman then asked her to demonstrate how she communicates with Sharon. The transcript reflected the following breakdown:

Ms. ADAMSKI: How are you doing today? This kind of overwhelming? Do you understand everything that's going on here today? A little bit. Sharon, what sport do you like to play? Can you spell it out for me? What sport do you like to play? Sharon, are you okay? Are you okay? Are you in pain, yes or no? Are you in pain? Where did you grow up? What city did you grow up in? . . . Can you spell it out for me? What city? Did you grow up in Nashwauk? Is that where you grew up, Nashwauk? Am I saying it right? Yeah, okay, good. Where did you go to college, what city? Where did you go to college? Spell it out for me. Where did you go to college? In St. Cloud, yeah, okay. What did you major in? What did you get a degree in?

MR. FRIEDMAN: Can you ask her something that gives me a no answer. Ask her something like a leading question. Like did you go to school at North Carolina or did you major in biology, anything that gets a no answer.

THE WITNESS: Sharon I have got a question for you. Do you like Toyotas? Sharon, are you okay?

THE COURT: Have you seen this type of a response?

THE WITNESS: Never.

THE COURT: You have never seen this type of response?

THE WITNESS: Never. I think it's her toe, honestly; her left toe, the toenail came off all the way.

THE COURT: When?

THE WITNESS: A couple of nights ago on p.m. shift when they took the sock off. . . .

THE COURT: This is unintelligible so it's not going down on the record.

THE WITNESS: I am just asking her if her toe hurts.

THE COURT: Ask her again.

THE WITNESS: Does your toe hurt?

THE COURT: There are times when Sharon chooses not to respond?

THE WITNESS: I believe so.

THE COURT: All right. . . . Ask her if she would like to come back tomorrow. . . .

THE WITNESS: She can say yes or no but if she is in pain, if she chooses not to answer the question, she won't, and there isn't anything anybody can do to make her respond. She is able to make that choice. . . .

KAREN THOMPSON: Can I ask her?

THE COURT: Sure.

> Karen Thompson: Are you all right? Are you okay? Are you okay? There is
> something wrong.
> The Court: Okay.
> Mr. Friedman: Ms. Adamski, I have got a couple more questions.
> The Court: All right. Now, I think the record should note that Karen Thomp-
> son has attempted to communicate with Sharon and at this time Sharon indi-
> cated a sign of distress and let out a cry of distress and pulled her shirt over
> her head.
> Mr. Friedman: I agree with that.[30]

After another attempt to talk to Sharon was equally unsuccessful, the judge decided to move on with the next witness, since Sharon's van was due to pick her
up in ten minutes.

After testimony from two more health care witnesses, Sue Wilson had
called her last witness of the day, so Judge Campbell allowed Fred Friedman
to call a witness out of turn — the social worker Margaret Grahek, appointed
to Sharon's case by Judge Campbell in 1988. Grahek had been visiting Sharon
once a quarter, more frequently when she went on other trips to the Twin
Cities. She testified that she had seen positive communication with Sharon in
her encounters with Thompson, the Kowalski family, and Tomberlin. She had
never herself asked Sharon questions about preference. When Grahek stopped
in Nashwauk on her way to Minneapolis, the Kowalskis indicated to her that
they would not be at the hearing, that they had seen their daughter over
Thanksgiving, and that they felt "a great deal of frustration" with the court
process. When Friedman asked if they had voiced their preference for a
guardian, Wilson's objection of hearsay was overruled, Grahek answering that
in the past they had voiced their desire for a neutral third party. On cross-examination, Sue Wilson asked Grahek if she ever had difficulty communicating
with her client. Grahek testified that Karen sometimes "becomes very concerned and at times almost angry" when she thinks Sharon's needs are not
being met. "Karen seems to feel that she is the only one who could possibly
know what is in the best interest of Sharon," Grahek told the court.[31] After
Margaret Grahek's testimony, Judge Campbell called it a day, ordering court
to reconvene the next morning at eight-thirty.

Law and Medicine

Dr. Gail Gregor of the Sister Kenny Institute had testified at the hearing in 1985
that led to Donald Kowalski's appointment as guardian by Judge Douglas. Back

on the stand on December 6 in Minneapolis, the feisty Gregor had been following Sharon since her arrival in the Twin Cities in 1989 but had also
reviewed her records for possible admission to Sister Kenny in 1984. As she
explained it, Sharon had suffered a severe brain injury that manifested itself
neurologically as spastic quadriplegia, affecting the left side of her body more
significantly than the right. She still had a feeding tube and had just had a surgical procedure done to correct the opening of that tube into her stomach. At
this time she also had a prolific thrush infection in her mouth. Sharon's muscle
contracture and spasticity were new since the 1984 review, she noted.[32]

"I think that she didn't receive adequate and proper care to prevent complications or to correct complications of the brain surgery," Dr. Gregor boldly
began. She declared "within a reasonable medical certainty" that the contracture of Sharon's muscles could have been prevented with proper physical therapy when she was in Hibbing. She did state that the surgery on Sharon's
tendons, once done, was very successful. Her feet were now in a position where
they could be placed on the foot pedal of her wheelchair, and the hand and
wrist surgery had relieved much of the spasticity there. Even with the surgery,
however, Gregor told the court, Sharon was still not able to do what she could
do in 1984.[33]

Dr. Gregor concurred with previous assessments of Sharon's mental capacity. Her memory "impairment" was "severe." The right side of Sharon's
brain — the frontal lobe and temporal lobes — was the main area of injury. "So
Sharon has severe impairment of attention and concentration and is very selective in ways in which she interacts with her environment and other people,"
Dr. Gregor reminded the court, frustrated by the events of the previous day.
"She does have the capacity to be communicative," the doctor continued. "I
have communicated with her; she communicates, is very aware and observant
of her environment but she has communication and cognitive problems as well
as behavioral changes."[34]

When asked about the effect on Sharon of the deprivation of contact with
Karen Thompson for three and a half years, Dr. Gregor poignantly replied,
"devastating," emphasizing that Sharon's level of response to one person over
all others — in this case Karen Thompson — was one of the most extreme she
had ever seen. She speculated that this connection was probably clear from the
time Sharon came out of her coma. "It's very common that a person recovering from coma will only be awake and out of their coma with one other person, the one other person that's the most important person in their life."[35]

Having established the connection between Karen and Sharon, Wilson was
now required to broach its dehiscence. Gregor told the court that Thompson's

romantic involvement with Patty Bresser was not unusual for a partner of someone with a disability because the noninjured partner also needs to continue her
life and make it the best she can. "And we commonly see divorces occurring but
continued involvement with the brain-injured partner," she noted. When Fred
Friedman continued to ask on cross-examination about Karen's new romance,
Dr. Gregor testified that Karen and Sharon had to make a decision themselves
about how much to share about Karen's new sexual involvement. "That's not
for me as a physician to advise or recommend. I don't think it would be harmful
for Sharon to know about Karen's relationships with other people. But I think
it would be a very private and personal thing and for them to choose. Certainly,
not for me as a doctor or the courts to decide that." The doctor had been
involved in the last ten years with very creative and novel solutions to situations
created by a brain injury or spinal cord injury.[36]

Dr. Gregor had not seen the patient in the company of her parents, but on
redirect by Sue Wilson, she opined that it was not harmful to Sharon for Karen
to come out to the Kowalskis when she did. Judge Campbell immediately questioned whether the doctor had the ability to answer that question, since she was
not there at the time. Gregor insisted that "it was natural and necessary" to
share that kind of information at the time of a medical crisis, in fact beneficial
to the care providers, though, in her estimation, the Kowalskis had no idea of
how much Karen's disclosure meant to Sharon. "And my impression of the sister and the father, that day in court [in 1985], was that they were responding in
a common way of shock and denial."[37] Friedman's cross-examination led to
further questions about outing:

> MR. FRIEDMAN: Dr. Gregor, didn't Sharon Kowalski have the right to decide
> for herself whether to tell her parents about her sexual orientation?
> DR. GREGOR: I don't know. The issue of rights is such a legal term. From a
> medical context, it was necessary for Karen to reveal her relationship with
> Sharon in order to help her parents cope with the tragedy of Sharon's acci-
> dent and illness and to permit continued involvement of Karen, who loved
> Sharon, with Sharon.
> Q: Do you believe —
> A: Under the threat of parental —
> Q: So that decision was taken away from Sharon?
> A: What was taken away?
> Q: The decision to —
> A: Sharon was in coma when this all happened.
> Q: That's correct. So the decision to tell her parents was taken away from
> Sharon?
> A: My understanding is that Karen came out, revealed herself to Sharon's par-

ents for the purpose of not coming out or revealing to Sharon's parents lifestyle preference, sexuality, but to help the parents know why Karen was involved with Sharon. What their relationship was . . .

THE COURT: As a physician, do you have a responsibility to your patient to keep confidences that they divulge to you? Yes or no?

A: Yes. If they request that confidence to be maintained.

Q: And even if they don't request that confidence to be maintained, do you feel that you have a right to divulge those confidences?

A: I don't know what you're asking

Q: Okay. Do you know —

A: I know that most of my communication, as a physician, with my patient, Sharon, is through Karen because Sharon has chosen that. . . . It is difficult for me to deliver health care to Sharon because, you, as a guardian, are not accessible to Sharon and cannot communicate with me on what her current state of activities and affairs are, and I need to rely on Karen as Sharon's friend.

Q: Have you ever talked to me by phone, Doctor?

A: I have talked with your —

Q: Have you ever talked to me by phone?

A: No.

Q: Could I inform you that —

A: I have called you several times. I have left messages several times. . . .

Q: Are other people there, are other patients of yours at Trevilla or Caroline Center under guardianship?

A: A few are, yes. And I communicate with their guardians in the same way.

Q: Are some of them under state guardianship?

A: I don't know of anyone else who has the Court as a guardian. Most of them are lucky enough to have a real person who cares about them.

Q: Counsel.

Ms. WILSON: Excuse me, your honor.

Q: All right.

Ms. WILSON: I apologize to the court.

THE WITNESS: Excuse me. I may be — I am not understanding what — I am not —

THE COURT: I guess not, doctor.

THE WITNESS: I am sorry for anything that I have done to —

THE COURT: That's all right, doctor.

A: But I honestly don't know what I have said that's offensive to the court.

Q: One thing, doctor, why don't you let me finish a sentence or a question before you start answering. I want to go back, doctor, and ask you, again, about Sharon's right or request to her physician not to disclose her sexuality to her parents. Now, we know she can reliably express certain decisions. You have said that, correct?

A: Yes.

Q: Are you aware that she has expressed a desire not to tell her parents of her sexuality today? Or within the past—

A: I am not aware of that.

Q: You're not aware of that? All right. If you were aware of that today—

A: If Sharon asked me not to reveal?

Q: Correct. Would you respect that request?

A: Absolutely, I would respect that request.[38]

The relationship between Dr. Gregor and the court, even in the previous hearing in 1985, had the flavor of acerbity — given the traditional disdain between the two professions — but toward the end of this testimony the civility of the courtroom began to break down.

Thompson v. Thompson

After Dr. Gregor's tumultuous testimony, Sue Wilson put her client on the stand. Karen Diane Thompson, the next witness, was born in Parkersburg, West Virginia, grew up in Ohio, and had spent the last fifteen years in St. Cloud, Minnesota, where she taught physical education, recreation, and sports science. She continued to be ABD at Ohio State with an unfinished dissertation in learning motivation. She was now also an adjunct professor in human relations, which allowed her to teach classes in social activism. Sharon Kowalski enrolled in Karen's "Competitive Sports for Women" class in 1976 and later took basketball officiating. Karen gave her a job as assistant track and field coach in 1978.

The rest was history, which Thompson recounted once again — the story she had told so many times, had written a book about, had again and again revealed to reporters, lawyers, doctors, judges. Her romantic attachment, her fundamentalism, her fierce attachment to the closet, and her dedication to the wild Iron Ranger who had come into her life. "Sharon had a love/hate relationship with the Iron Range," Karen told the court. "She loved the land, the beauty of the land and things up there, and she enjoyed taking me up there cross-country skiing and other things, camping and things within the area. She despised what they were doing to the land, the scars on the land, and was very concerned with what was happening to the Iron Range itself."[39]

As for the people on the Iron Range, Thompson testified that she and her partner had frequently talked about "the Iron Range mentality." Sharon found it hard "to break away from the Iron Range," but "she felt she had to do that for her own survival." Her partner "was very bitter," Thompson testified, "about how women were treated on the Iron Range," and she had lots of strong feelings about the many friends she had made growing up. "But in a very interesting conversation just a couple of weeks ago she labeled them as negative friends to me," Thompson asserted, mentioning the heavy "partying there was; how much drinking there was; how much smoking pot there was." Karen told the court that Sharon "was on pot a lot when I met her. And she felt that she was, you know, burning herself out and she needed to get away from the people that she did that with." Sharon would often go home for a vacation, "and she would be back before the vacation was over. And she said, 'they just won't change. They don't understand, you know, the things I am doing.' "[40]

Characterized by long, uninterrupted answers, Karen's testimony was briefly held up in the afternoon by the return of Sharon Kowalski and the interjection of the testimony of Nancy Brennan, a professor of social work and women's studies at St. Cloud State. Nancy herself had grown up on the Range and lived in Coleraine until 1961. Professor Brennan, in her admittedly biased but professional way, stated that she recognized in Karen Thompson only one motivation: "a total and complete love for another human being. I base it [my answer] on all of my contact with Karen. All of my observation of Karen and Sharon together. I base it on knowing how rare that kind of love is in our culture." The witness concurred that the Range was "not a hotbed of feminism," and as a result it was fair to say that "Karen Thompson has broken every rule that has to do with how women are supposed to be on the Iron Range. That means, don't make waves. You know, don't—certainly don't stand up for your rights. Fit in, and yeah, I think as a woman." In contrast Karen Thompson was "speaking out," taking a stand, and pointing out injustice. "If one added homophobia and the way lesbians are forced to live in the closet on the Range," Brennan opined, the reaction to Thompson became more culturally understandable. Brennan pointed out that the Range was the only area in Minnesota that had no one testifying to the governor's task force on gays and lesbians when the committee came to Grand Rapids. In fact, the police were called when someone tried to disrupt the meeting, which was eventually held in private—an event the professor thought telling.[41]

Karen's afternoon narrative resumed, with little drama until the witness was asked to compare Sharon's condition in August 1985 to that in February 1989. She broke out in tears as she remembered the reunion, trying to maintain her professional composure. "As I said, Sharon had lost the ability to do standing pivot transfers. I could take hold of her ankle and I couldn't move it. It was like there was no joint there any more. And I could not stretch it out at all," she spoke with quiet dismay. Sharon had lost the use of her left hand and wrist from muscle contraction. "Sharon's mouth," the witness continued, "she lost teeth from gum disease. She had fungus growing on her tongue from lack of proper oral care. She could eat before. She no longer could eat."[42]

The crying Thompson refused the court's offer to recess, proceeding to describe the changes in her life: her activism, her increased friendships, her prominence as a public figure, and most recently the building of the wheel-chair-accessible house where Sharon could still come only two nights a month. Sharon has a waterbed in the house, and the cat has adopted her, even though Sharon has never been a cat person. The judge then adjourned for the day, saying good night to Sharon and asking the witnesses to return at nine o'clock on the following day. The hearing was to last more than two days.

On the morning of December 7, Karen Thompson's direct examination proceeded in its narrative format, but there was a new combative edge to the testimony. At one point the court again became the adversary in this unopposed hearing when Karen, at the request of her lawyer, began to express her misgivings about having to ask Sharon questions in court the day before. Attempting to use the privacy argument to her own advantage, Thompson testified that she thought "it was a set-up situation" to ask other people questions about Sharon while Sharon could hear them and answer herself. "I feel that discounts who Sharon is, and I know it embarrasses me when Sharon is treated like that, and I can only guess how Sharon must feel about it." When asked by her lawyer to explain her own sensitivity to putting Sharon "on display" at the NOW convention in San Francisco, Thompson replied that she specifically asked Sharon many times if she wished to go on stage, and her completely amenable partner "was fascinated by the type of support that she felt from the people out there."[43]

When the subject turned to religion, Judge Campbell decided predictably to interrupt Thompson's discussion of her break from the Presbyterian Church and pose some questions for Sharon on his own. The judge asked Sharon if she remembered going through the Kennedy Program, a Catholic rehabilitation program for people with disabilities, with Karen during which they "accepted Christ." Sharon nodded her head affirmatively. When Sharon was asked what her church was, Sharon apparently typed "Newman" on her synthesizer, although the court transcript registered some difficulty in reading the synthesizer's display. Karen told the court that Sharon spoke the word "Newman," though others did not record their hearing of it.[44]

The morning's testimony moved methodically on. Thompson detailed the purchases the Karen Thompson Legal Fund had made — speech synthesizer, Hoyer lift, portable ramp, electric wheelchair ($8,000), and portable bed. Karen detailed her departure from Sharon in 1985, after Sharon pleaded with her partner to take her home. "I lived for years with the love and the trust that I saw in

Sharon's eyes at that moment when she looked at me. If I really loved her, I would get her out, and she trusted me to do that. And I went through day after day after day feeling like I had totally failed Sharon," an emotional Thompson told the court. Karen wanted nothing more than to give Sharon "the chance to live," but Sharon, she realized, "had to want it from within herself. I can't do that for her." Karen wanted "a lot for Sharon Kowalski, I want this to end. I don't want to go through another year like the past seven."[45]

Karen Thompson v. Karen Tomberlin

Karen broke down again at the close of her long statement about her dreams for her partner. The court took a short recess, but when the witness returned, the rest of her direct testimony was anticlimactic. Fred Friedman's cross-examination was interrupted by the appearance of another medical professional, Dr. Carolyn Herron, a licensed clinical psychologist, who had met with Sharon forty times since her arrival in Minneapolis. She also testified to Sharon's remarkable transformation in the presence of Karen. During Herron's testimony, Karen Tomberlin and Rose Jones arrived, and Tomberlin sat within the purview of Sharon. Judge Campbell pointedly interrupted the witness's testimony to pursue the following line of questioning:

> Ms. WILSON: I don't have any more questions [for Dr. Herron].
> Mr. FRIEDMAN: Nor do I.
> THE COURT: I might have a couple, doctor, just a minute. While you have been testifying, doctor, have you observed Sharon?
> DR. HERRON: I have looked at her a couple of times.
> THE COURT: Have you observed anything that you want to share with me?
> A: She looks attentive, I might say. I found myself focusing on Sue as I talked, more than Sharon at that point, but as I looked, she looked attentive. I saw her and Karen sharing expressions back and forth.
> THE COURT: You didn't observe her sharing expressions with the other woman sitting next to her?
> A: Not in my field of view. As I found myself going like this, I guess I didn't see that as much.
> THE COURT: Well, I am going to let the record show right now, that she did, 90 percent of the time during your testimony, focus her attention on Karen Tomberlin, who is seated next to her.[46]

Some pleasant adversarial sparring took place after Carolyn Herron stepped down, since the hearing was about to move from the petitioner's case to Fred Friedman's, on behalf of the ward. Because Karen Thompson was not going anywhere, the court was willing to accommodate Friedman's witnesses before the cross-examination of the petitioner continued. The only stickler to this arrangement was Friedman's desire to call a third witness besides the already deposed Tomberlin and Jones. Sue Wilson objected to the testimony of a witness who was not on the list, of whom she had been given no notice or an opportunity to examine before the hearing. Judge Campbell, relying on the informality of domestic relations hearings, ruled that the possible benefits of the testimony of the proposed new witness, one Becky Muotka, far outweighed the procedural inconvenience for Sue Wilson. He also allowed Wilson a greater scope of examination when she cross-examined.

Becky Muotka was a thirty-three-year-old part-time physical therapy aide and housecleaner presently residing in south Minneapolis. She had come out to Sharon when she was in junior college and thought at that time that Sharon was not gay. In fact, Becky thought her own disclosure made Sharon "distance" herself from their previous closeness, so she was surprised to find out Sharon had been a lesbian as far back as Karen Thompson suggested. They were blood sisters in high school, and Becky was very close to the Kowalskis, a family she liked. Guilty about visiting Sharon only rarely since the accident, she explained, "I was so afraid that I would pull the plug because of this promise that we had made to each other when we were in 9th grade."

Becky wanted the court to know that the Sharon she knew was a very private, unpolitical, well-liked person who did not want to hurt her family by coming out. "And I don't believe that Sharon would want to be put in this kind of position that her name is all over the country because that's not the Sharon that I know." In her opinion, Sharon had "been outed before outing even came out," and she felt that was not fair. Being a lesbian and a friend of the Kowalskis, Becky had struggled with these issues. She had not seen Sharon for three years but had talked to the Kowalskis recently. When the court asked, "What do you think best?" Sue Wilson immediately objected that there was no foundation for the witness to make a judgment about Sharon's best interest. Campbell overruled the objection immediately, and Wilson laughed in disbelief and frustration — the court had not even allowed her to state why there was a lack of foundation, why she thought the witness was not qualified to testify to that kind of legal conclusion. "The objection is overruled. You can laugh now, counsel," Campbell snapped back from the bench — displaying some of his own capacity for sarcasm. Muotka said the best guardian would be someone "like myself, who is lesbian, but who also knows Sharon as a person and understands the family, where they're coming from and who can — who is willing to let in both sides."[47]

Friedman's next witness was Rose Jones, whom Sue Wilson had deposed, and who on the stand said nothing of substance different from what she revealed to Sue in Duluth. What was different, of course, was the contentious manner in which her testimony was presented, not from the witness but from the attorneys and judge:

> Mr. Friedman: Did she [Sharon] ever indicate an interest or display an interest in being active in political issues, either lesbian political issues or, you know, political issues in general?
> Ms. Jones: No she didn't. And I guess that's partly why I am here today and—
> Ms. Wilson: Objection. I don't know the scope.
> The Court: Just a minute. The objection is not responsive and your objection is sustained.
> Ms. Wilson: The first part was responsive. The second part I am objecting to.
> Mr. Friedman: So the answer is no?
> The Witness: No.
> Q: All right. And you have — she did talk to you about homosexuality or issues of lesbian[ism]?
> A: Yes. She talked to me about her relationship, becoming involved with Karen Thompson. And that it was very private and she wanted to keep it that way, and was very discreet about it.
> Q: She made that clear to you?
> A: Very clear.[48]

Jones also did not believe Sharon was "really capable of making all these decisions everybody is sitting here and saying she is," and had strong misgivings about Sharon's "life being displayed throughout the media. And I don't feel she has had a choice in it." Fred Friedman interrupted his witness at this point to ask her where she thought Sharon should live. The answer — "a private residence with other physically handicapped people her age" in Duluth — precluded Karen Thompson's home, in part because Karen had become interested in other women, because Sharon knew many people who would not come to Karen's home, including herself, because Karen was "very controlling and manipulative" and thought she was the only person in Sharon's life.[49]

On cross-examination, Sue Wilson used Jones's previous testimony to attempt to discredit her. Jones was forced to admit that she did not think the Kowalskis had acted in Sharon's best interest in terminating visitation with Thompson, even though she had previously stated that the Kowalskis always acted in their daughter's best interest. Wilson wanted to know if Jones would change her mind about disapproving of Sharon's move to St. Cloud if the witness knew that a group of disinterested professionals had determined that Sharon could express her wishes and wants to live with Karen Thompson. Jones refused to change her mind; she believed "you could probably find people that would also say Sharon is not capable" of making a decision. At this point she did not "know what to believe." The lesbian lawyer had finished examining an adverse lesbian witness about the validity of a lesbian relationship.[50]

Next on the stand was Karen Tomberlin. She had essentially the same message as her friend, Rose Jones, but it came across in a more nostalgic, less combative tone. A mother of six and a longtime, popular physical education teacher in Greenway High School in Coleraine, Tomberlin was a well-known fixture on the Range — a kind of sports den mother for many athletic girls whom she had guided over the years. She had known Sharon for twenty years and thought of her as her own child. She talked about the love of the Kowalskis and over an objection by Sue Wilson, spoke of Della's daily visits to Leisure Hills. (Dr. Gregor had testified that the Kowalskis had not been frequent visitors even in Hibbing.) Karen Tomberlin was opposed to the petition, of course, "because of her [Sharon's] long-term memory and the fact that it is so keen." Tomberlin wanted Sharon to be surrounded by family and friends. "I think she should have the opportunity to sit in the backyard where she shot baskets by the hour, take a nap in the bed she slept in the room she grew up in, sit with the family in the kitchen, you know, that she had enjoyed many, numerous hours of happy times."[51]

Tomberlin, who had volunteered to be co-guardian, said she would not restrict access to Karen Thompson if appointed. She did not feel the Kowalskis had excluded Thompson for three and a half years out of any "vindictive" motive. They were acting on "the advice of medical professionals." If Thompson becomes guardian, Tomberlin stated, Sharon would lose the visitation of her family. "Leisure Hills in Hibbing was giving Sharon care far above and beyond the call of duty," Tomberlin remarked, recommending her return to the place where she was getting a "shower and a shampoo" once a day instead of the perfunctory once a week, which for Tomberlin showed they had the "TLC" that a small institution can provide.[52]

Although Tomberlin fully agreed with Don's decision to terminate Thompson's visitation in 1985, she now believed Karen's visits were not detrimental to Sharon's mental health. The witness was not sure whether or not Sharon should have a say about who her guardian should be, because she was not sure how reliable Sharon's answers were. "What you're telling the court," Sue Wilson stated, "is that you want to be made her guardian but you don't even know whether the experts who have treated her think she can reliably express her wishes, is that what you're telling us?" The court objected to the question as argumentative. Tomberlin had to agree that if the experts, whom she had not consulted, stated Sharon could state her wishes, then her preference would be important.

Ms. WILSON: Okay. . . . Now would you say as between you and Ms. Thompson that Ms. Thompson has spent a lot more time with Ms. Kowalski since she was injured?

KAREN TOMBERLIN: Yes.

Q: And would you say she has been a lot more involved in her care, in her therapy and in her rehabilitation than you have?

A: Than I have but—

Q: Yes. Well, you're the one who is requesting to be guardian so I am asking.

A: Okay. But I am—people seem to be forgetting what her parents did and particularly her mother and—

Q: Let me—

A: I would say her mother was a comparable caregiver to what Karen Thompson is doing now.

Q: Is her mother petitioning for guardianship that I am not aware of it? . . .

A: They can't.

Q: So they do not want to be guardians, correct?

A: That doesn't mean they don't want to be in close contact.

Q: Okay. So they cannot be guardians, and then of all the people that are left in the world, besides those people who have excluded themselves, Mr. and Mrs. Kowalski, can you name one person who has shown more interest or commitment to Sharon Kowalski's care and rehabilitation than Ms. Thompson?

A: No.[53]

The court did not allow Tomberlin to answer Wilson's last speculative question: "What if Karen Thompson were to get on the stand and say that if Sharon were placed in Northern Minnesota, that she wouldn't visit?" Friedman objected without stating why, and the judge sustained it without stating why, but the question was—albeit speculative and hypothetical—one that established an important perspective.

After the personable Tomberlin stepped down, Sue Wilson stated, "Your honor, for the record I would like, at least my observation was, that when Ms. Tomberlin was testifying, Ms. Kowalski was making extensive eye contact with Ms. Thompson. . . . And that I don't know the percentage of time but I would say it was 50% or more of the time, she was looking at Ms. Thompson instead of Ms. Tomberlin." Judge Campbell answered matter-of-factly, "I will note your observation for the record, counsel, and I will also indicate that I also have observed and have marked down in my notes, that there has been eye contact. . . . Sharon is looking at Karen and then up at Ms. Tomberlin." Ms. Wilson asked if it was still the judge's desire to have nonparties like Tomberlin sitting at the counsel table, to which the judge replied in the affirmative.[54]

Fred Friedman finally got his chance to cross-examine the petitioner. He asked how Thompson would react if the court put restrictions on her guardian-ship, not allowing Sharon to be taken to awards dinners or "television shows." Karen stated she "would obey the order," though she might attempt to change "any portion of that court order" that she "felt was not in Sharon's best inter-ests. She likes to go to those workshops. She enjoyed Susan Farr at that Creat-ing Change Workshop, who gave a wonderful talk, and Sharon interacted with her well during that speech. . . . I think that Sharon should be allowed to live her fullest life, doing types of activities that can enrich it."[55]

When Friedman then asked about the other woman, Karen admitted that she was in a relationship "of sorts," which she had discussed with Sharon "in a way. She has been around us on occasions and I answer whatever questions Sharon asks." Friedman probed no further; Karen Thompson was not a wit-ness that Friedman at this juncture decided to impugn. He had elicited her pen-chant to challenge court orders, but he could not undermine her willingness to include the Kowalskis if she did become guardian. Thompson offered to trans-port Sharon to the Range for visits and stated that the Kowalskis and their friends would always be welcome in St. Cloud. When Karen's testimony was finished at the end of the third day, Judge Campbell put one more observation on the record. He had noticed that Karen was wearing two rings, one on her left hand from Sharon and one on her right hand from Patty Bresser. "The com-mitment that I have made to Sharon Kowalski," Karen explained passionately, "will always be the primary commitment and anyone who is a part of my life must always understand that my life revolves around Sharon Kowalski."[56] The hearing concluded, Judge Campbell asked the attorneys to submit their final arguments in writing by December 21, promising a decision within the statu-tory ninety days from the time of that submission.

The Duluth paper excerpted the Associated Press story "Lesbian Testifies in Custody Case: Thompson Says She'd OK Visits by Disabled Partner's Par-ents" (*Duluth News-Tribune*, December 7, 1990, sec. A, p. 4). Karen's statement on the stand that she would never keep Sharon from seeing her parents was the main part of the story, along with Dr. Gregor's testimony that "Karen is the key to her [Sharon's] past self and the window into who she is now." The St. Cloud paper told the same Associated Press story with a tellingly different headline: "Thompson: Revealing Love Was Agonizing." Here the emphasis was on the difficulty Karen had in coming out to the Kowalskis: "There is no way I would ever have told anyone about either of our sexual orientations except for the extraordinary circumstances," Karen was quoted as testifying, in response to Judge Campbell, who, the article stated, "frequently has returned to that issue during the hearing" (*St. Cloud Times*, December 7, 1990, sec. B, p. 1).

Hibbing Hearing

Final arguments turned out to be premature. On December 29 Fred Friedman was asking for yet another hearing, this time in Hibbing. He reportedly had heard from at least seventeen witnesses who wanted to testify to the superior quality of Sharon's treatment on the Range, many having felt that the reputation of the northern Minnesota health care profession had been maligned during the hearings in Minneapolis. Karen Tomberlin also wanted the hearing, hoping to have Debbie Kowalski testify. On January 4 Campbell ordered the hearing in Hibbing, asking Friedman to present a witness list as soon as possible. Thompson's lawyers sought a writ of prohibition preventing the hearing, but they were unsuccessful. Meanwhile, in a telephone conference the judge and the two lawyers explored the potential scope of the new hearing — including two days of testimony and many depositions. Friedman assured the court and Wilson that many of the witnesses would not testify, and lawyers for Leisure Hills were actually counseling against going into court to discuss their reputation.[57]

It was not over until it was over, but the last hurrah, which took place on March 22, turned out to be somewhat of a tempest in an iron teapot. Besides a few health care workers, the main witness was Debbie Kowalski, the thirty-two-year-old sister of Sharon who was adamantly opposed to the petition. Her testimony highlighted the divide that now existed between the petitioner and the Kowalski family. She had prepared a statement to explain why she was "scared" at the idea of Thompson becoming guardian. She was worried about what would happen to Sharon while Karen was "out promoting gay rights." Debbie had seen *The Joan Rivers Show* during which Karen stated that she "had other lovers since the accident," and Sharon's sister worried about the impact. "If they were truly involved as she says they were, is this good for Sharon to see other lovers or lover of Karen's with her in the house?" Debbie asked the court. Karen had also said on the show that "resuming a sexual relationship" was something that they might try, and it worried Debbie "that Sharon would be sexually abused. But I understand there is a Vulnerable Adult Act law that, you know, to me it's sexual abuse on somebody that isn't fully capable of stuff like that." There were other considerations — the money Karen had raised, the displaying of her sister at gay pride events, and, most important, the assured boycott of the Rangers from any appearances at Thompson's house. If Karen were to take Sharon to her house to live, Debbie knew "there wouldn't be many people from Sharon's past — friends, family — that will go to see her."[58]

MR. FRIEDMAN: All right. Now, I need to know why, why do you say that?

DEBRA KOWALSKI: I don't think you really have any understanding of how hate—how strong the hatred is.

Q: That's what I'm asking you.

A: The hatred for Karen Thompson of what she has done to Sharon and her family is so deep and she is so—it's like she is so domineering and stuff that nobody can handle being around her. I have heard all of Sharon's friends talk. They can't handle even seeing her, being—

MS. WILSON: Objection, hearsay.

THE COURT: The objection is overruled.

Q: When you say, her friends, you're talking about friends from the Nashwauk/Hibbing area, right?

A: Right, her college friends, high school friends. It's the way they feel.[59]

As a final volley on direct, Debbie wanted the court to know that Sharon's family had not given up on her even though they had not come to the hearings. They still truly loved her.

Cross-examination, naturally, was a little rockier. Debbie had visited her sister only twice in the last two years at Trevilla, and she herself did not want to be guardian and was not familiar with the recent expert testimony.

MS. WILSON: Do you know what homophobia is?

DEBRA KOWALSKI: Yes. . . . It's a prejudice against gays.

Q: And you just testified that you said, "where does it say that if you're gay you get to be a guardian"?

A: What I mean by that is, where is it written that if you're gay, if you have a lover, that automatically you should be guardian because you were gay, because you were with them. I don't care if somebody is gay. . . .

Q: Now you said, "what would happen if Karen gets tired taking care of her"—that's a concern you have?

A: Right.

Q: And don't you think that if Karen Thompson was going to get tired she would be tired by now after eight years?

THE COURT: Just a minute. Just a minute. It's argumentative. You don't have to answer that question. . . .

Q: Now, you have said that if Karen Thompson would kill her baby, what she would do with Sharon, correct?

A: Correct.

Q: So what you're saying is that any woman who would have an abortion, no matter when it was, would be disqualified to be guardian of someone?

A: No.

MR. FRIEDMAN: Excuse me, I am going to object to the question as vague, argumentative, irrelevant.

THE COURT: It's argumentative. You don't have to answer it.

MS. WILSON: Ms. Kowalski, I do not understand why a woman making a decision to have an abortion, a decision she has a legal right to, would have any impact at all on her qualifications to be guardian. You seem to think it does. Why?

MR. FRIEDMAN: Same objection.

THE COURT: Sustained.

MS. WILSON: Your honor, she has made the statement. I believe I have a right to find out what she is talking about.

THE COURT: Is this your belief?

THE WITNESS: My belief is not — I said — when I said she had the abortion, I said, which is her choice. What I am saying is, I feel that if she —

THE COURT: Ms. Kowalski, are you Roman Catholic?

THE WITNESS: Yes.

THE COURT: Are abortions contrary to your faith?

THE WITNESS: That — well, to the Catholic faith they are. But, myself, I feel it's an independent decision. . . .

Q: Now, you said that you don't think that Sharon would ever want to let her — that she would never want anyone to know about her lesbianism, if she were lesbian, correct?

A: Well, apparently she didn't tell anybody before. I mean, as far as her family, she didn't tell us about it before, so apparently she didn't want us to know.

Q: Do you have any idea why she wouldn't want to tell her family?

A: No.

Q: Would you say that your family, overall, is not sympathetic to homosexuals?

A: I can't say what they feel. I myself, don't care if somebody is gay. It's up to them.

Q: You don't know whether your sister was a lesbian, do you?

A: No, I don't.

Q: Are you aware that your sister wanted to go to lesbian events and lesbian bars before the accident?

A: No.

Q: Is it correct that you testified that you personally hate Karen Thompson?

A: Yes.[60]

The protracted hearings concerning Karen Thompson's second petition for guardianship ended with Debbie Kowalski's testimony. The court again took the case under submission and spent another month deliberating before producing a decision that surprised journalists, lawyers, and experts. On April 23,

1991, Judge Campbell denied Karen Thompson's petition for guardianship and named Karen Tomberlin guardian of Sharon Kowalski.

On Thursday, May 29, I talked to Barb Newberg at Sara's Table, the women's café and bookstore in Duluth. Her impression was that the case taught single people that they had to protect themselves from eventualities. A nurse who had taken care of Sharon at one point, Newberg was more forthcoming about handicapped issues than lesbian ones. The care of the disabled, she assured me, was labor-intensive. Her only feeling about the Range that she would express to me was that the people had not changed. The dispute might not be decided any differently today given the climate in Hibbing, though she felt Duluth was progressing somewhat.

After leaving Sara's Table, I began wondering whether the case was principally about disabled rights or homosexuality. Were the two "conditions" at odds with one another? Was disability a closet? Or did disability create another way of not talking about being queer? Maybe the real issues in the case were autonomy and freedom from being exploited for any condition or orientation. I could not help thinking that the tendency to generalize about disability and care was a way of sweeping the queer issue under the table. The AIDS pandemic was showing how one designated "queer" disability incited deep-seated scapegoating that gays and lesbians could only avoid if they stayed in the closet and were not outed. The designation "disabled" was functioning as another way of aligning homosexuality with disease while at the same time hiding queerness under the broader rubric of illness. Sharon — a disabled woman who was also a lesbian — faced a triple handicap in a world that commodified and condemned the abnormal, the incapacitated, and the weak (still falsely attributed to women). Was being lesbian itself a handicap just as being handicapped was a kind of queerness? Only in the eyes of those who designated and disapproved. What, after all, was a lesbian or gay person other than a practitioner of certain acts who had been designated and stigmatized by a discourse — produced, packaged, and hidden on the bottom shelf?

I left Duluth heading south toward Minneapolis, and distracted by traffic, soon found myself entering the outskirts of the Twin Cities, the homogenized suburbs, wondering if the packaging of America was not in some way connected to the packaging of ourselves, if the labels gay, straight, handicapped, lawyer, doctor, judge were shrunk-wrapped generalizations that produced and consumed us in ways that obscured the living particularities in our differences. Karen had become "landlady," "lesbian," "activist," the Kowalskis struggling rural "homemakers" and "retirees" — each categorized and understood through a narrative that began with a careless man getting drunk and putting his key into the ignition. As the comatose Sharon lay in the hospital, incapable of defining herself, those around her began the process of labeling. When Karen used the word "lesbian" to describe her partner, her family found that term discomfiting, and professionals found it uncertain or indeterminable. They resisted this generalization in much the same way Sharon may have done in some point in her life — by closeting her difference in the role of a tomboy who liked to ride motorcycles and shoot hoops. Although largely unnamed, the closet itself became another form of packaging, another container for identity.

Cars whipped by on the highway, while unresolved questions raced through my brain. Why did Rose Jones and her friends appear to dismiss Karen Thompson as controlling and manipulative? Why did they, as lesbians, seemingly adopt the very stereotypes of domination and control that very likely had hounded them their entire lives — in and out of the closet? Did Karen Thompson, in fact, embody the very generalizations — possessive, controlling, and judgmental — that I was so loath to employ? Or was Rose Jones suffering from internalized homophobia; was she so protective of the valor of her discretion and her insistence that she did not advertise that she was willing to adopt the very labels of disapproval that no doubt would be applied to her if she'd dared to speak the name of her love? Was it possible that that she and her friends were actually jealous of Karen Thompson, possessive of Sharon, and angry about the apparent strength of their love — instead of merely skeptical of Karen's declared commitment? Or did they, in fact, understand Sharon in ways that no one else could?

Neither lawyers nor doctors nor I could tell. Nor could the injured Sharon. Nor could those still living in the closet, hunkering down beneath the reproachful gaze of an intolerant and labeling society.

ELEVEN

Judgments

> We do not expect American society to give us some seal of approval. It is
> not within the scope of government to do that. We have our own approval.
> What we do want is equal protection of the laws and *all* that implies, and we
> want our fellow citizens to acknowledge that our constitutionally protected
> choices about what is, after all, our own business should not disqualify us
> from equal membership in the multitude of American communities.
>
> Michael Nava and Robert Dawidoff,
> *Created Equal: Why Gay Rights Matter to America*

Judge Campbell's order appointing general guardian of person and estate came
down on April 23, 1991. It included eighty-two findings of fact, twenty-three
conclusions of law, and a memorandum of law. The decision to make Karen
Tomberlin guardian was based on the best interest of the ward as defined by
the Minnesota Guardianship Statute Sections 525.56, subd.3, and 525.539, subd.
7, and the right of privacy under the Minnesota Constitution, which the court
found that Karen Thompson had violated by outing Sharon.[1]

Campbell's factual determinations about Sharon's "mental condition and
memory" laid the groundwork for a decision that saw Sharon's living in a place
of neutral access as the key to a resolution of this matter. In his findings of fact,
he emphasized that Sharon "requires much repetition to remember even simple new things and instructions," and even though she "has learned to recognize several health care providers," she "forgets them within days or weeks."
Campbell found that Dorothy Rappel "reports that Sharon responded posi-
tively to Karen Thompson's visits and parents' visits," but he concluded that
Sharon's interaction with others was "inconsistent" (31).

In the past, the judge noted, Sharon had "indicated a preference for her
father to be her guardian and to remain at Leisure Hills," but for the past two
years "when asked where she would like to live Sharon has consistently said,
'St. Cloud with Karen.'" For Campbell, the evidence was not clear "whether
Sharon's statements regarding living in St. Cloud with Karen are based on
long, constant contact, lack of constant contact with other visitors, or a reference to her memory of her pre-accident relationship and living situation. The

statements are not tantamount to a preference of who should be her guardian." The judge added that his own observations both at Trevilla and at the hearing in Minneapolis showed that Sharon responded more favorably to Karen Tomberlin than to Karen Thompson, but he agreed that what he saw was also "not determinative nor is it tantamount to Sharon's preference of who should be her guardian." Before the accident, the judge found, Sharon was "independent and decisive. However, she was struggling with her identity, her relationships, and her career. She loved her parents and family" (46). And although Sharon had a "loving, intimate relationship with Karen Thompson," Campbell stated "the evidence is contradictory as to whether that relationship was intact or in the process of breaking up at the time of the accident" (47).

The judge also made a separate set of findings about the petitioner and what he called the "involuntary 'outing' of Sharon Kowalski." He detailed Karen Thompson's "constant commitment and devotion"; her awareness of Sharon's medical, material, and social needs; and her building of a handicapped-accessible home to accommodate Sharon, but the judge also found "Ms Thompson is described by some witnesses as possessive, authoritative, inflexible, and committed to her own political agenda" (52). Under the heading "involuntary outing," Campbell found that before the accident, Sharon "never revealed her sexual orientation to her parents, sister, or many close acquaintances. She expressed more than a firm desire not to inform her family or people in general" and "had never participated in political activism whatsoever, including any public advocacy of gay and lesbian rights. Sharon was private then and remains so to this day." The judge also asserted that the Kowalskis "did not accept Karen's 'outing' of their daughter. They have been outraged and hurt by the public invasion of Sharon's privacy and their privacy." Moreover, he stated, "witnesses of both sexual orientations have testified that Sharon's appearances at public meetings and political events are not what Sharon would want, are contrary to her personality and not in her best interest. Such appearances are, they claim, putting her on display" (58–62).

The judge's selective set of findings of fact contained some conspicuous exclusions as well as some emphasized inclusions that pointed to the judge's view of the case. The testimony that Sharon was the one pushing Karen to come out at the time of the accident was not noted; the earlier finding that Sharon was inconsistent and unreliable about her preference as to almost everything, including a guardian, was controverted by the determination of her consistency about wanting to remain in the closet; the testimony that Karen came out because the Kowalskis were threatening to curtail her visitation was omitted; the testimony by third parties that Sharon enjoyed public outings was overlooked in favor of testimony by those who saw her as being put "on display."

Judge Campbell was also building his case for Thompson's tortious interference of Sharon's right of privacy, which in this case was her right to remain in the closet about her love for Karen. The ironic outcome was that if Karen had complied with Sharon's supposed insistence on keeping her love secret, Sharon's right to a private life of love with Karen would probably have been fully abrogated by the same people who claimed it did not exist at all. Under this scenario, Karen Thompson was given the choice of hurting Sharon by outing her or losing the very love the right of privacy was designed to protect by her silence.

The judge's conclusions of law were a set of twenty-three statements arrived at by applying the relevant law in the case to the fact findings. Foremost, in denying Karen's petition, Campbell found that Sharon's "short-term memory undercuts the reliability of her stated preference" to live with Thompson, and therefore Sharon belonged in a neutral setting where she could obtain "constant, long-term medical supervision," such as a nursing home other than Leisure Hills (12, 6). He concluded that Thompson had "demonstrated a lack of understanding of Sharon's consanguineous family and the family's Minnesota Iron Range cultural background. This lack of understanding is injurious to Sharon's social and emotional well-being" (13). He also ruled as a matter of law that Thompson was "incapable of providing, as a single caretaker, the necessary health care to Sharon at the petitioner's home in St. Cloud, Minnesota," and that the petitioner's "[s]plit loyalties to her past domestic partner and other present domestic partners will diminish time the petitioner may devote to Sharon and will have an uncertain effect upon Sharon that cannot be considered completely beneficial to Sharon" (18).

The boldest move by Judge Campbell was his appointment of Karen Tomberlin in place of the petitioner without holding a hearing on her qualifications. Tomberlin had filed no formal petition, so her status remained that of a witness in this proceeding. In his conclusion, the judge reiterated that "Sharon smiled and expressed great pleasure in court in December, 1990, at Ms. Tomberlin's presence next to her during part of the guardianship hearings." She "enjoys the friendship and respect of Sharon's parents and siblings" and "earned the respect of the petitioner" (19). Even though Tomberlin had expressed her wish that Sharon return to the dubious Leisure Hills, the judge concluded that she was maintaining "a current understanding of Sharon's physical and mental status and needs" (20).

Judge Campbell's ten-page memorandum of law began with a review of the common law of guardianship in Minnesota.[2] Although a presumption lay in favor of family members in such a case, the judge cited the precedent of nominating a trust officer at a local bank in an internecine dispute over guardianship within a family. He also cited a case that stated "sexual misconduct" of a petitioner, while not enough to disqualify a guardian, was relevant if it had bearing on the welfare of the ward. In this case, he concluded, "the presence of Ms. Thompson's other domestic partners will have an uncertain effect upon Sharon" (7).

The section of the judge's memorandum on the right of privacy argued that Karen's disclosure of her "sexual orientation" to Sharon's parents and "the world" without Sharon's consent "constituted an invasion of Sharon's privacy by the petitioner" (5). The judge held that the right of privacy made the disclosure of the secret of homosexuality an actionable civil wrong. "The civil tort of invasion of privacy includes the public disclosure of embarrassing but truthful facts," the judge wrote, admitting that Minnesota had not yet recognized this tort. The judge relied on *Sipple v Chronicle Publishing Company* (154 Cal App3d 1040, 201 CalRptr 665 [Cal App 1984]), a California case, for his authority. In *Sipple* the defendant, a gay ex-marine who foiled an assassination attempt against Gerald Ford at the St. Francis Hotel, sued the *San Francisco Chronicle* for declaring him the "center of attention" of a gay bar he frequented. The California Supreme Court upheld a summary judgment against Oliver Sipple because it agreed that his gay identity was already public: he had marched in gay parades, was friends with Harvey Milk, and had been mentioned in gay newspapers. Although the *Sipple* case did not hold that the disclosure would be actionable if Sipple's sexual orientation were private or discuss what "private" constituted, Judge Campbell, by analogy, argued that Sharon Kowalski had not publicly disclosed her homosexuality (4).

The *Sipple* analogy became the foundation for the judge's decision that Karen's actions were an invasion. "The right of privacy," Campbell wrote, "protects the essence of the human individual. Privacy is a right deeply entrenched, yet transcendent beyond the mortal shell of the body. Sexual orientation lies at the core of human existence, an indispensable strand of one human fiber. This disclosure by Karen Thompson, known colloquially as 'outing,' constituted an invasion of Sharon's privacy by the petitioner" (5). Some central questions arose in relation to the reasoning of Judge Campbell in his decision: Was being a lesbian "considered highly offensive by a reasonable person" for purposes of invasion of privacy? If the right of privacy was "deeply entrenched, yet transcendent beyond the mortal shell of the body," and "sexual orientation lies at the core of human existence," why should this "indispensable strand" of sexuality be something that would be offensive to disclose? Was the core of human existence something the law needed to protect from public disclosure?

Judge Campbell lamented the three-and-a-half-year hiatus in Karen's contact with her lover, but he foresaw a similar foreclosure of the Kowalskis' participation should the petition be granted. To prevent that outcome, he chose what he considered to be a neutral third party — a close friend of the Kowalskis from the Range and a role model for the ward — Karen Tomberlin. The neutrality of Tomberlin, however, would become an issue on appeal.

Campbell's controversial decision was reported in the *Hibbing Daily Tribune, New York Times,* and *Gay Community News,* among many other newspapers across the country. The headlines focused on Karen Thompson's defeat: "Activist Loses Custody Fight: Judge Appoints Third Party as Kowalski's Guardian" (Candace Renalis, *Duluth News-Tribune,* April 25, 1991, sec. A, p. 1); "2 Sides Are Bypassed in Lesbian Case" (Nadine Brozan, *New York Times,* April 26, 1991, sec. A, p. 12); "Kowalski Guardianship Assigned to Neutral Party" (*Hibbing Daily Tribune,* April 5, 1991, p. 1); "Judge Denies Thompson Guardianship" (Jacob Smith Yang, *GCN,* May 5–11, 1991, p. 1). Donald Kowalski and Karen Tomberlin refused to talk to the press about the decision, but Thompson told reporters it was a "terrible order," which she planned to appeal *(Duluth News-Tribune).* Thompson told Nadine Brozan of the *New York Times,* "Karen Tomberlin is just a stand-in for the parents."

Speaking to the *New York Times,* Lambda's Tom Stoddard called the decision "a deep offense not only to all lesbians and gay men, but to all Americans who choose their partners and household by their own terms and not the legal rules imposed by society." *Outweek,* a gay and lesbian publication, published an editorial on the case in its May 15 issue. "The legal fiction that, because Thompson has a new lover, she is somehow incapable of caring for Kowalski is sadly familiar to every lesbian — indeed every woman — who has ever been denied custody of her children on similar grounds," Carrie Wofford wrote. "The strange notion that participation in an adult relationship is proof of selfishness and disqualifies one as a potential care-giver is worse than perverse. It's a precise reversal of the truth, which is that the capacity to love and partake in a relationship is a strong argument *in favor of* emotional health and the capacity to give selflessly." Wofford called the outing argument even more "bizarre," the judge in effect proposing that "if you come out of the closet to claim your rights," as Karen did, "you will be punished" (Carrie Wofford, "Citing 'Outing,' Judge Keeps Lesbian Lovers Apart," *Outweek,* May 15, 1991, p. 14).

In Atlanta, where she spoke the following week, Karen Thompson and her lawyers called a press conference. Judge Campbell, Thompson pronounced, was "homophobic," his ruling made in blatant disregard for the rights of lesbians and gay men to live as they choose (Margaret Zack, "Ruling Is Disputed in Guardianship Case," *Minneapolis Star Tribune,* May 9, 1991, sec. B, p. 2). Rosemary Dempsey of the National Organization for Women told reporters, "I know that none of us will stand for this. We have, out of this tragedy, an absolute obligation to take further action. This is an affront to all of us. It is a major setback of civil rights" ("Women's Groups to Fight Decision in Kowalski Case," *St. Cloud Times*, April 28?, 1991). On May 8 Sue Wilson held a press conference in Minneapolis, announcing an appeal by the end of the month (Marie Beunaiche, "Thompson Decries Judicial Homophobia," *Equal Time*, April 26–May 10, 1991, p. 1). Wilson said that the appeal would address two areas of Campbell's decision. The first was the failure of Tomberlin to submit a required court petition or be examined about her qualifications. Wilson likened this part of the decision to granting a divorce to someone who never filed for it. The second part of the appeal, Wilson stated, would deal with the criteria of the guardianship statute: the ward's preference, the quality of interaction between petitioner and ward, and the ability of the petitioner to provide care. Wilson said that the evidence was overwhelmingly in Karen Thompson's favor on each of these points.

The disrespect that Karen supposedly showed for the Kowalskis' Iron Range cultural background, Wilson stated, in fact masked a disrespect on the part of the parents. The family was "blackmailing" Karen by threatening to abandon their daughter if guardianship went to Wilson's client. Wilson reminded reporters that Dr. Eckman had called the parents' actions selfish and unfair. "Karen Thompson has been denied guardianship so the parents can visit three times a year," Wilson told Beunaiche. Wilson also decried Judge Campbell's finding that Karen had "outed" Sharon and thereby invaded her privacy. Karen, Wilson stated, made a complex ethical decision. Besides, the attorney remarked, "There are worse things in the world than having someone know you're a lesbian. One of those things might be getting cut off from the person you've chosen to live your life with" (*Equal Time*, April 26–May 10 1991, p. 3). Wilson expected oral arguments on the appeal to occur within twelve weeks of the expected filing date in the first week in August. A decision would come down within six months.

After a pro forma dismissal of a motion for a new trial, Thompson's lawyers began the arduous process of preparing the appeal, which involved many hours of legal research and writing, as well as coordination of the various amici who wished to file arguments on behalf of Karen Thompson's petition. By July, Fred Friedman was feeling some of the pressure from the mounting documentation that the petitioner's appeal was beginning to generate. He wrote to Judge Wozniak on the Court of Appeals, claiming that he had yet to be paid for any of his representation and was now being asked to file an appellate brief in reply to Thompson's war machine: "I expect the Minnesota Appellate court to receive at least five Amicus briefs on this matter on behalf of the petitioner, Karen Thompson. Ms. Thompson is attempting to raise $25,000 to $30,000, which is advertised by Thompson as the cost of the appeal." He claimed his own legal bills were over $9,000 and that he had never received any payment.[3]

The state capitol complex in St. Paul, an expansive set of neoclassical buildings and green grounds on the east side of Constitutional Avenue, houses a judicial building, its inside hushed, carpeted, and removed from the hustle and bustle of downtown Minneapolis or the crowded working-class neighborhoods and churches of St. Paul. There, on August 5, the Court of Appeals received the hundreds of pages of documents from the appellant Karen Thompson, the respondents Sharon Kowalski and Karen Tomberlin — as well as a host of amici, including the MCLU and women's, lesbian, and gay organizations.[4] In addition to these briefs, the appellant Karen Thompson filed a reply to the respondents' filings.

The foundation of Sue Wilson's argument on appeal was that Judge Campbell had failed to follow the recommendations of the very experts he himself had named for advice in the case, namely, Dr. Eckman and his team at Miller-Dwan.[5] Though the judge felt their conclusion that Sharon could reliably express her preference was unduly influenced by Karen Thompson's presence, the uninterested experts who worked with Sharon testified Karen Thompson's presence was beneficial and unintrusive. As Sue Wilson stated at the end of her statement of facts, "All of the court-appointed experts who testified," from Eckman to physical therapists, stated that Sharon "responds in a more affirmative and responsive way to Karen Thompson than to any other individual," that Karen Thompson had "consistently shown the highest degree of commitment and concern for Sharon's welfare," and that "Sharon consistently and reliably expresses a desire to live once again with Karen Thompson in St. Cloud, Minnesota." Despite this overwhelming evidence provided by the court's own experts, Wilson wrote, Judge Campbell still ruled "that Sharon could not reliably express her wishes about where she wanted to live and with whom she wanted to live."[6]

Appellants normally argued "abuse of discretion" when they believe that determinations made by a trial court were wholly inconsistent with the evidence before the court. Sue Wilson used this standard of review to show that the facts clearly demonstrated that Karen Thompson had met the statutory requirements for guardianship, most notably being the person reasonably preferred by the ward. In the face of this overwhelming evidence, Campbell committed error by finding that Sharon's stated preference was unreliable because her choice was influenced by Thompson's constant contact. If experts stated that Sharon had the ability to make the choice, then the basis for her decision was irrelevant, Wilson contended. "Why does the court have the right to tell this adult woman that she cannot return to the environment which she feels and states is 'home' to her? For the court to give it no weight is degrading and dehumanizing to Sharon," counsel wrote. "Sharon wants to live with the woman whom she chose to be her lesbian partner," and the court, Wilson declared, "must not be allowed to abuse its power by substituting its own values and attitudes for Sharon's."[7]

In turning to the issues of outing, the appellant argued that Karen Thompson had no choice but to disclose the nature of her relationship. First of all, counsel questioned the judge's determination that Sharon was as fiercely closeted before the accident as he claimed. Wilson cited testimony that Sharon was attempting to get Karen to come out more fully at the time of the accident and also detailed all the medical experts that Sharon was willing to tell about her lesbian relation with Karen. Experts testified that the information was necessary for a complete understanding of the patient and that Sharon's trips were beneficial to her psychological well-being. "What if Karen had not come forward? What if Karen had not struggled for all of these years on Sharon's behalf?" Wilson asked. Sharon would still be in Leisure Hills Nursing Home, an institution for elderly, dying patients, "receiving the substandard care which has resulted in the deterioration in her condition." Sharon would not have "access to technical advances such as her speech synthesizer, which enables her to communicate and interact with others. She would not be going on the outings which give her so much happiness. But, most importantly, she would not be seeing the one person she loves and wants to be with."[8]

On the issue of putting Sharon on display at political events against what the court determined unequivocally to be her personality and her best interest, Wilson pointed out again that the judge was relying on his own predilection and the judgments of biased witnesses rather than those of experts and other eyewitnesses of Sharon's participation. Experts like Dr. Gregor and Kathy King, staff coordinator at Trevilla, stated that these outings were enjoyable for Sharon. The judge himself had approved in advance Sharon's attendance at the NOW convention, so his inconsistent disapproval in his final decision evidenced either a need to justify his unreasonable decision or a reliance on unreliable testimony.[9]

Wilson also argued that it was not Karen Thompson who misunderstood the family's "Minnesota Iron Range cultural background," but the Kowalskis who did not understand Sharon and Karen's lesbian love. Wilson insisted that gay ambivalence about the Range came from Karen's assessment of Sharon's own "love/hate" relationship with the place where she grew up, with Sharon's need to break away from a culture that the ward saw as homophobic and chauvinistic. "Sharon chose to remove herself from the Iron Range culture years before the accident. Is it now a requirement that guardians have some sort of innate anthropological knowledge of a ward's *former* culture, even when the ward rejected that culture?" Thompson's lawyers asked rhetorically.[10]

The testimony of experts also dispelled the court's conclusion that Karen's subsequent relationships could harm Sharon. Karen Tomberlin's "split loyalties" as a married mother of four were completely overlooked in her appointment, while Karen's other domestic partner had suddenly become an impediment to Sharon's best interests, even though Thompson had testified that Sharon would always be her first priority and Drs. Rappel and Gregor had testified that the taking on of another sexual relationship by the partner of a handicapped person was not an uncommon occurrence.

Wilson's fifty-page legal brief then challenged the judge's reliance on the testimony of lay witnesses from the Range, including the hearsay statements of the Kowalskis, who never attended the hearings and rarely visited their daughter at this point. Dr. Gregor had testified that the Kowalskis were no longer interested in being involved, yet the court, Wilson pointed out, was relying on their absence as a reason to deny Karen Thompson's petition. As Debbie Kowalski testified, it was her parents' "hatred" of Karen Thompson that was preventing a reconciliation. "This hatred is derived in part from their own unwillingness to accept Sharon's sexuality. Perhaps this hatred is fueled by their own anger at the tragedy of Sharon's disability. While we may comprehend and even sympathize with their pain, we cannot sympathize with their unwillingness to set aside their hatred and act in Sharon's best interest. It is tragic that they would rather see Sharon institutionalized than living in the community. It is incomprehensible that they would choose to never see their sister and daughter again if Karen were made guardian."[11]

Wilson concluded with an attack on the appointment of Tomberlin, which she criticized as procedurally erroneous and evidentially unconscionable. Tomberlin, she argued, was unqualified (she wanted Sharon back in Leisure Hills), lacking neutrality (she considered herself a close friend of the Kowalskis), untested (there was no hearing as to her qualifications), and unpreferred (Sharon never expressed her desire to have Tomberlin as guardian). She saw Sharon less than four times a year. "It is apparent from the court's decision that it felt called upon to protect the Kowalskis' interests," Wilson stated in conclusion, "even where those interests conflicted with Sharon's best interests."[12]

The most eloquent of the amicus briefs was the work of Sonja R. Peterson of Horton and Associates of Minnesota in combination with Linda B. Berg of NOW.[13] Their argument, necessarily more political and provocative, contended that Campbell's decision was "impermissibly based upon sex stereotyping and bias against Ms. Thompson's political beliefs, activism, and lesbian lifestyle."

Beginning with a reminder to the appellate court that the standard of proof in guardianship cases is clear and convincing evidence (more than a preponderance of the evidence but less than the criminal-law standard of beyond a reasonable doubt), the drafters of this brief discussed how a "parade of 15 health care professionals with intimate knowledge of Ms. Kowalski's medical records and treatment, all of whom were chosen by the court as the court's own experts," gave witness to the "profound benefits" that flowed from the devotion of Karen Thompson and established "clear and convincing evidence that Karen Thompson is the most suitable and best qualified person." Peterson and Berg ironically described the incomprehensible outcome of the case:

> Guardianship was granted to a woman who only visited Sharon Kowalski approximately three times a year instead of to a woman who sees Sharon on almost a daily basis despite the fact that she has to drive many hours to make the trip. Guardianship was granted to a woman who, over the eight years that Sharon Kowalski has been institutionalized, has attended two case conferences, instead of to a woman who has been intimately and consistently involved in decisions about Sharon's care. Guardianship was granted to a woman who has testified that she is not willing to take Sharon Kowalski into her home and intends to institutionalize her, instead of to a woman who has remodeled her home in order to make it comfortable and accessible to Sharon.[14]

Within this rhetorical framework, the lower court's decision appeared capricious and arbitrary, in spite of Judge Campbell's careful deliberation and preparation of findings. This probate court judge might have taken special umbrage at the attempt of this brief to cast his decision as "sex stereotyping." Citing *Price Waterhouse v Hopkins* (490 US 228 [1989]), a job discrimination case in which comments by partners that the female employee was too "macho" and should "walk more femininely" in order to deserve promotion were actionable sex stereotyping, appellate counsel analogously pointed to the judge's conclusion that Karen Thompson was "possessive, authoritative, inflexible, and committed to her own political agenda." Besides pointing out that this conclusion was borne out by none of the health care experts, counsel also argued that "aggressiveness" was a necessary component of patient advocacy and that the court curiously had never berated Donald Kowalski for his inflexibility or possessiveness. Donald Kowalski, according to experts, "disagrees with everything" — "ranting and raving" — while Karen Thompson is "punished for a mere allegation of such behavior," the lawyers wrote. "Such a double standard is as patently unfair and discriminatory when applied to Karen Thompson as it was when applied to the woman partnership candidate at Price Waterhouse."[15]

Counsel also decried Campbell's characterization of the heterosexual Tomberlin as a "role model" for Sharon. Not only was Tomberlin anything but a neutral third party, as the court characterized her, but she was also a close Kowalski family friend. "And yet," the brief continued, "although the court is not offended by Karen Tomberlin's clear advocacy of Sharon Kowalski's parents' viewpoint, it criticizes Karen Thompson for being committed to 'her own political agenda.' Perhaps the Kowalski family agenda is more palatable to the court because it incorporates more stereotypical feminine values."[16]

Suzanne Born of Minneapolis and Paula Ettelbrick of the Lambda Legal Defense Fund were authors of another amicus brief that focused primarily on the expanding legal definition of family to include same-sex domestic partners. "Karen and Sharon share a family relationship that is highly relevant to the determination of Sharon's best interests," their argument stated, as they narrated a different version of the Kowalskis' behavior than lower courts were willing to acknowledge. "After receiving Karen's letter, the Kowalski family responded by calling Karen crazy and sick. They totally prevented Karen from seeing Sharon. Several years later, when the court finally gave effect to Sharon's wish to see Karen, the Kowalskis virtually abandoned their relationship with their daughter rather than accept Sharon for who she is."[17] Lambda lawyers were familiar with the metaphors of insanity and sickness that permeated the lives of lesbians and gay men and were conversant with the abandonment of gay and lesbian children by homophobic parents. In this brief, however, Born and Ettelbrick were contending that some of this opprobrium was lifting, that a "shift to a broader concept of family is the result of the increasing visibility and acceptance of lesbian and gay relationships as legitimate and healthy families."

Their argument continued to describe this social and cultural shift. "Approximately ten percent of the population of this country, or twenty-five million men and women, are lesbian and gay," the brief stated, and "although lesbians and gay men in the United States are generally prohibited from formalizing their family relationships through marriage or other means, millions of couples, like Sharon Kowalski and Karen Thompson, live in families that are functionally indistinguishable from heterosexual families." They informed the appellate court that nearly 75 percent of all lesbians live with a partner in a committed, long-term relationship. "Lesbian and gay couples love and care for each other, share the economic, social, and emotional necessities of life and regard one another as family," the lawyers insisted, citing celebrations of "lifetime commitment" ceremonies across the country.[18]

Lambda's assimilatory argument, controversial among many gays and lesbians who saw their sexual orientation as an alternative to historically discriminatory social structures like marriage, functioned as a tool to suggest that Karen and Sharon were married de facto if not de jure, and therefore as spouses should be given a preference in questions of guardianship. In anticipation of the same-sex marriage controversy that would surface nationally in a year or two, Lambda argued that "some cities" had adopted laws allowing unmarried partners to register their relationships and receive health insurance and sick leave for domestic partners. In August 1991, the lawyers cited, a New York state court had upheld the claims of lesbian and gay teachers to health benefits for their domestic partners. The brief cited the overturning of hospital visitation policies that barred admission to unmarried heterosexual partners in Michigan, the expansion of "single-family" covenants in housing developments to non-consanguineous units in Wisconsin, the provision of unemployment benefits in California to a man who left his job to care for his partner who was dying of AIDS. Slowly courts were waking up to the changing "societal realities" of what Judge Campbell himself had described as a "family of affinity."[19]

The relevance of this sociology lesson to the matter at bar, the brief argued, arose from the failure of the lower court "to consider the significance of these women's family relationship," which was germane to a determination of the best interests of the ward. By refusing to recognize Sharon and Karen's relationship as equivalent to a marriage, the court "held Karen Thompson to a double standard that, one would hope, no court would require of any other family member, spouse or petitioner." Counsel wondered whether or not the court would have dismissed Sharon's expressed wishes with such alacrity if Karen had been married to Sharon and they were living together in a relationship "as fulfilling and satisfying as other adult relationships."[20]

In discussing the "double standard" issue, Lambda lawyers contended that Campbell's decision had accepted "vicious, insupportable attacks on Karen's character as fact" and "consistently blames Karen Thompson for the Kowalski family's inability to accept the fact—revealed repeatedly by Sharon herself—that Sharon is a lesbian." Ironically, the brief noted, Karen could gain the legitimacy she needed to fight on Sharon's behalf only by revealing the nature of her relationship, a revelation for which she is now being blamed. "Oddly enough, the lower court most likely would never have considered them a 'family of affinity' without knowing of their lesbian relationship. By using the very inflammatory reference to 'outing' in order to describe Karen's revelation of her sexual orientation and her relationship with Sharon, the court once again exhibits its bias against an expression of one's sexual orientation."[21]

A third amicus brief came from the Minnesota Civil Liberties Union and, in particular, its volunteer attorney Brian O'Neill, whose stake in the case had started as early as 1986. The basis of his legal argument (by O'Neill in conjunction with

John Bedosky and Michael Ponto) was that a constitutional right of all persons to choose their own partners should be part of the existing constitutional right of privacy that had developed in the federal courts at least since Justice William Douglas's opinion in the *Griswold* case, preventing the government from banning the use of contraceptive devices. O'Neill insisted that there was ample evidence that Sharon had chosen Karen as a partner and guardian but no evidence that she had chosen Karen Tomberlin. Citing Justice Louis Brandeis, the brief argued that the constitutional "protection of Americans in their beliefs, their thoughts, their emotions and their sensations" included the right to pursue same-sex love without government interference — the right to choose one's intimate partners as Justice Harry Blackmun had stated in the dissent to *Bowers v Hardwick*. There was "no excuse for discounting the fundamental importance" of Karen and Sharon's lesbian relationship just because it fell outside of heterosexual norms.[22]

Thomas Sjogren of Duluth agreed to take Karen Tomberlin's appeal pro bono. He read the voluminous briefs and did his best to write a compelling argument. The statement of facts detailed his client's acceptance of guardianship and oath of acceptance on May 8, 1991. "The reaction of the Kowalski family [to Karen's disclosure of her lesbian relationship with their daughter], coupled with the widespread media attention arising from Karen Thompson's repeated legal maneuvers and her nationwide fund-raising efforts utilizing Sharon Kowalski's name, has resulted in inflexible positions on both sides which have resisted all attempts at mediation."[23] Sjogren's brief followed the judge's opinion closely, notably agreeing with Campbell that "Karen Thompson was placing her own concerns before those of Sharon Kowalski." Thompson, he argued, admitted undergoing a transformation from, in her own words, "a very private, closeted woman" to a "very famous person." It could not therefore "be seriously questioned," counsel stated, "that Ms. Thompson's change and present stature as a nationally known personality has taken place at the expense of Sharon Kowalski's own right to privacy and that this has contributed to the animosity between Ms. Thompson and Sharon's natural family." Sjogren reiterated the substantial evidence that Sharon did not want to reveal her sexual orientation before the accident, testimony that neither "an appreciation of the music of Chris Williamson nor a visit to a gay bar" could overcome. Though Sharon might have come out to her health care providers, she still did not want to tell her parents.

Tomberlin's lawyer made some other points before closing. The probate court's discretion gave it wide authority in appointing guardians, and Judge Campbell had made specific findings as to the neutrality and competency of Karen Tomberlin to serve as a guardian who would provide access to all the parties. The court also had the authority to determine that the place where

Sharon was presently residing, Trevilla, was quite beneficial to her health and well-being and worthy of her continued residence. Relying on an appellate court's traditional reluctance to second-guess the judgment of the trier of fact, Thomas Sjogren concluded that "Ms. Thompson has failed to meet her burden of establishing that the trial court failed to properly apply the law or otherwise abused its discretion by appointing Karen Tomberlin as successor guardian."[24]

Fred Friedman's brief on behalf of his client, Sharon Kowalski, was in essence a document in support of the judge's decision, which was also closely aligned with a letter he wrote to the judge in April. He called Thompson and the Kowalskis "hostile camps" that required a neutral third party as guardian to avoid a breakup. While not explicitly discussing the testimony of the fifteen experts hired by the court, Friedman admitted that even if many witnesses testified to Sharon's desire to live with Karen, their testimony was "not dispositive" of her preference, which in his view was "still an open question." Friedman argued that the practical effect of granting the petition would be an elimination of contact with the Kowalski family and many other friends from the Range. The court's remedy, he stated, avoided that eventuality.[25]

In contrast to the Lambda brief, Friedman insisted that Thompson's announcement of her lesbian relation "created a rift between herself and Sharon's family which may never be mended." He stated that had Thompson respected Sharon's desire for confidentiality with regard to her sexual orientation, "she would still have had visitation, although it would have been more difficult to effect because of the distance involved." Friedman continued to concentrate on the importance of Sharon's family to her emotional well-being. "Debra Kowalski," the brief noted, "testified that if such a move [to Thompson's home] occurred there 'wouldn't be many people from Sharon's past, friends, family, that will go to see her.' If all contact with her family was cut off — notwithstanding who was responsible for such a cutoff — it seems clear that this would have an emotional effect." From Friedman's perspective, the court correctly found it unacceptable that the Kowalskis should be left out and "in its sound judgment appointed an individual who had no axe to grind, with the hope that all parties would then participate in Sharon's social life."[26]

Wilson's reply moved from an initial reiteration of her strongest position — the weight of the expert testimony — to a refutation of some of Friedman's arguments about Thompson's suspect qualifications. On the right-of-privacy issue, she stated flatly that Sharon's privacy was not violated by Karen's coming out. Friedman's argument that Karen does not understand the Iron Range cultural background, she pointed out, is a euphemistic legitimation of homophobia. "Disclosure of the truth about one's lesbianism is something one should not do on the Iron Range" was the court's message, and for Wilson that attitude completely discounted "the depth of the commitment Sharon and Karen have for each other." What if Karen were a black male married to Sharon without her parents' knowledge? "Would anyone under those circumstances," Wilson asked, "suggest that Karen should remain silent or that we should respect the racism of Sharon's parents? Would anyone claim that Karen, in that case, should not be guardian?"

Contrary to Friedman's assessment, both sides were *not* equally inflexible, the appellant argued. Thompson had offered to mediate with the Kowalskis from the start, but they refused. "The Kowalskis are the ones who are intransigent," Wilson argued, "and, by the court's Order, are being rewarded for their intransigence." In the final analysis, Thompson's lawyer concluded, "something very shocking has occurred in this case. It appears that a 35-year-old handicapped lesbian woman, who can reliably express her wishes . . . , is being denied what she wants and what she needs because the trial court wants to please her parents." Wilson could only hope that "the truth of this case has finally come to light, and that this court will act in a way which will restore Sharon Kowalski to the dignity which has been taken away from her over the last eight years."[27]

Election Day came on Tuesday, November 6, 1991. By its end, voters in the Twin Cities had battled more than two feet of snow with ice underneath to get to the polls. About forty-six thousand voters turned out in St. Paul to defeat an initiative to repeal the city council's recently enacted gay rights ordinance, which was made law originally in 1974 in an effort to prohibit discrimination based on sexual orientation in housing, public accommodation, jobs, and education. The 1974 ordinance was repealed in 1978 in a similar referendum but was restored by the city council in 1990. A group called Citizens Alert had gathered more than six thousand signatures to get the referendum on the ballot, but its attempt to overturn the statute was defeated when 54.3 percent of voters rejected the measure that Tuesday in 1991 ("B. J. Metzger, the Head of Campaign 90s, Which Fought the Repeal Effort, Declared a Victory for Gay Rights in Minnesota's Capital," *Duluth News-Tribune*, November 6, 1991).

In a related matter on the same day, lawyers faced snowy conditions to appear before the Minnesota Court of Appeals for oral arguments *In re Guardianship of Sharon Kowalski, Ward* (File No. C2-91-1047) ("St. Paul Upholds Gay Rights Ordinance" and "Battle over Sharon Kowalski Back before Court," *Duluth News-Tribune*, November 6, 1991, sec. A, p. 6). In three-piece suits, dark-colored dresses, and overcoats, a parade of lawyers came once again to St. Paul that first Tuesday after the first Monday in November to argue about who would take care of Sharon Kowalski: Fred Friedman, Sue Wilson, Thomas Sjogren, Suzanne Born, Brian O'Neill, and Sonja Peterson appeared before a three-judge panel of the Court of Appeals consisting of Judges Thomas Forsberg (presiding), Gary Crippin, and Jack Davies. Judges Wozniak and Popovich were not part of this panel. In the short time allotted for oral argument, Sue Wilson made her strongest point. She told the judges that Campbell had ignored the testimony of fifteen medical experts who all said Sharon Kowalski was able to reliably express a preference for where she wants to live and has made that preference clear: with Karen Thompson in St. Cloud. "If that's not an abuse of discretion, I don't know what is," Wilson asserted ("Kowalski Custody Case Goes Back Before Court of Appeals," *St. Cloud Times,* November 6, 1991).

Tomberlin's lawyer, Thomas Sjogren, on the other hand, argued that where Sharon says she wants to live now should not be the determining factor; rather, the court needs to go back to the situation eight years ago, before the accident. Then, he claimed, Sharon was "delicately balancing the maintenance of a relationship with her parents and with Karen Thompson by avoiding telling her parents what her relationship was." Friedman stated that he recommended a neutral third party as guardian because of the open hostility between the petitioner and Sharon's parents, but Wilson countered that the statute on guardianship does not contemplate neutrality but looks for the most committed person to be guardian. The court took the case under submission; by law it had ninety days to make its decision.

Judge Davies's opinion came down less than six weeks later on December 17, 1991. The court's swift decision stated, "The trial court abused its discretion in denying Thompson's petition where there was uncontradicted expert testimony as to appellant's suitability, and where there was insufficient evidence as to the qualifications or neutrality of the named guardian. We remand for an order, consistent with this opinion, appointing Karen Thompson guardian."[28] The unanimous opinion featured a court much more willing to accept the lesbian relationship of the partners. The statement of facts openly characterized Sharon and Karen as a "lesbian" couple living together for four years before the accident. It also made a point of emphasizing that Thompson "exercised little choice as to which medical witnesses were called," since the lower court itself had approved the appointment of the Miller-Dwan team. The witnesses in opposition to the guardianship (Debbie Kowalski, Rose Jones, and Karen Tomberlin), the court noted, had no medical training, were infrequent visitors, and had accompanied Sharon on none of her recent public outings.

On the ward's expressed preference, the court relied on the judge's erroneous refusal to follow the advice of his experts that Sharon was capable of expressing her preference. "This court finds," Davies wrote, "that, in the absence of contradictory evidence about Sharon's decision-making capacity from a professional or anyone in daily contact with her, the trial court's conclusion was clearly erroneous."[29] The testimony of Debbie Kowalski and other lay witnesses was, in short, insufficient to counteract the weight of the professional opinions. Once the capacity of the ward to make a decision was established, the court stated, the ward's choices could be denied by the court only if found not to be in the ward's best interest.

Judge Davies then considered the qualifications of the petitioner. Again relying on the testimony of the health care professionals, the court stated that Thompson had an extreme interest and commitment in promoting Sharon's welfare, "has an exceptional current understanding of Sharon's physical and mental status and needs, . . . and is strongly equipped to attend to her emotional needs." The court recognized the goal of the medical team that Sharon live outside an institution and noted that Karen Thompson was fully equipped to reach that goal. When asked whether they found Thompson "troublesome or overbearing in her demands for Sharon," no medical witness "responded that Thompson caused trouble, but rather each said she is highly cooperative and exceptionally attentive to what treatments and activities are in Sharon's best interests."[30] The court also reprimanded Campbell because he had substituted his judgment that Sharon remain institutionalized for the advice of the medical experts that she would best be helped outside a nursing home.

As far as the neutrality of the guardian, Judge Davies's opinion wondered why the court had not explored Thompson's offer to drive Sharon to the Range periodically, suggesting that Thompson's camp was not as hostile as the court concluded. "Thompson's appointment as guardian would not, of itself, result in the family ceasing to visit Sharon," the court wrote. "The Kowalskis are free to visit their daughter if they wish. It is not the court's role to accommodate one side's threatened intransigence, where to do so would deprive the ward of an otherwise suitable and preferred guardian." Not only did Davies find that the lower court ignored "Thompson's demonstrated willingness to facilitate all parties' involvement with Sharon"; it also questioned the neutrality of the named guardian — Tomberlin, who "[b]oth in her deposition and at the hearing . . . testified that her first and primary goal as guardian is to relocate Sharon to the Iron Range, close to her family. This testimony undermines the one 'qualification' relied on by the trial court in appointing Tomberlin — her role as an impartial mediator."[31]

Davies took issue with a number of Campbell's conclusions about the petitioner, including issues of invasion of privacy, public display, and emotional as well as financial conflicts of interest. "While the extent to which Sharon had publicly acknowledged her sexual preference at the time of the accident is unclear," Davies stated, "[s]ince the accident, Sharon's doctors and therapists testified that Sharon has voluntarily told them of her relationship with Thompson." The court agreed that most of the evidence showed that Sharon's attendance at public events was positive, not harmful or exploitative. There was no firsthand evidence that Sharon disliked these outings. The court also found that changes in a guardian's personal life, even if the ward was a spouse, were not uncommon, and in Thompson's case were clearly made with the proviso that Sharon would always be Karen's first responsibility.

Perhaps most important, the court concluded by calling Karen and Sharon "a family of affinity which ought to be accorded respect." Davies not only reversed the trial court and granted Thompson's petition but also disallowed the possibility of restrictions on the guardianship by the trial judge. Thompson "is free to make whatever decisions she and the doctors feel are necessary to achieve Sharon's best interests, including decisions regarding Sharon's location. Thompson is, however, directed to continue efforts at accommodating visitation between Sharon and the Kowalskis, without unreasonable restrictions."[32]

Thompson's victory was truly remarkable, but the Associated Press quoted Karen herself as saying, "Today's decision is not a victory. It is a right decision, a just decision that should have been made eight years ago" ("Lesbian Wins Appeal to Be Guardian of Ailing Lover," *Los Angeles Times,* December 18, 1991). But Karen's attorney, Sue Wilson, called the ruling a victory for the disabled and PWAs (people living with AIDS), as well as "a significant affirmation that moves gays and lesbians and the way the law treats them in this state into the 20th Century." While Suzanne Born, attorney for the Lambda Legal Defense Fund, cautioned that the state court ruling did not set precedent outside of Minnesota, this was the first case she knew of in which a gay or lesbian partner's guardian petition was contested by the ward's parents and met with defeat.

Hailed as a landmark by gay rights activists, the case was reported in the gay and straight media. *Time,* in its American Notes section, called the decision "A Victory for Gay Rights," quoting Paula Ettelbrick that the ruling "begins the process of recognizing that lesbian and gay couples share the kind of commitment that married couples do" ("A Victory for Gay Rights," *Time,* December 30, 1991, 25). Karen's attorney, Sue Wilson, made a broader claim: "Gay men, lesbians, handicapped people are safer. The court said gay and lesbian relationships count and it will acknowledge them." Linda Berg, who penned the NOW brief, was quoted by the *Star Tribune* as commenting, "It's not the usual practice to consider a gay or lesbian couple to be a family which is 'accorded respect.' Legally it's only applicable within Minnesota, [b]ut judges all over the country look at judges in other courts to see how they deal with difficult cases" (Margaret Zack and Kurt Chandler, "Breaking Tradition: Lesbian Guardianship Ruling May Aid Status of Gay Couples, Observers Say," *Minneapolis Star Tribune,* December 18, 1991, sec. B, p. 1).

The decision "comes 12 years to the day after Thompson and Sharon Kowalski exchanged rings and vowed to love each other for the rest of their lives," *St. Cloud Times* reporters wrote ("Thompson Wins Custody Appeal," December 17, 1991, sec. A, p. 1). Thompson was now free to discuss the possibility of moving Sharon to the St. Cloud area and eventually to her own home. "I need to talk to the doctors, therapists and Sharon," Karen told the *St. Cloud Times,* still unsure if there were any issues left to appeal in the case. "Is the nightmare over? I certainly hope so," she said. "This case never seemed to be over." Tomberlin was reported as still considering an appeal to the Supreme Court of Minnesota.

"A Family of Affinity Affirmed" was the lead editorial in the *Star Tribune* the next day (editorial, *Minneapolis Star Tribune,* December 19, 1991, sec. A, p. 26). While the editor claimed that the court should be "proud" of its "sensitive ruling" and Thompson's vindicated "grit and dedication" should be admired, the victory would be hollow unless hearts "soften" and the Kowalskis restore visitation with their daughter. Calling Campbell's ruling "intemperate" and "highly and unfairly critical of Thompson," the editors praised the "respect" accorded to this lesbian "family of affinity," an affirming statement "years of heartache overdue." The other "heartache" — the Kowalskis' refusal to see their daughter — remained. "However tired and hurt the parents may feel as a consequence of the court battle, they should reconsider," the editors felt. "Sharon Kowalski needs Karen Thompson, but she needs also love and affection from Donald and Della Kowalski of Nashwauk, Minn., whose child she will always be."

Candace Renalis, staff writer for the *Duluth News-Tribune,* added details to the story of Karen's reaction to the ruling. Besides noting that Judge Campbell refused to comment on the ruling because of ethics rules, she observed that Thompson on Monday expressed little joy with the decision, at times weeping. "I don't feel really good about this," Thompson said. "There's been too much hurt and pain." The forty-three-year-old Thompson also stated that she hoped the "healing process" could start because she did not "want to antagonize Sharon's parents any further." Karen Tomberlin expressed surprise at the decision, noting that she was "optimistic" until the news came. She was not sure she could appeal because she did not have unlimited resources, as she claimed Thompson did (Candace Renalis, "Gay Activist Named Guardian of Kowalski," *Duluth News-Tribune,* December 17, 1991, sec. A, p. 2).

Equal Time created a curious juxtaposition in its December 20 headline: "Pivotal Legal Rulings Issued: Thompson Granted Guardianship in Landmark Ruling; Military Ban on Gays Upheld in Steffan Case" (Cynthia Scott, December 20, 1991–January 3, 1992, p. 1). "A federal judge on December 9 upheld the

Pentagon ban on gays in the military, saying the armed forces must have that power if they are to protect soldiers and sailors from AIDS," one column read. The other stated: "Karen Thompson and Sharon Kowalski's eight-year battle to live together ended Tuesday." Joseph Steffan, of Warren, Minnesota, had challenged his dismissal from the U.S. Naval Academy after he disclosed to the chaplain his homosexuality six weeks before graduation. Oliver Gasch, a federal judge in Washington who had referred to Steffan as a "homo" three times during the hearing, ruled that the armed forces have the power to protect their soldiers from HIV. Sharon Kowalski had a disability other than AIDS, of course, but her case and Steffan's proved that gays and lesbians would continue to face discrimination.

In an exclusive interview, Phil Johnson, GAZE-TV field producer, wrote of the "shared eye contact" and "smiles" between Karen and Sharon as they sat in front of living room windows that framed "a picture postcard winter scene" overlooking the Mississippi River, where Karen had built her new home. In response to Karen's frequent questions to Sharon about how she was handling the attention, Sharon would give one of her "microscopic nods." When Johnson asked about reconciliation with the Kowalskis, Karen responded that "it's easier to continue to hate me and blame me than it is to start that process." She still held out hope for eventual reconciliation, however, especially for Sharon's sake. "She's lost too much and she shouldn't have to choose between her biological family and her chosen family," Thompson told Johnson (Phil Johnson, "Karen Thompson Appointed Guardian; Appeals Court Panel Agrees with Medical, Professional Testimony," *GAZE*, December 26, 1991, p. 1).

Sue Wilson and her client were not completely surprised by the news that greeted them one month after Judge Davies's opinion. On January 17, 1992, Thomas Sjogren, Karen Tomberlin's attorney, filed a petition for review with the Minnesota Supreme Court, arguing that the Court of Appeals "went beyond its function as an appealing court and has substituted its judgment for the trial court," thereby "intruding upon the fact-finding of the trial court." Because the case raised issues of statewide importance, Sjogren argued, the Minnesota Supreme Court should hear it. "I feel this is a form of harassment," Thompson told David Southgate, reporter for *Equal Time* (David Southgate, "Minnesota Supreme Court Asked to Review Kowalski's Guardianship," *Equal Time*, January 31, 1992–February 14, 1992, p. 1). Sue Wilson called the challenge "ridiculous" and remained optimistic the Supreme Court would uphold the Court of Appeals. "We thought it was over, but it's not," Thompson's public relations spokesperson told the *Lesbian News* (Corinna Radigan, "Custody of Kowalski Now in Doubt," *Lesbian News*, February 1992). The supreme court had thirty days to decide whether or not to hear the petition.

In the meantime, Karen Thompson proceeded as if her guardianship was secure, traveling with Sharon to Old Dominion University in Norfolk, Virginia, and publicly thanking the gay community for its support during the legal battle. "This case may end and we may go on with our lives, but now it's a time for us to pay back the community that supported us," Thompson told the crowd, which gave the women two standing ovations ("Lesbian Couple Say Thank You," *Duluth News-Tribune,* February 3, 1992, sec. A, p. 2). Sharon pointed to letters on a lapboard to spell "good" when asked how she felt about the decision.

On February 14 the Minnesota Supreme Court, as it had on numerous previous occasions, refused to review the ruling in the Kowalski case (Candace Renalis, "State High Court Refuses to Hear Appeal in Lesbian Guardianship," *Duluth News-Tribune,* February 13, 1992, sec. A, p. 2). The court's upholding of Davies's opinion brought the case to an end, to the degree any guardianship case is ever ended. Sjogren had no plan to appeal to the United States Supreme Court, the only other legal avenue available to Karen Tomberlin. Thompson told Renalis, "I'm told that, technically, they could still try to appeal to the U.S. Supreme Court. But it's not a constitutional issue, so I think realistically this is over." Tomberlin and the Kowalskis were not available for comment. Karen had won her case.

Jason is a traumatic brain-injured person who wants to be liked for who he is, not for what he is. He is a Montana native in his thirties who lives in Missoula and works at Rockin' Rudy's, the local head shop and record store, while remaining active in the disabled and queer communities. When eighteen and working as a male model in Phoenix, he took a ride without a helmet on the back of his friend Woody's motorcycle. He didn't want to get his hair flattened. He got hit by a driver who was so drunk he didn't even know his name when the cops picked him up. Jason, who has never met the guy, remained in a coma for sixteen months, showing few ostensible signs of movement other than returning the kisses of his mother, who now, after his recovery, is his guardian. He had his head "sewn up" after the accident, referring to the brain surgery he underwent as a result of the collision.

Since coming back from Los Angeles and getting involved in the gay community in Montana, I had wanted to interview Jason about what it was like to be TBI, especially as a gay man. I knew he was in better shape than Sharon — he was ambulatory and more articulate (he used a synthesizer, though he could voice some words) — but they had some things in common. "I talk to my bird," Jason said, "he's the only one that listens." I had known Jason for a while, maybe three or four years. We worked together on the Missoula AIDS Prevention Project, making condom packs and distributing safe-sex paraphernalia. He marched in the Montana PRIDE parades. We joked a lot.

I had never sat down and talked to him about his life. I myself was guilty of not paying much attention to him, so I understood when he told me people ignored him. Jason thought gay men did not get close to him because they believed his condition would wear off on them. He was only half joking; many of the guys he knew before the accident in 1986 would never associate with him now because they thought he was a "retard." Jason knew what it was like to be vain, to be a gay man concerned with looks. He had been there and done that, but now he was the brunt of their snobbery, he said, holding his nose in the air.

He hated himself after he woke up following the accident, he remembered. He spent two years in Libby, a logging town in northwestern Montana that makes Hibbing look like Amsterdam, a location where queers did not exist, and in the end he tried to kill himself. He ended up on the psych ward at St. Pat's in Missoula — the best thing that ever happened, he told me while we ate lunch that winter afternoon in 1999. Now he was living in Missoula, which *was* the Amsterdam of Montana, and had his own apartment on West Sixth. He was living independently. He received Medicaid, had a case worker, and was in regular contact with his mom, who still lived in that corner of our state.

He still had moods — still got frustrated when people did not listen to him. He had tendon surgery to release his right arm, which at one point was stuck in an upward position with his hand against his head. He had rings on his fingers, which moved across the keyboard of his voice box like a daddy longlegs. He called himself a "mute" whom no one wanted to pay attention to, except for a few people. He was dating a lawyer in Helena. He liked his mom, even though she had control over his movements. He had a brother who knew, a sister who knew but didn't know. She interrupted the fag jokes that her husband liked to tell, which indicated a certain sensitivity, but beyond that she wasn't asking.

Who is Jason? A romantic with a streak of social conscience and a large dose of irony. What is he? A gay man who is handicapped — a TBI. Who am I? A guy writing a book about what it's like to try to be queer in a world that vacillates. What am I? A man in love with a man named David, a writer on my own synthesizer. Who is Sharon Kowalski?

TWELVE

Remedy

As a way of thinking about legal marriage, this notion of pure love, like so much else in contemporary U.S. politics, is an image of sentimental privacy. Love, it says, is beyond criticism and beyond the judgments of the law. Where law adjudicates conflict and competing claims, love speaks an inner truth, in a space where there is no conflict, no politics. It is the human heart, not ideology. Its intentions are pure. It has no unconscious.

I would argue that any politics based on such a sentimental rhetoric of privacy is not only a false idealization of love and coupling; it is an increasingly powerful way of distracting citizens from the real, conflicted and unequal conditions governing their lives, and that it serves to reinforce the privilege of those who already find it easiest to imagine their lives as private.

> Michael Warner, *The Trouble with Normal:*
> *Sex, Politics, and the Ethics of Queer Life*

Love's Labor

On March 20, 1992, a month after Karen Tomberlin's appeal to the Minnesota Supreme Court was rejected and the legal case put to rest for the foreseeable future, Karen Thompson and Sharon Kowalski appeared together on the *The Phil Donahue Show* as the only guests for an hour ("Kowalski, Thompson Appear on Phil Donahue TV Program," *St. Cloud Times,* March 20, 1992, sec. A, p. 4). Karen once again retold her story — the eight-year legal struggle, the three-and-a-half-year separation, the reunification after a legal victory. Sharon responded to short questions asked her by Phil Donahue, nodding or shaking her head. The feature was a crowning moment in the media limelight for the two women and marked an opportunity to discuss their trials and legacy.

That legacy was addressed more substantially in an article by Donna Halvorsen about the opening of the Lambda Justice Center in St. Paul. The article began anecdotally, alluding to the significance of the lawsuit for the gay male community. "A gay man goes to the hospital, gravely ill with AIDS. His longtime companion goes along to comfort him and make decisions about his care. But the companion has no legal rights. The sick man's parents do. Upset about their son's plight and hostile toward his companion, they take over the decision-making and ban their son's companion from his bedside." The article described this "familiar scenario" as one that could worsen as the AIDS crisis deepened, but if gay people did the kind of planning the new Lambda Justice Center was advocating, much of that suffering could be avoided (Donna Halvorsen, "Center Will Help Gays Plan Ahead," *Minneapolis Star Tribune,* June 24, 1992, sec. B, p. 5).

Karen Thompson had been making the same pitch, urging partners to sign living wills, which were now becoming available in software produced by Nolo Press. Halvorsen reported that the newly opened Lambda Justice Center, serving 250,000 gay and lesbian citizens of Minneapolis–St. Paul and run by Richard Sykora, a St. Paul lawyer, would emphasize mediation and family and estate planning. "[W]e do the kind of positive building to avoid situations like the Thompson-Kowalski matter that involved eight years of fighting in the courts," Sykora told the *Star.* He described the decision as "an exciting turning point in the established legal system in Minnesota, that the Court of Appeals recognized the dignity of a lesbian relationship." Sykora, like Thompson, said that the court battle could have been avoided if Sharon and Karen had filed a simple legal form designating each other as guardian if the other became ill. But the courts in Sharon and Karen's case were not avoided, and an inestimable number of same-sex couples — for reasons of economics or spontaneity or ignorance or uncertainty — would never take advantage of the legal planning needed to protect themselves from the eventualities of sickness and death that people did not want to think about. Heterosexual couples were already protected by the law; gays and lesbians had to create their own legal protection.

Judge Robert Campbell received the remanded order from Judge Davies of the Court of Appeals early in 1992, but he was seemingly in no hurry to sign it. In May, for inexplicable reasons, he removed himself from the case, turning the file over to Chief Judge Donovan Frank to administer; Campbell would retire the same year. Karen Thompson underwent the process of writing to the new judge to have the guardianship approved and the order signed. At the advice of her attorney, she also filed a motion of change of venue, and the case was transferred from St. Louis to Hennepin County, from Duluth to Minneapolis. Karen would file her yearly medical evaluations and accountings with the Hennepin County court from that time forward.

"Justice delayed," reported Mark Kasel, continued to be the hallmark of the Kowalski case ("What Will It Take to Finally Bring Sharon Home?" *GAZE,* May 3, 1993, p. 30). The change of venue did not end Thompson's attempt to realize full rights as guardian. The Hennepin District Court requested a final accounting of Sharon's assets from St. Louis County District

Court before the judges in Minneapolis would sign the order. Not until February 1993, almost ten years after the accident and a year after the Minnesota Supreme Court refused to hear the case, did Thompson receive her final order giving her the "power and ability" to act as guardian.

In the meantime, Karen was periodically bringing Sharon to their home overlooking the Mississippi River in Clearwater, south of St. Cloud. "Bay windows and a cedar deck overlook the wide, slow river," Jennifer Juarez Robles wrote in her featured interview, "Karen Thompson and Sharon Kowalski: 'A Family of Affinity'" (*Advocate*, October 20, 1992, p. 45). The disability-accessible home had lower light switches, higher electrical outlets, and a wheelchair ramp. Robles sat in the living room as Sharon celebrated her thirty-sixth birthday in August 1992. The women spent the afternoon watching the women's platform diving contest in the summer Olympics. Clear of any foreseeable legal challenges to their union for the first time in nine years, Thompson fielded Robles's questions about her crusade. She attributed her success to a lack of activism before the accident: "I was so afraid of who an activist was, who a feminist was. I thought these were negatives. I had swallowed the social control that's used to keep us in our place, to keep us from speaking out."

Now Thompson had embraced the political mantle and taught students about how she and they are "indoctrinated" by invalid versions of the truth, Robles reported. Karen stated that she was "saved" by being a teacher. "As a teacher you look for teachable moments in the classroom. For whatever reason, this case is a teachable moment," she told her interviewer. "Not to use it to help people try and understand these issues and their interconnections would be criminal." In her struggle, the gay and lesbian community supported her almost from the start. Her friendships, though, changed as a result of the ordeal. Some women were afraid of being seen with Karen now because of her high profile.

Her religious views had also evolved. Thompson had changed "radically" since the days when she "took Sharon through accepting Christ." She told Robles the "church to me is another economic, political institution that perpetuates the isms," even though she continued to "have a strong faith in a power bigger than me." Karen still prayed before every presentation she gave but no longer was sure whom she was praying to. "Something clearly has been worked on through this whole situation. It's much bigger than the two of us."

Karen continued the interview by speaking directly to her partner: "What you have, Sharon, is the past, before the accident, and then you have right now. You understand everything that's going on right now. In five minutes you'll forget. Yesterday is a blur to you, and the concept of tomorrow is hard to think about. And yet that's all any of us ever has—this moment." Sharon had taught Karen "to live this moment, live it to the fullest. Right now."

Homecoming

By the end of 1992, John Welsh, reporter for the *St. Cloud Times*, found Karen Thompson waxing less philosophic. He wanted to do a story about Sharon Kowalski's homecoming and received permission after pitching it to his editor. Welsh's impression of Karen from the beginning was that she was committed — if "somewhat abrasive." Thompson, he felt, was no different from many public figures who had to deal with the media on a regular basis. His access to Sharon was limited, and within that window the opportunity to catch her when she was able to answer questions made a formal interview even more difficult. Sharon's responses, however, did seem "genuine" to him, and her affection for Thompson also seemed unquestionable. What fascinated Welsh about following the case was the differences the legal struggle had produced in the two partners. The accident had radicalized Thompson but left Sharon arrested in the past because of her disability. Even though Karen had won the legal battle, she was also faced with the huge responsibility of caring for Sharon.

For Welsh, responding to interview questions in 1998, the case was not just about homophobia but also about drunk drivers and the damage they cause, about "the fragility of families — the interesting and unpredictable ways that life's hardships cause us to change." His article began as an interview with Sharon, who was spending the night at home with the woman who had fought for the last nine years to gain public recognition of their relationship:

> "How are you feeling today, Sharon?"
> Sharon Kowalski looks at the questioner intently and mouths a silent "fine."
> "Are you happy?"
> She nods, moving her head only slightly.
> "Do they treat you all right at the nursing home?"
> She nods.
> "But you would rather spend your life here?"
> She nods again.
> "Sharon, what do you want for Christmas?"

"This time neither her head nor mouth move," Welsh wrote. "Instead, she points. Moving just her right index finger off the board attached to her wheelchair, she points to Karen Thompson."

Thompson told John Welsh that she had modified the title of her book as a way of introducing her current stump speech: "Why can't Sharon Kowalski still come home?" she was now asking audiences. "Today, the enemy isn't Kowalski's friends or family who challenged Thompson for guardianship in the courts. Now the adversary is a faceless health care bureaucracy," Welsh reported. Karen was facing the loss of state medical assistance because of how often Sharon was coming home on weekends and traveling away from Trevilla of Robbinsdale. State law, Karen explained, cuts off medical assistance for those who spend more than seventy-two nights a year away from homes that care for the brain-injured. By August 1992, Sharon had already spent sixty nights out of the nursing home. Thompson was forced to stop bringing Sharon home and concentrate on overcoming the government hurdles. She had to apply for a waiver through a state head-injury program that would pay Karen directly if she could prove that Sharon could receive equivalent health care at home and the costs of the care were no more than those at the nursing home. She remained hopeful but was still working on the application and evaluation.

Thompson was facing other difficulties associated with finally getting what she had fought long and hard for. First, Sharon's memory had left her living either in the immediate present or in the past before the accident. When Welsh asked Kowalski how old she was, he reported: "Thompson [meaning Kowalski] looks down at her portable computer and begins the long search for the right keys. After punching the numbers she wants, she hits a large red button that will make the computer speak. 'Twenty-six,' said the mechanical female voice." Ronald Reagan is still president in Kowalski's mind, and Thompson is still a shy, closeted lesbian, Welsh wrote. Today, none of that is true for Thompson. "I've changed. And I can't go back to being the person I was before — not for anyone, not even Sharon."

Karen also reported that the Kowalskis were visiting their daughter on occasion at the facility where Sharon resided when she was not at home in Clearwater, but there was still no contact between Thompson and Sharon's family. Donald had hung up on Welsh when he called for an interview, but Karen Tomberlin was willing to state that the Kowalskis were now reluctant to repeat their vow that they would never see their daughter again.

After Sharon answered about a half dozen yes-or-no questions, Welsh noted, her head slumped forward, her right arm locked up, and her hand grasped her shirt. She grimaced and let out a noise that seemed like a moan. These seizures could last a few moments or stretch into a half hour, Thompson said. Although Kowalski looked to be in pain during these episodes, Welsh reported, there was no way of telling because moments afterward she did not remember them. "It hurts me just looking," Thompson said. "But this is a part of Sharon as well" (John Welsh, "Almost a Year Later, Thompson, Kowalski Facing New Hurdles," *St. Cloud Times*, December 14, 1992, sec. A, p. 1).

Mark Kasel's front-page article in *GAZE* ("What Will It Take to Finally Bring Sharon Home?" May 3, 1992, p. 30) appeared three months later. The article was both an update and an advertisement for a lesbian couple or live-in person to be a care attendant for Sharon during certain times of the day. The pay for attendant care at home would be reimbursed by the Hennepin County health program, which allowed whatever monies would have been spent at the nursing home at Trevilla to be spent on attendant home care. Karen had finally received a waiver from the seventy-two-day limit on time away from disabled health care facilities, allowing her to remove Sharon from Trevilla and take her permanently home. Under the waiver, she would receive a combination of state and federal assistance. Karen found a boarder to live rent free in her home and located a rehabilitation center in St. Cloud, St. Benedict's, where Sharon could spend days, receive therapy, and see her family when visits were arranged.

The couple's April 1993 homecoming had coincided with a larger moment in the annals of lesbian and gay history, one that Sharon and Karen experienced firsthand. They were part of the million people who came to the nation's capital, and part of "hundreds of same-sex couples" who "jammed Constitution Avenue Saturday for a 'wedding' ceremony in which they defiantly demanded rights for homosexual couples. Thousands more joined hands, blew pink whistles and encircled the U.S. Capitol in an angry call for more AIDS research funding." In a "ceremony of commitment," the *St. Cloud Times* reported, nearly a thousand couples "drew hearts on Constitution Avenue, where they exchanged vows, rings and kisses." Men wearing bridal veils and women in tuxedos "cheered when Thompson announced she was taking disabled companion Sharon Kowalski home." They were introduced at the rally on Saturday as the "most famous lesbian couple in the United States." Thompson told the crowd it was "time right now to pass legislation to protect our rights" ("Gay-Rights Activists Cheer St. Cloud Pair," *St. Cloud Times*, April 25, 1993, sec. A, p. 1).

" 'I . . . Will Not Let Her Down': Thompson Takes Kowalski Home to Stay," the front-page headline of the *Minneapolis Star Tribune* read on April 29, 1993. Kurt Chandler and Carol Byrne also wrote a feature piece that reviewed the history of the case, beginning with an account of a conversation between the two lovers:

> "What kind of accident were you in?" Thompson asked, pulling Kowalski's wheelchair closer. "You remember?" Kowalski pecked at a speech synthesizer with an index finger, spelling out her thoughts letter by letter.
> "C-A-R." She tapped a red button and a monotone computerized voice —
> female — sounded out her response.
> "Who hit you? Who were you hit by?" Thompson said.
> "Drunk driver," Kowalski answered through her electronic interpreter.
> "And how do you feel about that?"
> "Pisses me off."

The article, ostensibly about the homecoming and the standing ovation at the Washington march, served as a colorful history and update of the saga. "They were the classic odd couple — Kowalski the free spirit who crisscrossed the country on her motorcycle, Thompson the introverted college professor who lived for her work," the staff writers penned. Kowalski had been nicknamed "Killer" — an "outdoorsy, athletic girl who set a free-throw record in the state high school basketball tournament. She liked to play poker and drink beer. She was an expert on birds and wildflowers, but panicked in a boat. She collected Garfield cartoons and stuffed animals." Thompson they described as a "work-aholic — teaching, coaching, studying the motivation of winning" — who was devoted to her spirituality and family.

Thompson was "excited and angry" about Sharon's homecoming. Even though their almost ten-year journey had been "exhausting" and "filled with losses," Karen saw more hardship ahead. She was using the honoraria from her speaking engagements to supplement her $36,000 teaching salary to pay off the remaining portion of her over $200,000 legal fees. But "juggling a teaching career and speaking tours with Kowalski's care and medical appointments" would be no simple task, the reporters noted. Sharon had to be turned in bed every three hours each night to avoid pressure spots, so Karen had taken in a boarder, exchanging rent for health care. In spite of the ongoing problems, Karen looked forward to the routine activities that the two had missed — "fishing for rock bass, going to concerts and softball games at campus, maybe someday sharing pizza and beer." Thompson looked at her partner and said: "We're gonna live, aren't we Sharon? Just do normal everyday things that we haven't been allowed to do."

John Welsh was the only reporter to appear at the scene on April 29, 1993 — Sharon's homecoming. "No crowds, no lawyers, no doctors, no television cameras showed up," the story opened. "Instead, just a couple of friends helped unpack." By the time Welsh and his photographer arrived, Sharon had already had a full day, traveling to Minneapolis for a doctor's examination and packing her belongings at Trevilla. The photographer captured what appeared to be a tired Sharon being lowered in the Hoyer lift from the van. The endless trips to Robbinsdale were for the time being coming to an end (John Welsh, "A Quiet End to a Long Ordeal," *St. Cloud Times,* April 29, 1993, sec. A, p. 1).

Three years later, on Sharon's birthday, the *St. Paul Pioneer Press* reported that "a landmark Minnesota legal struggle was headed for the movies" (Chris Hewitt, "St. Cloud Couple's Story to Be Filmed," August 8, 1996, sec. D, p. 8). The movie, made for HBO, would be directed by Deborah Chasnoff, who won an Oscar for her documentary on General Electric (*Deadly Deception,* 1991), and written by Jan Oxenberg, who was best known for her appearance in *The Celluloid Closet,* in which she joked that the only time lesbians appear in movies is when they are vampires. "When Karen won [the right to care for her partner], I burst into tears," Chasnoff told *Variety* magazine. "And even though I've done documentaries exclusively, I felt if I was ever going to make a feature, this would be it." HBO later dropped the project after the company merged with Time, Inc., and Chasnoff has yet to make the film.

Three's Company

In 1995 Jean Swallow published a coffee-table book called *Making Love Visible: In Celebration of Gay and Lesbian Families*. All over the country, Swallow, a Seattle writer, conducted interviews with lesbians and gays, who in spite of the stereotypes of loneliness, the reality of being ostracized from biological families, and the ban on same-sex marriage, had created their own family units. Karen, Sharon, and Patty Bresser were featured in one of twenty-four interviews under the title "How Long Does Love Last?"[1] A close-up photo by Geoff Manasse showed Sharon in her wheelchair between an older Karen (forty-seven) and a younger Patty Bresser (thirty-eight). Both Patty and Karen had curly hair and large wire-rimmed glasses. Karen was shown helping Sharon use her computer, tube-feeding Sharon before the 1994 Minnesota Gay Pride parade, and wheeling Sharon with the central Minnesota lesbian contingent through the streets of Minneapolis, while Patty, in sunglasses and a T-shirt ("I am created in God's image, not in your image of God"), held an umbrella over Sharon to shade her from the sun. Patty posed for photos while playing the electric piano and making a layup on the backboard over the garage in Clearwater.

After detailing Thompson's "eight years of excruciating tests of her love, of having to come out publicly despite her Midwest reserve and political reticence," Swallow broached the issue of the ménage à trois that made resolution of the Kowalski case something other than a picture-book ending. Swallow wrote that Sharon and Karen had known Patty before she moved away a year before the accident. Karen linked up with Patty seven years later after giving a speech in Connecticut. "Without wanting to," Swallow wrote, "they had fallen in love. Karen cautioned Patty that she would never leave Sharon, but Patty already understood that. Two years later when Patty moved back to Minnesota to live with Karen, it was clear she was coming not only to be with Karen, but also to care for Sharon." Now the three of them were living quietly on the banks of the Mississippi.

Two interviews followed the introduction, the first with Karen Thompson, who stated categorically that "neither love takes away from the other love."

Without Patty's help as a nurse, Karen could not keep Sharon at home, she stated, but also insisting that without Sharon there, the house in Clearwater was not a home. "The hardest thing" was her regret about the time Sharon lost at the beginning: "There was a window of time for her to regain some skills, and that window was lost. Now we'll never know what Sharon could have done if she had been provided with adequate care," Karen lamented. Now, ten years after the accident, the chances of more progress were slim, though she has never given up hope. "In my heart," Karen told Swallow, "I hurt every time I look at her, how these people condemned her to this quality of life."[2]

Karen's resentment and anger were tempered by her assurance that there was nothing about "our family today" that was hurting Sharon, who had her own relationship with Patty. And Karen and Patty were very open with Sharon about their love. "I've given to myself that it's okay to love Patty and to receive what I can from her," Thompson told Swallow. It was "a juggling act sometimes, to know that it's okay for Sharon to go into respite care so Patty and I can have a weekend together." Karen admitted she was a "fortunate person to have two very special people who love me very much."[3]

Although Patty remembered calling Karen in 1983 after the accident, she lost track of Karen until 1990, when they linked up in Connecticut. "Things progressed such that by 1992, I moved out here to be with her." Patty's family thought she was "crazy," but Karen had "asked Sharon multiple times, in many different ways, if it is okay with her that I live here, and Sharon has always said yes," Bresser told the interviewer.[4] Karen's new partner was also acutely aware of the need to protect themselves legally. She and Karen had durable powers of attorney, but they were not prepared for what might happen to Sharon if Karen died. "I can't legally become successor guardian, but I would want that responsibility because I consider Sharon family," Bresser stated, though she would comply with Sharon's preference. "Sharon amazes me on a daily basis," Bresser stated. "She has such courage. I look at what she has gone through — the sheer isolation, institutional abandonment, surgery, lack of physical care — and she still kept her wits about her. She has not just survived. She has strength. . . . It's the biggest victory."

Between clichés and contradictions, Bresser's interview presented a picture of a qualified woman whose prosaic poise belied her supposed position as the disrupter of the Thompson-Kowalski romance. In some ways Patty was its facilitator as much as its interference. Yet her presence evidenced how even the resolution of this case of lesbian rights was fraught with particular twists. Patty, Karen, and Sharon's union was not only a critique of love as exclusively heterosexual but also a critique of its province within the couple. Even though this outcome was not unlikely in the annals of traumatic brain injuries, its emergence in the context of the struggle to expand the meaning of domestic partnership offered an added challenge to accepted notions of sexuality, disability, family, and marriage.

Sharon was not interviewed for Swallow's celebratory book. No words were provided to understand her feelings about Karen's new lover, about her status as a public figure, about her privilege to live with two caregivers outside a nursing home facility. Did she still make love to Karen? Was she jealous, angry, hurt? Or was she accepting, loving, and grateful? Was she often in pain? In her wheelchair, with her head tilted to the right, her straight, dark, boyish hair and large, closed mouth facing the viewer in the featured photo, Sharon's image spoke a thousand words, but they were words none of us could ever know.

At the turn of the millennium, Karen Thompson, Sharon Kowalski, and Patty Bresser were still living together in Clearwater — a family of affinities and no doubt disaffinities (invisible though they may be) — with economic, physical, emotional, and intellectual connections and disconnections. Sharon had made progress on standing pivot transfers, but her mental disability was about the same. On occasion, the Kowalski family visited Sharon in St. Cloud when she went there for respite care. Although Karen Thompson and the Kowalskis are still not speaking to one another, Sharon's nephew, Michael — the other survivor — was now visiting Sharon at her home in Clearwater whenever he could. The next generation, who had directly shared with Sharon the indiscriminate impact of a drunk driver, was willing to cross a boundary from north to south, from straight to gay, from nephew to aunt; was willing in the name of affection to cross the rough waters of hatred that were churned by an adversarial legal system.

Precedent

In re Guardianship of Sharon Kowalski is a story about law and love, separation and union, struggle and resolution. It narrates different claims of affinity based on categories of identification — parent, daughter, teacher, lover, spouse, judge, doctor, lawyer, writer — the subject positions that we inhabit and maintain whether we want to or not. The law is a method of generalization called upon to adjudicate between the priorities of these affiliations within the social, economic, and geographic variables that configure particular lives. Blindly and objectively, the icon of justice weighs, discriminates, and judges in a manner that often only approximates its own ideals of equality and fairness. The courtroom provides a forum for the articulation of conflicting positions, and judicial decisions, however arbitrary, act as cultural indicators of struggles for versions of justice.

Sharon Kowalski's case did not take place in a vacuum; it emerged within a cultural geography whose history laid a groundwork for its emergence. Minnesota is not only the home of Judge William O. Douglas and Paul Wellstone; it is also the state of our union that boasted the first openly gay man to hold state office — Allen Spear, who joined the Minnesota Senate in 1972 and fought for same-sex rights for twenty-five years before dying in 2000. A few years before Spear joined the state senate, Richard John Baker and James Michael McConnell applied to the clerk of Hennepin County District Court for a marriage license. The Minnesota Supreme Court ruled that there was no denial of equal protection under the law when these two gay men were refused a marriage license, in part because "the institution of marriage is a union of man and woman, uniquely involving the procreation and rearing of children within a family," a concept as old as the Book of Genesis.[5]

Spear and Baker were Thompson and Kowalski's predecessors, Michael Hardwick and Joseph Steffan their contemporaries. In the 1980s and early 1990s, these parallel legal struggles shadowed Sharon Kowalski's, signaling the setbacks that have accompanied the successes of the lesbian and gay rights movement. As the federal courts continued to refuse to overturn archaic sodomy laws or recognize gays and lesbians as an integral part of the armed forces, the state courts in Minnesota resisted acknowledging the validity, and in some cases even the existence, of Sharon and Karen's lesbian love. The secrecy of the closet served as the prison of the gay and lesbian body, the metaphor for passing that allowed courts to ignore and erase same-sex love under the legal conclusion of a lack of evidence. Sharon was silenced by a legal judgment of incapacity; Karen was silenced, paradoxically, by her outspokenness. Karen asked and told, and as a result her love for Sharon was legally dismissed and made conditional; she was reduced to the tenuous subject position of roommate — or closetmate.

But about the same time that Donald and Della Kowalski were running out of money and patience in their fight to keep their daughter at home, Nina Baehr and Genora Dancel applied for a marriage license with the Hawaii Department of Health. Their case would lead to a judicial decision that the refusal to allow same-sex couples the rights associated with marriage was unconstitutional under Hawaii law. This bow shot from the Hawaii Supreme Court in 1993 set the stage for a series of legal actions and reactions that have characterized the tumultuous course of the struggle for lesbian and gay civil rights. In spite of the passage of federal and state Defense of Marriage Acts, the governor of Vermont in July 2000 signed a "civil union" law allowing gays and lesbians to obtain many of the benefits and burdens conferred by a state marriage license. His signature coincided with a decision from the United States Supreme Court that the Boy Scouts of America, because they are a private group that seeks to instill its moral values in boys, was free to bar those whose lifestyle conflicts with its message, including James Dale, a gay Eagle Scout

Karen Thompson and Sharon Kowalski's legal struggle, at once more personal, local, and heartrending than those of Hardwick or Dale, found itself making headlines in the midst of these successes and failures in the last three decades. Thompson's perseverance, itself a model for making justice, has become both legal and political precedent for the equality and respect that gays and lesbians insist upon receiving from intransigent institutions — law, medicine, religion, media, government. Karen's own intransigence made her struggle more difficult on a personal level, but ironically that stridency heightened the drama of a romance that captured the imagination of a country reeling from the domestic complications and tragedy of AIDS.

The guardianship of Sharon Kowalski acts as a metaphor for the stewardship of a political and social struggle for legal rights, whether those be health benefits for same-sex partners, employment discrimination laws, or hate crimes statutes. Unless the lesbian and gay community states its preference out loud in every venue, it will continue as a ward of a state that depends on that community's incapacity and confines that queer ward in a closet. While living in the Leisure Hills of secrecy may avoid conflict and produce a shared code of discretion and insidership, it is built on a foundation of intolerance and fear that Sharon's traumatic accident has exposed and undermined. In spite of this state-sanctioned and internalized inertia, the best interests of the gay and lesbian community continue to call for more outings, more mobility, more independent living.

Lesbians and gays must get out more in every geography, not passing as assimilated and normal humans, not just fleeing to the havens of urban ghettos, but also celebrating their own cultural and social heritage of same-sex love while demanding freedom from state-sanctioned intolerance. The struggle for a queer-accessible world involves not only filing lawsuits like those of Karen Thompson and James Dale but also building social and cultural bridges through acts as simple as introducing partners or holding hands on Main Street. Karen Thompson has spoken often of the price of silence; we need now to recognize the benefits of speaking out.

Remaking Justice

In response to the murder of Matthew Shephard in 1998, together with threats by Montana legislators to cut funding for the university if a proposed class called "Queer Stories" took place, a group of teachers, staff, and graduate students at the University of Montana met to form a response. The Outfield Alliance was created — a coalition of GLBT faculty, staff, graduate students, and their supporters, whose goals were to promote queer studies, civil rights, and acceptance of lesbians and gays on and off campus. By the fall of 1999, Outfield meetings usually consisted of seven or eight of us gathering in a classroom at five in the evening. The decision to seek health insurance for same-sex domestic partners was made unanimously, though the single members of our group must have felt somewhat de-emphasized. My work on Sharon Kowalski's case made me realize how important the issue was. Had Sharon been able to pay into Karen's health insurance plan at St. Cloud State University in the 1980s, had they signed a joint declaration stating that they were living together in a long-term committed relationship, such an affidavit would have provided evidence of partnership between them that the courts refused to recognize.

Our research showed that many other universities (even North Dakota) and corporations (even Kodak) had extended the benefits with little or no cost. We did discover, however, since health benefits were provided to the entire university system in Montana, that the Inter-Unit Benefits Committee of the Office of the Commissioner of Higher Education would have to recommend the change, and the board of regents would have to approve it. In a state like Montana, that glitch made a difference. Getting the approval of the university community at Missoula was one thing; getting the approval of the statewide board of regents, we knew, would be another, especially with a commissioner of higher education notorious for sympathizing with right-wing legislators.

After developing a packet that addressed frequently asked questions (premature babies cost up to a million, the average AIDS case $200,000), we drafted a proposal, using a declaration of domestic partnership based on one used at the University of Minnesota, which provided health benefits to same-sex domestic partners who held joint assets, residence, and a commitment to living together. The proposal asked that "qualified same-sex domestic partners" receive the same health benefits as their heterosexual counterparts in order to avoid discrimination, attract and keep the best employees, and foster an atmosphere of tolerance for all employees. At first we met with success. After we explained to union members that unmarried heterosexual couples, who were not included in the proposal, at least had the option of marrying, which we did not, the executive board endorsed the proposal unanimously. In the faculty senate, the proposal was sponsored by two of my straight colleagues, who spoke of their lesbian and gay friends and their desire to work in an environment of acceptance. At the meeting of the Associated Students of the University of Montana, I heard testimony from student senators about prejudice and cruelty against gays in high schools, of uncles who had AIDS. These groups endorsed the proposal overwhelmingly. Even the regents' own advisory board, the Inter-Unit Benefits Committee, endorsed it twenty to one, leaving it up to the commissioner to determine the political ramifications of the coverage.

My new partner and I had mixed feelings about the proposal. What about universal health care? What about single gays and lesbians? Did the proposal cover same-sex partners living together who were not gay and lesbian? Was this proposal a first step toward same-sex marriage, toward assimilation of the gay community into the norms of heterosexual society? I thought of a quotation by Pat Califia I had run across: "I can fight for gay marriage if that fight is about making straight people recognize queer love and devotion. I can't fight for it if it's about passing. . . . Identifying with the oppressor is a great temptation: Homogenize, blend in, cut off whatever makes the majority uncomfortable, and you'll be safe. This is the false promise that is always held out to minorities. Until it's safe to be different, we will have no real freedom — no genuine equality" (*Out*, July 1999, 41). Polemical though Califia was, this quotation spoke to some of the misgivings I had about our campaign for equality, which was often confused with sameness.

There was, however, something pleasantly Socratic about the pursuit of our goal, something in-your-face that made the push worthwhile, something exciting about the activism Karen Thompson had modeled. We were circulating petitions at union meetings, at the law school, in the hallways; we were getting press coverage; we were making those who thought we were deviant or nonexistent or unnatural feel uncomfortable and often times ridiculous in their pronouncements about the decline and fall of American civilization.

On Friday, February 25, 2000, I rode my bicycle home from my office in the liberal arts building on the University of Montana campus. My partner, David, a high school Spanish teacher and faculty adviser for the school's Gay Straight Alliance, was already home. He told me that the television news wanted to interview us about the commissioner of higher education's announcement that he had rejected the Proposal for Same-Sex Domestic Partner Health Benefits. Dick Crofts had stated he rejected the proposal for political reasons; for one, the Christian Coalition had targeted it. Camera-ready in the backyard, David and I told the reporter we were not surprised, given the notoriety of the commissioner. We would appeal to the board of regents as a next step, though we held out little hope of a different decision from the board, which was, in our estimation, a lapdog for the commissioner. Eventually we would probably have to go to court, I continued, stating there was some precedent for the recognition of same-sex partnership in domestic relations from other states like Minnesota. The *Kowalski* case, though not precedent in Montana, stood for the proposition that same-sex families deserve respect and legal protection, including, arguably, the right to avail themselves of the same compensation package as heterosexual families.

The reporter seemed more interested in filming us as we threw the stick for our dog than discussing the commissioner's decision or collateral precedent. He wanted to put a face on a same-sex domestic partnership. We were supposed to be just like everybody else: a middle-class suburban household with one dog in the yard and a garden full of delphiniums. "They're just like you," was the reporter's angle. We weren't just like them, of course, and we weren't just like Karen and Sharon, but we were refusing to be discriminated against because of our difference; we were demanding equal treatment by the law.

"Benefits for Gay Partners Denied," the front-page headline in the *Missoulian* read on Saturday, May 20, 2000. Michael Jamison reported on the board of regents meeting at Flathead Valley Community College in Kalispell, north of Missoula, where I had argued the appeal after driving to the junior college in the rain. School was out for summer, so there were only a few cars in the parking lot of the single-story campus on the outskirts of the old logging town turned right-wing enclave adjacent to Glacier National Park. Could it have been Hibbing? Except for administrators, union representatives, student supporters, and reporters who attended the two-day board meeting, the school was abandoned, especially when I arrived at eight in the evening.

Although not particularly sanguine about the outcome of the appeal, I was not prepared for the virulent outcry against the proposal. There seemed to be three camps in the neon-lit classroom where the board sat in a makeshift square with microphones. The first included myself and the students from the University of Montana who were in favor of the appeal. The second was a group of bureaucrats — university presidents and their financial advisers in gray and blue suits — there to report on their campus's activities to the board. In the hushed tones of a one-on-one political huddle, many of them quietly voiced their private support to me after the hearing; publicly, however, they remained silent. The third was the Christian Coalition, which showed up en masse after I testified — with Bibles and Exodus pamphlets. There were about twelve of them — three of them elected officials — and they marched in at the commissioner's cue.

Jamison summarized the discussion in his article. "According to Charles, more than 160 American universities now extend benefits to same-sex partners, including many in the Pacific Northwest." The proposal would promote equality, diversity, and tolerance, "which are cornerstones of a university education. Fairness requires that the university system not discriminate against employees on the basis of the gender of their partners, he said." On the other side, the article noted, "Julie Millam, executive director of the Christian Coalition of Montana, warned against the dangers of accepting unnatural relationships that could include 'any imaginable combination of people.'" Millam, he reported, said homosexuality was a perversion and as such should not be a state-sponsored activity. She wondered if the regents would extend partner coverage to the "guy who wants to marry his horse." Sexual revolutions, the Christians argued, had resulted in societal collapse and chaos, and so should be resisted rather than encouraged by the educational system. Scott Orr, a Republican legislator from Libby, said that in God's eyes, homosexuality is no different than lying, cheating, adultery, or murder.

In the end, Jamison wrote, "many regents said the testimony of proponents and opponents had little to do with their unanimous decision [to uphold the commissioner's rejection of the benefits proposal]. Instead, they said during a break after the vote, the financially strapped university system simply could not afford to put any more people on benefit rolls" (*Missoulian*, May 20, 2000, sec. A, p. 1). Ironically, the regents' own consultants stated that the coverage might make the insurance plan more solvent because of the increased premiums from lesbians, who were traditionally one of the healthiest of demographic groups. Of course, an occasional lesbian or gay man did have an accident, but drunk drivers did not discriminate in the way insurers did, and in the event tragedy did befall us indiscriminately, we did not deserve to be separated from or unable to provide for those we loved because of social assumptions about affinity. The board members used financial woes to hide behind their combination of homophobia and fear of political reprisal from a reactionary legislature. At least the Christian Coalition was able to call us names; the bureaucrats on the board were unwilling to acknowledge our existence as anything but a financial drain. Karen Thompson spent ten years seeking to gain guardianship of her disabled lover, some had also argued, because of her desire for money.

On July 21, 2000, I received a phone call from Holly Franz, the lawyer in Helena who had been lead counsel in the case that had overturned Montana's sexual deviancy code in 1996 and who had helped write the appeal to the board of regents. She told me the Gay and Lesbian Project of the ACLU had agreed to file suit on our behalf. On February 4, 2002, plaintiffs from the Outfield Alliance sued the Board of Regents of the University of Montana for denial of equal protection under the law. Four days later, after receiving threats in the mail, plaintiffs Carla Grayson, Adrienne Neff, and their son narrowly escaped from their home in the middle of the night after an arsonist set fire to their house. The hate crime is still under investigation.

Notes

Introduction: Making Justice

1. The Kowalski case is treated in Marc A. Fajer, *Can Two Real Men Eat Quiche Together? Storytelling, Gender-Role Stereotypes, and Legal Protection for Lesbians and Gay Men*, 46 University of Miami Law Review 511, 577 (1992); Ruthann Robson, *Lesbian (Out)law: Survival Under the Rule of Law* (Ithaca, N.Y.: Firebrand Books, 1992), 117–21; Robson, *Gay Men, Lesbians, and the Law* (New York: Chelsea House, 1997), 69–72; Casey Charles, "Making Justice: Same-Sex Partnership in the Kowalski Case," *disClosure: A Journal of Social Policy* 6 (1997): 9–34; Arthur S. Leonard, *Chronicling a Movement: 20 Years of Lesbian/Gay Law Notes*, 17 New York Law School Journal of Human Rights 415, 454–56 (2000); Joyce Murdoch and Deb Price, *Courting Justice: Gay Men and Lesbians v. the Supreme Court* (New York: Basic Books, 2001), 260–70.

2. Though critical legal studies represents a vast area of theoretical inquiry, one of its accomplishments is an introduction of tenets of deconstruction and cultural materialism into traditional notions of the objectivity of justice. For an introduction to critical legal studies, see Roberto Mangabeira Unger, *The Critical Legal Studies Movement* (Cambridge, Mass.: Harvard University Press, 1986); Jerry Leonard, ed., *Legal Studies as Cultural Studies: A Reader in (Post)Modern Critical Theory* (Albany: State University of New York Press, 1995); Peter Goodrich, *Legal Discourse: Studies in Linguistics, Rhetoric and Legal Analysis* (New York: St. Martin's, 1987).

3. For critiques of legal objectivity, see Iris Marion Young, *Justice and the Politics of Difference* (Princeton, N.J.: Princeton University Press, 1990); Samuel Weber, "In the Name of the Law," in *Deconstruction and the Possibility of Justice,* ed. Drucilla Cornell, Michel Rosenfeld, and D. G. Carlson (New York: Routledge, 1992); Deborah Rhode, *Justice and Gender* (Cambridge, Mass.: Harvard University Press, 1989); Michael Sandel, *Liberalism and the Limits of Justice* (Cambridge: Cambridge University Press, 1982).

4. The structure of this book is indebted to Michel Foucault's notion of the archive as "systems that establish statements as events" or the laws by which "enunciability" occurs (Michel Foucault, *The Archaeology of Knowledge,* trans. A. M. Sheridan-Smith [New York: Pantheon 1972] 128–29). Statements about lesbians and gays emerge within the context and modes of certain discourses or fields of knowledge (law, medicine, personal testimony, journalism). In this account I present texts of these discourses in relation to events surrounding the Kowalski case.

5. For discussions of law and narrative, see Paul Gewirtz, "Narrative and Rhetoric

in the Law," *Law's Stories: Narrative and Rhetoric in the Law* (New Haven, Conn.: Yale University Press, 1996); Richard Delgado, *Storytelling for Oppositionists and Others: A Plea for Narrative*, 87 Michigan Law Review 2411 (1989); Mari J. Matsuda, *Looking to the Bottom: Critical Legal Studies and Reparations*, 22 Harvard Law Review 323 (1987).

6. Judith Butler, *Gender Trouble: Feminism and the Subversion of Identity* (New York: Routledge, 1990), ix.

7. Patricia J. Williams, *The Alchemy of Race and Rights* (Cambridge, Mass.: Harvard University Press, 1992); see also Peter Goodrich, *Oedipus Lex: Psychology, History, Law: Philosophy, Social Theory, and the Rule of Law* (Berkeley: University of California Press, 1995). For autoethnography within the context of other academic discourse, see, for example, Frederick C. Corey and Thomas K. Nakayama, "Sextet," *Text and Performance Quarterly* 17 (1997): 58–68.

8. Foucault, *Archaeology*, 21.

9. For accounts of the lesbian and gay political struggle, see John D'Emilio, *Sexual Politics, Sexual Communities: The Making of a Homosexual Minority in the United States, 1940–1970* (Chicago: University of Chicago Press, 1983); Mark Blasius, *Gay and Lesbian Politics* (Philadelphia: Temple University Press, 1994); Barry Adam, *The Rise of a Gay and Lesbian Movement* (New York: Twayne, 1995); James W. Button, Barbara A. Rienzo, and Kenneth D. Wald, *Private Lives, Public Conflicts: Battles over Gay Rights in American Communities* (Washington, D.C.: Congressional Quarterly Press, 1997); Diane Helene Miller, *Freedom to Differ: The Shaping of the Gay and Lesbian Struggle for Civil Rights* (New York: New York University Press, 1998); Dudley Clendinen and Adam Nagourney, *Out for Good: The Struggle to Build a Gay Rights Movement in America* (New York: Simon and Schuster, 1999); Ellen D. B. Riggle and Barry L. Tadlock, eds., *Public Policy, Public Opinion, and Political Representation* (New York: Columbia University Press, 1999); Craig A. Rimmerman, Kenneth D. Wald, and Clyde Wilcox, eds., *The Politics of Gay Rights* (Chicago: University of Chicago Press, 2000); John D'Emilio, William B. Turner, and Urvashi Vaid, eds., *Creating Change: Sexuality, Public Policy, and Civil Rights* (New York: St. Martin's, 2000); Mary Bernstein and Renate Reimann, *Queer Families, Queer Politics: Challenging Culture and the State* (New York: Columbia University Press, 2001).

10. For the right to privacy in relation to lesbians and gays, see David Link, *The Tie That Binds: Recognizing Privacy and the Family Commitments of Same-Sex Couples*, 23 Loyola L.A. Law Review 1055 (1990); Kendall Thomas, *Beyond the Privacy Principle*, 92 Columbia Law Review 1413 (1992).

11. Eve Kosofsky Sedgwick, *Epistemology of the Closet* (Berkeley: University of California Press, 1990), 67.

12. Scott Tucker, "Our Right to the World," *Body Politic*, July/August 1982, 32, quoted in Larry Gross, *Contested Closets: The Politics of Ethics and Outing* (Minneapolis: University of Minnesota Press, 1993), 148. Gross discusses the *Kowalski* case at 148–49.

13. Michael W. McCann, *Rights at Work: Pay Equity Reform and the Politics of Legal Mobilization* (Chicago: University of Chicago Press, 1994), 283. Frances Zeman's

"Legal Mobilization: The Neglected Role of Law in the Political System," *American Political Science Review* 77 (1983): 690–703, was published the same year as the Kowalski case began.

14 . Rhonda R. Rivera, review of *Sexual Politics, Sexual Communities: The Making of a Homosexual Minority in the United States, 1940–1970,* by John D'Emilio, 132 University Pennsylvania Law Review 391, 398 (1984). Rivera researches case law that coincides with D'Emilio's history. See also William N. Eskridge, *Gaylaw: Challenging the Apartheid of the Closet* (Cambridge, Mass.: Harvard University Press, 1999), 139. Minnesota actually enacted a sodomy statute in 1977, but the courts repealed it ten years later in *State v Gray,* 413 NW2d 107 (1987).

15. David L. Chambers, "Couples: Marriage, Civil Union, and Domestic Partnership," in *Creating Change,* 288.

16. Clendinen, *Out for Good,* 473.

17. Leonard, *Chronicling a Movement,* 422, includes an entry from *Lesbian/Gay Law Notes,* a monthly digest, from September 1983, announcing AIDS law as a growing field of litigation.

18. Michel Foucault, *The History of Sexuality: Volume I: An Introduction,* trans. Robert Hurley (New York: Vintage, 1980) 92.

19. David A. J. Richards, *Identity and the Case for Gay Rights: Race, Gender, Religion as Analogies* (Chicago: University of Chicago Press, 1999), and his *Women, Gays and the Constitution: The Grounds for Feminism and Gay Rights in Culture and Law* (Chicago: University of Chicago Press, 1998).

20. Murdoch and Price, *Courting Justice,* 269.

21. For a more sober view of the movement's accomplishments, see the "Opening Remarks" in *Gay Rights as Human Rights,* 64 Albany Law Review 893–1019 [2001]).

22. William B. Rubinstein, ed., *Lesbians, Gay Men, and the Law* (New York: Free Press, 1993) (a casebook that includes the last *Kowalski* appeal); Alba Conte, *Sexual Orientation and Legal Rights* (New York: Wiley, 1998), is an updated digest. See also Arthur S. Leonard, ed., *Homosexuality and the Constitution* (New York: Garland, 1997); Nan D. Hunter, Sherryl E. Michaelson, and Thomas B. Stoddard, *The Rights of Lesbians and Gay Men: A Basic ACLU Guide to a Gay Person's Rights* (Carbondale: Southern Illinois University Press, 1992). *Lesbian/Gay Law Notes* is an essential monthly digest. A sampling of law review articles includes Fajer, *Storytelling* (1993); Rhonda R. Rivera, *Recent Developments in Sexual Preference Law,* 30 Drake Law Review 311 (1980–81); and Rivera, review of *Sexual Politics, Sexual Communities* (1984); Editors of Harvard Law Review, *Sexual Orientation and the Law* (Cambridge, Mass.: Harvard University Press, 1990); Leonard, *Chronicling a Movement; Gay Rights as Human Rights,* 64 Albany Law Review (2001). Some of the experts in the field include Ruthann Robson, William N. Eskridge Jr., Arthur Leonard, and David A. J. Richards; see Patricia Cain, *Rainbow Rights: The Role of Lawyers and Courts in the Lesbian and Gay Civil Rights Movement* (Boulder, Colo.: Westview, 2000); Tulane University publishes *Law and Sexuality: A Review of Lesbian and Gay Issues.*

23. Editors of Harvard Law Review, *Sexual Orientation,* 8 ff.

24. In *Recent Developments in Sexual Preference Law,* Rivera details military cases in the late 1970s at 319; *Gay Student Services v Texas A.&M. University,* 612 F2d 160 (5th Cir 1980); nonprofit status (Rivera, *Recent Developments in Sexual Preference Law,* 341); lesbian mother cases (Rivera, *Recent Developments in Sexual Preference Law,* 327).

25. 382 NW2d 681 (cert. denied 475 US 1085) (1986); 392NW2d 310 (1986); 478 NW2d 790 (1991).

26. As a signifier of the crime that dare not speak its name, the word "lesbian" is difficult to locate in the case law before the late 1970s (Rivera, *Book Review,* 399, 402). See also Editors of Harvard Law Review, *Sexual Orientation,* 121 ff.

27. Rivera, review of *Sexual Politics, Sexual Communities,* 406, and *Recent Developments in Sexual Preference Law,* 328.

28. Editors of Harvard Law Review, *Sexual Orientation,* 120.

29. Ibid., 121.

30. Ibid., 128 ff.

31. *ACLU Guidebook,* 160.

32. In 1993, NGLTF reported that eleven states had laws that make sexual orientation irrelevant in custody matters; eleven states had laws making gay and lesbian parents unfit for custody, and seventeen statutes making sexual orientation a factor but not a decisive one. See also the famous case of *Bottoms v Bottoms,* 457 SE2d 102 (Virginia Supreme Court 1993), denying a mother custody for active lesbianism.

33. Conte, *Sexual Orientation,* vol. 1, sec. 16.1, p. 593; sec. 16.2 discusses *Kowalski.* See also David L. Chambers, "What If? The Legal Consequences of Marriage and the Legal Needs of Lesbian and Gay Male Couples," in *Queer Families,* 310.

34. Chambers in *Queer Families,* 311.

35. Robson, *Lesbian (Out)law,* 120–21.

36. Hayden Curry et al., *A Legal Guide for Lesbian and Gay Couples,* 10th national ed. (Berkeley: Nolo Press, 1999).

37. For an introduction to the same-sex marriage legal debate, see William N. Eskridge Jr., *The Case for Same-Sex Marriage: From Sexual Liberty to Civilized Commitment* (New York: Free Press, 1996); Andrew Sullivan, ed., *Same-Sex Marriage: Pro and Con* (New York: Vintage, 1997); Michael Warner, *The Trouble with Normal: Sex, Politics, and the Ethics of Queer Life* (New York: Free Press, 1999).

38. The *Baker* case is discussed in Chambers, *Creating Change,* 282.

39. Curry et al., *A Legal Guide,* 1/5.

40. See Button, Rienzo, and Wald, *Private Lives,* 58–100.

41. Cain, *Rainbow Rights,* 257 ff.

42. "California Expands Rights of Domestic Partners," *Lesbian/Gay Law Notes,* November 2001, 1.

43. The domestic partnership story is told in Chambers, *Creating Change,* 299 ff.

44 . Cain, *Rainbow Rights,* 269.

45. One-quarter of corporations with over five hundred employees provide insurance benefits to same-sex domestic partners (Chambers, *Creating Change,* 302).

46. Eskridge, *Gaylaw,* 289.

47. Ibid., Appendix B3—Minnesota Statutes Section 363.021, subds. 2–3.
48. Miller, *Freedom to Differ,* 139.
49. Eskridge, *Gay Law,* 2.

1. Injury

1. For a firsthand account of the events surrounding the accident, see Karen Thompson and Julie Andrzejewski, *Why Can't Sharon Kowalski Come Home?* (San Francisco: Spinsters/Aunt Lute, 1988), 3–17. Thompson's account is an important source for events in the case during the period between 1983 and 1988; other sources include periodicals and court records.

2. Arnold R. Alanen, "Years of Change on the Range," in *Minnesota in a Century of Change: The State and Its People Since 1900,* ed. Clifford E. Clark Jr. (St. Paul: Minnesota Historical Society Press, 1989).

3. For the details of early Iron Range history, see Robert I. Vexler and William F. Swindler, eds., *Chronology and Documentary Handbook of the State of Minnesota* (Dobbs Ferry, N.Y.: Oceana); *The WPA Guide to the Minnesota Arrowhead Country* (St. Paul: Minnesota Historical Society Press, 1988); William E. Lass, *Minnesota: A Bicentennial History* (New York: Norton, 1977); Paul Henry Landis, *Three Iron Mining Towns* (New York: Arno Press, 1970).

4. *WPA Guide,* 110–11.
5. Landis, *Three Iron Mining Towns,* 22.
6. Alanen, "Years of Change."

2. Counsel

1. See Winsor C. Schmidt Jr., *Guardianship: Court of Last Resort for the Elderly and Disabled* (Durham, N.C.: Carolina Academic Press, 1995), 5–7.

3. Guardians

1. State of Minnesota, County of Sherburne, District Court, Probate Division, *In re Guardianship of Sharon Kowalski, Ward,* File No. 4497, Petition for Appointment of Guardian, March 2, 1984, p. 2. Unless otherwise indicated, further references to other official documents of the District Court of Sherburne County, Probate Division, File No. 4497 (*In re Guardianship of Sharon Kowalski*), will be cited by document name, date of filing, and page number where relevant.

2. Copies of Thompson's handwritten letters to Don and Della Kowalski are attached to Responsive Affidavit, Karen Thompson, November 28, 1984. The letters were written in the first months of 1984.

3. Affidavit, Kevin A. Spellacy and Jack Fena, November 2, 1984, p. 1. Angie Workman herself filed an affidavit on November 7, 1984. The conversastion with Karen Thompson took place in February 1984.

4. Judge Bruce R. Douglas, Order Appointing General Guardian of the Person and Estate, May 11, 1984 (filed).

5. Affidavit, Mary Hallberg, June 20, 1984 (physical therapist); Affidavit, Delores Lenner, June 25, 1984 (occupational therapist).

6. Transcript of Proceedings, June 26, 1984, pp. 4–14.

7. Letter from Jack Fena to Thomas D. Hayes, Exhibit C to Notice of Motion and Motion, August 31, 1984.

8. Handwritten Letter of Donald Kowalski to Tom Hayes, Exhibit A to documents filed September 6, 1984.

9. Affidavit, Donald Kowalski and Della Kowalski, Exhibit A to Affidavit of Prejudice, August 31, 1984.

10. Supplemental Affidavit, Della Kowalski, September 6, 1984.

11. Affidavit, Karen Oberrath, September 4, 1984 (date notarized).

12. Affidavit, Deb Hauge, September 5, 1984 (date notarized).

13. Affidavit, Mary Wild, September 9, 1984 (date notarized).

14. This hearing appears in Transcript of Proceedings, September, 13, 1984, pp. 15–101. The balance of the chapter follows the hearing chronologically.

15. A copy of Dr. Goff's report and letter, which includes the Polinsky report and earlier medical records in the case, is attached as Appendices, pp. 1–47 to State of Minnesota, Court of Appeals, *In re Guardianship of Sharon Kowalski, Ward,* File No. C6-86-176, Respondent Donald Kowalski's Brief and Appendix, March 25, 1986. The Polinsky report is also Exhibit 9 to Transcript of Proceedings, October 18, 1984.

16. George M. Cowan, M.D., medical report of October 15, 1984, in Respondent Donald Kowalski's Brief and Appendix, p. 37. It is also attached as Exhibit 9A to Transcript of Proceedings, October 18, 1984.

17. Linda Prout's statement is reproduced in *Why Can't,* 70. It is also an affidavit filed in Sherburne County, District Court, Probate Division, File No. 4497, November 28, 1984.

18. Affidavit, Theophanis Hortis, November 28, 1984.

19. Affidavit, Judy Belcastro, October 16, 1984 (notarized).

20. Affidavit, Joan Thralow, October 1984.

21. Kathy Sim's affidavit is cited in *Why Can't,* 60.

22. Affidavit, Karen Wright Tomberlin, August 1984.

23. Transcript of Proceedings, pp. 102–61.

24. Judge Douglas's findings are quoted in *Why Can't,* 74.

4. Injunction

1. Letter of Jack Fena to WDIO-TV, November 4, 1984 (filed in the Sherburne County District Court).

2. Affidavit, Kevin A. Spellacy, October 30, 1984 (signed), attached as Exhibit A to Application for Temporary Restraining Order, November 2, 1984.

3. Affidavit, Kevin A. Spellacy and Jack Fena, and Exhibits 1–4, November 2, 1984.

4. The affidavit of Thompson and the modified restraining order are reproduced in *Why Can't*, 89–90.

5. Responsive Affidavit, Stephen N. Vincent, November 29, 1984.

6. Responsive Affidavit, Dr. Charles Chmielewski, November 28, 1984.

7. Responsive Affidavit, Gail Romthun, November 28, 1984; Responsive Affidavit, Pat Larson, November 30, 1984, with attached letters of Sharon Kowalski.

8. Responsive Affidavit, Patricia L. Larson, November 28, 1984; Responsive Affidavit, Mary Wild, November 28, 1984.

9. Letter to Judge Douglas from J. [*sic*] King, November 26, 1984.

10. Brief of Amicus Curiae, November 30, 1984. See also *Why Can't*, 101–2.

11. Kim R. Johnson, Order, December 3, 1984.

12. Letter from Ristvedt, December 21, 1984.

13. Report from Dr. Moller, December 20, 1984, is part of a set of exhibits filed with the District Court, Probate Division, County of St. Louis, File No. 11146, when *In re the Guardianship of Sharon Kowalski* changed venue from Sherburne to St. Louis County on June 1, 1987.

14. Karen Thompson's version of the testing event is related in *Why Can't*, 122–24; for the nurses' versions, see Deposition of Ann Pellman, April 24, 1985, and Deposition of Jane Russell, April 24, 1985 (Exhibit 1 to the Deposition contains the nurse's note). The Catherine Anderson report is attached to Affidavit of Elizabeth A. Ristvedt, February 15, 1985.

15. Affidavit, Kathleen T. Wingen and Carla M. Hansen, February 15, 1985.

16. Letter from Jack Fena along with newspaper clippings, April 5, 1985.

17. *Baehr v Lewin*, 852 P2d 44 (Hawaii Supreme Court 1993).

18. *Congressional Record*, 1996, vol. 142, S10101.

19. *Congressional Record*, 1996, vol. 142, H7496.

5. Hearing

1. Affidavit, Kathleen T. Wingen and Carla M. Hansen, February 15, 1984.

2. Deposition of Karen Thompson, April 22, 1985, pp. 24–25, 44, 47, 74–75.

3. Transcript of Proceedings, May 5, 1985, pp. 166–317, at 166. Page numbers of further testimony in this chapter will refer to the proceeding transcript for May 5.

4. Examination of Debbie DiIorio, Transcript of Proceedings, pp. 170–204.

5. Transcript of Proceedings, pp. 186–90.

6. Transcript of Proceedings, pp. 193–94.

7. Transcript of Proceedings, pp. 200–2.

8. Examination of Dr. George Cowan, Transcript of Proceedings, pp. 204–28, at 206.

9. Transcript of Proceedings, pp. 208–13.

10. Transcript of Proceedings, p. 215.

11. Transcript of Proceedings, pp. 218–20.

12. The APA deleted homosexuality from the *Diagnostic and Statistical Manual of Mental Disorders* in 1973, and in 1975 the American Psychological Association resolved that homosexuality per se implies no impairment of reliability or general social and vocational capabilities.

13. Transcript of Proceedings, pp. 221–25.

14. Examination of Donald Kowalski, Transcript of Proceedings, pp. 231–66.

15. Transcript of Proceedings, pp. 232–38.

16. Transcript of Proceedings, pp. 247–51.

17. Transcript of Proceedings, pp. 264–65.

18. Deposition of Mary Kay Hewitt, April 24, 1985.

19. Deposition of Bruce Erickson, April 24, 1985.

20. Affidavit, Joan Shelhon, May 3, 1985.

6. Continued Hearing

1. Attachment to Deposition of Karen Thompson, April 22, 1985.

2. Examination of Dr. Gail Gregor, Transcript of Proceedings, May 3, 1985, pp. 267–97, 270.

3. Transcript of Proceedings, pp. 273–75.

4. Transcript of Proceedings, p. 276.

5. Transcript of Proceedings, pp. 281–83.

6. Transcript of Proceedings, pp. 283-85.

7. Transcript of Proceedings, pp. 289–91.

8. Examination of Karen Thompson, Transcript of Proceedings, pp. 299–371, 299.

9. Transcript of Proceedings, pp. 305–9.

10. Transcript of Proceedings, May 9, 1985, pp. 321-23.

11. Transcript of Proceedings, pp. 326–27.

12. Transcript of Proceedings, pp. 346–47.

13. Transcript of Proceedings, pp. 354–55, 359.

14. Transcript of Proceedings, pp. 361–63.

15. Reports of Dr. Goff and Dr. Moller became Guardian's Exhibits 7 and 8 to Transcript of Proceedings, May 9, 1985.

16. Transcript of Proceedings, pp. 367–70.

17. Affidavit, Donald Kowalski, May 7, 1985.

18. Affidavit, Kenneth Krossen, May 7, 1985.

19. Affidavit, Dr. Gail Gregor, June 14, 1985.

20. Deposition of Dr. J. C. Moller, June 3, 1985.

21. Deposition of Dr. Stephen K. Goff, probably also taken on June 3, 1985. Goff"s deposition is quoted in *Why Can't*, 150.

22. Final argument, Beth Ristvedt, June 17, 1985.

23. Letter from Bromberg, June 14, 1985.

24. The press release comes from the records of the Office of Deborah Chasnoff, San Francisco, California. The committee is discussed in *Why Can't*, 116.

25. Judge Bruce R. Douglas, Order Confirming Appointment of Guardian of the Person and Estate and Other Matters, July 23, 1985.

7. Appeal

1. The "Times Poll" was published in "Parents Should Get Custody of Disabled Adult, 49% Report," *St. Cloud Times*, September 23, 1985, sec. C, p. 1. For the letter to the editor, see Paul Reichert, "Poll Question Distorted Facts of Custody Battle," *St. Cloud Times*, September 30, 1985.

2. Progress notes of the nurses at Leisure Hills in Hibbing, Minnesota, August 14, 1985. These documents were produced for Karen Thompson's attorney, Sue Wilson, and are referred to in the deposition of Dr. William L. Wilson on October 7, 1985.

3. Letter of Dr. William Wilson to Jack Fena, August 20, 1985, attached as Exhibit 1 to the Deposition of William L. Wilson, October 7, 1985.

4. Affidavit, Donald Kowalski, August 12, 1985 (notarized).

5. State of Minnesota, Court of Appeals, Order, *In re Guardianship of Sharon Kowalski, Ward*, File Nos. C1-85-1502, C2-85-1590, C1-85-1595, September 17, 1985.

6. State of Minnesota, Supreme Court, Order, *In re Guardianship of Sharon Kowalski, Ward*, File Nos. C1-85-1502, C2-85-1590, C1-85-1595, and C5-85-1664; November 4, 1985; State of Minnesota, Supreme Court, Order, *In re Guardianship of Sharon Kowalski, Ward*, File No. C1-85-1502, November 25, 1985; United States Supreme Court, *In re Guardianship of Sharon Kowalski, Ward*, cert. denied, March 24, 1986.

7. The Minnesota *Civil Liberties Union* article is quoted in *Why Can't*, 172–73, as is the *Ms.* piece (Jeann Linsley, "A Right to Care," *Ms.*, September 19, 1985, 19).

8. Deposition of Dr. William L. Wilson, October 7, 1985, pp. 1–6.

9. Deposition of Dr. William L. Wilson, pp. 31–34.

10. Deposition of Dr. William L. Wilson, pp. 77–82.

11. State of Minnesota, Court of Appeals, *In re Guardianship of Sharon Kowalski, Ward*, File No. C1-85-1595, Chief Judge, Peter S. Popovich, Order, October 11, 1985.

12. State of Minnesota, Sherburne County, District Court, Probate Division, *In re Sharon Kowalski, Ward*, File No. 4497, M. Sue Wilson, Notice of Motion and Motion, December 3, 1985.

13. Affidavit, Jack Fena, December 26, 1985 (notarized).

14. Affidavit, Donald Kowalski, December 27, 1985 (notarized); probably filed December 31, 1985.

15. Transcript of Proceedings, File No. 4497, December 20, 1985, pp. 1–9.

16. Transcript of Proceedings, December 20, 1985, pp. 14–18.

17. Transcript of Proceedings, December 20, 1985, pp. 25–30.

18. Judge Kim R. Johnson, Order, January 3, 1986.

19. State of Minnesota, Court of Appeals, *In re Guardianship of Sharon Kowalski, Ward*, Respondent Donald Kowalsk's Brief and Appendix, File No. C6-86-176, March 25, 1986, pp. 4–5.

20. Court of Appeals, File No. C6-86-176, Respondent's Brief, pp. 8, 11, 24.

21. State of Minnesota, Court of Appeals, File No. C6-86-176, *In re Guardianship of Sharon Kowalski, Ward*, M. Sue Wilson, Letter, February 26, 1986, pp. 5–6.

22. Court of Appeals, File No. C6-86-176, Sue Wilson, Letter, February 26, 1986, pp. 10–11.

23. State of Minnesota, Court of Appeals, File No. C1-85-1595, *In re Guardianship of Sharon Kowalski, Ward*, Brief of Amicus Curiae, Minnesota Civil Liberties Union, November 11, 1985 (signed), p. 13.

24. Court of Appeals, File No. C1-85-1595, Brief of Minnesota Civil Liberties Union, p. 4.

25. State of Minnesota, Court of Appeals, File No. 01-85-1995, *In re Guardianship of Sharon Kowalski, Ward*, Karen Thompson's Brief, November 18, 1985 (signed), pp. 21–24.

26. This is the appeal from the July 23, 1985, order of Judge Bruce R. Douglas, appointing Donald Kowalski guardian (District Court File No. 4497). *In re Guardianship of Sharon Kowalski, Ward*, 382 NW2d 861 (Minn App 1986) (cert denied March 24, 1986 [See 106 S.Ct. 1467], review denied April 18, 1986) is Appellate Court File No. C1-85-1595.

27. 382 NW2d 861, 863–64.

28. 382 NW2d 861, 865.

29. 382 NW2d 861, 865.

30. 382 NW2d 861, 867.

31. Judith Butler, *Excitable Speech: A Politics of the Performative* (New York: Routledge, 1997), 121.

8. Publicity

1. This is the appeal from Judge Kim R. Johnson's January 3, 1986, order (District Court, File No. 4497), which became Appeals Court File No. C6-86-176 (*In re Guardianship of Sharon Kowalski, Ward*, 392 NW2d 310 [Minn App 1986] [review denied October 17, 1986]).

2. 392 NW2d 310, 311.

3. 392 NW2d 310, 313.

4. 392 NW2d 310, 313–14.

5. Ann Phibbs, "Karen Thompson Talks About the Battle to Care for Her Lover: Coming Out to Save a Life," *GCN*, August 1986 (the interview was conducted on July 27, 1986, when Karen Thompson began her first speaking tours).

9. Petition

1. *In re Guardianship of Sharon Kowalski, Ward,* changed venue from Sherburne County to St. Louis County District Court by order of the Sherburne County District Court on May 11, 1987. St. Louis County District Court, Probate Division, File No. P4-87-11146, received the Petition for an Order Restoring Sharon Kowalski to Capacity and Other Relief on September 16, 1987. Unless otherwise indicated, the remainder of the chapters refer to this file number when citing affidavits, letters, transcripts of proceedings, and other documents.

2. M. Sue Wilson, Memorandum of Law, November 16, 1987.

3. Jack Fena, Momorandum of Law, November 13, 1987. The attachments to Fena's Memorandum (Exhibits A through S) present a documentary history of the appeals in the case.

4. Affidavit, Jack Fena, November 13, 1987; Affidavit, Harry A. Sieben, November 13, 1987.

5. Letter, Dr. William Wilson, November 2, 1987, attached to Affidavit, Jack Fena, November 13, 1987.

6. Transcript of Proceedings, November 18, 1987.

7. Transcript of Proceedings, November 18, 1987, pp. 23–38 (Fena's Argument).

8. Transcript of Proceedings, November 18, 1987, p. 33.

9. Transcript of Proceedings, November 18, 1987, pp. 35–36.

10. Transcript of Proceedings, November 18, 1987, pp. 45-46.

11. Partial Transcript Only, February 5, 1988, pp. 6-9.

12. Partial Transcript Only, February 5, 1988, pp. 8-9.

13. Partial Transcript Only, February 5, 1988, p. 14.

14. Judge R. V. Campbell, Order, July 6, 1988.

15. State of Minnesota, County of Mille Lacs, District Court, Personal Injury, *Sharon Kowalski and others v D. J. Enterprises and others,* File No. C3-84-843, Order Approving Settlement and Distribution, July 19, 1988.

16. Letter, Jack Fena, August 18, 1988 (signed). This document is probably part of Notice of Motion and Motion, August 22, 1988.

17. Affidavit, William L. Wilson, December 29, 1989 (notarized).

18. Letter from Human Rights Campaign by Karen Thompson, 1989. The letter is part of the documents on the Sharon Kowalski case at the One Institute in Los Angeles, California.

10. New Trial

1. "Bitter Quarrel—Test of Love," *West 57th Street,* CBS News, February 25, 1989 (videotape).

2. Medical Reports from 1988, filed June 7, 1989 (miscited in the District Court

Receipt as 1988). The report is also quoted in John Ritter, "Kowalski Moved; Father Resigns as Guardian," *Equal Time,* July 5, 1989, p. 1.

3. Judge R. V. Campbell, Order, June 21, 1989.

4. State of Minnesota, Court of Appeals, *Star Tribune v Honorable R. V. Campbell,* File No. C2-91-1047, Order, July 11, 1989.

5. News Releases, National Organization for Women, Washington, D.C., July 12, 1990, and August 1, 1990. These documents are part of the archives of the One Institute, Los Angeles, California, on Sharon Kowalski. See also "NOW Conference Honors Karen and Sharon; Passes Resolution Against Outing," *Equal Time,* August 3, 1990, p. 1.

6. I have changed the name of this person to protect her anonymity, as requested in an interview. Issues of outing and privacy remain extant in this retelling.

7. Letter, Fred T. Friedman, August 16, 1990.

8. Affidavit, Karen Tomberlin, August 15, 1990.

9. Peter J. Nickitas, Memorandum to Judge Campbell, October 19, 1990.

10. Deposition, [Rose Jones], November 2, 1990.

11. Deposition, November 2, 1990, pp. 9–11.

12. Deposition, November 2, 1990, pp. 13, 23, 31.

13. Deposition, Karen Rae Wright Tomberlin, November 2, 1990, pp. 7–9, 13.

14. Deposition, Karen Rae Wright Tomberlin, November 2, 1990, pp. 21–22.

15. Transcript of Proceedings, vol. 1, November 8, 1990, pp. 7–9.

16. Transcript of Proceedings, vol. 1, November 8, 1990, Examination of Dr. Matthew Eckman, pp. 10–46, 18–25.

17. Transcript of Proceedings, vol. 1, November 8, 1990, p. 22.

18. Transcript of Proceedings, vol. 1, November 8, 1990, Examination of Dorothy Rappel, pp. 46–69, at 49–54.

19. Transcript of Proceedings, vol. 1, November 8, 1990, pp. 63–69.

20. Transcript of Proceedings, vol. 1, November 8, 1990, Examination of Rachael Komarek, pp. 69–89, 73–80.

21. Transcript of Proceedings, vol. 1, November 8, 1990, Re-examination of Dorothy Rappel, pp. 89–100.

22. Notice of Motion in Limine, Memorandum and Consent, December 3, 1990.

23. Transcript of Proceedings, vol. 1, December 5, 1990, pp. 126–29.

24. Transcript of Proceedings, vol. 1, December 5, 1990, pp. 129–38.

25. Transcript of Proceedings, vol. 1, December 5, 1990, Examination of Mary Anne Connell, pp. 139–51.

26. Transcript of Proceedings, vol. 1, December 5, 1990, p. 151.

27. Transcript of Proceedings, vol. 1, December 5, 1990, Examination of Kathy King, pp. 151–71.

28. Transcript of Proceedings, vol. 1, December 5, 1990, Examination of Anita Johnson, pp. 179–87, 186–87.

29. Transcript of Proceedings, vol. 1, December 5, 1990, Examination of Jackie Nelson, pp. 188–202, 194–95.

30. Transcript of Proceedings, vol. 1, December 5, 1990, Examination of Jennette Adamski, pp. 203–31, 214–18.

31. Transcript of Proceedings, vol. 1, December 5, 1990, Examination of Margaret Grahek, pp. 269–84.

32. Transcript of Proceedings, vol. 2, December 6, 1990, Examination of Dr. Gail Gregor, pp. 290–388, 294–95.

33. Transcript of Proceedings, vol. 2, December 6, 1990, pp. 296–302.

34. Transcript of Proceedings, vol. 2, December 6, 1990, pp. 304–5.

35. Transcript of Proceedings, vol. 2, December 6, 1990, p. 310.

36. Transcript of Proceedings, vol. 2, December 6, 1990, pp. 321–22, 355–56.

37. Transcript of Proceedings, vol. 2, December 6, 1990, pp. 376–81.

38. Transcript of Proceedings, vol. 2, December 6, 1990, pp. 383–88.

39. Transcript of Proceedings, vol. 2, December 6, 1990, Examination of Karen Thompson, pp. 389–416, 403–5. Karen Thompson's examination was continued at 456–508, moving into Transcript of Proceedings for December 7, 1990.

40. Transcript of Proceedings, vol. 2, December 6, 1990, pp. 404–6.

41. Transcript of Proceedings, vol. 2, December 6, 1990, Examination of Nancy Brennan, pp. 417–47.

42. Transcript of Proceedings, vol. 2, December 6, 1990, Examination of Karen Thompson Continued, pp. 464–65.

43. Transcript of Proceedings, vol. 2, December 7, 1990, pp. 485–86.

44. Transcript of Proceedings, vol. 2, December 7, 1990, pp. 488–91.

45. Transcript of Proceedings, vol. 2, December 7, 1990, p. 508.

46. Transcript of Proceedings, vol. 2, December 7, 1990, Examination of Dr. Carolyn Herron, pp. 512–29, 525–26.

47. Transcript of Proceedings, vol. 2, December 7, 1990, Examination of Becky Muotka, pp. 531–49.

48. Transcript of Proceedings, vol. 2, December 7, 1990, Examination of [Rose Jones], pp. 551–89, 555.

49. Transcript of Proceedings, vol. 2, December 7, 1990, pp. 565–67.

50. Transcript of Proceedings, vol. 2, December 7, 1990, pp. 578–79.

51. Transcript of Proceedings, vol. 2 , December 7, 1990, Examination of Karen Tomberlin, pp. 589–623, 594–97.

52. Transcript of Proceedings, vol. 2, December 7, 1990, pp. 599–600.

53. Transcript of Proceedings, vol. 2, December 7, 1990, pp. 613–14.

54. Transcript of Proceedings, vol. 2, December 7, 1990, pp. 622–23.

55. Transcript of Proceedings, vol. 2, December 7, 1990, pp. 659–60.

56. Transcript of Proceedings, vol. 2, December 7, 1990, pp. 660–70.

57. Transcript of Proceedings, vol. 3, January 15, 1991, Telephone Conference, pp. 685–98.

58. Transcript of Proceedings, vol. 3, March 22, 1991, Examination of Debra Kowalski, pp. 727–63, 737–42.

59. Transcript of Proceedings, vol. 3, March 22, 1991, pp. 742–43.
60. Transcript of Proceedings, vol. 3, pp. 749–50, 754–56, 759–60.

11. Judgments

1. Judge R. V. Campbell, Order Appointing General Guardian of Person and Estate, April 23, 1991. Further references to this document are made within the text and cite the numbered paragraphs of the order's findings of fact and conclusions of law.

2. The memorandum is attached to the order of April 23, 1991. Further citations within this chapter refer to page numbers.

3. State of Minnesota, Court of Appeals, *In re Guardianship of Sharon Kowalski, Ward*, File No. C2-91-1047, Exhibit A-1 to Reply Brief and Appendix of Appellant Karen Thompson (Letter from Fred Friedman to Judge Wozniak, July 2, 1991).

4. Lambda Legal Defense and Education Fund, Inc., All God's Children Metropolitan Community Church, Friends of AIDS Ministry, Gay and Lesbian Advocates and Defenders, Gay and Lesbian Community Action Council, Minnesota Affirmation/United Methodists, Minnesota Alliance for Progressive Action, Minnesota Democratic Farm Labor Lesbian and Gay Caucus, National Center for Lesbian Rights, National Gay and Lesbian Task Force, National Gay and Lesbian Health Foundation, Parents and Friends of Lesbians and Gays (P-FLAG), Spirit of the Lakes United Church of Christ, Wingspan Ministry of St. Paul/Reformation Lutheran Church.

5. State of Minnesota, Court of Appeals, *In re Guardianship of Sharon Kowalski, Ward*, File No. C2-91-1047, Brief and Appendix of Appellant Karen Thompson, August 5, 1991 (signed). Notice of Appeal of the April 23, 1991, Order (File No. 11146) was filed June 10, 1991.

6. Court of Appeals, Brief of Appellant Karen Thompson, pp. 3–5.

7. Court of Appeals, Brief of Appellant Karen Thompson, pp. 11–12.

8. Court of Appeals, Brief of Appellant Karen Thompson, pp. 21–22.

9. Court of Appeals, Brief of Appellant Karen Thompson, pp. 25–28.

10. Court of Appeals, Brief of Appellant Karen Thompson, pp. 28–29.

11. Court of Appeals, Brief of Appellant Karen Thompson, p. 20.

12. Court of Appeals, Brief of Appellant Karen Thompson, pp. 46–48.

13. State of Minnesota, Court of Appeals, *In re Guardianship of Sharon Kowalski, Ward*, File No. C2-91-1047, Brief of Amici Curiae of National Organization for Women, Inc., and others, August 21, 1991 (signed).

14. Court of Appeals, Brief of National Organization for Women and others, pp. 1–4.

15. Court of Appeals, Brief of National Organization for Women and others, pp. 5–9.

16. Court of Appeals, Brief of National Organization for Women and others, p. 10.

17. State of Minnesota, Court of Appeals, *In re Guardianship of Sharon Kowalski, Ward*, File No. C2-91-1407, Brief of Amici Curiae of Lambda Legal Defense and Education Fund, Inc., and others, August 23, 1991 (signed), pp. 16, 2.

18. Court of Appeals, Brief of Lambda Legal Defense and others, pp. 4–7.

19. Court of Appeals, Brief of Lambda Legal Defense and others, pp. 7–11.

20. Court of Appeals, Brief of Lambda Legal Defense and others, p. 11.

21. Court of Appeals, Brief of Lambda Legal Defense and others, pp. 17–20.

22. State of Minnesota, Court of Appeals, *In re Guardianship of Sharon Kowalski, Ward*, File No. C2-91-1047, Brief of Amicus Curiae of Minnesota Civil Liberties Union, August 5, 1991 (signed).

23. State of Minnesota, Court of Appeals, *In re Guardianship of Sharon Kowalski, Ward*, File No. C2-91-1047, Karen Tomberlin's Brief and Appendix, September 9, 1991 (signed), pp. 6–7.

24. Court of Appeals, Brief of Karen Tomberlin, pp. 10–16.

25. State of Minnesota, Court of Appeals, *In re Guardianship of Sharon Kowalski, Ward*, File No. C2-91-1047, Respondent's Brief, September 4, 1991 (signed), pp. 4–8.

26. Court of Appeals, Respondent's Brief, pp. 11–14.

27. State of Minnesota, Court of Appeals, *In re Guardianship of Sharon Kowalski, Ward*, File No. C2-91-1047, Reply Brief and Appendix of Appellant Karen Thompson, September 20, 1991 (signed).

28. *In re Guardianship of Sharon Kowalski, Ward* 478 NW2d 790, 795 (Minn App 1991). This is the third published decision of the case in the Minnesota Court of Appeals (File No. C2-91-1047).

29. 478 NW2d 790, 793.

30. 478 NW2d 790, 794.

31. 478 NW2d 790, 795.

32. 478 NW2d 790, 797.

12. Remedy

1. Jean Swallow, *Making Love Visible: In Celebration of Gay and Lesbian Families* (Freedom, Calif.: Crossing Press, 1995), 96–101.

2. Ibid., 98.

3. Ibid., 99.

4. Ibid., 100.

5. *Baker v Nelson*, 191 NW2d 185 (Minn Supreme Court, 1971).

Bibliography

The bibliography consists of five sections. The first provides the locations of many of the legal, medical, and periodical records. The second is a list of principal periodicals commonly cited within the body of the book, including lesbian and gay newspapers, Minnesota newspapers, and national media. The third section lists the persons interviewed. The fourth section cites books and articles substantially quoted within the text, including a list of reference sources for the introduction. Finally, a table of cases gives citations to legal decisions, including the three published appeals in the Kowalski case and relevant United States Supreme Court cases.

All the documents I have photocopied will be donated to the One Institute in Los Angeles, California, upon publication of the book. The legal documents in the Kowalski case, apart from three published Minnesota Court of Appeals cases, are unpublished public documents that are located in the probate divisions of the district courts of Minnesota, specifically Sherburne County, St. Louis County, and Hennepin County. *In re Guardianship of Sharon Kowalski, Ward* began in Sherburne County in 1984, was transferred to St. Louis County (Duluth) in 1987, and is currently in Hennepin County District Court in Minneapolis, Minnesota.

Documents

LEGAL

The principal legal documents concerning *In re Guardianship of Sharon Kowalski, Ward,* come from two probate courts in Minnesota: State of Minnesota, County of Sherburne, District Court, Probate Division, File No. 4497, March 2, 1984–June 1, 1987; and State of Minnesota, County of St. Louis, District Court, Probate Division, File No. 11146, June 1, 1987–June 15, 1992 (transferred to County of Hennepin, District Court, Probate Division, which is the current jurisdiction of the guardianship).

Files 4497 and 11146 gave rise to a number of appeals to the Minnesota Court of Appeals in St. Paul. The principal appeals include File Nos. C1-85-1502, C1-85-1595 (published as 382 NW2d 861 [Minn App 1986] [cert. denied 475 US 1085]), C2-85-1590, C5-85-1664, C6-86-176 (published as 392 NW2d 310 [Minn App 1986]), C2-91-1047 (published as 478 NW2d 790 [Minn App 1991]).

OTHER DOCUMENTS
Minnesota Historical Society, St. Paul, Minnesota
Quatrefoil Library, St. Paul, Minnesota (periodicals)
Offices of Deborah Chasnoff, San Francisco, California
One Institute and Archives, Los Angeles, California

Periodicals

Duluth News-Tribune (1984–92)
Equal Time (Minneapolis) (1985–93)
Gay Community News (GCN) (1985–92)
(Twin Cities) GAZE (1987–93) (cited as *GAZE* in the text)
Los Angeles Times (1988–92)
Minneapolis Star Tribune (1985–93)
New York Times (1988–92)
St. Cloud Times (1984-1993)
St. Paul Pioneer Press (1987–92)
Washington Blade (1985–93)
Washington Post (1988–92)

Interviews

Unless otherwise indicated, interviews took place in 1997.
Jason Burrell, activist (1999)
Judge R. V. Campbell
Judge Bruce Douglas
Dr. Matthew Eckman
Fred Friedman, attorney
Amy Bromberg Funk, attorney
Judge Thomas Hayes (by phone)
[Rose Jones — anonymous], witness
Mark Kasel, reporter
Judge Gary Pagliaccetti
Dr. Dorothy Rappel
Mark Stodghill, reporter
John Welsh, reporter (by mail, 1998)

Articles and Books

Adam, Barry. *The Rise of a Gay and Lesbian Movement.* New York: Twayne, 1995.
Alanen, Arnold R. "Years of Change on the Range." In *Minnesota in a Century of*

Change: The State and Its People Since 1900, ed. Clifford E. Clark Jr. St. Paul: Minnesota Historical Society Press, 1989.

Anderson, Shelley. "Til Catastrophe Do Us Part . . . A Minnesota Woman Fights for Her Injured Lover's Best Interests." *Washington Blade,* January 17, 1986, p. 1.

Andrzejewski, Julie. "The Trampled Rights of Sharon Kowalski." Editorial. *Minneapolis Star Tribune,* March 25, 1986, sec. A, p. 19.

Bernstein, Mary, and Renate Reimann, eds. *Queer Families, Queer Politics: Challenging Culture and the State.* New York: Columbia University Press, 2001.

"Bitter Quarrel — Test of Love." *West 57th Street.* CBS News. February 25, 1989 (videotape).

Blasius, Mark. *Gay and Lesbian Politics.* Philadelphia: Temple University Press, 1994.

Browning Cole, Eve. "There Are No Clear-Cut Answers in the Tragedy of Sharon Kowalski." Editorial. *Duluth News-Tribune,* March 2, 1989, sec. D, p. 10.

Brozan, Nadine. "Gay Groups Are Rallied to Aid 2 Women's Fight." *New York Times,* August 7, 1988, p. 26.

Burch, Mariel Rae. "Lesbian Couple Torn Apart by the Court: Help Needed from Lesbian Community." *Lesbian Inciter,* February/March 1986, 12–15.

Butler, Judith. *Excitable Speech: A Politics of the Performative.* New York: Routledge, 1997.

———. *Gender Trouble: Feminism and the Subversion of Identity.* New York: Routledge, 1990.

Button, James W., Barbara A. Rienzo, and Kenneth D. Wald. *Private Lives, Public Conflicts: Battles over Gay Rights in American Communities.* Washington, D.C.: Congressional Quarterly, 1997.

Cain, Patricia. *Rainbow Rights: The Role of Lawyers and Courts in the Lesbian and Gay Civil Rights Movement.* Boulder, Colo.: Westview, 2000.

Califia, Pat. Editorial. *Out,* July, 1999, 41.

Chambers, David L. "Couples: Marriage, Civil Union, and Domestic Partnership." In *Creating Change: Sexuality, Public Policy, and Civil Rights,* edited by John D'Emilio, William B. Turner, and Urvashi Vaid. New York: St. Martin's, 2000.

Chandler, Kurt, and Carol Byrne. "'I . . . Will Not Let Her Down': Thompson Takes Kowalski Home to Stay." *Minneapolis Star Tribune,* April 29, 1993, sec. A, p. 1.

Charles, Casey. "Making Justice: Same-Sex Partnership in the Kowalski Case." *disClosure: A Journal of Social Policy* 6 (1997): 9–34.

Clendinen, Dudley, and Adam Nagourney. *Out for Good: The Struggle to Build a Gay Rights Movement in America.* New York: Simon and Schuster, 1999.

Conte, Alba. *Sexual Orientation and Legal Rights.* 2 vols. New York: Wiley, 1998.

Corey, Frederick C., and Thomas K. Nakayama. "Sextet." *Text and Performance Quarterly* 17 (1997): 58–68.

Cuniberti, Betty. "Just Whose Life Is It?" *Los Angeles Times,* August 5, 1988, p. 1.

Curry, Hayden, et al. *A Legal Guide for Lesbian and Gay Couples.* 10th national ed. Berkeley: Nolo Press, 1999.

Delgado, Richard. *Storytelling for Oppositionists and Others: A Plea for Narrative.* 87 Michigan Law Review 2411 (1989).

D'Emilio, John. *Sexual Politics, Sexual Communities: The Making of a Homosexual Minority in the United States, 1940–1970.* Chicago: University Press of Chicago, 1983.

"Disabled Rights Issues Raised in Kowalski Case." *GCN,* February 15, 1986, p. 1.

"Disabled Woman's Parents, Professed Lover Battling in Court over Rights to Her Custody." *Duluth News-Tribune,* October 30, 1984, sec. A, p. 2.

Editors of Harvard Law Review. *Sexual Orientation and the Law.* Cambridge, Mass.: Harvard University Press, 1990.

Eskridge, William N. *The Case for Same-Sex Marriage: From Liberty to Civilized Commitment.* New York: Free Press, 1996.

———. *GayLaw: Challenging the Apartheid of the Closet.* Cambridge, Mass.: Harvard University Press, 1999.

Faderman, Lillian. *Surpassing the Love of Men.* London: Women's Press, 1985.

Fajer, Marc A. *Can Two Real Men Eat Quiche Together? Storytelling, Gender-Role Stereotypes, and Legal Protection for Lesbian and Gay Men.* 46 University of Miami Law Review 511–651 (1992).

Feinberg, Leslie. "Lesbian Supporters Campaign to Bring Sharon Kowalski Home." *Workers World,* 19 November 1987.

Foucault, Michel. *The Archaeology of Knowledge.* Translated by A. M. Sheridan-Smith. New York: Pantheon, 1972.

———. *The History of Sexuality: Volume I: An Introduction.* Translated by Robert Hurley. New York: Vintage, 1980.

Gay Rights as Human Rights. 64 Albany Law Review 64 (2001).

Gerwirtz, Paul, ed. *Law's Stories: Narrative and Rhetoric in the Law.* New Haven, Conn.: Yale University Press, 1996.

Goodrich, Peter. *Legal Discourse: Studies in Linguistics, Rhetoric and Legal Analysis.* New York: St. Martin's, 1987.

———. *Oedipus Lex: Psychology, History, Law: Philosophy, Social Theory, and the Rule of Law.* Berkeley: University of California Press, 1995.

Guderian, Brenda. "Attorney Wants Other Side of Story to Be Heard." *St. Cloud State University Chronicle,* April 1, 1986, p. 3.

Halvorsen, Donna. "Center Will Help Gays Plan Ahead." *Minneapolis Star Tribune,* 24 June 1992, sec. B, p. 5.

Hunter, Nan D., Sherryl E. Michaelson, and Thomas B. Stoddard. *The Rights of Lesbians and Gay Men: A Basic ACLU Guide to a Gay Person's Rights.* Carbondale: Southern Illinois University Press, 1992.

Jagose, Anne-Marie. *Queer Theory: An Introduction.* New York: New York University Press, 1993.

Jamison, Michael. "Benefits for Gay Partners Denied." *Missoulian,* May 20, 2000, sec. A, p. 1.

Jay, Karla, ed. *Out of the Closets.* New York: New York University Press, 1992.

Johnson, Phil. "Karen Thompson Appointed Guardian; Appeals Court Panel Agrees with Medical, Professional Testimony." *(Twin Cities) GAZE*, December 26, 1991, p. 1.

Kahn, Emily Matilda. "Minnesota Court Rejects Another Thompson Appeal." *Philadelphia Gay News*, September 5, 1986, 5.

Kasel, Mark. "Judge Rules Kowalski to Be Tested for Competency." *(Twin Cities) GAZE*, February 11, 1988.

———. "What Will It Take to Finally Bring Sharon Home?" *(Twin Cities) GAZE*, May 3, 1993, p. 30.

Keen, Lisa M. "High Court Rejects Appeal from Lesbian, Set to Hear Sodomy Challenge Monday." *Washington Blade*, March 28, 1986, sec. A, p. 1.

Kennedy, Tony. "Gay Issue Clouds Fight for Custody." *St. Cloud Times*, October 18, 1984, sec. A, p. 1.

Laclau, Ernesto. *New Reflections on the Revolution of Our Time*. London: Verso, 1990.

Landis, Paul Henry. *Three Iron Mining Towns*. New York: Arno Press, 1970.

Lass, William E. *Minnesota: A Bicentennial History*. New York: Norton, 1977.

Leonard, Arthur S. *Chronicling a Movement: 20 Years of* Lesbian/Gay Law Notes. 17 New York Law School Journal of Human Rights 415 (2000).

———, ed. *Homosexuality and the Constitution*. New York: Garland, 1997.

Leonard, Jerry, ed. *Legal Studies as Cultural Studies: A Reader in (Post)Modern Critical Theory*. Albany: State University of New York Press, 1995.

Lewis, Sinclair. *Main Street: The Story of Carol Kennicott*. New York: Harcourt, Brace, 1921.

Lindgren, Amy. "Nightmare Leads Karen Thompson into Struggle for Rights, Reunion." *Minnesota Women's Press*, (May 12, 1987) 1.

Link, David. *The Tie That Binds: Recognizing Privacy and the Family Commitments of Same-Sex Couples*. 23 Loyola L.A. Law Review 1055–1151 (1990).

Livingston, Nancy. "A Silent Ordeal." *St. Paul Pioneer Press*, June 14, 1987, sec. D, p. 1.

Matsuda, Mari J. *Looking to the Bottom: Critical Legal Studies and Reparations*. 22 Harvard Law Review 323 (1987).

McCann, Michael W. *Rights at Work: Pay Equity Reform and the Politics of Legal Mobilization*. Chicago: University of Chicago Press, 1994.

McFadden, Cyra. "Karen and Sharon and the Spirit of the Law." *San Francisco Examiner*, November 29, 1987, sec. E, p. 1.

Miller, Diane Helene. *Freedom to Differ: The Shaping of the Gay and Lesbian Struggle for Civil Rights*. New York: New York University Press, 1998.

Murdoch, Joyce. "Fighting for Control of a Loved One: Guardianship Dispute Pits Disabled Woman's Partner, Family." *Washington Post*, August 5, 1988, sec. A, p. 1.

Murdoch, Joyce, and Deb Price. *Courting Justice: Gay Men and Lesbians v. the Supreme Court*. New York: Basic Books, 2001.

Nava, Michael, and Robert Dawidoff. *Created Equal: Why Gay Rights Matter to America*. New York: St. Martin's, 1994.

Olson, Debra. "Interest Grows in Battle over Rights of Gay, Disabled." *St. Cloud Times,* July 30, 1988, sec. A, p. 3.

Renalis, Candace. "Gay Activist Named Guardian of Kowalski." *Duluth News-Tribune,* December 17, 1991, sec. A, p. 2.

Rhode, Deborah. *Justice and Gender.* Cambridge, Mass.: Harvard University Press, 1989.

Richards, David A. J. *Identity and the Case for Gay Rights: Race, Gender, Religion as Analogies.* Chicago: University of Chicago Press, 1999.

———. *Women, Gays and the Constitution: The Grounds for Feminism and Gay Rights in Culture and Law.* Chicago: University of Chicago Press, 1998.

Riggle, Ellen D. B., and Barry L. Tadlock, eds. *Public Policy, Public Opinion, and Political Representation.* New York: Columbia University Press, 1999.

Rimmerman, Craig A., Kenneth D. Wald, and Clyde Wilcox, eds. *The Politics of Gay Rights.* Chicago: University of Chicago Press, 2000.

Ritter, J. C. "Karen Thompson: Still Fighting, Despite Stress." *Equal Time,* February 19, 1986, 9.

Rivera, Rhonda R. *Recent Developments in Sexual Preference Law.* 30 Drake Law Review 311 (1980–81).

———. Review of *Sexual Politics, Sexual Communities: The Making of a Homosexual Minority in the United States, 1940–1970,* by John D'Emilio. 132 University of Pennsylvania Law Review 391 (1984).

Robles, Jennifer Juarez. "Karen Thompson and Sharon Kowalski: 'A Family of Affinity.'" *Advocate,* October 20, 1992, 45.

Robson, Ruthann. *Gay Men, Lesbians, and the Law.* New York: Chelsea House, 1997.

———. *Lesbian (Out)law: Survival Under the Rule of Law.* Ithaca, N.Y.: Firebrand Books, 1992.

Rubinstein, William B., ed. *Lesbians, Gay Men, and the Law.* New York: Free Press, 1993.

Salinas, Mike. "Free Sharon Kowalski!" *New York Native,* April 6, 1987, p. 1.

Sandel Michael. *Liberalism and the Limit of Justice.* Cambridge: Cambridge University Press, 1982.

Schmidt, Winsor C., Jr. *Guardianship: Court of Last Resort for the Elderly and Disabled.* Durham, N.C.: Carolina Academic Press, 1995.

Sedgwick, Eve Kosofsky. *Epistemology of the Closet.* Berkeley: University of California Press, 1990.

Solomon, Alisa. "Activist by Accident." *Village Voice,* October 20, 1987, 29.

Stoddard, Thomas B. "Gay Adults Should Not Be Denied the Benefits of Marriage." Editorial. *Minneapolis Star Tribune,* March 7, 1989, sec. A, p. 11.

Stodghill, Mark. "Custody." *Duluth News-Tribune,* November 17, 1987, sec. A, p. 1.

———. "Ellen's Sex Life Is Not My Concern." *Duluth News-Tribune,* May 11, 1997, sec. E, p. 1.

Sullivan, Andrew, ed. *Same-Sex Marriage: Pro and Con.* New York: Vintage, 1997.

Swallow, Jean. *Making Love Visible: In Celebration of Gay and Lesbian Families.* Freedom, Calif.: Crossing Press, 1995.

Thomas, Kendall. *Beyond the Privacy Principle.* 92 Columbia Law Review 1413 (1992).

Thompson, Karen. "Why Can't Sharon Kowalski Come Home?" *Sojourner,* October 1986, 21.

Thompson, Karen, and Julie Andrzejewski. *Why Can't Sharon Kowalski Come Home?* San Francisco: Spinsters/Aunt Lute, 1988.

Tucker, Scott. "Our Right to the World." *Body Politic,* July/August 1982, 32. Reprinted in Larry Gross, *Contested Closets: The Politics of Ethics and Outing,* 148. Minneapolis: University of Minnesota Press, 1993.

Unger, Roberto Mangabeira. *The Critical Legal Studies Movement.* Cambridge, Mass.: Harvard University Press, 1986.

Vexler, Robert I., and William F. Swindler, eds. *Chronology and Documentary Handbook of the State of Minnesota.* Dobbs Ferry, N.Y.: Oceana, 1978.

Warner, Michael. *The Trouble with Normal: Sex, Politics, and the Ethics of Queer Life.* New York: Free Press, 1999.

Weber, Samuel. "In the Name of the Law." In *Deconstruction and the Possibility of Justice.* Edited by Drucilla Cornell, Michel Rosenfeld, and D. G. Carlson. New York: Routledge, 1992.

Weisberg, Robert. "Proclaiming Trials as Narratives." In *Law's Stories: Narrative and Rhetoric in the Law,* 61–83. New Haven, Conn.: Yale University Press, 1996.

Welsh, John. "Almost a Year Later, Thompson, Kowalski Facing New Hurdles." *St. Cloud Times,* December 14, 1992, sec. A, p. 1.

———. "Thompson-Kowalski Case Gave Inspiration to Others." *St. Cloud Times,* August 5, 1989, sec. A, p. 10.

Williams, Patricia J. *The Alchemy of Race and Rights.* Cambridge, Mass.: Harvard University Press, 1992.

Wofford, Carrie. "Citing 'Outing,' Judge Keeps Lesbian Lovers Apart." *Outweek,* May 15, 1991.

The WPA Guide to the Minnesota Arrowhead Country. St. Paul: Minnesota Historical Society Press, 1988.

Yewell, John. "After Tug of War Ends, Sharon Kowalski Is Sure to Be the Loser." *St. Paul Pioneer Press,* December 2, 1990, sec. E, p. 1.

Young, Iris Marion. *Justice and the Politics of Difference.* Princeton, N.J.: Princeton University Press, 1990.

Zeman, Francis. "Legal Mobilization: The Neglected Role of Law in the Political System." *American Political Science Review* 77 (1983): 690–703.

Table of Cases

Baehr v Lewin, 852 P2d 44 (Hawaii Supreme Court 1993).

Baker v Nelson, 191 NW2d 185 (Minnesota Supreme Court 1971).

Baker v State, 74 A2d 864 (Vermont Supreme Court 1999).

Bowers v Harowick, 478 US 168 (United States Supreme Court, 1986).

In re Guardianship of Sharon Kowalski, Ward, 382 NW2d 861 (Minnesota Court of Appeals, 1986).

In re Guardianship of Sharon Kowalski, Ward, 392 NW2d 310 (Minnesota Court of Appeals, 1986).

In re Guardianship of Sharon Kowalski, Ward, 478 NW2d 790 (Minnesota Court of Appeals, 1991).

Olmstead v United States, 277 US 438 (United States Supreme Court, 1928).

Price Waterhouse v Hopkins, 490 US 228 (United States Supreme Court, 1989).

Romer v Evans, 517 US 620 (United States Supreme Court, 1984).

Sipple v Chronicle Publishing Company, 154 CalApp3d, 201 CalRptr 665 (California Court of Appeals, 1984).

Index

ACLU. *See* American Civil Liberties
    Union
Act Up (AIDS Coalition to Unleash
    Power), 7, 25
Adamski, Jenette, 210–11, 212
Adoption, 9, 12, 73–74
  second parent, 11
Advocate, 110, 121, 254
Agnos, Art, 175
AIDS (acquired immune deficiency
    syndrome), 3, 4, 6, 68, 257
  disability and discrimination, 9, 14,
    148, 169, 247
  medication, 8
  song, 141
AIDS Coalition to Unleash Power (Act Up),
    7, 25
Aikane, 73, 74
Alioto, Angela, 192
Allerton, Robert Henry, 73–74
American Civil Liberties Union
    (ACLU), 6, 7
  Gay Rights Project, 6, 174, 268
  See also Minnesota Civil Liberties
    Union
American Psychological Association
    Humanitarian Award, 191
Anderson, Catherine, 69
Andrzejewski, Julie, 3, 30–31, 58, 67, 71,
    110, 114–15, 121, 126, 129–30, 132,
    140, 143, 154. *See also Why Can't
    Sharon Kowalski Come Home?*
Anger, David, 199
Antidiscrimination law (Fla.), 6
Antigay evangelical forces, 6

Arrowhead region (Minn.), 21
Artificial insemination, 11
Aspen (Co.), 8
Associated Press, 59, 139, 180, 192, 198,
    199, 205, 224, 247

Baehr, Nina, 262
Baehr v Lewin (Hawaii 1993), 12, 56, 74,
    262
Baker, Richard John (Jack), 11, 262
Baker v Nelson (Minn. 1971), 11,
    128–129. *See also* Baker, Richard
    John (Jack)
Baker v State (Vermont 1999), 12
Baraga, Elizabeth, 143
Becker, Jaime, 174
Bedosky, John, 242
Bennett, William, 75
Berg, Linda B., 238–39, 247
Berkeley (Cal.), 13
"Best interests" standard, 10
Beunaiche, Marie, 235
Bill (gay trucker), 100–1
Blackmun, Harry, 242
Bloomquist, Gary, 125–26
Blue Goose. *See* Kowalski, Sharon,
    accident and injury
Born, Suzanne, 240–41, 244, 247
Boston Gay Pride Committee, 170
Bowers v Hardwick (1986), 5, 139, 242
Boy Scouts of America, 8, 263
Brennan, Nancy, 217
Bresser, Patty (new partner of Karen
    Thompson), 7, 13, 112, 200, 214,
    259, 260

Briggs Lake (Minn.), 1
Britt, Harry, 169
Brix, Dr., 42, 90
Bromberg, Amy, 108, 109, 118, 120, 121, 130–31
Browning Cole, Eve, 187
Brozan, Nadine, 174, 234
Bryant, Anita, 6
Burnes, Karen, 183, 184, 185
Butler, Judith, 137
Buyer, Steve, 75
Byrne, Carol, 257

Califia, Pat, 265
California, 8, 12–13
Campbell, Robert V. (judge), 161–62, 164, 166, 168, 170–71, 172, 175, 177, 178, 179, 187, 188, 189, 193, 194–95, 198, 203, 205, 207–8, 224, 230–34, 253
    judgment criticized, 236, 240, 241, 245, 246
Canada, 13
Can Two Real Men Eat Quiche Together? Story-telling, Gender-Role Stereotypes, and Legal Protectionism for Lesbians and Gay Men (Fajer), 25, 26, 58
Center for Feminist Research (CFR) (University of Southern California), 73, 93.
CFR. *See* Center for Feminist Research
Chambers, David, 11
Chandler, Kurt, 257
Charles, Casey, 3–4, 24–25, 57, 251
    domestic partnership proposal, 264–68
    and HIV, 25, 57, 93, 228, 265
    law class and Kowalski case, 33–34, 57
    research on Kowalski case, 73, 74, 93–94, 111–13, 135–38, 153–54, 181–82, 228–29
Chasnoff, Deborah, 94, 258, 259

Chemberlin, Peg, 31, 35, 67, 71, 122
Chippewa/Ojibwa, 21, 153
Chmielewski, Charles, 28, 63
Christian Coalition, 267
Civil disobedience, 158
Civil rights, 25, 115. *See also* Lesbian and gay rights
Civil union (Vermont), 12, 262
Clinton, Bill, 74
Clinton, Kate, 157
Closet gays and lesbians, 4–5, 14, 162, 194, 201
Collinson, Peter S., 119
Committee for the Right to Recovery and Relationships, 71, 110, 132, 152
Committees to Free Sharon Kowalski, 7, 94, 141, 146, 161, 164, 170, 189
"Common benefits" clause (Vermont), 12
Common-law marriage, 31
Connell, Mary, 208
Conservatism, 4, 6, 7
Contested Closets: The Politics of Ethics and Outing (Gross), 5
Contracts, 10–11
Corporations and same-sex domestic partners insurance, 13, 264, 272(n45)
Country Manor Nursing Home, 43, 47, 55, 76
Cowan, George, 53, 54, 83–87, 104–5, 107, 129, 133, 164
Coyle, Brian, 198
Crippin, Gary, 245
Crofts, Dick, 266
Cuniberti, Betty, 173
Custody, 6, 9, 12, 14

Dade County (Fla.), 6
Dakota Sioux, 21
Dale, James, 8, 263
Dancel, Genora, 262

Daniels, Terry, 168
Davies, Jack (judge), 7, 9, 245, 246–47, 253
Defamation, 60
Defense of Marriage Acts (DOMAs), 8, 12, 14, 74–75, 93
DeGeneres, Ellen, 8, 159
Democratic Party, 6
Dempsey, Rosemary, 199, 234–35
Denmark, 13
DiIorio, Debbie Kowalski (sister of Sharon), 1, 79, 81–83, 90, 134, 150, 225–27, 245
Disabled persons, 1, 3, 4, 7, 9, 11, 41–42, 108, 109, 115, 133, 140, 167, 228, 247, 250–51
    rights, 145, 146, 134, 192
DOMAs. *See* Defense of Marriage Acts
Domestic partnership
    and courts, 44–45
    and family law, 9
    health benefits, 10, 263, 265
    legislation (Minneapolis), 7, 13
    movement, 13, 121
    rights, 11–13
    and taxes and insurance, 9, 13
    violence, 8, 268
    See also Same-sex partnership
Donahue, Phil, 252. *See also The Phil Donahue Show*
Donohue, Peter S. (lawyer for Karen Thompson), 31, 32, 35, 37, 40, 42, 47, 116, 118, 119
"Don't-ask-don't-tell policy," 8, 14, 72, 197, 249
Douglas, Bruce R. (judge), 37–38, 40, 42, 43, 44, 47, 49, 50, 55, 56, 59, 64, 65, 66, 72, 76, 79, 82, 91, 92, 97, 110, 111, 120, 122, 128, 133
Douglas, William O. (judge), 242, 262
Due process, 120
Duluth Clinic, 171
Duluth News-Tribune, 59, 61, 79, 95,

100, 101, 110, 158, 159, 187, 189, 192, 205, 248, 250
Dylan, Bob, 23

Ebenezer Caroline Center (Minneapolis), 187
Eckman, Matthew, 168, 171, 175, 176, 177, 188, 202–3, 235
Ellen (television show), 8, 159
Encephalopathy, 203
Equal protection, 11, 12, 268
Equal Time (Twin Cities gay and lesbian newspaper), 7, 79, 110, 116, 121, 132, 179, 190, 199, 248, 249
Erickson, Bruce, 92
Eskridge, William, 14
Estate planning, 11, 12, 14
Ettelbrick, Paula, 199, 240–41, 247

Faderman, Lillian, 155
Faegre and Benson (law firm), 108–9, 156, 162–63
Fajer, Mark, 25
Family law, 9, 45
Family of affinity, 7, 13, 241, 247, 261
Fasano, Michael, 169
Federal Rehabilitation Act, 77
Feinberg, Leslie, 158
Feinstein, Diane, 169
Feminists, 7, 30–31
Fena, Jack (lawyer for Donald Kowalski), 29–30, 35, 37, 40, 44, 47, 48, 51, 53, 59–60, 61, 66, 70, 72, 77, 79, 80, 81–82, 83–85, 89, 90, 91, 92–93, 95, 96, 97–98, 100, 101, 102, 103–4, 105–6, 108, 110, 115, 116, 121, 125, 126, 128, 131–32, 140, 142, 143, 156–57, 161, 163–66, 168–69, 173
    and conflict of interest, 126, 127
    friends, 152
    and publicity, 147, 150, 178
    and res judicata, 156, 164

Fena, Jack, *continued*
 on Thompson, Karen, 164, 172
 withdrawal from case, 176–77
 writ of prohibition, 171
Fierstein, Harvey, 157
Film proposal, 258–59
Finklestein, Arthur, 93
Finnish Temperance Union, 22
First Amendment, 6, 65, 66, 131, 150,
 189, 193
Fjell, Judy, 7, 141
Florida, 6
Ford (company), 13
Forsberg, Thomas, 245
Foucault, Michel, 3
Fourteenth Amendment, 120
Frank, Donovan, 253
Franz, Holly (attorney), 267–68
Freedom to associate, 6, 11, 116, 130, 131,
 133, 150–51
Free Sharon Day, 172
Free Sharon Kowalski. *See* Committees
 to Free Sharon Kowalski
"Free Sharon Kowalski"
 T-shirts, 145
 wreath, 175
Friedman, Fred (lawyer for Sharon
 Kowalski), 193–95, 199, 206–
 7, 208, 209, 210, 211, 214,
 221, 223–24, 225, 226–27, 235,
 243, 244

Garland, Judy, 21
Gay and Lesbian Community Center,
 147
Gay, lesbian, bisexual, and
 transgendered (GLBT), 7, 8, 9, 144,
 264
Gay Community News (GCN), 7, 121,
 132, 144, 146, 170, 178, 234
Gay Pride Parade (NYC 1987), 7
Gay Straight Alliance (Big Sky High
 School), 265

Gay Women's Alternative, 147
GAZE (Twin Cities), 7, 144, 199, 249,
 256
GCN. See Gay Community News
Gekas, George, 75
General Motors (company), 13
Georgia, 5
GLBT. *See* Gay, lesbian, bisexual, and
 transgendered
Goff, Steven K., 51, 52, 53, 54, 56, 60, 61,
 84, 104–5, 106, 107, 111, 129, 131,
 133
Goldman, Janlori, 118, 121, 139
Grahek, Margaret, 193, 212
Grayson, Carla, 268
Gregg, John, 73–74
Gregor, Gail, 96–99, 107, 212–16, 222,
 237
Griswold v Connecticut (1965), 242
Gross, Larry, 5
Guardianship, 13, 31, 32, 39, 200
 joint, 40
 and kinship, 32, 200
 and spousal ties, 131
 See also under In re Guardianship of
 Sharon Kowalski, Ward

Halvorsen, Donna, 252, 253
Handicapped Bill of Rights, 103
Hansen, Carla M., 71
Hardwick, Michael, 139, 140, 190,
 262
Hate crimes, 9, 14, 268
Hatten, John, 171
Hawaii, 8, 12, 73, 74, 262
Hayes, Tom (Thomas) (lawyer for
 Sharon Kowalski), 38–39, 40, 43,
 44, 47, 50, 56, 79, 83, 86–87, 96, 99,
 100, 102–3, 108, 119, 126, 127, 139,
 142, 154
 as associate, 131
 denied visitation, 114
 and Fena, Jack, 45, 47

and Kowalski, Donald, 45–46
withdrawal from case, 156
Health insurance, 12, 264–65
Hennepin County District Court, 253
Herron, Carolyn, 219
Hewitt, Mary Kay, 90, 91, 107
Hibbing Daily Tribune, 234
HIV (human immunodeficiency virus), 25
Hixson, Emma, 190
Hoagland, David, 141
Homophobia, 4–5, 6, 14–15, 39, 59, 103, 109, 115, 118, 131, 143, 152
Homosexuality, 6, 8–9, 12
 on campus, 6, 9
 and custody, 9, 10
 as disorder, 86–87
 and guardianship, 10 *(see also In re Guardianship of Sharon Kowalski, Ward)*
 and the law, 6, 9–10, 14, 25
 and marriage rights, 6, 11, 240
 and molestation, 10
 sex as crime, 57, 75
 See also Lesbian and gay rights
Hortis, Theophanis, 53
Horton and Associates (law firm), 238
HRC. *See* Human Rights Campaign
Human rights, 77, 122, 191
Human Rights Campaign (HRC), 6, 180, 188
 Fund, 188
Humphrey, Hubert, 21
Hunter, Nan, 6, 10, 174
Huspeni, Doris (judge), 120

Immigration law and homosexuality, 6, 9
Incapacity, 31
Incompetence, 31
In re Guardianship of Sharon Kowalski, Ward (1984–1993), 1, 2, 3, 11, 14, 25, 261–63
 affidavits, 77–78, 87, 106–7, 117–18, 126, 156, 171, 178
 amicus briefs, 7, 65–66, 108, 119–21, 139, 235, 238–39
 appeals, 7, 115–16, 119, 126, 128–32, 133, 139, 141–43, 235
 appellate brief, 235–45
 change of venue petition, 155, 157, 253
 and discrimination, 15
 as domestic rights case, 6, 11
 expert witnesses, 83
 and gay rights issue, 105–6, 128
 and guardianship, 6, 7, 8–9, 12, 13, 38, 40–41, 79, 101, 115–16, 126–27, 129, 133–35, 140, 156, 162, 189, 191, 193, 194–200, 202–28, 239, 244–50
 hearings, 38, 40, 42, 47, 79–93, 95–99, 101–8, 202–12
 judges, 37–38, 62 *(see also individual names)*
 legal legacy, 14, 198
 lower court decision overturned (1992), 7, 245
 media coverage, 58–60, 62, 77, 100, 101, 110–11, 114, 121, 132–33, 140, 144, 157–61, 169, 172–75, 186–87, 197–98, 205–6, 234–35, 247–49
 as medical issue, 128
 and outing, 194, 231, 233
 and personal injury liability, 80, 163
 and privacy rights, 116, 230, 232–33
 publicity, 140, 141, 145–53, 157–58
 writ of prohibition, 189
Insurance law, 9, 12, 13, 272(n45)
Iron Range, 1, 3, 4, 21, 22, 109, 138, 153, 216–17, 237

Jackson, Jesse, 157, 170
Jackson, Jesse, Jr., 75
Jagim, Ryan, 69
Jamison, Michael, 266, 267

Jason, 250–51
Johnson, Anita, 209
Johnson, Kim, 62, 65, 77, 126, 127, 128, 156, 169
Johnson, Phil, 249
Jones, Rose, 194, 195–97, 201, 210, 220–22, 245
Justice, 2

Kahn, Emily, 144
Kasel, Mark, 144, 170, 171, 190, 191, 253, 256
Keen, Lisa, 139, 169
Kennedy, Edward, 74
Kennedy, Tony, 58, 180
Kentucky, 6
King, Kathy, 64–65, 209, 237
Kinship, 32, 200
Koch, Ed, 175
Komarek, Rachel, 204
Kowalski, Della (mother), 16, 19, 20, 23, 26, 27–28, 29–30, 32, 33, 36–37, 38, 39, 41, 44, 121, 148–49, 151, 160, 199, 212, 222, 235
    alleged assault on Karen Thompson, 44, 46
    and daughter's rehabilitation, 43, 46, 47, 186, 230
    extreme emotional distress, 45, 48, 49, 66, 68, 157
    hospitalized, 66
    and publicity, 147, 149–50
    testimony, 48
    visits to Trevilla, 256
Kowalski, Donald (father), 1, 2, 4, 6, 7, 19, 20, 22, 23, 26, 27–28, 29–30, 32–33, 36–37, 38–39, 121, 148–49, 151, 160, 176–77, 212, 222, 235, 239
    attorneys (*see* Fena, Jack; Spellacy, Kevin)
    and Charles, Casey, 181
    and daughter's rehabilitation, 43, 47, 48, 60, 185–86, 230

expenses, 47, 149
extreme emotional distress, 45, 49, 157
guardianship of daughter, 40–41, 55, 60, 76, 80, 111, 117–18, 122, 126, 127, 129, 131, 133, 141–42, 143, 152, 156, 187
guardianship of daughter relinquished, 189, 198
and Hayes, Tom, 45–46
health, 157
letter from Karen Thompson, 61, 103, 128
press interviews, 58–59, 173
and publicity, 147, 149–50, 158
refusal to believe daughter's lesbianism, 68, 77, 106, 107–8, 118, 126, 128, 131, 149, 173, 179–80, 184–85, 240, 243
television interviews, 172–73, 184
testimony, 48, 88–91, 92–93, 168
visits to Trevilla, 256
on *West 57th Street*, 184–85
Kowalski, Mark (brother), 151
Kowalski, Sharon
    accident and injury, 1, 16, 19–20, 24, 26, 28, 41, 52–53, 168
    appearance on television, 252
    assets, 253
    attendant home care, 257
    attorneys (*see* Friedman, Fred; Hayes, Tom; Pagliaccetti, Gary)
    auto insurance, 41
    birthday celebrations, 174, 254
    case (*see In re Guardianship of Sharon Kowalski, Ward*)
    cognitive functioning ability, 52, 68–69, 71, 98, 105, 117, 143, 188, 203, 204
    communication skills, 133, 157, 178, 188, 191, 204, 210, 211, 213
    at daytime rehabilitation center, 257
    depression, 70, 71, 77, 84, 95, 105, 133, 191, 209

estate of, 128, 178, 230

evaluation, annual, 128, 156, 162–72, 174, 175

evaluation at Miller-Dwan Hospital, 175–76, 178, 179, 188, 202

evaluation at Polinsky, 51–54, 55

evaluation by Collinson, 119

evaluation by Moller, 68–69, 129

evaluation by TRICAP, 71

featured in book, 259–60, 261

friends of, 63–65, 195–96, 206, 220

functioning, 9, 53, 55–56, 71, 84, 176, 203, 213, 217–18, 230, 260

guardianship of, 1, 9–10, 40–41, 55, 111, 114, 189, 198–99, 228, 230, 245–50

"home" location, 36, 203, 205

legal fees, 199

medical assistance, 256

medical evaluations, 253

medical records, 62, 133

medical recovery, 7, 51–54, 55

medical testimony on, 2, 51–54, 55, 142, 203

niece and nephew, 1, 16, 24, 261

in nursing homes, 45, 46, 56, 108, 187–88, 256

outing of, 5, 118, 131, 159, 200, 205, 214, 231, 233, 237, 242

parents (*see* Kowalski, Della; Kowalski, Donald)

at parents' home for Christmas (1988), 178

partner (*see* Thompson, Karen D.)

personal injury award, 171

possessions, 95–96

press interviews, 255–56, 257

psychological evaluations of, 63, 69, 133, 178, 185

rehabilitation of, 41, 42–43, 46–47, 48, 50–51, 53, 61, 63, 64–65, 96, 97, 104–5, 117, 132, 135, 148–49, 166, 177, 188, 191, 209, 213, 237 (*see also*

Thompson, Karen, and Sharon's rehabilitation)

rights, 130–31, 151, 203, 230, 232, 233

San Francisco trip, 192, 218, 237

as sexual person, 205

siblings, 19, 20, 30, 54, 79 (*see also* DiIorio, Debbie Kowalski; Kowalski, Mark)

social worker appointed for, 193, 212

spasms, 210

tendon surgery, 190, 213

Virginia trip, 250

visit from Robert Campbell, 161

as ward of the court, 38, 134

Kowalski family doctor, 117

Krossen, Kenneth, 106–7, 123

Lambda Legal Defense and Education Fund, 6, 7, 11, 14, 72, 174, 191, 199, 234, 240

Justice Center (St. Paul), 252, 253

Landsman, Maury, 198

Larson, Keith, 42–43, 49, 50

Larson, Pat, 63

Law and literature, 24–25

Law schools, and sexual orientation, 8–9

Lawyers Professional Responsibility Board, 125, 126

Leisure Hills (Hibbing nursing home), 108, 115, 116, 117, 119, 121, 123, 132, 161, 166, 178, 222, 237

Lesbian and gay media, 7, 133, 144, 151, 234

Lesbian and gay rights, 1, 4, 5–6, 8, 9, 13, 37, 77, 186, 188, 190, 240, 244, 257, 262–63

and biological children, 14

on campuses, 6, 9, 264

and Democratic Party, 6

and disability, 133

and employment, 14

in military, 8, 9, 14, 100, 249

national organizations, 6

Lesbian and gay rights, *continued*
    and television and film
        representations, 8
    See also American Civil Liberties
        Union; *In re Guardianship of
        Sharon Kowalski, Ward;* Same-sex
        partnership
Lesbian/Gay Law Notes, 8
Lesbian Inciter (San Francisco), 133
Lesbian News, 249
Life and Times of Harvey Milk, The
    (film), 141
Linda (sister of Karen Thompson), 36,
    53
Lindquist, Judy, 166
Livingston, Nancy, 148–50
Living wills, 253
Los Angeles Times, 172, 173
Lutheran Social Services, 166

Main Club (Superior), 110
*Main Street: The Story of Carol
    Kennicott* (Lewis), 35
Makepeace, James, 115
"Making Justice: Same-sex Partnership
    in the Kowalski Case" (Charles),
    73
*Making Love Visible: In Celebration of
    Gay and Lesbian Families*
    (Swallow), 259
Manning, Charley, 93
Marital trusts, 12
Marks, Wayne, 23, 163
Marriage rights. *See under*
    Homosexuality; Same-sex
    partnership
Marvin v. Marvin palimony, 9, 12
McCaffrey, Stephen, 49
McConnell, James Michael, 262
McFadden, Cyra, 166
MCLU. *See* Minnesota Civil Liberties
    Union
Medical decision making, 6, 14

Medical records access, 40, 62
Metropolitan Community Church, 7
Mexico, 13
Michigan Women's Music Festival, 7
Mikulski, Barbara, 75
Military, gays and lesbians in, 8, 9, 14,
    100, 249
Milk, Harvey, 141, 190
Millam, Julie, 267
Miller-Dwan Hospital (Duluth), 171,
    175, 179, 187, 188, 202
Minneapolis (Minn.), 21
    Department of Civil Rights, 190
    domestic partnership legislation
        (1991), 7, 13
    gay and lesbian community, 110
Minneapolis Star Tribune, 59, 77, 157,
    166, 172, 174, 186, 189, 193, 247,
    248, 253, 257–58
Minnesota, 262
    conservative and progressive areas, 4,
        20–21, 109, 138, 154, 237
    constitution, 230
    DOMA (1997), 14
    early economy, 21–22
    explorers in, 21
    guardianship law, 10, 230, 232
    human rights statute, 77
    and same-sex marriage, 6, 12, 14
    and sexual orientation, 14
    Supreme Court, 249, 250, 262
    See also Patients' Bill of Rights
Minnesota Alliance for Progressive
    Action, 7
Minnesota Civil Liberties Union
    (MCLU), 11, 65, 108, 109, 110, 114,
    115, 118, 119, 120, 126, 130, 131, 139,
    140, 241
Minnesota Gay and Lesbian Legal
    Assistance, 110–11
Minnesota Office of Health Facility
    Complaints, 118
Minnesota Women's Press, 148

Miscegenation statute unconstitutional, 186
Missoulian, 266
Moller, Julie, 68, 71, 89, 103–4, 105, 106, 107, 111, 131, 133
Mondale, Walter, 6, 21
Montana, 8, 57, 72, 267–68
Moral slavery, 7
Ms., 121
Muotka, Becky, 206, 220
Murdoch, Joyce, 173

National Committee to Free Sharon Kowalski. *See* Committees to Free Sharon Kowalski
National Gay and Lesbian Health Care Providers Conference, 148
National Gay and Lesbian Rights March on Wash ington, 157
National Gay and Lesbian Task Force (NGLTF), 6
National March on Washington for Women's Equality, Women's Lives, 188
National Organization for Women (NOW), 7, 175, 199, 234, 238
  Long Distance Runner Award, 148
  Woman of Courage Award, 192
Native Americans, 21, 153
Neff, Adrienne, 268
Nelson, Jackie, 210
Netherlands, 13
Netland, Marge, 206
Newberg, Barb, 228
Newsday, 172
New York City, 7, 13
New York Native, 151–52
New York Times, 7, 172, 179, 186, 234
NGLTF. *See* National Gay and Lesbian Task Force
Nickitas, Peter J., 200
Nistler, Mike, 189

Nolo Press, 11, 253
Northwestern Hospital. *See* Sister Kenny Institute
NOW. *See* National Organization for Women

Ojibwa, 21
Old Dominion University (Va.), 250
Olson, Clyde, 171
Olson, Deborah, 158, 172
O'Neill, Brian, 156, 162, 163, 184, 241–42, 244
One Institute (Los Angeles), 94
On the Issues, 146
Oral sex, as crime, 14
Oregon Citizens Alliance, 57
Orr, Scott, 267
Orrock, Pam, 64
Outfield Alliance (University of Montana), 264, 268
Outing, 5, 28–29, 109, 192, 194. *See also under* Kowalski, Sharon; Thompson, Karen D.
Outweek (gay and lesbian publication), 234
Oxenberg, Jan, 258

Pagliaccetti, Gary (lawyer for Sharon Kowalski), 153, 166–68, 169, 170, 171, 173–74, 193
  and personal injury award, 171
  visit to Sharon Kowalski, 168
Palimony, 9, 31
Parents and Friends of Lesbians and Gays (PFLAG), 7
Park Point Manor Nursing Home (Duluth), 56, 60–61, 62, 76, 92, 101, 102, 103, 108
Patients' Bill of Rights (Minn.), 64, 119, 142
Patty. *See* Bresser, Patty
Paull, Dolores, 166
Pellman, Ann, 69–70, 90, 102

People Are Talking (television
    program), 172
People living with AIDS (PWAs), 247
Perpich, Rudy, 152, 158
Personal injury action, 132, 163, 171
Peterson, Sonja R., 238–39, 244
PFLAG. *See* Parents and Friends of
    Lesbians and Gays
Phibbs, Anne, 146
Philadelphia (film), 8
Phil Donahue Show, The (television
    program), 147, 252
PLGC. *See* Presbyterians for
    Lesbian/Gay Concerns
Polinsky, Nat G., Memorial
    Rehabilitation Center (Duluth), 50,
    51, 76
  Adult Rehabilitation Division, 204
Polygamy, 13
Polyparenting, 11, 13
Pomerene, Toni (lawyer for Karen D.
    Thompson), 121, 122, 162, 165, 166
Ponto, Michael, 242
Popovich, Peter (judge), 120, 125, 133,
    134, 135, 142, 152, 154, 245
Powers of attorney, 147, 198
  medical, 11
Presbyterians for Lesbian/Gay
    Concerns (PLGC), 67
Price Waterhouse v Hopkins (1989), 239
Pringle, Gary, 131
Privacy rights, 4, 5, 60, 109, 118, 130,
    139, 140, 165, 230, 232, 233
Probate, 6, 10–11
Professional Responsibility Board, 167
Publishers Weekly, 177
PWAs. *See* People living with AIDS

Quadriplegia, 213

Raphael, Sally Jesse, 147–48
Rappel, Dorothy, 179, 185, 203–5, 230
Reagan, Ronald, 6

"Reciprocal beneficiaries" (Hawaii), 12
Rehabilitation restoration theory, 175
Reichert, Paul, 115, 116
Renalis, Candace, 178, 205, 248, 250
Res judicata, 156, 164
Richards, David A. J., 7
Right-wing politics, 12
Ristvedt, Beth (Elizabeth) (lawyer for
    Karen D. Thompson), 40, 42, 46,
    47, 48, 49, 50, 53, 55, 59, 63, 66, 79,
    80, 82, 83, 85–86, 88, 89, 90, 91, 96,
    99, 101–2, 104, 105, 106, 107–8, 116,
    119
  and Charles, Casey, 112
Ritter, John C., 110, 116, 132–33, 188,
    190
Rivera, Geraldo, 172
Rivera, Rhonda, 9
Robles, Jennifer Juarez, 254
Roe, Roger (attorney), 162, 163, 165
Robson, Ruthann, 11
Rogers, Ellen, 59
Romer v Evans (1996), 8
Romthun, Gail, 63
Rosenthal, Arnold, 103
Russell, Jane, 90, 102, 107

St. Benedict's rehabilitation center (St.
    Cloud), 257
St. Cloud (Minn.), 4, 21
St. Cloud State University Chronicle, 140
St. Cloud Times, 58, 59, 60, 77, 79, 114,
    115, 158, 172, 189, 197, 198, 248, 255,
    257
St. Patrick's Cathedral (NYC), 175
St. Paul (Minn.), 6, 21, 244
St. Paul Pioneer Press, 148–51, 157,
    205–6, 258
Salinas, Mike, 151–52
Same-sex partnership, 4, 5, 8, 13, 190,
    264
  domestic partnership legislation, 7, 12,
    13, 14

and guardianship, 39, 131
issues, 6, 265
and marriage rights, 6, 8, 9, 11, 12–13,
    14, 74, 131, 137, 186, 241, 257, 262
not gay, 265–66
San Francisco Chronicle, 177, 233
Save Our Children Network, 6
Schmeichen, Richard, 141
Schmidt v Hebeisen (Minn. 1984), 200
Security clearances, 9
Sedgwick, Eve Kosofsky, 4, 133
Sex discrimination, 12, 100, 170, 239. *See
    also* Homophobia
Sexual harassment law, 25
Sexual orientation, 207
    law (*see under* Homosexuality)
Sharon Kowalski Day (August 8), 175
"Sharon Will Wheel Free" T-shirts, 174
Shelhon, Joan, 92
Shephard, Matthew, 264
Sherburne National Wildlife Refuge, 63
Sieben, Harry A., 156, 162
Siegesmund, Kristin (attorney), 162
Sims, Kathi, 49, 54
Sioux, 153
Sipple v Chronicle Publishing Company
    (Cal. 1984), 233
Sister Kenny Institute (Minneapolis),
    156, 190, 212
60 Minutes (television program), 147
Sjogren, Thomas (lawyer for Karen
    Tomberlin), 242, 243, 244, 245, 249,
    250
Sodomy law, 9, 120
    Georgia, 6
    Montana, 57
    repealed, 6
South Africa, 13
Southgate, David, 249
Spear, Allen, 262
Speech synthesizer, 188, 191
Spellacy, Kevin (lawyer for Donald
    Kowalski), 35, 37, 38, 40, 44, 47, 48,

49–50, 55–56, 60, 61, 79, 89, 90, 92,
    100, 101
Spinsters/Aunt Lute (women's press),
    170
Spousal-equivalent commitment, 10
Spousal presumption, 11, 37
Spousal rights, 116
Steffan, Joseph, 249, 262
Steinem, Gloria, 188
Stoddard, Tom, 14, 174, 186–87, 234
Stodghill, Mark, 158–61, 185
Stone Butch Blues (Feinberg), 158
Stonewall Riots (N.Y.) (1969), 4
Supreme Court (U.S.), 120, 139, 140,
    186, 263
Surrogate mothering, 11
Surrogate parenting, 9
Survivor's benefits, 12
Susens, Joann, 60–61
Swallow, Jean, 259–60
Sykora, Richard, 253

Take Back the Night rally
    (Minneapolis), 122, 152
Tax law, 9, 12
TBI. *See* Traumatic brain injury
Televangelists, 143–44
Temporary restraining order (TRO),
    60, 115, 116
Texas A&M University, 9
Thompson, Karen D., 1, 4, 5, 8, 187–88
    as activist, 254, 255
    anonymous letter about, 61–62
    alleged assault by Della Kowalski, 44,
        46
    attorneys (*see* Donohue, Peter S.;
        Pomerene, Toni; Ristvedt, Beth;
        Wilson, Sue)
    on Campbell, Robert, 234
    character, 54, 61, 90, 123, 138,
        194–95, 196, 201, 206, 221, 226, 239,
        242
    and Charles, Casey, 93–94, 112–13

Thompson, Karen D., *continued*
  as closet lesbian, 17, 18–19, 28, 101
  as coauthor, 3, 145, 169–70, 177
  on Cowan as expert witness, 88
  as defense witness, 156–57
  deposition, 77–78
  depression, 143
  disability accessible home, 254
  editorial, 145
  featured in book, 259–260
  friendship/relationship with Sharon
    Kowalski, 17–19, 63–64, 81, 82–83,
    91–92, 102, 119, 125–26, 131, 134,
    135, 140–41, 145, 150, 151, 162,
    184, 190, 191, 187–98, 204–5, 215,
    216, 218–19, 221, 223, 231, 232, 240,
    247
  grand marshal at NYC Gay Pride
    Parade, 7, 148
  guardianship denied, 228
  guardianship granted, 245–50, 254
  and hospital psychologist, 28
  hospital visitations, 16–17, 24, 26–28,
    36, 38, 40, 41
  hysterectomy, 129
  legal bills, 11, 125, 132, 143, 158, 170,
    188, 235, 258
  lesbian opponents, 194, 195–96
  letter to Donald Kowalski, 61, 103,
    128
  life insurance policy, 63
  lovers, 225, 233, 234
  and NOW, 148, 192
  outing, 28–29, 30, 35–36, 59, 145, 201,
    214–15
  parents, 66–67, 72
  partners (*see* Bresser, Patty; Kowalski,
    Sharon)
  and *The Phil Donahue Show*, 147,
    252
  as political conservative, 6, 158
  psychiatric testimony on, 2
  psychological evaluation on, 63
  publicity campaign, 140, 141, 145–53,
    157–58, 160, 170, 172, 177, 191
  religion, 17, 67, 143–44, 254
  sexual abuse allegation by others, 10,
    38, 59, 77, 101, 106, 107, 117,
    123–24, 162
  and Sharon's medical information, 76
  and Sharon's rehabilitation, 41, 42, 43,
    49, 50, 51, 54, 55, 62, 92, 95, 99, 107,
    176, 191, 202, 208, 212, 213, 219, 237
  sister, 36, 53, 79
  support for, 11–12, 58, 63, 64, 67–68,
    71–72, 110–11, 121, 132, 141,
    145–46, 157–58, 170, 188, 191, 238,
    250
  as teacher, 17, 19, 62
  testimony, 99–100, 104, 105–6,
    117–18, 208–9, 210, 212, 216–19,
    224
  on Tomberlin's guardianship, 234
  videotape of, 144
  and visitations, 16–17, 24, 26–28, 36,
    38, 40, 41, 61, 76, 80, 85, 87, 104,
    105, 106, 114, 116–17, 120, 123, 126,
    163, 178, 179, 180, 181, 186, 190,
    204, 210, 230
  visitation TRO, 60
  on *West 57th Street*, 183–84
Thompson, Karen, Legal Fund, 67, 110,
  132, 218
Thralow, Joan, 54
Time (magazine), 247
Tomberlin, Karen, 23, 54, 194, 195, 199,
  201–2, 210, 212, 219, 220, 222–23,
  225, 231, 240, 256
  guardianship cancelled, 245, 248, 250
  guardianship of Sharon Kowalski
    (1991), 220, 230, 232, 234, 235
  lawyer (*see* Sjogren, Thomas)
Torch Song Trilogy (Fierstein), 157
Traumatic brain injury (TBI), 10, 250
Trevilla (Robbinsdale extended care
  facility), 187–88, 190, 193, 237, 256

TRICAP. *See* Tri-County Action
    Programs, Inc.
Tri-County Action Programs, Inc.
    (TRICAP), 71, 110
TRO. *See* Temporary restraining order
Twentieth District Ethics Committee,
    125
Twin Posts Gay/Lesbian Pride Week
    (University of Minnesota), 188

UHC. *See* Uniform Health Care
    Decisions Act
Uniform Health Care (UHC) Decisions
    Act (1993), 10
Uniform Probate Code, 10–11
United Ministries of Higher Education,
    31
University of Alaska, 13
University of California, 13
University of Minnesota, 171, 188, 264
University of Montana, 72, 112, 264, 265
University of North Dakota, 13, 264
University of Southern California, 73
University of Washington, 13
USA Today, 172
U.S. Student Association National
    Congress, 191

Vermont, 8, 12, 262
Village Voice (NYC), 157
Vincent, Stephen, 63, 66
Visitation, 6, 9, 12, 13, 14, 16
Vulnerable Adult Act, 225

Washington, 6
Washington Blade, 7, 110, 121, 132, 139,
    169
Washington Post, 172, 173–74
WDIO (Duluth), 59
Wellstone, Paul, 262

Welsh, John, 197, 198, 255–56, 258
West 57th Street (television program), 2,
    7, 147, 172, 183–85
West Hollywood (Calif.), 13
*Why Can't Sharon Kowalski Come
    Home?* (Thompson and
    Andrzejewski), 3, 169–70, 177
    review, 177
Wild, Mary, 47, 64
Williams, Patricia, 3
Wilson, Jay, 169
Wilson, Sue (lawyer for Karen
    Thompson), 121, 122, 123, 124–25,
    126, 127, 128, 129, 131, 135, 141, 142,
    143, 144, 171. 192, 194, 199, 201–2,
    205, 207, 209, 210, 214, 216, 220,
    221, 222, 223, 227
    appeal, 235, 236–38, 243–44, 247,
        249
    and personal injury settlement, 171
    and petition to restore capacity, 189
    writ of prohibition, 189, 225
Wilson, William, 49, 117, 118, 157, 171,
    178–79, 180, 186
    deposition, 122–25, 126, 127, 129, 131
Wingen, Kathleen, 71
Wofford, Carrie, 234
Workers World, 158
Workman, Angie, 37, 77
Wozniak, D. D. (Court of Appeals
    judge), 120, 133, 142, 143, 144, 152,
    193, 235, 245
Wrongful death claims, 12

Yard, Molly, 175, 192
Yeager, Gary, 23, 24, 29, 80, 163
Yewell, John, 205–6

Zeman, Frances, 5
Zygo machine, 204